P9-CLY-898

# LET'S GO

## PAGES PACKED WITH ESSENTIAL INFORMATION

"Value-packed, unbeatable, accurate, and comprehensive."

—*The Los Angeles Times*

"The guides are aimed not only at young budget travelers but at the independent traveler; a sort of streetwise cookbook for traveling alone."

—*The New York Times*

"Unbeatable; good sight-seeing advice; up-to-date info on restaurants, hotels, and inns; a commitment to money-saving travel; and a wry style that brightens nearly every page."

—*The Washington Post*

## THE BEST TRAVEL BARGAINS IN YOUR BUDGET

"All the dirt, dirt cheap."

—*People*

"Let's Go follows the creed that you don't have to toss your life's savings to the wind to travel—unless you want to."

—*The Salt Lake Tribune*

## REAL ADVICE FOR REAL EXPERIENCES

"The writers seem to have experienced every rooster-packed bus and lunar-surfaced mattress about which they write."

—*The New York Times*

"[Let's Go's] devoted updaters really walk the walk (and thumb the ride, and trek the trail). Learn how to fish, haggle, find work—anywhere."

—*Food & Wine*

"A world-wise traveling companion—always ready with friendly advice and helpful hints, all sprinkled with a bit of wit."

—*The Philadelphia Inquirer*

## A GUIDE WITH A SPIRIT AND A SOCIAL CONSCIENCE

"Lighthearted and sophisticated, informative and fun to read. [Let's Go] helps the novice traveler navigate like a knowledgeable old hand."

—*Atlanta Journal-Constitution*

"The serious mission at the book's core reveals itself in exhortations to respect the culture and the environment—and, if possible, to visit as a volunteer, a student, or a teacher rather than a tourist."

—*San Francisco Chronicle*

# LET'S GO PUBLICATIONS

## TRAVEL GUIDES

Australia
Austria & Switzerland
Brazil
Britain
California
Central America
Chile
China
Costa Rica
Eastern Europe
Ecuador
Egypt
Europe
France
Germany
Greece
Hawaii
India & Nepal
Ireland
Israel
Italy
Japan
Mexico
New Zealand
Peru
Puerto Rico
Southeast Asia
Spain & Portugal with Morocco
Thailand
USA
Vietnam
Western Europe

## ROADTRIP GUIDE

Roadtripping USA

## ADVENTURE GUIDES

Alaska
Pacific Northwest
Southwest USA

## CITY GUIDES

Amsterdam
Barcelona
Boston
Buenos Aires
London
New York City
Paris
Rome
San Francisco
Washington, DC

## POCKET CITY GUIDES

Amsterdam
Berlin
Boston
Chicago
London
New York City
Paris
San Francisco
Venice
Washington, DC

# LET'S GO

# BUENOS AIRES

**NICHOLAS TRAVERSE** EDITOR
**JAKE SEGAL** ASSOCIATE EDITOR

RESEARCHER-WRITERS
**INGRID GUSTAFSON**
**NATALIE SHERMAN**

**R. DEREK WETZEL** MAP EDITOR
**LAURA M. GORDON** MANAGING EDITOR

RICE PUBLIC LIBRARY
8 WENTWORTH ST.
KITTERY, MAINE 03904
207-439-1553

ST. MARTIN'S PRESS ✦ NEW YORK

**HELPING LET'S GO.** If you want to share your discoveries, suggestions, or corrections, please drop us a line. We appreciate every piece of correspondence, whether a postcard, a 10-page email, or a coconut. Visit Let's Go at **http://www.letsgo.com,** or send email to:

> **feedback@letsgo.com**
> **Subject: "Let's Go: Buenos Aires"**

**Address mail to:**

> **Let's Go: Buenos Aires**
> **67 Mount Auburn St.**
> **Cambridge, MA 02138**
> **USA**

In addition to the invaluable travel advice our readers share with us, many are kind enough to offer their services as researchers or editors. Unfortunately, our charter enables us to employ only currently enrolled Harvard students.

Maps by Let's Go copyright © 2009 by Let's Go, Inc.
Maps by David Lindroth copyright © 2009 by St. Martin's Press.

Distributed outside the USA and Canada by Macmillan.

**Let's Go: Buenos Aires** Copyright © 2009 by Let's Go, Inc. All rights reserved. Printed in the United States of America. No part of this book may be used or reproduced in any manner whatsoever without written permission except in the case of brief quotations embodied in critical articles or reviews. Let's Go is available for purchase in bulk by institutions and authorized resellers. For information, address St. Martin's Press, 175 Fifth Avenue, New York, NY 10010, USA.

ISBN-13: 978-0-312-38576-7
ISBN-10: 0-312-38576-5
First edition
10 9 8 7 6 5 4 3 2 1

**Let's Go: Buenos Aires** is written by Let's Go Publications, 67 Mount Auburn St., Cambridge, MA 02138, USA.

**Let's Go**® and the LG logo are trademarks of Let's Go, Inc.

**ADVERTISING DISCLAIMER.** All advertisements appearing in Let's Go publications are sold by an independent agency not affiliated with the editorial production of the guides. Advertisers are never given preferential treatment, and the guides are researched, written, and published independent of advertising. Advertisements do not imply endorsement of products or services by Let's Go, and Let's Go does not vouch for the accuracy of information provided in advertisements.

If you are interested in purchasing advertising space in a Let's Go publication, contact: Let's Go Advertising Sales, 67 Mount Auburn St., Cambridge, MA 02138, USA.

# CONTENTS

# HOW TO USE THIS BOOK

Once, there was a time—yes, fair reader, a dark time—a time before the glories of this here modern age, when the rich *Pampas* knew not the ticklish grazing of a happy cow's tongue. Our time, fortunately, is not that time. Nay, the varied and mysterious sections of those plains-dwelling cows now populate the plates and cutting boards of Buenos Aires' gastronomical miracles, the *parillas*. This is but one of many reasons you, dear reader, have come to us: to find them. And together, we will. This book will be your Maradona, leading you (cleanly) to victory across the city's streets. It will guide you through the tourist hordes on the Calle Florida to loving *bife* in the hidden basement cafes of Recoleta. It will show you where to shop, where to dance, and where to find a really, really big rubber ▄tree. From the banks of the mud-colored river to the wooden floors of sweaty *milongas*, from huge public parks to a massive, metallic, sun-powered flower, our gritty, dutiful researchers have fanned out across the city and beyond to bring you this: the freshest, most thorough, most awesome-tastic travel guide ever created. Open this bad boy up and choose your own adventure. ▄Buenos Aires is waiting. Here's how to use the guide:

**COVERING THE BASICS.** The first chapter is **Discover** (p. 1), meant to help you—ahem—discover BA with short overviews of the city's *barrios* and **suggested itineraries** to help you plan your journey. The **Essentials** (p. 17) chapter gets down to the nitty-gritty, detailing the stuff you'll need to get around and stay safe on your adventure—not to mention stay on ▄budget. **Life and Times** (p. 53) provides valuable cultural and historical background that you can use to impress your friends, and not look like an idiot at dinner. **Beyond Tourism** (p. 83) suggests some non-standard ways to experience Argentina, helping you study, work, and volunteer your way around the country. Our delightful **Appendix** (p. 257) helps bolster your 9th grade Spanish with a **pronunciation guide,** a **phrasebook,** and a **glossary.** And don't forget to check out the sweet ▄conversion charts.

**COVERAGE LAYOUT.** Here's the meat of the book. The **Accommodations** (p. 101), **Food** (p. 117), **Sights** (p. 139), **Museums** (p. 171), **Entertainment** (p. 183), **Shopping** (p. 195), and **Nightlife** (p. 203) chapters are broken down into neighborhood groupings—the order of those neighborhoods swings in a graceful spiral from **Monserrat** south to **San Telmo** and **La Boca,** then jumping back up to **Puerto Madero** before curving through **Retiro, Recoleta, Palermo,** and the **Outer Barrios** beyond. The basic **Daytrips** (p. 217) section details short journeys to towns and cities near BA, while the **Excursions** (p. 229) chapter covers "daytrips," such as Iguazú Falls, that will likely require more than one day to see. Throughout the book, you will also find **tipboxes** with **warnings (▄), helpful hints and resources (▄), fun facts (▄),** and other things you should know. We've also prepared a mouthwatering selection of **sidebar feature articles** for your reading pleasure.

---

**A NOTE TO OUR READERS.** The information for this book was gathered by Let's Go researchers from January through August of 2008. Each listing is based on one researcher's opinion, formed during his or her visit at a particular time. Those traveling at other times may have different experiences since prices, dates, hours, and conditions are always subject to change. You are urged to check the facts presented in this book beforehand to avoid inconvenience and surprises.

---

Our researchers list establishments in order of value from best to worst; our favorites get the Let's Go **thumbs-up** (🖒). However, because the best value is not always the cheapest price, we have incorporated a system of price ranges based on a rough expectation of what you'll spend. For **accommodations,** we base our range on the cheapest price for which a single traveler can stay for one night. For **restaurants** and other dining establishments, we estimate the average amount one traveler will spend in one sitting. The table below tells you what you'll *typically* find in BA at the corresponding price range, but keep in mind that no system can allow for the quirks of individual establishments.

| ACCOMMODATIONS | RANGE | WHAT YOU'RE *LIKELY* TO FIND |
|---|---|---|
| ❶ | under AR$30 | Dorm rooms, or dorm-style rooms, with some remarkably cheap singles and doubles mixed in. For the dorms, expect bunk beds, a communal bath, linens, towels, and breakfast. |
| ❷ | AR$30-61 | Similar to ❶, but with more guaranteed amenities and elaborate common facilities. Some of the more affordable hotels in the city sneak in here, too. |
| ❸ | AR$62-91 | The offerings are purely hotels at this point, so if you're not getting a basic private room, you're grossly overpaying. |
| ❹ | AR$92-121 | Amped up versions of the hotels from ❸, with more sumptuous accommodations and amenities. The location may be more central than other lower options. |
| ❺ | over AR$122 | Very little separates rooms at this level from ❹, facilities-wise, save for the location—most of our ❺ listings are based in glitzy areas of the city, such as Recoleta. |

| FOOD | RANGE | WHAT YOU'RE *LIKELY* TO FIND |
|---|---|---|
| ❶ | under AR$15 | Mostly all-you-can-eat *tenedor libres*, cheap pizza joints, *empanada* shops, and cafe sandwich/salad fare. |
| ❷ | AR$15-24 | Save for pizza, which is almost universally a ❶, the ❷ offerings are just more upscale versions of ❶ fare—classier *parrillas* instead of buffets, for example, along with some pricier cafes. |
| ❸ | AR$25-36 | Around ❸, you're starting to hit the realm of the city's fancier restaurants and chic ethnic offerings, which are all still amazingly affordable thanks to the favorable exchange rate. |
| ❹ | AR$37-48 | More upscale than ❸, but still well within reach of the budget traveler's wallet. Location plays a big role, too—trendier areas of the city, such as Palermo, translate to more ❹-type offerings. |
| ❺ | over AR$49 | These are simply some of *the* fanciest restaurants in the city, all of which are viable splurges and decent bang-for-your-buck deals. |

# ABOUT LET'S GO

## NOT YOUR PARENTS' TRAVEL GUIDE

At Let's Go, we see every trip as the chance of a lifetime. If your dream is to grab a machete and forge through the jungles of Costa Rica, we can take you there. If you'd rather bask in the Riviera sun at a beachside cafe, we'll set you a table. We write for readers who know that there's more to travel than sharing double deckers with tourists and who believe that travel can change both themselves and the world—whether they plan to spend six days in Bangkok or six months in Europe. We'll show you just how far your money can go, and prove that the greatest limitation on your adventures is not your wallet but your imagination.

## BEYOND THE TOURIST EXPERIENCE

To help you gain a deeper connection with the places you travel, our fearless researchers scour the globe to give you the heads-up on both world-renowned and off-the-beaten-track attractions, sights, and destinations. They dive into the local culture only to emerge with the freshest insights on everything from festivals to regional cuisine. We've also opened our pages to respected writers and scholars to hear their takes on the countries and regions we cover, and asked travelers who have worked, studied, or volunteered abroad to contribute first-person accounts of their experiences. In addition, each guide's Beyond Tourism chapter shares ideas about responsible travel, study abroad, and how to give back while on the road.

## FORTY-NINE YEARS OF WISDOM

Let's Go got its start in 1960, when a group of creative and well-traveled students compiled their experience and advice into a 20-page mimeographed pamphlet, which they gave to travelers on charter flights to Europe. Almost five decades later, we've expanded to cover six continents and all kinds of travel—while retaining our founders' adventurous attitude. Laced with witty prose and total candor, our guides are still researched and written entirely by students on shoestring budgets, experienced travelers who know that train strikes, stolen luggage, food poisoning, and marriage proposals are all part of a day's work.

## THE LET'S GO COMMUNITY

More than just a travel guide company, Let's Go is a community. Our small staff comes together because of our shared passion for travel and our desire to help other travelers see the world the way it was meant to be seen. We love it when our readers become part of the Let's Go community as well—when you travel, drop us a postcard (67 Mt. Auburn St., Cambridge, MA 02138, USA), send us an e-mail (feedback@letsgo.com), or sign up online (http://www.letsgo.com) to tell us about your adventures and discoveries.

**For more information, visit us online: www.letsgo.com.**

# RESEARCHER-WRITERS

**Ingrid Gustafson**  *Buenos Aires, Iguazú Falls, Mendoza, San Antonio de Areco, San Isidro, Tigre*

Oh, Ingrid—the superlatives in the dictionary are not numerous enough to sing her praises. After churning out legendary, pristine copy, pithy marginalia, and cartographer-quality hand-drawn maps for the core *barrios* of Buenos Aires during the low season, this former Eastern Europe editor rejoined the team for high season coverage of Palermo, the outer *barrios*, and Argentine excursions, and did nothing less than continue her reign of dominance over the research-writing trade. For those of you who think it's impossible to transcend legend status, think again—she pulled it off with style.

**Natalie Sherman**  *Buenos Aires, Colonia del Sacramento, Montevideo*

Writing a first edition travel guide can be a scary proposition. Researcher-writers like Natalie take that scariness, turn it upside down, and make it a veritable walk in the park. A fellow recipient of legendary status, Natalie, a former Associate Editor, joined Team Buenos Aires for the high season, and attacked the incredibly difficult task of generating raw copy head on, sending back page after page of sparkling coverage from around Argentina and Uruguay. Ask her how it went and she would say merely "OK"; her editors, on the other hand, had a different take—they were floored by her kick ass-ness and dedication.

# CONTRIBUTING WRITERS

**N. Aaron Pancost** is an economic research assistant at the Federal Reserve Bank of Boston. He spent time in Argentina learning Spanish while studying at the University of Maryland College Park.

**Martín L. Gaspar** is a doctoral candidate in the Romance Languages and Literatures Department at Harvard University.

# ACKNOWLEDGMENTS

# LET'S GO

**NICK THANKS:** LG, captain of the flagship Buenos Aires: most people would see the job of writing a first edition and say "uh… no thanks." For me, when I knew it would be working with you, I didn't need to think about it for a second—it was a pure joy. BAH! Jake: you carried this book team through its formative stages. It just wouldn't be the same without the brilliant foundation you laid. See you in Finland for the Santa's Workshop visit. BAlove. City Pod (Frank, Lauren, and guests): you guys are pretty awesome, I guess… and by "pretty awesome," I mean the best podmates imaginable. Derek: your map wizardry will go down in the history tomes. Jonathan: the only word I can think of for your typesetting: magic. Blockmates, roommates, fellow '08ers: sorry I vanished for three months. I'll be back. Thank you for being your usual, loving, incredible selves. Dad, Ben, and Hannah: I love you very much. Let's go to Buenos Aires together? Denly's PDI1. Border PDI1. Last, but not least, to all of my dear friends here at the office: it makes me even sadder to leave Harvard and Let's Go knowing I won't see you everyday. Hence, once again: I'll be back. Thank you for being you. With much love, NPT.

**JAKE THANKS:** To NPT, for everything, ▄BAlove, finishing; LoGo, for rockzone; █LG, for tenacity; █▓▓Cec, for all and all; fam, assembled!; roomies; bcgas. To ARG for BA, and Ponts. ◤, ◥, ◰: renegades all. RIP Frame.

**Publishing Director**
Inés C. Pacheco
**Editor-in-Chief**
Samantha Gelfand
**Production Manager**
Jansen A. S. Thurmer
**Cartography Manager**
R. Derek Wetzel
**Editorial Managers**
Dwight Livingstone Curtis,
Vanessa J. Dube, Nathaniel Rakich
**Financial Manager**
Lauren Caruso
**Publicity and Marketing Manager**
Patrick McKiernan
**Personnel Manager**
Laura M. Gordon
**Production Associate**
C. Alexander Tremblay
**Director of IT & E-Commerce**
Lukáš Tóth
**Website Manager**
Ian Malott
**Office Coordinators**
Vinnie Chiappini, Jenny Wong
**Director of Advertising Sales**
Nicole J. Bass
**Senior Advertising Associates**
Kipyegon Kitur, Jeremy Siegfried,
John B. Ulrich
**Junior Advertising Associate**
Edward C. Robinson Jr.

**Editor**
Nicholas Traverse
**Associate Editors**
Jake Segal
**Managing Editor**
Laura M. Gordon
**Map Editor**
R. Derek Wetzel
**Typesetter**
Jonathan Reed

**President**
Timothy J. J. Creamer
**General Manager**
Jim McKellar

# DISCOVER BUENOS AIRES

Buenos Aires is a city reborn. Eight years after Argentina declared the largest foreign debt default in history, the city is reinventing itself as Latin America's trendiest and most exciting capital. That sucking, whooshing sound you hear is the rush of tourists heading to the Argentine metropolis. As many will explain, Buenos Aires is a cosmopolitan city, and that cosmopolitanism plays out in ways both delicious and downright confusing. It's a city where high-heeled fashionistas and broken down garbage drivers inhabit the same fifty-year-old streets, where incessant arrays of protesters in front of the Casa Rosada mix with innumerable German expats in new bars carved out of old, luxurious townhouses, and where trendy boutiques in Palermo Soho get busy only after the bakery next door has sold its daily fresh bread. As it has transitioned from one of the most expensive cities in Latin America to one of the cheapest, it's become a magnet for bohemians and backpackers without losing that feel that makes it one of the world's most exciting cities.

## FACTS AND FIGURES

**METRO AREA POPULATION:** 13,044,800.

**AS PERCENT OF ARGENTINA'S POPULATION:** Over 40%.

**TOTAL AREA:** 4758 sq. km.

**LARGEST BARRIO:** Palermo, at 17.4 sq. km. Also the most populous, with 252,312 people.

**RELIGIOUS AFFILIATION:** Roman Catholic 92%.

**PRACTICING ROMAN CATHOLICS:** Under 20%.

**POPULATION BELOW POVERTY LINE:** 23.4%.

**NUMBER OF LANES IN AVENIDA DE JULIO:** A whopping 16. Don't forget to look both ways before crossing.

**COLOR OF THE RÍO DE LA PLATA:** Brown. Very brown.

**ANNUAL MEAT CONSUMPTION PER CAPITA:** 68kg.

**NUMBER OF TRAFFIC DEATHS ANNUALLY:** 7500.

**APPROXIMATE NUMBER OF ARGENTINE TOURIST INDUSTRY JOBS:** 2,000,000.

**NUMBER OF SOCCER TEAMS:** Over 24, the highest concentration of soccer teams in any one city in the world.

**PERCENT OF HOUSEHOLDS THAT DRINK MATE:** 92%.

**NUMBER OF WORLD CUP TITLES:** 2 (1978 and 1986).

That feel springs up from a cultural legacy at once expansive and unique. Between the sweaty *milongas* of San Telmo and the cheap leather wallets and knock-off jerseys on Calle Florida, there's a life in Buenos Aires that's all its own. And though chic bohemian artists and hard-drinking expatriates own more than their fair share of the city, the bombardment of tourists and immigrants in the last half decade has done nothing but reinforce a culture that's based on jumbled ethnicities in the first place. Maybe, even, it's that mixed cultural legacy—the legacy that makes Argentine pizza the best in the world and Argentine *fútbol* (read: soccer) fans some of the craziest—that makes travel here so compelling. To the visitor, it's a pseudo-European city of cheap Malbec and **larger-than-reasonable steaks.** It's also an odd-couple pairing of Paris or

**DISCOVER**

Italy, complete with ice cream-and-espresso modernity, with tall white ancestry and a distinctly South American flair—from ad-hoc construction to suicidal no-lane driving and large, pink government buildings that could only be found in the subtropics, or perhaps a Floridian retirement community. To the *porteño*, it's a proud capital brought to its knees by 2001's unprecedented economic disaster. But surrounding the pomp and poverty of it all is a tremendous Argentine culture, forged in the bowls of *mate* gourds and in art galleries and in divebars—a culture both slow-paced and passionate, created of a people of strong and sometimes strangely conservative opinions—that makes Buenos Aires a city of captivating complexity and irresistible beauty.

# WHEN TO GO

The first thing to know—and we hope you've already realized this; if you haven't, you might want to sit down—is that Buenos Aires is in the **Southern Hemisphere.** Hence, the seasons are the reverse of those up in the Northern Hemisphere. Relatively moderate, the weather in Buenos Aires fluctuates from season to season, though it's enjoyable all months of the year. The city is at its most pleasant during the fall and spring months, between March and May and September through November, but there's often more rain during these months (for weather specifics, see **Appendix,** p. 257). During the summer, more hotels are booked, and many city-dwellers head to beach resorts such as Mar del Plata and sandy spots in Uruguay (p. 242), as temperatures average around 28°C and spike to 40°C in January. During the Argentine winter, temperatures drop as low as 0°C, but the rain abates. If you're going north to Iguazú (p. 237), the most tropical region in Argentina, go during the winter (June-August) when you won't have to bring ice packs and a spray bottle to keep cool.

**NOT BUENOS AIRES-IANS OR -ITES.** Citizens of Buenos Aires are known as **porteños,** Spanish for "people of the port." Since its inception, BA has been a major port city, after all, and, as the title of this box suggests, the alternatives are pretty miserable.

# NEIGHBORHOOD OVERVIEWS

Buenos Aires proper is divided into a whopping 48 neighborhoods, known as *barrios.* Some, such as San Telmo (pop. 26,000), are relatively tiny, while others, like Palermo (pop. 252,000), are truly epic in scale. Fear not, weary-legged travelers: most visitors don't stop in every *barrio*, although it's certainly possible, if slightly crazy. Most travelers stick to the easily accessible easternmost group of districts along the **Río de la Plata,** which offers the majority of sights, restaurants, and hotels. For coverage in this so-called **zona turística,** we will start with what is often seen as the heart of the modern city, San Nicolás, often referred to as **Microcentro,** and work outward in a counterclockwise spiral, hitting **Monserrat, San Telmo,** and **La Boca** to the south before turning northward for **Puerto Madero, Retiro, Recoleta, Palermo,** and **Belgrano.** The city beyond is compiled under the single banner of **Outer Barrios.**

# BASP

**BUENOS AIRES SPANISH SCHOOL**

The best place
to study Spanish
in Buenos Aires.

- Taylor-Made courses
- Friendly atmosphere
- 5 students per class
- Competitive prices
- Touristic activities
- Excellent location

Av. Rivadavia 1559 2° "C" | (1033) | Cap. Fed. | Argentina
Tel.: (54 - 11) 4381-2076
info@baspanish.com | www.baspanish.com

DISCOVER

## MICROCENTRO

see map p. 269

Microcentro gets down to business. It's BA's central neighborhood in more than one way: it's the financial district, home to important government buildings, and where most tourists stay. Formally named **San Nicolás,** it's more commonly known as **Microcentro** (little center), and the area east of the canyon-like **Avenida 9 de Julio**—the city's main banking district—is generally referred to, in a stroke of genius, as **La City.** There are a few telltale signs that you're in Microcentro: the sidewalks are clogged with businesspeople and shoppers, and there are a stunning number of Christian Dior vendors. Its most crowded thoroughfare is the tourist-packed pedestrian **Calle Florida** (p. 145), home to knockoffs of everything and three-peso *chorizo*, not to mention some cheap eats and a high-class mall. Nearby are some of the city's most famous sights. Though it's technically not within Microcentro, the **Plaza de Mayo,** the city's main square, is just across **Avenida Rivadavia** in Monserrat (p. 139). Just a kilometer northwest from the Plaza along **Avenida Roque Sáenz Peña** is the iconic **Obelisk of Buenos Aires,** also known simply as **Obelisco** (p. 146). The 49-meter-tall monument, located in the **Plaza de la Independencia,** where the Argentine flag was first flown, was built in 1936 to commemorate the 400th anniversary of the city. Running east and west from Obelisco is yet another major thoroughfare, **Avenida Corrientes,** the street for tangos, huge post offices inspired by French architecture (read: **Correo Central,** p. 145, at the eastern end of Corrientes), bookstores, and cafes.

DISCOVER

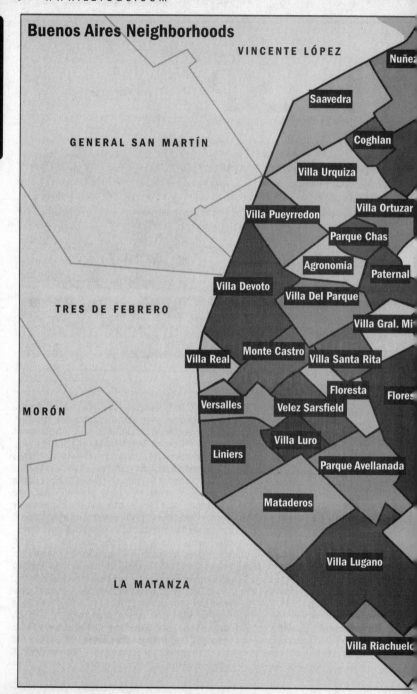

# Buenos Aires Neighborhoods

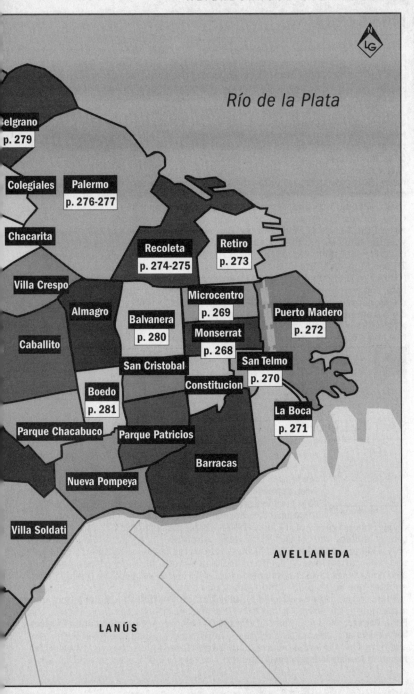

Río de la Plata

Belgrano
p. 279

Colegiales

Palermo
p. 276-277

Chacarita

Recoleta
p. 274-275

Retiro
p. 273

Villa Crespo

Almagro

Microcentro
p. 269

Puerto Madero
p. 272

Balvanera
p. 280

Monserrat
p. 268

Caballito

San Cristobal

San Telmo
p. 270

Boedo
p. 281

Constitucion

La Boca
p. 271

Parque Chacabuco

Parque Patricios

Nueva Pompeya

Barracas

Villa Soldati

AVELLANEDA

LANÚS

DISCOVER

## MONSERRAT

see map p. 268

Neither the European-imported name nor the colonial history of **Monserrat,** the city's oldest *barrio*, just south of El Centro, should come as any surprise in cosmopolitan Buenos Aires. Tucked away in the northeast corner of the *barrio* is one of Buenos Aires' biggest tourist magnets—the **Plaza de Mayo** and its accompanying bevy of buildings, including the **Casa Rosada** (the Presidential Palace; p. 139), the **Cabildo** (the colonial-era city council building; p. 140), the **Metropolitan Cathedral** (p. 140), **City Hall,** and the headquarters of the **Banco Nación** (p. 141). Several major arteries radiate from the Plaza, including **Avenida de Mayo,** named, along with the Plaza, after the 1810 May Revolution (p. 144). The east-west street, perhaps Buenos Aires' most Parisian, is a wide, tree-lined thoroughfare with cafes and restaurants. At the western terminus of the avenue is **Plaza del Congreso** and **Congreso de la Nación** (p. 144), the legislative branch of the Argentine government. For really old buildings and signs of Buenos Aires' colonial past, stray south of the Casa Rosada-Congreso axis. Back in the day, when Argentina was the Viceroyalty of the Río de la Plata and the English came knocking (p. 55), Monserrat was the defensive center of the Argentine resistance. Some of the district's old churches and buildings still bear the scars and bullet holes of the conflict. To see Monserrat in all its colonial glory, check out the **Manzana de las Luces** ("Block of Enlightenment"; p. 141), bordered by *calles* **Alsina, Bolívar, Moreno** and **Perú,** and containing some of the city's oldest buildings. Stroll through the city's oldest church, crumbling **Iglesia San Ignacio** (p. 141), built in 1734, see the naval flags from the 1806-1807 British invasion in the **Basílica Santo Domingo** (p. 144), and walk through the galleries and (somewhat creepy) 18th-century tunnels of the Jesuit museum and the **Sala de Representantes.**

 **A HAIRY SITUATION.** Law in Buenos Aires forbids *paseoperros* (dog walkers) from walking more than 15 dogs at a time. For some reason, 14 is fine, but hit 15 and you are in huge trouble.

## SAN TELMO

see map p. 270

**San Telmo** is beloved by tourists and mostly avoided by everyone else, except on Sundays. Old, colonial-style mansions and wrought-iron lanterns—relics of the wealth that made San Telmo the city's ritziest *barrio* until 1871's **yellow fever epidemic** sent monied families northward—line narrow cobblestone streets, which have only recently started to go upscale. Known for nearly half a century as the dirty, dangerous neighbor of its fancier *barrios* to the north, San Telmo, fueled by tourist dollars and its Old World feel, is renovating its crumbling buildings and widening its sidewalks, all the while trying hard not to disturb the colonial feel tourists love. This effort results in beautifully restored mansions, but also sometimes gives a strangely inauthentic feel to some of the freshly paved cobblestone and rapidly multiplying tango bars.

Back to the aforementioned Sunday buzz in San Telmo—the most popular attraction in the *barrio* is the **feria** (flea market; p. 167). Six days a week, the **Plaza Dorrego,** the focal point of the neighborhood, at the intersection of **Humberto Primo** and **Defensa,** is a relatively quiet square, albeit one filled with cafes and bars. On Sundays, however, authorities close Defensa between **Avenida San Juan** and **Avenida Independencia,** and the Plaza turns into a giant antiques market from around 9am to 5pm. Many of San Telmo's most famous sights are near the Plaza, including **La Casa Mínima** (p. 148), the city's narrowest house at two-meters wide by 50-meters long, and a string of imposing buildings: the **Edificio del Libertador**, a military complex flanked by tanks and cannons; the **Aduana,** home to customs services; the **Secretaría de Agricultura,** Argentina's Ministry of Agriculture; and, the largest and scariest-looking, **La Facultad de Ingeniería** (the School of Engineering) of the **University of Buenos Aires,** a cross between Athens' Parthenon and a big, windowless cube of granite. San Telmo is also home to some quirky museums, not the least of which is the **Museo del Traje** (p. 172), which houses clothes and costumes from over the last 100 years. There's also this whole **tango** (p. 183) thing. San Telmo is a hotbed for it, whatever it is.

## LA BOCA

see map p. 271

For many, the multi-colored walls and balconies of **El Caminito** (p. 149), a pedestrian alleyway in **La Boca,** are the icons by which they recognize Buenos Aires. In some ways, they're right to see Boca as archetypical Buenos Aires. Beyond the romanticized blue collar feel of the handful of sights gawked at by tourists on buses are the slums and tenements of a neighborhood outside the reach of Microcentro's tourist dollars. This *barrio*, built around the final U-shaped arm of the river **El Riachuelo** (formally **La Matanza,** "The Slaughter River") before it spills into the Río de la Plata, is marked by old warehouses and sunken freighters along its highly polluted and stinky waters. Modest *cantinas* and crumbling houses define this side of Boca—the Boca that began in poverty and has consistently remained poor, the Boca that seceded from Argentina in 1882, the Boca of loud soccer fans and street crime, of Diego Maradona and **Benito Quinquela Martín** (p. 149). It's sometimes beautiful, but it's not somewhere to go after dark.

 **LA BOCA SAFETY.** Boca can be very unsafe, both during the day and night. Exercise caution and consider using cabs to travel to destinations outside of the *barrio*'s more touristy sectors.

The other Boca is something built off of the grit and history of this neighborhood, and in many ways it is the more charming of the two. Tourist-friendly Boca is still covered in the many-colored paints that once defined the sector as a whole. When early Italian, Greek, and Slavic immigrants took over this port on El Riachuelo, they used the remainders of barge paint to cover their homes, creating the carnival-esque color scheme that now defines tourist streets such as El Caminito. Those same immigrants, and their varied ethnicities, still define the neighborhood. Perhaps the strongest group were the Genoese, whose flag the rebellious neighborhood flew during their (very brief) secession from the country in 1882. Even the name of the *barrio* may come from Genoese roots: though it's often stated that the name "La Boca" (the mouth) comes from the neighborhood's location at the river's mouth, it may well come from the Genoese neighborhood of Boccadasse, instead.

The line between the two Bocas isn't always clear, either. Fanny-pack-toting tourists make their way to **La Bombonera** (p. 149), home to the world-famous **Boca Juniors** *fútbol* club that produced Maradona and a host of other greats, and squeeze their way between auto mechanics wearing the signature blue and yellow of the club. Even the tourist areas along the river, the Disney-like El Caminito, or the corridors of the creepy wax museum, **Museo de Cera** (p. 173), of **Del Valle Iberlucea** street are never wholly owned by the bus groups

DISCOVER

DISCOVER

that photograph them. Throughout all is a rowdy feeling of community that permeates the vendor stalls and helps to make the dangers and poverty of the neighborhood a thing both tragic and romantic.

# PUERTO MADERO

see map p. 272

Seventy years ago, the main port of Buenos Aires moved away from **Puerto Madero** to Puerto Nuevo, a mile north, and the riverside warehouses and apartments of this *barrio* were nearly abandoned. But since the early 1990s, Puerto Madero has been on the up-and-up as one of the most successful urban renovation projects in the world, and this riverside neighborhood has transformed into the latest hot spot of young professionals and increasingly expensive restaurants. The red brick apartments—housed in buildings that once stored ship parts and cut wood for siding—attract a large crowd of expats and wealthy artists, while the recent construction of skyscrapers around the former port's four *diques* (docks) constitute one of the latest architectural trends in the city. In some ways, the *barrio* feels cut off from the rest of the city: few bus routes make their way to the old port, and no subway line reaches it. Nevertheless, one of Puerto Madero's main streets, **Avenida Juana Manso** (named, as are all the streets in the neighborhood, after a woman) still brings crowds of those wealthy enough to afford it to Puerto Madero's high-tech cinemas, quality theaters, luxury hotels, and classy eateries. Not all of the port redevelopment focused on glam and glitz. On the far eastern edge of the *barrio*, right along the Río de la Plata, is the **Reserva Ecológica Costanera Sur** (p. 150), a sliver of untamed nature reserve that provides an escape from the vast metropolis to the west.

# RETIRO

see map p. 273

Just a stone's throw north of the Microcentro, **Retiro** is well removed from all of the craziness of its southerly neighbor, making it the perfect haunt for top-notch hotels, foreign embassies, and a few super-classy restaurants. Though it doesn't offer much lodging for the budget traveler, Retiro's relaxing park and impressive buildings—many of which were private mansions during the early 20th-century boom, but are now owned by the government or have become foreign embassies or private hotels—offer a lot to see. The center of the neighborhood is Buenos Aires' second most important square after Plaza de Mayo, the **Plaza de San Martín** (p. 151). The leafy park is centered around a giant statue of **El Libertador, José de San Martín** (p. 55)—still revered throughout the country—rearing on a horse in a fashion typical for great liberators. Foreign dignitaries still leave wreaths at the foot of the monument, marking the ground where the general once trained his Granderos corps. The park slopes downward towards another memorial, this one commemorating the dead of the 1982 Falkland Islands War. Between the giant monuments and well-kept ground, the Plaza also serves as a main picnic and relaxation ground for many of the city's residents. On a summer weekend, it can fill up pretty quickly.

Surrounding the Plaza are some of the city's most spectacular buildings. The **Palacio Paz** (p. 151), built for José Paz, sugar baron and founder of the newspaper *La Prensa*, is perhaps the most extravagant and beautiful palace in the country. **Palacio San Martín** (p. 152), just off the western edge of the Plaza, is smaller but nearly as beautiful, and in better shape. Nearby are the 120-meter-tall **Edificio Kavanagh** and the French-style **Basílica de Santísimo Sacramento** (p.

152). Right in the middle of the Plaza is the **Torre de Los Ingleses** (British Clock Tower; p. 153), a 76-meter miniature replica of Big Ben—which, unsurprisingly, became an object of controversy during the Falklands War, leading to a temporary name change. The northern edge of the park is home to one of the largest transportation hubs in the country, including the decaying and enormous **Estación Retiro,** the city's main train terminal, and the major long-distance bus station, **Terminal de Omnibus** (p. 151), The area just north of the station, however, Villa 31, has long been home to one of the city's slums, and is best avoided.

# RECOLETA

see map p. 274-275

Like it's neighbor, Retiro, **Recoleta** is one of the glitziest and most exclusive residential areas in the city. When yellow fever hit San Telmo in the 1870s, the rich went north and chose Recoleta as the place to be. Strangely, and morbidly, the most expensive properties in one of the city's most prestigious *barrios* are the one-story, non-air-conditioned mausolea of **La Recoleta Cemetery** (p. 153). Once a public cemetery, this nearly 200-year-old burial ground is home to former Presidents and noblemen and -women: the most famous and tourist-crowded tomb is that of **Eva Perón,** whose black marble resting place is marked only as "Duarte," her maiden name. Just outside of the cemetery is the colonial-style church **Nuestra Señora del Pilar** (p. 153), a simple structure with an impressive interior. More impressive still is the monstrous rubber tree (as in a natural rubber tree, not a fake tree made out of rubber) in the square facing the cemetery. Known as the **Gran Gomero,** it's 150 years old and over 50 meters wide. No, you can't climb it.

Recoleta is an artistic and cultural center, too. Beyond the **Museo Nacional de Bellas Artes** and **Centro Cultural Recoleta** (p. 175) is an architectural opulence that's just absurd, with early 20th-century palaces and Art Deco mansions—now fancy storefronts and unbelievably expensive hotels—lining the **Avenida Alvear** and the **Plaza Carlos Pellegrini.** East of the cemetery is the **United Nations Park,** where the **Floralis Genérica** (p. 155), a giant metallic flower, opens and closes its petals daily. Farther west, the neighborhood becomes more residential and more difficult to reach by public transportation; it's also farther from the sights, besides the massive **Biblioteca Nacional** (p. 155), Latin America's largest library with five million books, and perhaps its ugliest building. You'll understand once you see it. Then again, Recoleta is closer to the ultra-trendy bar scene and restaurants of Palermo, our next stop on the *barrio* parade.

# PALERMO

see map p. 276-277

**Palermo** is the place to be in Buenos Aires. At the epicenter of the city's recent cultural explosion, it's today's culinary capital and nightlife hot spot. It's also filled with enormous, elegant mansions, well-designed and much-used parks, and some of the best boutique shopping in the country. At over 17 square kilometers, it's the city's biggest neighborhood—except that it's really a few different neighborhoods combined. **Alto Palermo** is the *barrio*'s center and the main shopping district, with the **Alto Palermo Shopping Centre** (p. 200) as its home base. **Palermo Viejo** (Old Palermo) contains the giant palaces of turn-of-the-19th-century elites, filled with beautiful Spanish-style architecture and a number of former residences now open to the public, including the former homes of **Jorge Luis Borges** (p. 159) and **Che Guevara. Palermo Soho**—so named for its bohemian atmosphere and teeming boutiques—is a small section of Palermo Viejo near **Plaza Serrano** (p.

DISCOVER

159), whose low houses, weekly crafts fair, and many cafes and bars make it a happening area at all hours. Farther west are the restaurants and nightclubs of **Palermo Hollywood,** home to many TV and radio producers during the 1990s. The fanciest area of the neighborhood is **Palermo Chico** (Small Palermo) and nearby **Barrio Parque** (p. 155), where many of the rich and famous live. **Las Cañitas,** once a slum in the northernmost section of Palermo, has joined the trendy train, and now serves food and drink to young professionals.

**PALERMO SOHOLLYIEJO.** Palermo is a neighborhood so big, it has its own neighborhoods. Here's a rundown on where to find them.
**Alto Palermo:** Centered around Avenida Santa Fe.
**Palermo Viejo:** Centered on Plaza Palermo Viejo, it's defined by Avenida Santa Fe, Avenida Coronel Diaz, Avenida Córdoba, and Carranza.
**Palermo Soho:** Centered on Plaza Serrano (formally Plazoleta Cortázar), at the intersection of Avenidas Serrano/Borges and Honduras.
**Palermo Hollywood:** Located between Avenidas Córdoba, Santa Fe, Dorrego and Juan B. Justo.
**Palermo Chico:** Located between Avenida del Libertador and the river.

Besides chowing down on tastebud-tingling gnocchi and guzzling imported beer, Palermo offers a fantastic set of parks, where you can bring said gnocchi and beer on picnics. The **Jardín Zoológico, Jardín Botánico, Jardín Japonés,** and **Parque Tres de Febrero** (p. 156) were all built in the 1870s out of land confiscated from Juan Manuel de Rosas (p. 56) and serve as a good spot to let your stomach settle between lunch and second lunch. Sure enough, outside the parks, there are an astounding number of museums, churches, and giant-palaces-turned-embassies, all waiting to be explored for cheap.

# THE OUTER BARRIOS

Like we said before, Buenos Aires is a big place, with 48 *barrios* within the Capital Federal district alone. Never mind the sprawling metropolis beyond. Though most tourists stay in the aforementioned neighborhoods in the city center, there are many other *barrios*—which we'll refer to as the **Outer Barrios**—that show a quieter side to BA only seen by *porteños* and ambitious travelers.

### THE NORTH

Contrary to popular belief, there is life beyond Palermo in northern Buenos Aires. Just northwest of Palermo, **Belgrano** is a leafy residential district with a large amount of local traffic. Named after **Manuel Belgrano,** the politician who designed the Argentine flag, the *barrio* was originally a separate town, and then—after sizeable growth—its own city. In 1880, during the national turbulence (p. 57), it served as the nation's capital, and it was here that the law was signed to make Buenos Aires Argentina's federal capital. Shortly thereafter, the federal district expanded to officially include Belgrano. It has been a part of Buenos Aires proper ever since. Locals come to shop among the department stores and eat at the numerous cafes scattered along the **Universidad de Belgrano,** a private liberal arts college. Belgrano is also home to the city's small **Chinatown** and to the **Barrancas de Belgrano,** a landscape park designed by Carlos Thays, who also designed the Parque San Martín and the Jardín Botánico.

Two more neighborhoods even farther north receive some degree of tourist traffic—**Núñez** and **Saavedra.** Núñez, which lies right along the Río de la Plata at the farthest northern section of Capital Federal, is a prosperous residential *barrio* best known as the home of **River Plate** (p. 74), one of BA's top soccer clubs and rival of the Boca Juniors to the south. **Saavedra,** just to the west of Núñez, is a neighborhood with little to see, save for its large, relaxing parks.

## THE WEST

The western sector of BA begins with **Balvanera,** just beyond the borders of Microcentro and Monserrat. A commercially important *barrio,* it's overcrowded and ugly. However, there are a few gems, including a handful of fine museums and shopping centers, as well as some viable accommodations options for those who want to be near the center without being in the thick of things. Thankfully for the budget traveler, this usually involves cheaper prices. Balvanera is also further divided into several well-trafficked sub-neighborhoods, including **Once,** home to one of the city's major train stations and one of its largest immigrant populations, and **Abasto,** where you'll find an enormous shopping center and a shrine to one of Argentina's tango legends, **Carlos Gardel** (p. 181). **Congreso** also overlaps a bit with Balvanera; it hums with busy office workers.

Almagro, just to the west of Balvanera, is similar to its neighbor—a little too commercial and unattractive as far as *barrios* go. It's not the best of haunts for tourists, though it does have some highlights, including a celebrated **"off-Corrientes" theater district. Caballito,** even further west, is a middle-class neighborhood with scant tourist offerings, but it's a fine place to wander, with several beautiful parks, tree-lined cobblestone streets, and rows of townhouses. Due north of Caballito is **Chacarita,** which takes its name from the word *chácara,* meaning "small farm"—in the late 18th century, before they were expelled, the neighborhood was home to farm-tending Jesuits. Today, Chacarita is better known for its eponymous, enormous cemetery, which puts its counterpart in Recoleta to shame in terms of sheer scope.

## THE SOUTH

For a taste of real, gritty *porteño* life, southern Buenos Aires is the place to be. There has been no attempt to doll up this district for tourist traffic. It's as simple and down-to-earth as Buenos Aires gets. **Barracas,** which sprawls west from La Boca, was originally a shantytown on the banks of the Riachuelo. This impoverished past explains the root of the *barrio*'s name, the word *barracas,* which refers to a temporary construction of hovels. Though the neighborhood had a brief period of wealth in the 19th century, a yellow fever epidemic brought the prosperity to an end, leading to today's grittiness.

Just west of San Telmo and south of Monserrat, **Constitución** (p. 168) has a utilitarian feel to it. The *barrio* purely serves as a residential neighborhood for the working class. Appropriately, few tourists venture out here. There are a couple of sights, including a massive pink train station and one of the city's oldest buildings, but little else to do beyond wandering the streets.

 **SOUTHERN SAFETY.** Similar to nearby Boca, many of BA's southern *barrios* can be unsafe, especially at night. Exercise caution.

**Boedo** and **San Cristóbal,** due west of Constitución, have a different feel than the rest of the south. Boedo is a trendy *barrio* on the rise, led by an alternative, artsy crowd of bohemians that frequent the neighborhood's many cafes, restaurants, and theaters. San Cristóbal, which is often lumped together with Boedo, is in a similar condition. Many tourists have started to mosey through the streets of this up-and-coming district, and the tourist industry has responded with a number of new hostels, eateries, and attractions.

DISCOVER

## LET'S GO PICKS

**MOST QUESTIONABLE CHOICE OF COLOR FOR A PRESIDENTIAL MANSION: Casa Rosada's** (p. 139) blazing, but distinctive, pink.

**NARROWEST HOUSE: Casa Mínima,** at a painful 2m wide (p. 148).

**BEST PLACE TO WATCH OTHER PEOPLE TANGO—AND MAYBE JOIN IN YOURSELF:** The informal *milonga* following the **Feria de San Telmo** (p. 147).

**BEST PLACE TO GO CRAZY AND UNLEASH YOUR INNER SOCCER FAN, WITHIN THE BOUNDS OF THE LAW: La Bombonera,** the raucous home of the **Boca Juniors** (p. 149).

**BEST ESCAPE: Reserva Ecológica Costanera Sur,** in Puerto Madero, is an oasis of wildlife in the heart of the city (p. 150).

**BEST PLACE TO UTTER THE PHRASE "I WISH I LIVED HERE":** Retiro's opulent **Palacio Paz,** inspired in part by France's Palace of Versailles (p. 151).

**BEST ALTERNATIVE TO HANGING OUT WITH LIVING HUMAN BEINGS:** Hang out with the dead at the massive **La Recoleta Cemetery** (p. 153), or the even bigger **La Chacarita Cemetery** (p. 164).

**MOST WORTHWHILE CAVITY:** A stop for some **dulce de leche** at one of the city's many *heladerías,* which serve mind-blowingly delicious ice cream (p. 122 and p. 129).

**BEST PLACE TO VIEW GREAT LATIN AMERICAN ART, RATHER THAN THE OLD MASTERS FOR THE MILLIONTH TIME:** The **MALBA** (p. 176).

**MOST BEEF: Cuatro Hojas,** where you can order all the *bife* you want for one low price (p. 128).

**BEST PLACE FOR JAZZ AND A DRINK:** Palermo's **Thelonius** (p. 187).

**BEST PLACE TO PARTY OVERNIGHT AND WELL INTO THE NEXT DAY: Caix,** which opens Saturday night and doesn't close until Sunday afternoon, is your place (p. 212).

**TREATMENT BEST FOR QUILMES EXHAUSTION SYNDROME (QES):** Try **Cossab,** a regular old pub in the heart of BA with a fine selection of brews other than the Argentine staple (p. 214).

**THE MOST BREATHTAKING SIGHT YOU WILL EVER SEE:** The thundering cascades of **Iguazú Falls** (p. 236).

# BA'S GREATEST HITS

La Chacarita Cemetery

Villa Crespo

Av. San Martin

Almagro

Balvanera

Av. Independencia

Av. San Juan

San Cristobal

Barracas

Av. Montes de Oca

La Boca

Recoleta

Av. Rivadavia

Av. Callao

Microcentro

Av. Belgrano

Av. de Mayo

Monserrat

Plaza de Mayo

San Telmo

Av. E. Madero

Av. Alicia Moreau de Justo

Puerto Madero

Retiro

Av. de Libertador

Autopista Arturo Illia

Av. Pueyrredón

### Parque Tres de Febrero
Visit Palermo, BA's trendiest *barrio*, and its massive system of relaxing **parks** (p. 156).

### MALBA
BA's top art museum, **MALBA** (p. 176), focuses only on Latin American artists. Take a hike, Old Masters.

### La Recoleta Cemetery
See Recoleta's city-like **cemetery** (p. 153) and hit up **La Biela** (p. 128) for coffee afterwards.

### Plaza de Mayo to Congreso
Take a stroll down BA's most famous thoroughfare, **Avenida de Mayo** (p. 144), and stop at **Cafe Tortoni** (p. 120).

### Calle Florida
Microcentro's hectic main artery, **Calle Florida** (p. 195), is a pedestrian way jam-packed with shops.

### San Telmo Feria and Defensa
Check out this old-school *barrio*'s center, **Plaza Dorrega**, and its fantastic Sunday flea market (p. 147).

### Plaza San Martín
BA's *other* plaza still manages to impress with stunning sights like **Palacio Paz** (p. 151).

### El Caminito and La Bombonera
Call it touristy, but La Boca's colorful street, **El Caminito,** is *classic* BA. See a Boca Juniors game at La Bombonera while you're there (p. 149).

DISCOVER

DISCOVER

# SLEEP BY DAY, PARTY BY NIGHT

La Chacarita Cemetery

Palermo

Villa Crespo

**Thursday**
Head to Palermo's **Niceto** (p. 212) for the drag dance troupe Club 69. They'll blow you away. There's also "Lost," a hip-hop night at **Club Araóz** (p. 211).

Av. Juan B Justo

**Sunday**
Still awake? **Calx** (p. 212) keeps partying until 2pm. Microcentro's Brazilian club, **Maluco Beleza** (p. 205), is also open late.

**Saturday**
Bar hop in Palermo, with a stop at **Congo** (p. 210), before **The Big One**, a popular electronica night at Monserrat's **Alsina** (p. 215).

Av. Cabildo

**Friday**
Load up on drinks and comfort food at Recoleta's **El Living** (p. 209) Next, start off the weekend right at one of the city's smaller electronica clubs, like nearby **Glam** (p. 214).

Almagro

Recoleta

Av. Córdoba

Balvanera

Av. Corrientes

Av. Rivadavia

Av. Independencia

Av. San Juan

Av. Callao

Av. Santa Fe

Av. de Mayo

Av. 9 de Julio

Microcentro

Retiro

**Tuesday**
Check out French cocktail night at **La Cigale** (p. 205). Then head to **Bahrein** (p. 205) for drum and bass.

**Monday**
Start off at the **La Bomba de Tiempo** percussion show in Balvanera (p. 188) followed by Monserrat's **Bar Seddon** (p. 204) for live music and drinks.

Av. Belgrano

Monserrat

**Wednesday**
Pay a visit to San Telmo's **La Puerta Roja** (p. 206), a traditional bar (read: great beer). Afterwards, stop at Monserrat's **Museum** (p. 204) for its post-work party.

San Telmo

Barracas

Av. Montes de Oca

Puerto Madero

Reserva Ecológica Costanera Sur

La Boca

## BEEF, SOCCER, AND TANGO

*Parque Tres de Febrero*

Diego Maradona was a big fan of the parrilla **El Pobre Luis** (p. 135). The house specialty: meat stuffed with cheese, peppers, and ham. We'll take it.

Looking for some beef? **La Cabrera** (p. 117), a Palermo *parrilla*, is the best option in the city.

Epic **La Chacarita Cemetery** (p. 164), bigger than Recoleta's, is the burial site of legendary tango crooner **Carlos Gardel** (p. 80).

**La Virutá** (p. 188) is one of the most popular tango venues in the city for lessons and *milongas*.

Av. Cabildo

Almagro

Av. Córdoba

Recoleta

Av. Pueyrredón

*La Recoleta Cemetery*

Autopista Arturo Illia

Av. Corrientes

Av. Rivadavia

Av. Callao

Av. Santa Fe

Retiro

Balvanera

Av. Independencia

Av. San Juan

**Microcentro**

Av. de Mayo

Av. 9 de Julio

A large cafe in the heart of Microcentro, **Confitería Ideal** (p. 122) has daily tango classes, evening shows, and, of course, coffee.

Av. Belgrano

San Cristobal

*Plaza de Mayo*

**Monserrat**

Av. San Juan

Constitucion

Sick of paying for tango? Try the Sunday **San Telmo Feria** (p. 147), where an informal *milonga* usually starts up after the market closes.

*Reserva Ecológica Costanera Sur*

Barracas

Av. Montes de Oca

**San Telmo**

**Puerto Madero**

**La Boca**

With its gritty fan base, the **Boca Juniors** are *the* classic BA soccer team. Be sure to catch a game at **La Bombonera** (p. 149).

# ESSENTIALS

## PLANNING YOUR TRIP

**ENTRANCE REQUIREMENTS**
**Passport** (p. 18). Required for citizens of Australia, Canada, Ireland, New Zealand, the UK, and the US.
**Visa** (p. 19). Required for citizens of Australia, Canada, Ireland, New Zealand, South Africa, the UK, and the US for stays longer than 90 days.
**Letter of Invitation** (p. 19).
**Inoculations** (p. 30).
**Work Permit** (p. 19).

## EMBASSIES AND CONSULATES

### ARGENTINE CONSULAR SERVICES ABROAD

**Australia:** John McEwen House, Level 2, 7 National Circuit, Barton, ACT 2600 (☎61 02 6273 9111; www.argentina.org.au). **Consulate:** 44 Market St., Lvl. 20, Sydney, NSW (☎61 02 9262 2933; www.argentina.org.au/consular_information.htm).

**Canada:** 81 Metcalfe St., Ste. 700, Ottawa, ONT K1P 6K7, (☎1-613-236-2351; www.argentina-canada.net). **Consulates:** 2000 Peel, Ste. 600, Montreal, QUE H3A 2W5, (☎1-514-842-6582; www.consargenmtl.com). 5001 Yonge St. Ste. 201, 2nd Floor, Toronto, ONT M2N 6P6 (☎1-416-955-9075; www.consargtoro.ca).

**Ireland:** 15 Ailesbury Dr., Ballsbridge, Dublin 4, Ireland (☎353 01 269 1546; embassyofargentina@eircom.net).

**New Zealand:** Lvl. 14, 142 Lambton Quay, Wellington (☎64 04 472 8330; www.arg.org.nz).

**United Kingdom:** 65 Brook St., London, W1K 4AH, United Kingdom (☎44 020 7318 1300; www.argentine-embassy-uk.org).

**United States:** 1600 New Hampshire Ave., NW, Washington, DC 20009-2512, United States (☎202-238-6401; www.embassyofargentina.us). **Consulate:** 12 West 56th St., New York, NY 10019, US (☎212-603-0400; www.congenargentinany.com).

**Uruguay:** Cuareim 1470, 11100, Montevideo, Uruguay (☎ 598 02 902 8166; emburuguay.mrecic.gov.ar). **Consulate:** Ave. General Flores 209, 70000, Colonia del Sacramento, Uruguay (☎598 522 2093; conccolo@adinet.com.uy).

### CONSULAR SERVICES IN BUENOS AIRES

**Australia:** Villanueva 1400, C1426BMJ, Buenos Aires, Argentina (☎011 4779 3500; www.argentina.embassy.gov.au).

**Canada:** Tagle 2828, C1425EEH, Buenos Aires, Argentina (☎011 4808 1000; geo.international.gc.ca/latin-america/argentina).

**Ireland:** Edificio Bluesky, 6th Floor, Av. del Libertador 1068, Recoleta, Buenos Aires, Argentina (☎011 5787 0801; www.embassyofireland.org.ar).

**New Zealand:** Carlos Pellegrini 1427, 5th Floor, CP1011, Buenos Aires, Argentina (☎011 4328 0747; www.nzembassy.com).

**United Kingdom:** Dr. Luis Agote 2412, C1425EOF, Buenos Aires, Argentina (☎011 4808 2200; www.britain.org.ar).

**United States:** Av. Colombia 4300, C1425GMN, Buenos Aires, Argentina (☎011 5777 4533; argentina.usembassy.gov).

**Uruguay:** Av. Las Heras 1907, Buenos Aires, Argentina (☎011 4807 3040; www.embajadadeluruguay.com.ar).

## TOURIST OFFICES

The government tourist agency, **Turismo de la Ciudad de Buenos Aires** (www.bue. gov.ar), runs **kiosks** throughout the city and at both **airports** (p. 36). The kiosks distribute free maps and guides on what's going on around Buenos Aires. In addition to free guided **tours** (usually Sa afternoons; check the website for more information), the office offers free audio tours that you can download at www. bue.gov.ar/audioguia and play on your iPod as you take in the sights. For information about museums, visit www.museos.buenosaires.gov.ar. For a complete listing of tourist office locations in Buenos Aires, see p. 18.

# DOCUMENTS AND FORMALITIES

## PASSPORTS

### REQUIREMENTS

Citizens of Australia, Canada, Ireland, New Zealand, the UK, and the US need valid passports to enter Argentina and to return home. Make sure that your passport is up to date and has been recently renewed before traveling; returning home with an expired passport is illegal and may result in a fine.

### NEW PASSPORTS

Citizens of Australia, Canada, Ireland, New Zealand, the UK, and the US can apply for a passport at any passport office or at selected post offices and courts of law. Citizens of these countries may also download passport applications from the official website of their country's government or passport office. Any new passport or renewal applications must be filed well in advance of the departure date, though most passport offices offer rush services for a very steep fee. Note that "rushed" passports still take up to two weeks to arrive.

### PASSPORT MAINTENANCE

Photocopy the page of your passport with your photo as well as your visas, traveler's check serial numbers, and any other important documents. Carry one set of copies in a safe place, apart from the originals, and leave another set at home. Consulates also recommend that you carry an expired passport or an official copy of your birth certificate in a part of your baggage separate from other important or official documents.

If you lose your passport, immediately notify the local police and your home country's nearest embassy or consulate. To expedite its replacement, you must show ID and proof of citizenship; it also helps to know all information previously recorded in the passport. In some cases, a replacement may take weeks to process, and it may be valid only for a limited time. Any visas stamped in your old passport will be lost forever. In an emergency, ask for immediate temporary traveling papers that will permit you to re-enter your home country.

# VISAS, INVITATIONS, AND WORK PERMITS

## VISAS

Citizens of Australia, Canada, Ireland, New Zealand, the UK, and the US do not need visas for stays of less than 90 days in Argentina. For longer stays, visas (US$30) are required. Contact the nearest Argentine consulate or embassy (listed under Argentine Consular Services Abroad, p. 17) for forms, more information on how to get a visa, and details on entrance requirements. US citizens can also consult http://travel.state.gov. Entering Argentina to study requires a special visa—for more information, see **Beyond Tourism,** p. 83).

## WORK PERMITS

A work permit is required to work in Argentina—this right is not guaranteed by admittance to the country. For more information, see **Beyond Tourism,** p. 83.

# IDENTIFICATION

When you travel, always carry at least two forms of identification on your person, including a photo ID. A passport and a driver's license or birth certificate will suffice. Never carry all of your IDs together; split them up in case of theft or loss and keep photocopies of all of them in your luggage and at home.

## STUDENT, TEACHER, AND YOUTH IDENTIFICATION

The **International Student Identity Card** (ISIC), the most widely accepted form of student ID, provides discounts on some sights, accommodations, food, and transportation; access to a 24hr. emergency help line; and insurance benefits for US cardholders (see **Insurance,** p. 29). Some discounts include savings at hostels, food establishments, and athletics facilities. Applicants must be full-time secondary or post-secondary school students at least 12 years old. Because of the proliferation of fake ISICs, some services (particularly airlines) require additional proof of student identity.

The **International Teacher Identity Card** (ITIC) offers teachers the same insurance coverage as the ISIC and similar but limited discounts. To qualify for the card, teachers must be currently employed and have worked a minimum of 18hr. per week for at least one school year. For travelers who are under 26 years old but are not students, the **International Youth Travel Card** (IYTC) also offers many of the same benefits as the ISIC.

Each of these identity cards costs US$22. ISICs, ITICS, and IYTCs are valid for one year from the date of issue. To learn more about ISICs, ITICs, and IYTCs, try www.myisic.com. Many student travel agencies (p. 33) issue the cards; for a list of issuing agencies or more information, see the **International Student Travel Confederation** (ISTC) website (www.istc.org).

The **International Student Exchange Card** (ISE Card) is a similar identification card available to students, faculty, and children aged 12 to 26. The card provides discounts, medical benefits, access to a 24hr. emergency help line, and the ability to purchase student airfares. An ISE Card costs US$25; call ☎800-255-8000 (in North America) or ☎480-951-1177 (from all other continents) for more information, or visit www.isecard.com.

ESSENTIALS

## CUSTOMS

Upon entering Argentina, you must declare certain items from abroad and pay a duty on the value of those articles if they exceed the allowance established by Argentina's customs service. Goods and gifts purchased at duty-free shops abroad are not exempt from duty or sales tax; "duty-free" means that you won't pay tax in the country of purchase. Duty-free allowances were abolished for travel between EU member states on June 30, 1999, but still exist for those arriving from outside the EU. Upon returning home, you must likewise declare all articles acquired abroad and pay a duty on the value of articles in excess of your home country's allowance. In order to expedite your return, make a list of any valuables brought from home and register them with customs before traveling abroad. It's a good idea to keep receipts for all goods acquired abroad.

Argentina has a **value added tax (VAT)** of 21%. Money spent on VAT in Argentina can be redeemed at the airport upon departure for purchases of over AR$70 made at tax-free shopping participant stores. Make sure to fill out the required forms at the airport or at participating stores.

# MONEY

## CURRENCY AND EXCHANGE

The currency chart below is based on August 2008 exchange rates between local currency and Australian dollars (AUS$), Canadian dollars (CDN$), European Union euro (EUR€), New Zealand dollars (NZ$), British pounds (UK£), and US dollars (US$). Check the currency converter on websites like www. xe.com or www.bloomberg.com for the latest exchange rates.

| CURRENCY (AR$) | | |
| --- | --- | --- |
| AUS$1 = AR$2.76 | | AR$1 = AUS$0.36 |
| CDN$1 = AR$2.90 | | AR$1 = CDN$0.34 |
| EUR€1 = AR$4.69 | | AR$1 = EUR€0.21 |
| NZ$1 = AR$2.18 | | AR$1 = NZ$0.46 |
| UK£1 = AR$5.93 | | AR$1 = UK£0.17 |
| US$1 = AR$3.04 | | AR$1 = US$0.33 |

As a general rule, it's cheaper to convert money in Argentina than at home. While currency exchange will probably be available in your arrival airport, it's wise to bring enough foreign currency to last for at least 24-72 hours.

When changing money abroad, try to go only to banks or *casas de cambio* that have at most a 5% margin between their buy and sell prices. Since you lose money with every transaction, it makes sense to convert large sums at one time (unless the currency is depreciating rapidly).

If you use traveler's checks or bills, carry some in small denominations (the equivalent of US$50 or fewer) for times when you are forced to exchange money at poor rates, but bring a range of denominations since charges may be applied per check cashed. Store your money in a variety of forms; ideally, at any given time you will be carrying some cash, some traveler's checks, and an ATM and/or credit card. All travelers should also consider carrying some US dollars (about US$50 worth), which are often preferred by local tellers.

# TRAVELER'S CHECKS

Traveler's checks are one of the safest and most convenient means of carrying funds. American Express and Visa are the most-recognized brands. Many banks and agencies sell them for a small commission. Check issuers provide refunds if the checks are lost or stolen, and many provide additional services, such as toll-free refund hotlines abroad, emergency message services and assistance with lost and stolen credit cards or passports. Traveler's checks are readily accepted in cities and towns throughout the Pampas and in rural areas of Buenos Aires province. Within Buenos Aires itself, you will have a harder time finding establishments that accept traveler's checks. Ask about toll-free refund hotlines and the location of refund centers when purchasing checks, and always carry emergency cash.

**American Express:** Checks available with commission at select banks, at all AmEx offices, and online (www.americanexpress.com; US residents only). AmEx cardholders can also purchase checks by phone (☎800-528-4800). Checks available in Australian, British, Canadian, European, Japanese, and US currencies, among others. AmEx also offers the Travelers Cheque Card, a prepaid reloadable card. Cheques for Two can be signed by either of 2 people traveling together. For purchase locations or more information, contact AmEx's service centers: in Argentina ☎011 4310 3000; in Australia ☎+61 2 9271 8666, in New Zealand +64 9 367 4567, in the UK +44 1273 696 933, in the US and Canada +1-800-221-7282; elsewhere, call the US collect at +1-336-393-1111.

**Travelex:** Visa TravelMoney prepaid cash card and Visa traveler's checks available. For information about Thomas Cook MasterCard in Canada and the US, call ☎+1-800-223-7373, in the UK +44 0800 622 101; elsewhere, call the UK collect at +44 1733 318 950. For information about Interpayment Visa in the US and Canada, call ☎+1-800-732-1322, in the UK +44 0800 515 884; elsewhere, call the UK collect at +44 1733 318 949. For more information, visit www.travelex.com.

**Visa:** Checks available (generally with commission) at banks worldwide. For the location of the nearest office, call the Visa Travelers Cheque Global Refund and Assistance Center: in the UK ☎+44 0800 895 078, in the US +1-800-227-6811; elsewhere, call the UK collect at +44 2079 378 091. Checks available in British, Canadian, European, Japanese, and US currencies, among others. Visa also offers TravelMoney, a prepaid debit card that can be reloaded online or by phone. For more information on Visa travel services, see http://usa.visa.com/personal/using_visa/travel_with_visa.html.

# CREDIT, DEBIT, AND ATM CARDS

Where they are accepted, credit cards often offer superior exchange rates—up to 5% better than the retail rate used by banks and other currency exchange establishments. Credit cards may also offer services such as insurance or emergency help and are sometimes required to reserve hotel rooms or rental cars. **MasterCard** and **Visa** are the most frequently accepted; **American Express** cards work at some ATMs and at AmEx offices and major airports.

The use of ATM cards is widespread in Argentina. Depending on the system your home bank uses, you can most likely access your personal bank account from abroad. ATMs get the same wholesale exchange rate as credit cards, but there is often a limit on the amount of money you can withdraw per day (usually around US$500). There is typically a surcharge of US$1-5 per withdrawal.

Debit cards are as convenient as credit cards but withdraw money directly from the holder's checking account. A debit card can be used wherever its associated credit card company (usually MasterCard or Visa) is accepted. Debit cards often also function as ATM cards and can be used to withdraw cash from associated banks and ATMs throughout Argentina.

ESSENTIALS

The two major international money networks are **MasterCard/Maestro/Cirrus** (for ATM locations ☎+1-800-424-7787 or www.mastercard.com) and **Visa/PLUS** (for ATM locations ☎+1-800-847-2911 or www.visa.com). Most ATMs charge a transaction fee that is paid to the bank that owns the ATM. The major national money networks within Argentina are **Banelco** (marked by red and white signs) and **Link** (marked by green and yellow signs). Link ATMs allow you to choose which network you wish to withdraw from, be it MasterCard/Maestro/Cirrus or Visa/PLUS. You should have little trouble withdrawing money from these machines. Banelco ATMs do not allow you to choose the network.

# GETTING MONEY FROM HOME

If you run out of money while traveling, the easiest and cheapest solution is to have someone back home make a deposit to your bank account. Otherwise, consider one of the following options.

## WIRING MONEY

It is possible to arrange a **bank money transfer,** which means asking a bank back home to wire money to a bank in Argentina. This is the cheapest way to transfer cash, but it's also the slowest, usually taking several days or more. Note that some banks may only release your funds in local currency, potentially sticking you with a poor exchange rate; inquire about this in advance. Money transfer services like Western Union are faster and more convenient than bank transfers—but also much pricier. **Western Union** has many locations worldwide. To find one, visit www.westernunion.com, or call in Australia ☎1800 173 833, in Canada and the US +1-800-325-6000, in the UK +44 0800 833 833, or in Argentina 011 4777 1940. To wire money using a credit card (Discover, MasterCard, Visa), call in Canada and the US +1-800-CALL-CASH, in the UK ☎+44 0800 833 833. Money transfer services are also available to **American Express** cardholders and at selected **Thomas Cook** offices.

## US STATE DEPARTMENT (US CITIZENS ONLY)

In serious emergencies only, the US State Department will forward money within hours to the nearest consular office, which will then disburse it according to instructions for a US$30 fee. If you wish to use this service, you must contact the Overseas Citizens Services division of the US State Department (☎+1-202-501-4444, from US ☎888-407-4747).

# COSTS

The cost of your trip will vary considerably, depending on where you go, how you travel, and where you stay. The most significant expenses will probably be your round-trip (return) airfare to Argentina (see **Getting to Argentina: By Plane,** p. 33). Before you go, spend some time calculating a reasonable daily budget.

## STAYING ON A BUDGET

To give you a general idea, a bare-bones day in Argentina (camping or sleeping in hostels/guesthouses, buying food at supermarkets) would cost about US$30 (AR$90); a slightly more comfortable day (sleeping in hostels/guesthouses and the occasional budget hotel, eating one meal per day at a restaurant, going out at night) would cost US$50 (AR$150); and, for a luxurious day, the sky's the limit. Don't forget to factor in emergency reserve funds (at least US$200) when planning how much money you'll need.

## TIPS FOR SAVING MONEY

Some simpler ways include searching out opportunities for free entertainment, splitting accommodation and food costs with trustworthy fellow travelers, and buying food in supermarkets rather than eating out. Bring a **sleepsack** (p. 24) to save on sheet charges in hostels and do your **laundry** in the sink (unless you're explicitly prohibited from doing so). Museums often have certain days once a month or once a week when admission is free; plan accordingly. If you are eligible, consider getting an ISIC or an IYTC (p. 19); many sights and museums offer reduced admission to students and youths. For getting around quickly, bikes are the most economical option. Renting a bike is cheaper than renting a moped or scooter. Don't forget about walking, though; you can learn a lot about a city by seeing it on foot. Drinking at bars and clubs quickly becomes expensive. It's cheaper to buy alcohol at a supermarket and imbibe before going out. That said, don't go overboard. Though staying within your budget is important, don't do so at the expense of your health or a great travel experience.

# TIPPING

Locals don't tip too much—about 10% at decent restaurants, usually when it's not included. More upscale and trendy bars and restaurants, however, charge a *cubierto* ("cover") for table service of approximately AR$5-6. In these circumstances, since the cover is small, make sure to tip more than usual. Tipping is never expected for taxis. Be sure to round up to the nearest peso, though, so the driver doesn't have to give you change.

# TAXES

See p. 20 for more information on Argentina's **value added tax (VAT).**

# PACKING

**Pack lightly:** lay out only what you absolutely need, then take half the clothes and twice the money. The Travelite FAQ (www.travelite.org) is a good resource for tips on traveling light. The online **Universal Packing List** (http://upl.codeq.info) will generate a customized list of suggested items based on your trip length, expected climate, planned activities, and other factors. Some frequent travelers keep a bag packed with all the essentials: passport, money belt, hat, socks, etc. Then, when they decide to leave, they know they haven't forgotten anything.

> **Luggage:** A sturdy **internal-frame backpack** is unbeatable for both the city and any day-trips you may take. A smaller **daypack** is indispensable for exploring the city.

> **Clothing:** By latitude, Buenos Aires is roughly as far south from the equator as Florida is north. It's warm during the summer, with average highs around 80°F/27°C, and rarely gets too cold during the winter, with average low temperatures never dropping below 45°F/7°C. Pack accordingly. No matter when you're traveling, it's a good idea to bring a warm jacket or wool sweater, a Gore-Tex® rain jacket, sturdy shoes or hiking boots, and thick socks (along with extra pairs aplenty). Flip-flops or waterproof sandals are must-haves for grubby hostel showers. You will want an outfit for going out and a nicer pair of shoes; jeans and flip-flops will get you kicked out of many clubs. Gearing up for an excursion to Iguazú Falls? Before packing, note that temperatures there are usually much higher than in Buenos Aires, given the tropical climate. Winter trips to interior and southern Argentina will bring cooler temperatures compared to Buenos Aires.

**Sleepsack:** Some hostels require that you either provide your own linen or rent sheets from them. Save cash by making your own sleepsack: fold a full-size sheet in half the long way, then sew it closed along the long side and one of the short sides.

**Converters and Adapters:** In Argentina, electricity is 220 volts AC, enough to fry any 120V North American appliance. 220/240V electrical appliances won't work with a 120V current, either. Americans and Canadians should buy an adapter (which changes the shape of the plug; US$5) and a converter (which changes the voltage; US$10-30). Don't make the mistake of using only an adapter (unless appliance instructions explicitly state otherwise). Australians and New Zealanders (who use 230V at home) won't need a converter but will need a set of adapters to use anything electrical. In general, to check appliance compatibility, see if there's any text on the appliance's adapter—this will usually specify what range of voltage levels is suitable. Most modern North American appliances, such as cell phones, digital cameras, and laptops, can still use Argentine 220V/50Hz electricity without conversion and will only require a plug adapter. For more on all things adaptable, check out http://kropla.com/electric.htm.

**Toiletries:** Condoms, deodorant, razors, tampons, and toothbrushes are often available, but it may be difficult to find your preferred brand; bring extras just in case. Contact lenses are likely to be expensive and difficult to find, so bring enough extra pairs and solution for your entire trip. Also bring your glasses and a copy of your prescription in case you need emergency replacements.

**First-Aid Kit:** For a basic first-aid kit, pack bandages, a pain reliever, antibiotic cream, a thermometer, a multifunction pocketknife, tweezers, moleskin, decongestant, motion-sickness remedy, diarrhea or upset-stomach medication, an antihistamine, sunscreen, insect repellent, burn ointment, and a syringe for emergencies.

**Other Useful Items:** For safety purposes, you should bring a **money belt** and a small **padlock.** Basic **outdoors equipment** (plastic water bottle, pocketknife, sunglasses, sunscreen, hat) may also be handy. Other things you're liable to forget include: an umbrella, sealable **plastic bags** (for damp clothes, soap, food, shampoo, and other spillables), an **alarm clock,** and earplugs. A **cell phone** can be a lifesaver (literally) on the road; see p. 43 for information on acquiring one that will work in Argentina.

**Important Documents:** Don't forget your passport, traveler's checks, ATM and/or credit cards, adequate ID, and photocopies of all of the aforementioned in case these documents are lost or stolen (p. 27). Also check that you have any of the following that might apply to you: a hosteling membership card; driver's license (p. 19); travel insurance forms (p. 29); ISIC (p. 19), and/or railpass or bus pass (p. 33).

# SAFETY AND HEALTH

## GENERAL ADVICE

In any type of crisis, the most important thing to do is **stay calm.** Your country's embassy abroad (p. 17) is usually your best resource in an emergency; registering with that embassy upon arrival in the country is a good idea. The government offices listed in the **Travel Advisories** box (p. 26) can provide information on the services they offer their citizens in case of emergencies abroad.

## LOCAL LAWS AND POLICE

Police officers are everywhere in Buenos Aires, stationed on nearly every street corner in the city center. The **Police Tourist Office** (436 Corrientes, Microcentro,

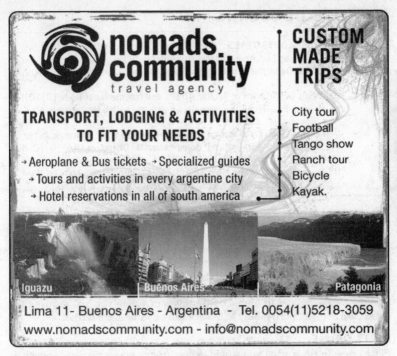

**nomads community** travel agency

**CUSTOM MADE TRIPS**

**TRANSPORT, LODGING & ACTIVITIES TO FIT YOUR NEEDS**

→ Aeroplane & Bus tickets → Specialized guides
→ Tours and activities in every argentine city
→ Hotel reservations in all of south america

City tour
Football
Tango show
Ranch tour
Bicycle
Kayak.

Iguazu · Buenos Aires · Patagonia

Lima 11- Buenos Aires - Argentina - Tel. 0054(11)5218-3059
www.nomadscommunity.com - info@nomadscommunity.com

ESSENTIALS

Ⓢ Florida. ☎4346 5748), with its English-speaking staff, can help with tourist-related crimes, such as theft. **Dial ☎101 for emergencies. For all other general emergencies, dial ☎911 for Police, ☎100 for Fire, and ☎107 for Ambulance.**

## DRUGS AND ALCOHOL

The legal **drinking age** in Argentina is technically 18 for purchasing alcoholic beverages in stores, bars, clubs, and restaurants. However, carding is rare in most establishments unless you look *really* young. Identification will always be checked in the few clubs that are 21+ only.

Argentina's legal **smoking age,** for purchasing and smoking cigarettes and other tobacco products, is 16, although some provinces, such as Buenos Aires, set the limit at 18. Smoking in bars, clubs, and restaurants is usually banned, unless the establishment has a smoking permit or a smoking section with suitable ventilation. On the other hand, in some clubs, everyone smokes everywhere—the rules can vary widely from place to place. Note that in BA in particular, smoking is outright prohibited in government buildings and in enclosed public spaces. Unlike many western countries, though, there is very little stigma against smoking—many people do it.

Although **drugs** are inexpensive and relatively easy to get, they are still very much illegal in Argentina, save, of course, for prescription medications. With some drugs, particularly **marijuana,** it's somewhat common to see people light up when they're in crowds and think they won't be found—in clubs, bars, and at soccer games. Such sights highlight a recent trend in Argentine law favoring a decriminalization of drug use. The debate, however, is ongoing.

# SPECIFIC CONCERNS

**TRAVEL ADVISORIES.** The following government offices provide travel information and advisories by telephone, by fax, or via the web:

**Australian Department of Foreign Affairs and Trade:** ☎+61 2 6261 1111; www.dfat.gov.au.

**Canadian Department of Foreign Affairs and International Trade (DFAIT):** Call ☎+1-800-267-8376; www.dfait-maeci.gc.ca. Call for their free booklet, *Bon Voyage...But.*

**New Zealand Ministry of Foreign Affairs:** ☎+64 4 439 8000; www.mfat.govt.nz.

**United Kingdom Foreign and Commonwealth Office:** ☎+44 20 7008 1500; www.fco.gov.uk.

**US Department of State:** ☎+1-888-407-4747; http://travel.state.gov. Visit the website for the booklet, *A Safe Trip Abroad.*

ESSENTIALS

## VIOLENT CRIME

Since the end of the Argentine economic crisis, violent crime has become less and less of a concern in Buenos Aires. Most *barrios* are quite safe during the day—violent crime is no worse here than in most big cities in North America and Europe. By Latin American standards, **Buenos Aires is one of the safest cities in South America. Kidnapping** is another concern, although it happens mainly to wealthy locals and not to tourists. Regardless of where you are, always take extra care at night, particularly in **La Boca** and other **southern barrios.**

## PETTY CRIME

Petty crime in BA is what you would expect from a major city—it happens in heavily trafficked areas, such as the *subte* and touristy thoroughfares. However, it is by no means a rampant problem. Take extra precaution around and in the city's major **bus** and **train stations.** Most robberies happen to visitors who do not closely watch their bags. Watch out for common distraction scams, such as an accomplice yelling at you while the thief steals your bag.

## RACISM

Argentina's population is largely **white** (97%), with most people being descendents of **Italian** and **Spanish** immigrants. The next largest group is **mestizo** (3%), which is a combination of European and indigenous Amerindian heritage. There is no notable **black** population to speak of. Anywhere along the white to brown spectrum will almost never garner much attention. Black visitors should expect to face no negative treatment, either. Due to the country's small black population, it will certainly be noticed, but perhaps only with a stare.

## DEMONSTRATIONS AND POLITICAL GATHERINGS

In its long history of coups, government upheaval, and regime change, Argentina has had periods of unrest marked by demonstrations and political gatherings, most recently, during the **economic crisis** of 1999-2002. When they happen, protests almost always center around the **Plaza de Mayo,** home of the **Casa Rosada,** the chief building of the Argentine executive branch. Many protest groups currently frequent the Plaza daily, but they are of no concern. For details on etiquette when discussing political issues, see p. 70.

**TERRORISM**

Terrorism has not been a serious problem in Buenos Aires as of late, although incidents have flared up in the past. The main period of terrorist activity in Argentine history occurred during the **Dirty War** of the late 1970s and early 1980s. However, terrorist groups from this time period have long since dissipated. The early 1990s saw some major attacks in Buenos Aires, including a **1992 strike** on the **Israeli Embassy** and a **1994 bombing** of the **Asociación Mutual Israelita Argentina (AMIA),** a Jewish community center. Both cases remain unsolved, though Hezbollah, the Lebanon-based terrorist group, is the most oft-cited culprit. Since then, no major terrorist incidents have occurred in Buenos Aires. The box below lists offices to contact and webpages to visit to get the most updated list of your home country's government's advisories about travel.

# PERSONAL SAFETY

## EXPLORING AND TRAVELING

To avoid unwanted attention, **try to blend in as much as possible.** Respecting local customs (in many cases, dressing more conservatively than you would at home) may ward off would-be hecklers. Familiarize yourself with your surroundings before setting out and carry yourself with confidence. Check maps in shops and restaurants rather than on the street. If you are traveling alone, be sure someone at home knows your itinerary and never tell anyone you meet that you're by yourself. When walking at night, stick to busy, well-lit streets. If you ever feel uncomfortable, leave the area as quickly and directly as you can. There is no surefire way to avoid all the threatening situations that you might encounter while traveling, but a good **self-defense course** will give you concrete ways to react to unwanted advances. **Impact, Prepare,** and **Model Mugging** can refer you to local self-defense courses in Australia, Canada, Switzerland, and the US. Visit www.modelmugging.org for listings of nearby chapters.

If you are using a **car,** learn local driving signals and wear a seatbelt. Children under 40 lb. should ride only in specially designed car seats, available for a small fee from most car-rental agencies. Study route maps before you hit the road and, if you plan on spending a lot of time driving, consider bringing spare parts. For long drives in desolate areas, invest in a cellular phone and a roadside assistance program. Park your vehicle in a garage or well-traveled area and use a steering-wheel locking device in larger cities. Sleeping in your car is the most dangerous way to get your rest, and it's also illegal in many countries. For info on the perils of **hitchhiking,** see p. 41.

## POSSESSIONS AND VALUABLES

Never leave your belongings unattended; crime can occur in even the most safe-looking place. Bring your own **padlock** for hostel lockers and don't ever store valuables in a locker. Be particularly careful on **buses** and **trains;** determined thieves who wait for travelers to fall asleep. Carry your bag or purse in front of you where you can see it. When traveling with others, sleep in alternate shifts. When alone, use good judgment in selecting a train compartment: never stay in an empty one and use a lock to secure your pack to the luggage rack. Use extra caution if traveling at night or on overnight trains. Try to sleep on top bunks with your luggage stored above you (if not in bed with you) and keep important documents and other valuables on you at all times.

There are a few steps you can take to minimize the financial risk associated with traveling. First, **bring as little with you as possible.** Second, buy a few combination **padlocks** to secure your belongings either in your pack or in a hostel or train-station locker. Third, **carry as little cash as possible.** Keep your traveler's checks and ATM/credit cards in a **money belt**—not a "fanny pack"—along with your passport and ID cards. Fourth, **keep a small cash reserve separate from your primary stash.** This should be about US$50 sewn into or stored in the depths of your pack, along with your traveler's check numbers, photocopies of your passport, your birth certificate, and other important documents.

In large cities, **con artists** often work in groups and may involve children. Beware of certain classics: sob stories that require money, rolls of bills "found" on the street, mustard spilled (or saliva spit) onto your shoulder to distract you while they snatch your bag. See p. 26 for details on common scam tactics and pickpocketing trouble spots in Buenos Aires. In general, follow this rule of thumb: **never let your passport and your bags out of your sight.** Hostel workers will sometimes stand at bus and train-station arrival points to recruit tired and disoriented travelers to their hostel; never believe strangers who tell you that theirs is the only hostel open. Also, be alert in public telephone booths: if you must say your calling card number, do so very quietly; if you punch it in, make sure no one can look over your shoulder.

If you will be traveling with electronic devices, such as a laptop, check whether your homeowner's insurance covers loss, theft, or damage when you travel. If not, consider purchasing a separate insurance policy. **Safeware** (☎+1-800-800-1492; www.safeware.com) covers computers and charges US$90 for 90-day comprehensive international travel coverage up to US$4000.

# PRE-DEPARTURE HEALTH

In your passport, write the names of people you wish to be contacted in a **medical emergency** and list any allergies or medical conditions. Matching a prescription to a foreign equivalent is not always possible, so if you take **prescription drugs,** consider carrying up-to-date prescriptions or a statement from your doctor stating the medication's trade name, manufacturer, chemical name, and dosage. While traveling, keep all medication with you in your carry-on luggage. For tips on packing a **first-aid kit** and other health essentials, see p. 24.

## IMMUNIZATIONS AND PRECAUTIONS

Travelers over two years old should make sure that the following vaccines are up to date: **MMR** (for measles, mumps, and rubella); **DTaP** or **Td** (for diphtheria, tetanus, and pertussis); **IPV** (for polio); **Hib** (for *haemophilus influenzae* B); and **HepB** (for Hepatitis B). Though it is not a requirement for travel, many visitors to **Iguazú Falls** (p. 236) get a **yellow fever** vaccine before leaving home. Due to the tropical location of the falls, there are many other remedies that may be pertinent, including, but not limited to, **typhoid** and **cholera** vaccinations and **malaria pills.** However, the area immediately around the falls is fairly developed and separated from the jungle, which makes most of these diseases of little concern. Be sure to consult with a doctor first before traveling to Iguazú. For recommendations on immunizations and prophylaxis, consult the **Centers for Disease Control and Prevention** (CDC; see below) in the US or the equivalent in your home country and check with a doctor for guidance.

**limehouse** Youth Hostel

1 Excellent Location
2 Big Sunny Terrace
3 Breakfast Included
4 Bar with beer on Tap
5 Pool Table & Games
6 Free Internet & Wi.Fi
7 Big Rooms with Lockers
8 Spacious Common Areas
9 Travel Agency in the Lobby

Lima 11 - Buenos Aires - C1073AAA
Argentina - 0054(11)4383-4561
www.limehouse.com.ar

**ESSENTIALS**

# INSURANCE

Travel insurance covers four basic areas: medical/health problems, property loss, trip cancellation/interruption, and emergency evacuation. Though regular insurance policies may well extend to travel-related accidents, you may consider purchasing separate travel insurance if the cost of potential trip cancellation, interruption, or emergency medical evacuation is greater than you can absorb. Prices for travel insurance purchased separately generally run about US$50 per week for full coverage, while trip cancellation/interruption may be purchased separately at a rate of US$3-5 per day, depending on length of stay.

**Medical insurance** (especially university policies) often covers costs incurred abroad; check with your provider. **Homeowners' Insurance** (or your family's coverage) often covers theft during travel and loss of travel documents (passport, plane ticket, railpass, etc.) up to US$500. **ISIC** and **ITIC** (p. 19) provide basic insurance benefits to US cardholders, including US$100 per day of in-hospital sickness for up to 100 days and US$10,000 of accident-related medical reimbursement (see www.isicus.com for details). Cardholders have access to a toll-free 24hr. helpline for medical, legal, and financial emergencies overseas. **American Express** (☎+1-800-338-1670) grants most cardholders automatic collision and theft car rental insurance on rentals made with the card.

# USEFUL ORGANIZATIONS AND PUBLICATIONS

The American **Centers for Disease Control and Prevention** (CDC; ☎+1-877-FYI-TRIP; www.cdc.gov/travel) maintains an international travelers' hotline and an informative website. Consult the appropriate government agency of your home country for consular information sheets on health, entry requirements, and other issues for various countries (see the listings in the box on **Travel Advisories**, p. 26). For quick information on health and other travel warnings, call the **Overseas Citizens Services** (M-F 8am-8pm from overseas +1-202-501-4444, from US ☎+1-888-407-4747; line open M-F 8am-8pm EST), or contact a passport agency, embassy, or consulate abroad. For information on medical evacuation services and travel insurance firms, see the US government's website at http://travel.state.gov/travel/abroad_health.html or the **British Foreign and Commonwealth Office** (www.fco.gov.uk). For general health information, contact the **American Red Cross** (☎+1-202-303-4498; www.redcross.org).

# STAYING HEALTHY

Common sense is the simplest prescription for good health while you travel. Drink lots of fluids to prevent dehydration and constipation and wear sturdy, broken-in shoes and clean socks.

## ONCE IN BUENOS AIRES

### ENVIRONMENTAL HAZARDS

**Heat exhaustion and dehydration:** Temperatures can get high in BA during the summer, particularly out on the plains. Exercise caution to prevent heat exhaustion during days with particularly hot conditions. Heat exhaustion leads to nausea, excessive thirst, headaches, and dizziness. Avoid it by drinking plenty of fluids, eating salty foods (e.g., crackers), abstaining from dehydrating beverages (e.g., alcohol and caffeinated beverages), and wearing sunscreen. Continuous heat stress may eventually lead to heatstroke, characterized by a rising temperature, severe headache, delirium, and cessation of sweating. Victims should be cooled off with wet towels and taken to a doctor immediately.

**Sunburn:** Always wear sunscreen (SPF 30 or higher) when spending a lot of time in the sun. If you get sunburned, drink more fluids than usual and apply an aloe-based lotion. Severe sunburns can lead to sun poisoning, a condition that can cause fever, chills, nausea, and vomiting. Sun poisoning should always be treated by a doctor.

**Hypothermia and frostbite:** During the winter, destinations in the Andes Mountains can get cold. Take extra precaution to avoid hypothermia and frostbite. A rapid drop in body temperature is the clearest sign of overexposure. Victims may also shiver, feel exhausted, have poor coordination or slurred speech, hallucinate, or suffer amnesia. Do not let hypothermia victims fall asleep. To avoid hypothermia, keep dry, wear layers, and stay out of the wind. In below freezing temperatures, watch out for frostbite. If skin turns white or blue, waxy, and cold, do not rub the area. Drink warm beverages, stay dry, and slowly warm the area with dry fabric or steady body contact until you can see a doctor.

**High Altitude:** This could be of concern in the Andes Mountains in western Argentina. Allow your body a couple of days to adjust to the lower oxygen levels before exerting yourself. Note that alcohol is more potent and UV rays are stronger at high elevations.

### INSECT-BORNE DISEASES

Many diseases are transmitted by insects—mainly mosquitoes, fleas, ticks, and lice. Be aware of insects in wet or forested areas, especially while hiking and camping. Wear long pants and long sleeves and tuck your pants into your socks. Use insect repellents such as DEET liberally. **Mosquitoes**—responsible for malaria, dengue fever, and yellow fever—can be particularly abundant in wet, swampy, or wooded areas, such as the Iguazú Falls region (p. 236).

**Malaria:** Transmitted by Anopheles mosquitoes that bite at night. The incubation period varies anywhere between 10 days and 4 weeks. Early symptoms include fever, chills, aches, and fatigue, followed by high fever and sweating, sometimes with vomiting and diarrhea. See a doctor for any flu-like sickness that occurs after travel in a risk area. To reduce the risk of contracting malaria, use mosquito repellent, particularly in the evenings and when visiting forested areas. See a doctor at least 4-6 weeks before a trip to a high-risk area to get up-to-date malaria prescriptions and recommendations. A doctor may prescribe oral prophylactics, like mefloquine or doxycycline. Mefloquine can have very serious side effects, including paranoia, psychotic behavior, and nightmares.

## FOOD- AND WATER-BORNE DISEASES

Prevention is the best cure: be sure that your food is properly cooked and the water you drink is clean. Watch out for food from markets or street vendors that may have been cooked in unhygienic conditions. Other culprits are raw shellfish, unpasteurized milk, and sauces containing raw eggs. Areas of Buenos Aires most frequented by tourists are practically first world—the drinking water, for the most part, is safe and clean. If you ever have any concerns about water quality, buy bottled water or purify your own water by bringing it to a rolling boil or treating it with **iodine tablets;** boiling, however, is more reliable.

**Traveler's diarrhea:** Results from drinking fecally contaminated water or eating uncooked and contaminated foods. Symptoms include nausea, bloating, and urgency. Try quick-energy, non-sugary foods with protein and carbohydrates to keep your strength up. Over-the-counter anti-diarrheals (e.g., Imodium) may counteract the problem. The most dangerous side effect is dehydration; drink 8 oz. of water with ½tsp. of sugar or honey and a pinch of salt, try uncaffeinated soft drinks, or eat salted crackers. If you develop a fever or your symptoms don't go away after 4-5 days, consult a doctor. Consult a doctor immediately for treatment of diarrhea in children.

**Cholera:** An intestinal disease caused by bacteria in contaminated food. Symptoms include diarrhea, dehydration, vomiting, and muscle cramps. See a doctor immediately; if left untreated, cholera can be lethal within hours. Antibiotics are available, but the most important treatment is rehydration. No vaccine is available in the US.

**Hepatitis A:** A viral infection of the liver acquired through contaminated water or shellfish from contaminated water. Symptoms include fatigue, fever, loss of appetite, nausea, dark urine, jaundice, vomiting, aches and pains, and light stools. The risk is highest in rural areas and the countryside, but it is also present in urban areas. Ask your doctor about the Hepatitis A vaccine or an injection of immune globulin.

**Typhoid fever:** Caused by the salmonella bacteria; common in rural areas of South America. While mostly transmitted through contaminated food and water, it may also be acquired by direct contact with another person. Early symptoms include high fever, headaches, fatigue, appetite loss, constipation, and a rash on the abdomen or chest. Antibiotics can treat typhoid, but a vaccination (70-90% effective) is recommended.

## OTHER INFECTIOUS DISEASES

The following diseases exist all over the world. Travelers should know how to recognize them and what to do if they suspect they have been infected.

**Hepatitis B:** A viral infection of the liver transmitted via blood or other bodily fluids. Symptoms, which may not surface until years after infection, include jaundice, appetite loss, fever, and joint pain. Transmitted through unprotected sex and unclean needles. A 3-shot vaccination sequence is recommended for sexually active travelers and anyone planning to seek medical treatment abroad; it must begin 6 months before traveling.

**Hepatitis C:** Like Hepatitis B, but the mode of transmission differs. IV drug users, those with occupational exposure to blood, hemodialysis patients, and recipients of blood transfusions are at the highest risk, but the disease can also be spread through sexual contact or sharing items like razors and toothbrushes that have traces of blood on them. No symptoms are usually exhibited. If untreated, Hepatitis C can lead to liver failure.

**AIDS and HIV:** For detailed information on Acquired Immune Deficiency Syndrome (AIDS) in Argentina, call the 24hr. National AIDS Hotline at ☎+1-800-342-2437.

**Sexually transmitted infections (STIs):** Gonorrhea, chlamydia, genital warts, syphilis, herpes, HPV, and other STIs are easier to catch than HIV and can be just as serious. Though condoms may protect you from some STIs, oral or even tactile contact can lead to transmission. If you think you may have contracted an STI, see a doctor immediately.

# OTHER HEALTH CONCERNS

## MEDICAL CARE ON THE ROAD

Medical care in Argentina is **free,** even for foreigners. If you want, you can pay more for a private hospital. Note that the free medical care is mediocre and the hospitals are in comparably mediocre condition. However, if you want free health care and are willing to deal with fine care, as opposed to great care, just show up at any public emergency room, ask for help, and you will be fine. There will probably be a doctor who speaks some English, but they won't necessarily have a medical professional who is fluent. Free 24hr. **public clinics** include **Hospital de Clínicas José de San Martín,** Av. Córdoba 2351 (☎5950 8000; www.hospitaldeclinicas.uba.ar). For better care, with regular walk-in business hours and a better chance of an English-speaking doctor being on hand, there are many private hospital options, such as **Hospital Britanico,** Perdriel 74, Barracas (☎4309 6400), and **Hospital Italiano,** Gascón 450, Almagro (☎4959 0200).

**Pharmacies** are nearly everywhere in Buenos Aires. One of the largest chains, **Farmacity,** has a good number of 24hr. branches. There are some medications and remedies that you can get here with no prescription that you can't get over the counter at home, such as valium, but foreign prescriptions may not always be accepted. For listings of pharmacy locations, see p. 32.

If you are concerned about obtaining medical assistance while traveling, there are several special support services. The **MedPass** from **GlobalCare,** Inc., 6875 Shiloh Rd. East, Alpharetta, GA 30005, USA (☎+1-800-860-1111; www.globalcare.net), provides 24hr. international medical assistance, support, and medical evacuation resources. The **International Association for Medical Assistance to Travelers** (**IAMAT;** US ☎+1-716-754-4883, Canada 519-836-0102; www.iamat.org) has free membership, lists English-speaking doctors worldwide, and offers detailed information on immunization requirements and sanitation. If your regular insurance policy does not cover travel abroad, you may wish to purchase additional coverage (p. 29).

Those with medical conditions such as diabetes, allergies, epilepsy, or heart ailments, may want to obtain a **MedicAlert** membership (US$40 per year), which includes a stainless-steel ID tag and a 24hr. collect-call number. Contact the MedicAlert Foundation International, 2323 Colorado Ave., Turlock, CA 95382, USA (☎+1-888-633-4298, outside US 209-668-3333; www.medicalert.org).

## WOMEN'S HEALTH

Women traveling in unsanitary conditions are vulnerable to **urinary tract** (including bladder and kidney) **infections.** Bring supplies from home if you are prone to infection, as they may be difficult to find on the road. And, since tampons, pads, and reliable contraceptive devices are sometimes hard to find when traveling, bring supplies with you. **Abortion** is **illegal** in Argentina and will result in punishment, including a possible jail sentence for the woman. However, several thousand abortions still occur in Argentina each year. Due to the illegality, most occur outside of official institutions, which dramatically increases the risk. Abortion is only allowed without punishment if it is performed to save the woman's life or if the pregnancy is the result of rape.

### TOILETS

Contrary to popular belief (or myth), toilets in the Southern Hemisphere do not flush in the opposite direction of Northern Hemisphere toilets. Gravity works similarly on both sides of the equator; there is no cause for panic or concern.

ESSENTIALS

# GETTING TO BUENOS AIRES

## BY PLANE

When it comes to airfare, a little effort can save you a bundle. Courier fares are the cheapest for those whose plans are flexible enough to deal with the restrictions. Tickets sold by consolidators and standby seating are also good deals, but last-minute specials, airfare wars, and charter flights often beat these fares. The key is to hunt around, be flexible, and ask about discounts. Students, seniors, and those under 26 should never pay full price for a ticket.

### AIRFARES

Airfares to Buenos Aires are almost always high, but they peak between December and February and July through August. Holidays are also expensive, particularly Easter and New Year's Day. The cheapest times to travel are March through June and September. Midweek (M-Th morning) round-trip flights run US$40-50 cheaper than weekend flights, but they are generally more crowded and less likely to permit frequent-flier upgrades. Not fixing a return date ("open return") or arriving in and departing from different cities ("open-jaw") can be pricier than round-trip flights. Patching several one-way flights together can be one of the most expensive ways to travel.

If Argentina is only one stop on a more extensive globe-hop, consider a **round-the-world (RTW)** ticket. Tickets usually include at least five stops and are valid for about a year; prices range US$1200-5000. Try **Northwest Airlines/KLM** (☎+1-800-225-2525; www.nwa.com) or **Star Alliance,** a consortium of 16 airlines including United Airlines (www.staralliance.com).

Fares for round-trip flights to Buenos Aires from the Canadian or US east coast cost US$900 in the low season and US$1300 in the high season; from the US or Canadian west coast US$1000/1400; from the UK, ₤650/₤900; from Australia AUS$2000; from New Zealand NZ$2100.

### BUDGET AND STUDENT TRAVEL AGENCIES

While knowledgeable agents specializing in flights to Buenos Aires can make your life easy, they may not spend the time to find you the lowest possible fare—they get paid on commission. Travelers holding **ISICs** and **IYTCs** (p. 19) qualify for big discounts from student travel agencies. Most flights from budget agencies are on major airlines, but during peak seasons and holidays, some may sell seats on less reliable chartered aircraft.

**STA Travel,** 5900 Wilshire Blvd., Ste. 900, Los Angeles, CA 90036, USA (24hr. reservations and info ☎+1-800-781-4040; www.statravel.com). A student and youth travel

ESSENTIALS

organization with over 150 offices worldwide (check their website for a listing of all their offices), including US offices in Boston, Chicago, Los Angeles, New York, Seattle, San Francisco, and Washington, DC. Ticket booking, travel insurance, railpasses, and more. Walk-in offices are located throughout Australia (☎+61 3 9207 5900), New Zealand (☎+64 9 309 9723), and the UK (☎+44 8701 630 026).

**Travel CUTS (Canadian Universities Travel Services Limited),** 187 College St., Toronto, ON M5T 1P7, Canada (☎+1-888-592-2887; www.travelcuts.com). Offices across Canada and the US including Los Angeles, New York, Seattle, and San Francisco.

**USIT,** 19-21 Aston Quay, Dublin 2, Ireland (☎+353 1 602 1904; www.usit.ie). Ireland's leading student/budget travel agency has 20 offices throughout Northern Ireland and the Republic of Ireland. Offers programs to work, study, and volunteer worldwide.

---

**FLIGHT PLANNING ON THE INTERNET.** The Internet may be the budget traveler's dream when it comes to finding and booking bargain fares, but the array of options can be overwhelming. Many airline sites offer special last-minute deals on the Web. Try **Aerolineas Argentinas** (www.aerolineas. com.ar) for tickets to Argentina from around the world.

**STA** (www.statravel.com) and **StudentUniverse** (www.studentuniverse.com) provide quotes on student tickets, while **Orbitz** (www.orbitz.com), **Expedia** (www.expedia.com), and Travelocity (www.travelocity.com) offer full travel services. **Priceline** (www.priceline.com) lets you specify a price and obligates you to buy any ticket that meets or beats it; **Hotwire** (www.hotwire. com) offers bargain fares but won't reveal the airline or flight times until you buy. Other sites with deals include www.bestfares.com, www.flights. com, www.lowestfare.com, www.onetravel.com, and www.travelzoo.com.

**SideStep** (www.sidestep.com) and **Booking Buddy** (www.bookingbuddy. com) are online tools that can help sift through multiple offers; these two let you enter your trip information once and search multiple sites.

**Air Traveler's Handbook** (www.faqs.org/faqs/travel/air/handbook) is an indispensable resource on the Internet; it has a comprehensive listing of links to everything you need to know before you board a plane.

---

# COMMERCIAL AIRLINES

The commercial airlines' lowest regular offer is the **APEX (Advance Purchase Excursion)** fare, which provides confirmed reservations and allows "open-jaw" tickets. Generally, reservations must be made seven to 21 days ahead of departure, with seven- to 14-day minimum-stay and up to 90-day maximum-stay restrictions. These fares carry hefty cancellation and change penalties (fees rise in summer). Book peak-season APEX fares early. Use **Expedia** (www.expedia.com) or **Travelocity** (www.travelocity.com) to get an idea of the lowest published fares, then use the resources outlined here to try to beat those fares. Low-season fares should be appreciably cheaper than the high-season (Dec.-Feb. and July-Aug.) fares listed here.

## TRAVELING FROM NORTH AMERICA

Basic round-trip fares to BA range from roughly US$900-1400. Standard commercial carriers like **American** (☎800-433-7300; www.aa.com) and **United** (☎800-538-2929; www.ual.com) will probably offer the most convenient flights, but they may not be the cheapest, unless you snag a special promotion or airfare-war ticket. There is no traditional discount airline that flies to Argentina. The major Argentine-based carriers are **Aerolineas Argentinas** (☎800-333-0276; www. aerolineas.com.ar) and **LAN** (☎866-435-9526; www.lan.com).

## TRAVELING FROM IRELAND AND THE UK

There are no direct flights to Buenos Aires from the UK—they must stop first at another destination in Europe, the United States, or South America. Ireland also has no direction connections to Buenos Aires. Flights from Ireland usually connect in London before continuing on to the Southern Hemisphere. The **Air Travel Advisory Bureau** in London (☎870 737 0021; www.atab.co.uk) provides referrals to travel agencies and consolidators that offer discounted airfares out of the UK. **Cheapflights** (www.cheapflights.co.uk) publishes airfare bargains. The following airlines can provide cheap connections from Ireland to the UK, and from the UK to connecting destinations prior to Buenos Aires:

**Aer Lingus:** Ireland ☎0818 365 000; www.aerlingus.ie.

**bmibaby:** UK ☎08702 642 229; www.bmibaby.com.

**easyJet:** UK ☎08712 442 366; www.easyjet.com.

**KLM:** UK ☎08705 074 074; www.klmuk.com.

**Ryanair:** Ireland ☎0818 303 030, UK 08712 460 000; www.ryanair.com.

## TRAVELING FROM AUSTRALIA AND NEW ZEALAND

The best way to fly to BA from Australia and New Zealand is through Aerolineas Argentinas or LAN via **Qantas** (Australia ☎13 13 13; New Zealand ☎0800 808 767; www.qantas.com) and **Air New Zealand** (www.airnewzealand.com). Most flights depart from Auckland, Melbourne, and Sydney and connect at another South American destination, such as Santiago, before continuing on to BA.

# AIR COURIER FLIGHTS

Those who travel light should consider courier flights. Couriers help transport cargo on international flights by using their checked luggage space for freight. Generally, couriers are limited to carry-ons and must deal with complex flight restrictions. Most flights are round-trip only, with short fixed-length stays (usually one week) and a limit of a one ticket per issue. Most of these flights also only operate out of major gateway cities, mostly in North America. Most flights leave from Los Angeles, Miami, New York, or San Francisco in the United States; and from Montreal, Toronto, or Vancouver in Canada. Generally, travelers must be over 18 (in some cases 21) to be eligible for courier flights. In summer, the most popular destinations usually require an advance reservation of about two weeks (you can usually book up to two months ahead). Super-discounted fares are common for "last-minute" flights (three to 14 days ahead).

# STANDBY FLIGHTS

Traveling standby requires considerable flexibility in arrival and departure dates. Companies dealing in standby flights sell vouchers rather than tickets, along with the promise to get you to your destination (or near your destination) within a certain window of time (typically 1-5 days). You call in before your specific window of time to hear your flight options and the probability that you will be able to board each flight. You can then decide which flights you want to try to catch, show up at the appropriate airport at the appropriate time, present your voucher, and board if space is available. Vouchers can usually be bought for both one-way and round-trip travel. You may receive a monetary refund only if every available flight within your date range is full;

if you opt not to take an available (but perhaps less convenient) flight, you can only get credit toward future travel. To check on a company's service record in the US, contact the **Better Business Bureau** (☎+1-703-276-0100; www. bbb.org). It is difficult to receive refunds, and clients' vouchers will not be honored when an airline fails to receive payment in time.

## TICKET CONSOLIDATORS

Ticket consolidators, or **"bucket shops,"** buy unsold tickets in bulk from commercial airlines and sell them at discounted rates. The best place to look is in the Sunday travel section of any major newspaper (such as *The New York Times*), where many bucket shops place tiny ads. Call quickly, as availability is extremely limited. Not all bucket shops are reliable, so insist on a receipt that gives full details of restrictions, refunds, and tickets, and pay by credit card (in spite of the 2-5% fee) so you can stop payment if you never receive your tickets. For more info, see www.travel-library.com/air-travel/consolidators.html.

### TRAVELING FROM CANADA AND THE US

Some consolidators worth trying are **Rebel** (☎800-732-3588; www.rebeltours. com), **Cheap Tickets** (www.cheaptickets.com), **Flights.com** (www.flights.com), and **TravelHUB** (www.travelhub.com). *Let's Go* does not endorse any of these agencies. As always, be cautious, and be sure to research companies before you hand over your credit card number.

## BY BOAT

Travel by boat to Buenos Aires is possible from destinations in Uruguay, such as Montevideo (p. 249) and Colonia (p. 244). The major ferry operator is **Buquebus** (www.buquebus.com). For more information on their routes, see p. 243.

# GETTING INTO BUENOS AIRES

## AIRPORTS

## EZEIZA INTERNATIONAL AIRPORT (EZE)

International flights to Buenos Aires land at **Ministro Pistarini International Airport,** better known as **Ezeiza International Airport (EZE),** 22km southwest of Buenos Aires. For more details on flights and facilities, call the information center (☎011 5480 6111) or visit the airport's website at www.aa2000.com.ar. The airport is replete with all of the normal international terminal services, including private exchange bureaus (which you should avoid) and ATMs. For immediate currency exchange, opt instead for the **Banco Nación** branch. The two cheapest and fastest ways to get into BA from Ezeiza are by **taxi** and **bus.**

### TAXI

It's easy to get a taxi in front of the airport—simply walk up to one of the official taxi stands and tell the operator, who will speak English, where you want to go. Fares into the city range from AR$60-80.

**BUS**

There are two bus options for traveling from Ezeiza into Buenos Aires. **Tourist buses** operated by companies such as Manuel Tienda León (☎011 4315 5115; www.tiendaloen.com) ferry visitors from the airport to the company's terminal in the city center at San Martín and Avenida Madero, right off the Plaza San Martín (p. 151; 2 per hr., 40min.; AR$40). From there, catch a local bus or a taxi to your hostel or hotel. **City buses** also run from Ezeiza to BA; **route #86** enters the city in La Boca and travels north through San Telmo, Monserrat, Microcentro, and Retiro (2hr.). Note that buses only accept change.

**AIRPORT CONNECTIONS.** There's no easy way to get between Ezeiza and Jorge Newbery—the only route is by road, and this can often lead to traffic nightmares (occasionally caused by protests, interestingly) and missed flights. Expect the worst. Manuel Tienda León offers a shuttle service between the two airports throughout the day for AR$45.

ESSENTIALS

# JORGE NEWBERY AIRPARK (AEP)

Domestic flights and routes from neighboring South American countries, such as Uruguay and Brazil, often arrive at **Jorge Newbery Airpark (AEP),** 6km from the city center and just north of Palermo on Costanera Norte along the Río de la Plata. For more details on flights and facilities, call the information center (☎011 5480 6111) or visit the airport's website at www.aa2000.com.

Exp. 4473/2005

VI·LUZ Y ENTRÉ
HOSTEL

**Small and cozy hostel managed by its owners**

• 3 double rooms and 2 dorms with low prices and best facilities.
• Breakfast, internet, WiFi and much more included.

VILUZ Y ENTRÉ HOSTEL

**2233 Mexico St. – Congreso – Buenos Aires**
**Phone: +54+11 4941-1155**
**MSN: amigos@viluzyentrehostel.com.ar**

www.viluzyentrehostel.com.ar

ar. To get into the city center, take a Manuel Tienda León **tourist bus** (20min., 1 per hr., AR$15) or opt for **city bus route #33**.

# BUS STATIONS

International and domestic buses arrive in Buenos Aires at the massive **Estación Terminal de Omnibus** in Retiro at the intersection of Avenida Antárida Argentina and Ramos Mejía (☎4310 0700; www.tebasa.com.ar). The station's website is incredibly helpful for finding all of the companies that go to your destination, their phone numbers, their location in the terminal, and their schedules.

The station itself is composed of two floors. The bottom floor has nearly 100 gates, while the top floor is where the almost 200 bus company **kiosks** are. Upon walking in via the ramp, go to the information booth immediately following it (unless you already checked in online) where you can find kiosk numbers of bus companies that travel to your final destination. For **purchasing tickets,** you can do it old school style and go to the bus station in advance, where you'll shop around at a few companies before buying tickets in person, or you can call (or have your hostel call) the company number and reserve a seat. In these cases, you're only required to show up about 2hr. in advance to pay for your ticket, which saves significant amounts of time. A final, efficient option for online ticket buying is www.plataforma10.com. A number of the major companies, such as **Andesmar** (www.andesmar.com), also have their own websites.

Bus travel in Argentina, in general, is a very pleasant experience. Coaches are much more comfortable and cheaper than those found in the US. Most buses have three classes. The bottom, called **Semi-Cama,** gives you a cozy seat that reclines about halfway. The next level up, **Cama,** which is still inexpensive, gives you a leather seat that reclines further back. Dinner and breakfast service are also included, along with some annoying games, like Bingo. Many budget travelers go even further and splurge for **First Class**—it only costs about US$8 more than Cama and the amenities, including a seat that will recline 180 degrees, are far superior. There's also more free food and better drinks.

# GETTING AROUND BUENOS AIRES

## BY PUBLIC TRANSPORTATION

### SUBTE

The **Buenos Aires Metro** (☎011 4555 1616; www.metrovias.com.ar), also called the **Subte** (Ⓢ) is the easiest way to get around the city, and also the most pleasant. The system is clean, efficient, and dirt cheap—fares run around AR$0.90 per trip. Yes, that's right, it's roughly US$0.30 for a subway ride. Veterans of the New York MTA and the London Underground will find this hard to believe, and borderline miraculous. Believe it. There are no long-term passes, so the best you can do is to buy multiple single ride tickets at once. This is usually a good strategy, since it will allow you to bypass ticket lines during your next trip. These can get quite long, especially during rush hour. The *subte* is in fairly decent condition, although it can get very crowded at times and uncomfortably hot during the summer. Note that there are no inbound or outbound directions on the lines—line direction is identified by the terminus station. Also, standard etiquette in Argentina mandates that passengers give up their seats to anyone who needs it more. Though this is usually a "only if you want to" rule in the US and Europe, it's often expected in Argentina.

The *subte* is usually open from 5am-10:30pm, depending on the line. On Sunday, it doesn't open until 8am. Service is frequent on weekdays, while you'll probably have to wait longer on weekends.

## BUSES

After the *subte*, bus is the next easiest way to get around the city. Tickets cost either AR$0.90 or AR$1, depending on the length of your trip. To travel, simply flag down a bus, get on, and tell the driver the amount you should pay. If you're not sure, just say your destination and the driver can figure out the fare for you. Next, put your change, or *monedas* (you still can't use bills on buses, although they are currently looking for ways to change this), in the machine behind the driver and take your ticket, which you must keep in case of official checks, which happen every once in a while. Since buses only accept change, it's wise to avoid spending it around the city, as you'll likely need it for transportation.

For short stays in Buenos Aires, stay away from the bus system. The system is complicated, with many, many routes, and is difficult to master during a brief trip. However, for some trips within Buenos Aires, you will most likely have to take a bus. The 86 from Plaza de Mayo, for example, is one of the only ways to get to Boca, unless you plan to take a taxi (p. 40). If you're staying in Buenos Aires for a longer time, or want to get to the outer suburbs, a **GUIA T** (AR$15), a comprehensive guide for the bus system, is essential. You can buy them from one of the kiosks in the city center. They have extensive maps of all of Buenos Aires, and detail the route of every single bus.

Bus stops are pretty well marked with the bus numbers and where they go. However, less trafficked *barrios* may just have stickers on trees with the bus number. Keep an eye out for such markings. Like everyone else in Buenos Aires, bus drivers can sometimes be maniacal drivers, so hold on tight or get a seat. Note that they will speed up quickly as soon as you get on, so sit tight or grab on to something. Steer clear of the bus system during rush hour if you don't know where you're going. The buses get packed and you'll have a hard time getting your bearings straight.

THE LOCAL STORY

### (SUB)WAY COOL

From the London Underground to Paris Metro, many (slightly nerdy?) travelers find a major city's **subway** system to be among the niftiest sights to see. With its rich history, Buenos Aires' **subte** ([S]) is no exception. The first station in the network opened in 1913, making the *subte* the first subway system in Latin America, in the Southern Hemisphere, and, most impressively, in all of the Spanish-speaking world. To this day, it remains the only metro in Argentina, though plans are currently in the works to build a system for **Córdoba,** Argentina's second biggest city.

The *subte*'s lines and stations are renowned for their elaborate murals and artwork, none of which would look out of place whatsoever in any of the city's museums. If, for some reason, you don't plan to use the subway for public transportation during your stay, you should still make a point of taking a brief trip down **Line A,** Buenos Aires' core line, from **Plaza de Mayo** to **Congreso.** Of the city's five lines, it's the only one that still uses the original carriages and somewhat unnervingly rickety wood-framed interiors.

The city has ambitious plans for the future of the *subte*. The existing lines are being outfitted with Wi-Fi, and four new lines are under construction or in planning, a project that would extend the network by nearly 30km and 35 stations. Construction may be complete by as soon as 2010.

# BY TAXI

There are two sides to the coin when it comes to taxis in Buenos Aires. Some people, including residents of Buenos Aires, believe all cabs hailed on the street are dangerous. This is true, to some extent—some theft schemes have been organized by taxi drivers in the past. However, most taxis are fine for the extra vigilant traveler. **Make sure the driver turns on the meter at the beginning of the trip.** Many will try to scam you with some story detailing a broken meter. If this happens, consider getting a new cab. Some taxi drivers will also do the typical scam of driving around unnecessarily to rack up the fare. Have an idea of where you're going and watch what you say while in the cab. There are many tell tale "I'm a tourist, please scam me" red-flag phrases, such as asking how much the trip will cost before leaving. This just opens the door for the taxi driver to make up an exorbitant fare.

Buenos Aires has two kinds of cabs, though it's difficult to tell, since both are black and yellow. There are **regular** taxis and **radio** taxis (radio taxis will be identified as such on the side). Radio taxis are considered to be safer, whether you call them or hail them on the street If you're away from the city center, where the only cars in the street seem to be taxis, in a dangerous area, or are nervous about taking taxis, you can call, or have someone else call, a radio taxi. In these cases, the rate will be fixed from your departure point to your destination. It's usually more expensive to travel this way, but it guarantees the fare beforehand. Taxis around the city center should cost AR$7-30, depending on how far you go; expect to pay AR$9-15 for a ride across the city center.

Cabs are common and easy to find in the central *barrios*. Safety should not be a concern in this area of the city. Drivers do not expect tips, although you should always round up to the nearest peso. Once again, do not give them change—you will need it for the bus system.

# BY BICYCLE

There are many places to rent bikes and mopeds around Buenos Aires. For more information, see p. 96. Note that biking is fairly uncommon for tourists. *Porteños* are notoriously crazy drivers and tend, on the whole, to ignore traffic rules, as well as pavement markers. It can be borderline suicidal to bike in these conditions. Drivers often don't give bikers and mopedists a full lane, although most bikers who brave the streets don't occupy a single lane anyway—they usually just zip in and out of traffic or stay on the sidewalk. Although the city center itself is not very biker friendly, some of the less populous northern *barrios* and the Reserva Ecológica (p. 150) can provide a nice, relatively tranquil ride. As a rule of thumb, just stay away from *porteño* drivers.

# BY FOOT

Buenos Aires is a walking city. Many people walk, and there are almost always people on the streets everywhere, even along the major thoroughfares. For walking tours of the city, see p. 139. Rules for walking safety are the same as any other city—first and foremost, make sure you know which way the traffic is going before you cross the street. Many *porteños* simply throw themselves out into the street. Though this may be a good way to fit in, it might be best to put it off until you're more familiar with the city and its crazy drivers.

# BY THUMB

**LET'S NOT GO.** Let's Go never recommends hitchhiking as a safe means of transportation, and none of the information presented here is intended to do so.

Let's Go strongly urges you to consider the risks before you choose to hitchhike. Hitching means entrusting your life to a stranger and risking assault, sexual harassment, theft, and unsafe driving. For women traveling alone (or even in pairs), hitching is just too dangerous. A man and a woman are a less dangerous combination; two men will have a harder time getting a lift, while three men will go nowhere.

# KEEPING IN TOUCH

## BY EMAIL AND INTERNET

Internet cafes and *locutorios*, which are call centers, are all over the city and have relatively inexpensive internet access. Rates usually run around AR\$1.50-5 per hour, depending on the speed of the connection. The vast majority of hostels, along with some restaurants, do have Wi-Fi, though *porteños* don't usually carry their laptops around the city.

Although in some places it's possible to forge a remote link with your home server, in most cases this is a much slower (and thus more expensive) option than taking advantage of free **web-based email accounts** (e.g., ◩www.gmail.com and www.hotmail.com). **Internet cafes** and the occasional free Internet terminal

Southern house ba

**Southernhouse ba**
hostel - buenos aires

www.hostel-buenos-aires.com

Lodging in southern house ba means staying in the most strategic point of te city, You'll find the comfort of superior hotel service combined with the fun and social life of a hostel, and the best rates in the market.

Southernhouse ba • T. M. de Anchorena 1117 (1425), Buenos Aires, Argentina • T.E.: (00 54) 11 4961 6933 • info@southernhouseba.com

ESSENTIALS

at a public library or university are listed in the **Practical Information** sections of major cities. For lists of additional cybercafes in Buenos Aires, check out www.cybercaptive.com and www.world66.com/netcafeguide.

Increasingly, travelers find that taking their **laptop computers** on the road with them can be a convenient option for staying connected. Laptop users can call an Internet service provider via a modem using long-distance phone cards specifically intended for such calls. They may also find Internet cafes that allow them to connect their laptops to the Internet. Lucky travelers with wireless-enabled computers may be able to take advantage of an increasing number of Internet "hot spots," where they can get online for free or for a small fee. Newer computers can detect these hot spots automatically; otherwise, websites like www.jiwire.com, www.wififreespot.com, and www.wifihotspotlist.com can help you find them. For more information on insuring your laptop while traveling abroad, see p. 29.

**WARY WI-FI.** Wireless hot spots make Internet access possible in public and remote places. Unfortunately, they also pose **security risks.** Hot spots are public, open networks that use unencrypted, unsecured connections. They are susceptible to hacks and "packet sniffing"—ways of stealing passwords and other private information. To prevent problems, disable ad hoc mode, turn off file sharing and network discovery, encrypt your email, turn on your firewall, beware of phony networks, and watch for over-the-shoulder creeps.

# BY TELEPHONE

## CALLING HOME FROM BUENOS AIRES

**Prepaid phone cards** are a common and relatively inexpensive means of calling abroad. Each one comes with a Personal Identification Number (PIN) and a toll-free access number. You call the access number and then follow the directions for dialing your PIN. To purchase prepaid phone cards, check online for the best rates; www.callingcards.com is a good place to start. Online providers generally send your access number and PIN via email, with no actual "card" involved. You can also call home with prepaid phone cards purchased in Argentina (see **Calling Within Argentina,** p. 43).

**PLACING INTERNATIONAL CALLS.** To call Argentina from home or to call home from Argentina, dial:

1. The **international dialing prefix.** To call from **Australia,** dial 0011; **Canada** or the **US,** 011; **Ireland, New Zealand,** or the **UK,** 00; **Argentina,** 00.
2. The **country code** of the country you want to call. To call **Australia,** dial 61; **Canada** or the **US,** 1; **Ireland,** 353; **New Zealand,** 64; the **UK,** 44; **Argentina,** 54.
3. The **city/area code.** *Let's Go* lists the city/area codes for cities and towns in Argentina opposite the city or town name, next to a ☎, as well as in every phone number. If the first digit is a zero (e.g., 020 for London), omit the zero when calling from abroad (e.g., dial 20 from Canada to reach London). **The city code for Buenos Aires is 011.**
4. The **local number.**

Another option is to purchase a **calling card,** linked to a major national telecommunications service in your home country. Calls are billed collect or to your account. To call home with a calling card, contact the operator for your service provider in Argentina by dialing the appropriate toll-free access number (listed below in the third column).

| COMPANY | TO OBTAIN A CARD: | TO CALL ABROAD: |
|---|---|---|
| AT&T (US) | 800-364-9292 or www.att.com | 800 555 4288 |
| Canada Direct | 800-561-8868 or www.infocana-dadirect.com | 800 222 1004 |
| Telecom New Zealand Direct | www.telecom.co.nz | 800 222 6400 |
| Telstra Australia | 1800 676 638 or www.telstra.com | 800 222 0061 |

Placing a collect call through an international operator can be expensive, but may be necessary in case of an emergency. You can frequently call collect without even possessing a company's calling card just by calling its access number and following the instructions.

## CALLING WITHIN ARGENTINA

As is the case in many world cities, payphones are virtually nowhere to be found anymore in Buenos Aires. This is no problem. Just pop into a *locutorio*, public call centers which are located throughout the city. They also have internet access, to boot (p. 41). At the *locutorio*, check their rates, both international and domestic. You then go into your private booth and make your call—a meter will tell you how much you've spent while you're talking. You pay for the call after it's completed. Take note of the **off-peak hours**—they're when international calls will become much cheaper.

**Calling cards** are an essential ally at *locutorios*, and for phone calls in general. To call cell phones, which costs more than a landline, the best option is **Hablemás**, which come in AR$5 or AR$10 denominations. To call other countries, it works best to walk up to a kiosk that sells phone cards (they can be found throughout the city) and ask for a card that has the best rates to a certain country. In general, it is most convenient to buy calling cards at kiosks.

## CELLULAR PHONES

**GSM PHONES.** Just having a GSM phone doesn't mean you're necessarily good to go when you travel abroad. The majority of GSM phones sold in the United States operate on a different frequency (1900) than international phones (900/1800) and will not work abroad. Tri-band phones work on all three frequencies (900/1800/1900) and will operate through most of the world. Additionally, some GSM phones are SIM-locked and will only accept SIM cards from a single carrier. You'll need a SIM-unlocked phone to use a SIM card from a local carrier when you travel.

Cell phone use is widespread in Buenos Aires. The reception is fine within the city and you should be able to purchase a SIM card for Argentina, either before departure or in Buenos Aires. In Argentina, you can get them at places that sell phones; such places are common in the city center. For making phone calls on your cell phone, you don't need a pre-paid plan. You can purchase cards for your phone so that you will have credit.

The international standard for cell phones is **Global System for Mobile Communication (GSM)**. To make and receive calls in Argentina, you will need a GSM-compatible phone and a **Subscriber Identity Module (SIM)** card, a country-specific, thumbnail-sized chip that gives you a local phone number and plugs you into the local network. Many SIM cards are prepaid, and incoming calls are frequently free. You can buy additional cards or vouchers (usually available at convenience stores) to "top up" your phone. For more information on GSM phones, check out www.telestial.com, www.orange.co.uk, www.roadpost.com, or www.planetomni.com. Companies like **Cellular Abroad** (www.cellularabroad. com) rent cell phones that work in a variety of destinations around the world.

## TIME DIFFERENCES

Contrary to popular belief, Argentina is actually well due east of the North American east coast, longitudinally. As such, Argentina is 3 hours behind Greenwich Mean Time (GMT), and usually observes Daylight Saving Time from January to mid-March.

The following table applies from mid-March to December.

| 4AM | 5AM | 6AM | 7AM | 8AM | 9AM | NOON |
|---|---|---|---|---|---|---|
| Vancouver Seattle San Francisco Los Angeles | Denver | Chicago | New York Toronto | Santiago La Paz | **BUENOS AIRES** | London |

# BY MAIL

## SENDING MAIL HOME FROM ARGENTINA

**Airmail** is the best way to send mail home from Argentina. **Aerogrammes,** printed sheets that fold into envelopes and travel via airmail, are available at post offices. Write "airmail," *"par avion,"* or *"correo aéreo"* on the front. Most post offices will charge exorbitant fees or simply refuse to send aerogrammes with enclosures. Surface mail is the cheapest and slowest way to send mail. It takes one to two months to cross the Atlantic and one to three to cross the Pacific—good for heavy items you won't need for a while, such as souvenirs that you've acquired along the way. These are standard rates for mail from Argentina to:

**Australia:** Allow 15 days for regular airmail home. Postcards/aerogrammes and letters up to 20g cost AR$4. Packages up to 0.5kg AR$22.25, up to 2kg AR$80.25.

**Canada:** Allow 12 days for regular airmail home. Postcards/aerogrammes and letters up to 20g cost AR$4. Packages up to 0.5kg AR$19.75, up to 2kg AR$71.25.

**UK:** Allow 15 days for regular airmail home. Postcards/aerogrammes and letters up to 20g cost AR$4. Packages up to 0.5kg AR$22.25, up to 2kg AR$80.25.

**US:** Allow 12 days for regular airmail home. Postcards/aerogrammes and letters up to 20g cost AR$4. Packages up to 0.5kg AR$19.75, up to 2kg AR$71.25.

## SENDING MAIL TO ARGENTINA

To ensure timely delivery, mark envelopes *"airmail," "par avion,"* or *"correo aéreo".* In addition to the standard postage system whose rates are listed below, **Federal Express** (Australia ☎+61 13 26 10, Canada and the US +1-800-463-3339, Ireland +353 800 535 800, New Zealand +64 800 733 339, the UK +44 8456 070 809; www.fedex.com) handles express mail services from most countries to Argentina. Sending a postcard within Argentina costs AR$1, while sending letters up to 150g domestically requires AR$4. Though the Argentina postal service has historically had trouble efficiently delivering mail, they are doing much better today, particularly within Buenos Aires.

There are several ways to arrange pick up of letters sent to you while you are abroad. Mail can be sent via **Poste Restante** (General Delivery; *lista de correos* in Spanish) to almost any city or town in Argentina with a post office, and it is quite reliable. Address **Poste Restante** letters for Buenos Aires like so:

Lionel MESSI

Lista de Correos

Correo Central

Sarmiento 189

(1003) Capital Federal

Argentina

The mail will go to a special desk in the central post office, unless you specify a post office by street address or postal code. It's best to use the largest post office, since mail may be sent there regardless. It is usually safer and quicker, though more expensive, to send mail express or registered. Bring your passport (or other photo ID) for pickup; there may be a small fee of AR$1.50. If the clerks insist that there is nothing for you, ask them to check under your first name as well. For more information on postal services, *Let's Go* lists post offices in the **Practical Information** section (p. 99) for Buenos Aires.

**American Express's** travel offices throughout the world offer a free **Client Letter Service** (mail held up to 30 days and forwarded upon request) for cardholders who contact them in advance. Some offices provide these services to non-cardholders (especially AmEx Travelers Cheque holders), but call ahead to make sure that you are eligible. *Let's Go* lists AmEx locations for most large cities in **Practical Information** sections; for a complete list, call ☎+1-800-528-4800 or visit www.americanexpress.com/travel.

ESSENTIALS

# THE GREAT OUTDOORS

Travelers interested in exploring the natural wonders that lie just outside of Buenos Aires (see **Excursions,** p. 229) should make sure to prepare for non-city life. The **Great Outdoor Recreation Page** (www.gorp.com) provides excellent general information for travelers planning on camping or enjoying the outdoors.

## CAMPING AND HIKING EQUIPMENT

### WHAT TO BUY

Good camping equipment is both sturdy and light. North American suppliers tend to offer the most competitive prices.

**Sleeping bags:** Most sleeping bags are rated by season; "summer" means 30-40°F (around 0°C) at night; "4-season" or "winter" often means below 0°F (-17°C). Bags are made of **down** (warm and light, but expensive, and miserable when wet) or of **synthetic** material (heavy, durable, and warm when wet). Prices range from US$50-250 for a summer synthetic to US$200-300 for a good down winter bag. **Sleeping bag pads** include foam pads (US$10-30), air mattresses (US$15-50), and self-inflating mats (US$30-120). Bring a **stuff sack** to store your bag and keep it dry.

**Tents:** The best tents are freestanding (with their own frames and suspension systems), set up quickly, and only require staking in high winds. Low-profile dome tents are the best all around. Worthy 2-person tents start at US$100, 4-person tents at US$160.

**ESSENTIALS**

Make sure yours has a rain fly and seal its seams with waterproofer. Other useful accessories include a **battery-operated lantern,** a plastic **ground cloth,** and a nylon **tarp.**

**Backpacks: Internal-frame** packs mold well to your back, keep a lower center of gravity, and flex adequately to allow you to hike difficult trails, while **external-frame** packs are more comfortable for long hikes over even terrain, as they carry weight higher and distribute it more evenly. Make sure your pack has a strong, padded hip belt to transfer weight to your legs. There are models designed specifically for women. Any serious backpacking requires a pack of at least 4000 cu. in. (16,000cc), plus 500 cu. in. for sleeping bags in internal-frame packs. Sturdy backpacks cost anywhere from US$125 to US$420—your pack is an area where it doesn't pay to economize. On your hunt for the perfect pack, fill up prospective models with something heavy, strap it on correctly, and walk around the store to get a sense of how the model distributes weight. Either buy a rain cover (US$10-20) or store all of your belongings in plastic bags inside your pack.

**Boots:** Be sure to wear hiking boots with good **ankle support.** They should fit snugly and comfortably over 1-2 pairs of **wool socks** and a pair of thin **liner socks.** Break in boots over several weeks before you go to spare yourself blisters.

**Other necessities: Synthetic layers,** like those made of polypropylene or polyester, and a pile jacket will keep you warm even when wet. A **space blanket** (US$5-15) will help you to retain body heat and doubles as a **ground cloth.** Plastic **water bottles** are vital; look for shatter- and leak-resistant models. Carry **water-purification tablets** for when you can't boil water. Although most campgrounds provide campfire sites, you may want to bring a small **metal grate** or **grill.** For places that forbid fires, you'll need a **camp stove** (starts at US$50) and a propane-filled fuel bottle to operate it. Also bring a **first-aid kit, pocketknife, insect repellent,** and **waterproof matches** or a **lighter.**

# SPECIFIC CONCERNS

## SUSTAINABLE TRAVEL

As the number of travelers on the road rises, the detrimental effect they can have on natural environments is an increasing concern. *Let's Go* promotes the philosophy of sustainable travel with this in mind. Through a sensitivity to issues of ecology and sustainability, today's travelers can be a powerful force in preserving and restoring the places they visit.

Ecotourism, a rising trend in sustainable travel, focuses on the conservation of natural habitats—mainly, on how to use them to build up the economy without exploitation or overdevelopment. Travelers can make a difference by doing advance research, by supporting organizations and establishments that pay attention to their carbon "footprint," and by patronizing establishments that strive to be environmentally friendly.

Argentina has a strong history of environmentally friendly practices. The country has low carbon dioxide emissions, despite the fact that it has a mostly developed economy, and has been an important player in many international conventions aimed at protecting the environment, including the 1992 Convention on Biological Diversity and the 1997 Kyoto Protocol. There are many opportunities available for travelers in Argentina who want to contribute to the greater mission of sustainability, from protecting endangered species in the jungles of Iguazú to working on an organic farm on the *Pampas.* For more information, see **Beyond Tourism** (p. 83).

ESSENTIALS

**ECOTOURISM RESOURCES.** For more information on environmentally responsible tourism, contact one of the organizations below:

**Conservation International,** 2011 Crystal Dr., Ste. 500, Arlington, VA 22202, USA (☎+1-800-406-2306 or 703-341-2400; www.conservation.org).

**Green Globe 21,** Green Globe vof, Verbenalaan 1, 2111 ZL Aerdenhout, the Netherlands (☎+31 23 544 0306; www.greenglobe.com).

**International Ecotourism Society,** 1333 H St. NW, Ste. 300E, Washington, DC 20005, USA (☎+1-202-347-9203; www.ecotourism.org).

**United Nations Environment Program (UNEP),** 39-43 Quai André Citroën, 75739 Paris Cedex 15, France (☎+33 1 44 37 14 50; www.uneptie.org/pc/tourism).

# RESPONSIBLE TRAVEL

Your tourist dollars can make a big impact on the destinations you visit. The choices you make during your trip can have powerful effects on local communities—for better or for worse. Travelers who care about the destinations and environments they explore should make themselves aware of the social, cultural, and political implications of their choices. Simple decisions such as buying local products, paying fair prices for products or services, and attempting to speak the local language can have very positive effects on the community.

**Community-based tourism** aims to channel tourist dollars into the local economy by emphasizing tours and cultural programs that are run by members of the host community. This type of tourism also benefits the tourists themselves, as it often takes them beyond the traditional tours of the region. *The Ethical Travel Guide* (UK£13), a project of Tourism Concern (☎+44 20 7133 3330; www.tourismconcern.org.uk), is an excellent resource for information on community-based travel, with a directory of 300 establishments in 60 countries.

Of course, part of the reason why Argentina is a popular destination today is because of the relative weakness of its currency, in large part due to the recent economic crisis of 1999-2002. Though the crisis is long over, its lasting effects can still be felt in some of Buenos Aires poorest *barrios*. While enjoying the city, many travelers choose to give back to the community and volunteer or work for an urban development organization aimed at helping the most disadvantaged sectors of Argentina's population. For more information on related volunteer opportunities, see **Beyond Tourism** (p. 83).

# TRAVELING ALONE

Traveling alone can provide you with a sense of independence and a greater opportunity to connect with locals. On the other hand, solo travelers are more vulnerable targets of harassment and street theft. If you are traveling alone, look confident, try not to stand out as a tourist, and be especially careful in deserted or very crowded areas. Stay away from areas that are not well lit. If questioned, never admit that you are traveling alone. Maintain regular contact with someone at home who knows your itinerary, and always research your destination before traveling. For more tips, pick up *Traveling Solo* by Eleanor Berman (Globe Pequot Press; US$18), visit www.travelaloneandloveit.com, or subscribe to **Connecting: Solo Travel Network,** 689 Park Rd., Unit 6, Gibsons, BC V0N 1V7, Canada (☎+1-604-886-9099; www.cstn.org; membership US$30-48).

ESSENTIALS

# WOMEN TRAVELERS

Women exploring on their own inevitably face some additional safety concerns. Single women can consider staying in hostels which offer single rooms that lock from the inside or in religious organizations with single-sex rooms. It's a good idea to stick to centrally located accommodations and to avoid solitary late-night treks or *subte* rides.

Always carry extra cash for a phone call, bus, or taxi. **Hitchhiking** is never safe for lone women, or even for two women traveling together. Look as if you know where you're going and approach older women or couples for directions if you're lost or feeling uncomfortable in your surroundings. Generally, the less you look like a tourist, the better off you'll be. Dress conservatively, especially in rural areas. Additionally, wearing a conspicuous **wedding band** sometimes helps to prevent unwanted advances.

Your best answer to verbal harassment is no answer at all; sitting motionless and staring straight ahead at nothing in particular will usually do the trick. The extremely persistent can sometimes be dissuaded by a firm, loud, and very public "go away," or just say *"véte."* Memorize the emergency numbers in places you visit, and consider carrying a whistle on your keychain. A self-defense course will both prepare you for a potential attack and raise your level of awareness of your surroundings (see **Personal Safety,** p. 27).

# GLBT TRAVELERS

Argentina as a whole, and Buenos Aires in particular, is a very welcoming destination for gay travelers. Buenos Aires province has laws that protect homosexuals from discrimination, and many provinces have provisions allowing same-sex civil unions. A current movement is pushing for all of the rights of marriage to be extended to same-sex couples. Argentine society embraces gay lifestyle, and visitors should expect to encounter no discrimination whatsoever. The following GLBT listings may prove useful for gay travelers in Buenos Aires.

## COMMUNITY CENTERS

**Comunidad Homosexual Argentina (CHA),** Tomás Liberti 1080 (☎4361 6382; www. cha.org.ar). In operation since 1984. The oldest and most politically active GLBT organization in Argentina. Offer free legal advice and a 24hr. hotline to report discrimination.

**La Fulana,** Av. Callao 339, 5th floor (☎4383 7413; www.lafulana.org.ar). An organization targeted at lesbian and bisexual women, which advocates a combination of feminism and socialism. They also provide health and legal services. Open Tu-Sa 8-10pm.

**Sociedad de Inegración Gay-Lésbica Argentina (SIGLA),** Pasaje del Progreso 949 (☎4922 3351; www.sigla.org.ar). Focus on STI and HIV/AIDS prevention.

## INTERNET RESOURCES

**Gay BA** (www.gay-ba.com). The website for this government sponsored group lists several gay establishments in the city. Maps are also available.

**Nexo** (www.nexo.org). First launched in 1992, this group publishes a magazine and offers a range of services, including HIV/AIDS tests. Works in partnership with groups like La Fulana with the umbrella organization **Federación Argentina LGTB** (☎4383 7413; www.lgbt.org.ar), which centralizes a wealth of information on GLBT life in Argentina.

Below are contact organizations, mail-order catalogs, and publishers that offer materials addressing specific travel concerns. **Out and About** (www.planetout.

com) offers a weekly newsletter addressing travel concerns and a comprehensive site addressing gay travel concerns. The online newspaper **365gay.com** also has a travel section (www.365gay.com/travel/travelchannel.htm).

**Gay's the Word,** 66 Marchmont St., London WC1N 1AB, UK (☎+44 20 7278 7654; http://freespace.virgin.net/gays.theword). The largest gay and lesbian bookshop in the UK, with both fiction and non-fiction titles. Mail-order service available.

**Giovanni's Room,** 345 S. 12th St., Philadelphia, PA 19107, USA (☎+1-215-923-2960; www.queerbooks.com). An international lesbian and gay bookstore with mail-order service (carries many of the publications listed below).

**International Lesbian and Gay Association (ILGA),** Avenue des Villas 34, 1060 Brussels, Belgium (☎+32 2 502 2471; www.ilga.org). Provides political information, such as homosexuality laws of individual countries.

**ADDITIONAL RESOURCES: GLBT**

*Spartacus 2005-2006: International Gay Guide.* Bruno Gmunder Verlag (US$33).

*Damron Men's Travel Guide, Damron Road Atlas, Damron Accommodations Guide, Damron City Guide,* and *Damron Women's Traveller.* Damron Travel Guides (US$18-24). For info, call ☎800-462-6654 or visit www.damron.com.

*The Gay Vacation Guide: The Best Trips and How to Plan Them,* by Mark Chesnut. Kensington Books (US$15).*Gayellow Pages USA/Canada,* by Frances Green. Gayellow Pages (US$20). They also publish regional editions. Visit Gayellow pages online at http://gayellowpages.com.

# TRAVELERS WITH DISABILITIES

Like many places in South America, accessibility for travelers with disabilities is still quite difficult in Buenos Aires. Few establishments, save for the most expensive, are accessible. However, several *subte* stops are, and the city is attempting to introduce buses that are lower to the ground. For a listing of handicap accessible *subte* stops, purchase a copy of the **GUIA T** (AR$15), found at kiosks throughout the city center. For accessible bus lines, there are no resources available save for calling the bus company and asking if they have low-riding buses for your stop. Currently, Buenos Aires is carrying out a massive plan to put ramps in every curb to make it easier to get around. Unfortunately, sidewalks in the city are in bad shape as is, so it is unclear if any significant progress will be made in the immdediate future with the ramp project.

## USEFUL ORGANIZATIONS

**Accessible Journeys,** 35 W. Sellers Ave., Ridley Park, PA 19078, USA (☎+1-800-846-4537; www.disabilitytravel.com). Designs tours for wheelchair users and slow walkers. The site has tips and forums for all travelers.

**Flying Wheels Travel,** 143 W. Bridge St., Owatonna, MN 55060, USA (☎+1-507-451-5005; www.flyingwheelstravel.com). Specializes in escorted trips to Europe for people with physical disabilities; plans custom trips worldwide.

**Mobility International USA (MIUSA),** P.O. Box 10767, Eugene, OR 97440, USA (☎+1-541-343-1284; www.miusa.org). Provides a variety of books and other publications containing information for travelers with disabilities.

ESSENTIALS

**Society for Accessible Travel and Hospitality (SATH),** 347 5th Ave., Ste. 610, New York, NY 10016, USA (☎+1-212-447-7284; www.sath.org). Advocacy group publishes free online travel information. Annual membership US$49, students and seniors US$29.

# DIETARY CONCERNS

Argentine cuisine is heavily based on two staples: beef and more beef, usually paired with a glass of red wine. Despite this reputation, though, the country is by no means a difficult place to eat for vegetarians, vegans, and those who keep kosher or halal. Our **Food** chapter (p. 117) lists several establishments that can cater to specific dietary needs without including beef.

The travel section of the **The Vegetarian Resource Group's** website, at www.vrg.org/travel, has a comprehensive list of organizations and websites that are geared toward helping vegetarians and vegans traveling abroad. For more information, visit your local bookstore or health food store and consult *The Vegetarian Traveler: Where to Stay if You're Vegetarian, Vegan, Environmentally Sensitive*, by Jed and Susan Civic (Larson Publications; US$16). Vegetarians will also find numerous resources on the web; try www.vegdining.com, www.happycow.net, and www.vegetariansabroad.com, for starters.

A worldwide kosher restaurant database at http://shamash.org/kosher/ lists several kosher establishments in the Buenos Aires metropolitan area. If you are strict in your observance, you may have to prepare your own food on the road. A good resource is the *Jewish Travel Guide*, edited by Michael Zaidner (Vallentine Mitchell; US$18). Travelers looking for halal restaurants abroad may find www.zabihah.com to be a useful resource.

# OTHER RESOURCES

*Let's Go* tries to cover all aspects of budget travel, but we can't put everything in our guides. Listed below are books and websites that can serve as jumping-off points for your own research.

# USEFUL PUBLICATIONS

**English-language newspapers:**

**Buenos Aires Herald** (☎4342-8476; www.buenosairesherald.com). Established in 1876 by a Scottish immigrant, and one of the premier daily English-language newspapers in the city.

**Argentimes** (☎4362 4799; www.theargentimes.com). *Argentimes*, a publication aimed at the youth market, is published every 2 weeks and distributed for free in Buenos Aires. There are currently plans to distribute it throughout the rest of the country.

**The Nose** (www.thenose.com.ar). Distributed at several locations throughout Buenos Aires, *The Nose* also has an online edition at its website.

# WORLD WIDE WEB

Almost every aspect of budget travel is accessible via the web. In 10 minutes at the keyboard, you can make a hostel reservation, get advice on travel hot spots from other travelers, or find out how transportation from Buenos Aires to Mendoza costs. Listed here are some regional and travel-related sites to start off your surfing; other relevant websites are listed throughout the book.

ESSENTIALS

ESSENTIALS

 **LET'S GO ONLINE.** Plan your next trip on our newly redesigned website, **www.letsgo.com.** It features the latest travel info on your favorite destinations as well as tons of interactive features: make your own itinerary, read blogs from our trusty researcher-writers, browse our photo library, watch exclusive videos, check out our newsletter, find travel deals, and buy new guides. We're always updating and adding new features, so check back often!

# THE ART OF TRAVEL

**Backpacker's Ultimate Guide:** www.bugeurope.com. Tips on packing, transportation, and where to go. Also tons of country-specific travel information.

**BootsnAll.com:** www.bootsnall.com. Numerous resources for independent travelers, from planning your trip to reporting on it when you get back.

**How to See the World:** www.artoftravel.com. A compendium of great travel tips, from cheap flights to self defense to interacting with local culture.

**Travel Intelligence:** www.travelintelligence.net. A large collection of travel writing by distinguished travel writers.

**Travel Library:** www.travel-library.com. A fantastic set of links for general information and personal travelogues.

**World Hum:** www.worldhum.com. An independently produced collection of "travel dispatches from a shrinking planet."

# INFORMATION ON ARGENTINA

**Buenos Aires Mapa Interactivo:** mapa.buenosaires.gov.ar. An interactive online map of Buenos Aires. Ideal for pre-trip planning and navigation on the road.

 **BUENOS AIRES ONLINE.** There are a number of excellent Buenos Aires websites, covering everything from *porteño* reviews of local restaurants and cafes, to listings of what's going on in the entertainment and nightlife scene. A smattering of some of the best ones follows:

**Óleo Guía de Restaurantes** (http://www.guiaoleo.com.ar/). This website provides an indispensable listing of restaurants in the greater Buenos Aires area, with feedback from *porteño* readers.

**What's Up Buenos Aires** (www.whatsupbuenosaires.com). The title says it all—this is the best English-language website for finding out what's going on lately in the arts and entertainment scene in Buenos Aires.

**Buenos Aliens** (www.buenosaliens.com). A Spanish-language website with details on upcoming events in Buenos Aires' bars and clubs.

**CIA World Factbook:** www.odci.gov/cia/publications/factbook/index.html. Tons of vital statistics on Argentina's geography, government, economy, and people.

**Geographia:** www.geographia.com. Highlights, culture, and people of Argentina.

**TravelPage:** www.travelpage.com. Links to official tourist office sites in Argentina.

**PlanetRider:** www.planetrider.com. A subjective list of links to the "best" websites covering the culture and tourist attractions of Argentina.

**World Travel Guide:** www.travel-guides.com. Helpful practical info.

# LIFE AND TIMES

For most, the history of Argentina is blurred by the catastrophe of the 1999-2001 economic crisis and a general lack of interest in Latin American history. Many people simply know the country for its soccer, the Peróns, and its propensity for going through long periods of political instability. Behind this veneer, though, is a complex and fascinating national trajectory, starting with a rich indigenous tradition and passing through a Spanish colonial era as the country moved on, post-independence, to become a 20th-century economic powerhouse and melting pot. The resulting culture is one that is both distinctly Latin American and European, mixing Argentine influences with an imported European touch brought over by immigrants—where else will you see tango dancers, pink mansions, and Parisian-style cafes side by side?

## HISTORY OF ARGENTINA

### ANCIENT TO COLONIAL

**ANCIENT, LARGELY IRRELEVANT GEOLOGIC HISTORY.** Allow me to spin a yarn for you. The landmass that today is **Argentina** has been around for a long time. Say, several billion years or so. At one point, back in the day, when all of the continents were still hanging out together as the supercontinent (so much better than a normal continent) **Pangaea,** Argentina sat next to Africa. Things didn't stay hunky-dory forever, though, and around 200 million years ago, South America started its drift away from Africa towards its current location, the space in between becoming the **Atlantic Ocean,** a body of water that would later inconvenience the globetrotting **Spanish.** More on that later. Today, as educators still like to say, you can see how the continents once fit together like a puzzle. A very large puzzle made of rocks and water sitting on top of a bed of hot **magma.** During this time, Argentina was inhabited by **dinosaurs** and other plants and animals that no longer exist. Then, one day, **humans** crashed the party.

**WORD TO YOUR MOMS.** The first records of human habitation in the land that is now Argentina date back to around 11,000 BC in the **Patagonia** region, South America's southern tip. Over the millennia, the original peoples coalesced into tribes, such as the clan-based **Diaguta,** the hunter-gatherer **Guraní** and **Quechua,** and the **Tehuelches,** who were known for their stature, so much so that they were identified by Portuguese explorer **Ferdinand Magellan** and his crew as giants ("patagons," hence the name of the region).

**HI HO, SILVER...AWAY!** Portuguese navigator **Juan Díaz de Solís,** who sailed for the Spanish crown, was the first Euro-

**4.6 Billion BC**
Earth forms.

**A very long time ago**
Continents disco boogie across the globe.

**100 million BC**
There be dinosaurs.

**11,000 BC**
First humans arrive in Patagonia.

**AD 1516**
Juan Díaz de Solís visits Argentina and hears rumors of a magical mountain of silver.

pean traveler to Argentina. Though his ill-fated 1516 expedition shipwrecked off the coast, some of his crew survived to hear tales of a "White King" and his **Mountain of Silver.** Predictably, an expedition was organized to find this King and steal his magical mound of silver. Predictably, again, all those in the expedition were killed in the attempt. They survived, however, just long enough to pass on the legend of the elusive "White King" to a group of Portuguese explorers, and the name **Argentina**—derived from the Latin *argentum*, meaning "silver"—stuck. So too did the hilariously incongruous name of the river Buenos Aires abuts, **Río de la Plata** (river of silver). Though the name would have you think that Buenos Aires lies next to a shiny, sparkly stream, the river is, in fact, an unremarkable shade of **brown.** So much for that.

**1536**
Pedro de Mendoza founds Buenos Aires v1.0.

**THE CITY OF GOOD AIRE.** In 1536, yet another Spanish expedition under **Pedro de Mendoza** arrived and created the first settlement at the mouth of the Río de la Plata. Named **Ciudad de Nuestra Señora Santa María del Buen Ayre** (usually translated "City of Our Lady Saint Mary of the Fair Winds"), it was located in the area of the modern-day *barrio* **San Telmo.** According to some accounts, many residents were dissatisfied with the extreme length of the city's original name. Thankfully, especially for our sake (*Let's Go: Ciudad de Nuestra Señora Santa María del Buen Ayre* just isn't very catchy), the name of the settlement was eventually shortened. After years of peace, the native Guaraní turned against Mendoza and wiped out much of the colony. Buenos Aires, version 1.0, was abandoned in 1541.

**1541**
Buenos Aires v1.0 fails amidst cannibalism.

**BUENOS AIRES RELOADED.** Mendoza's expedition wasn't a complete failure. Instead of returning to Spain, Pedro's brother, **Gonzalo de Mendoza,** sailed north to found **Asunción** (now the capital of Paraguay). After some time, the inhabitants of the new city decided to give establishing Buenos Aires another try. The second settlement, led by **Juan de Garay,** sailed down the Paraná River towards the Atlantic in 1580 and set up a new town that proved to be more successful than the last one—notably, Buenos Aires 2.0 managed to avoid getting wiped off the map, thanks in part to the **cattle** and **horses** brought by Pedro Mendoza's crew that had spread across the **Pampas** (plains) and flourished, providing a supply of food and equine transportation. Within 20 years, cattle had become the city's major industry, but for the next 200 years, BA would remain a sleepy outpost of the Spanish empire. Trade restrictions, which ordered all goods to travel through **Lima** to be taxed, created a thriving **black market** and sent increasingly independent **porteños** (people of the port) into the arms of British and Portuguese smugglers.

**1580**
Juan de Garay sails down from Paraguay and founds Buenos Aires v2.0. This time, it will last.

**1600-1776**
Buenos Aires is little more than a sleepy colonial outpost churning out beef. What else?

**1776**
Spanish King Carlos III establishes the Viceroyalty of the Río de la Plata and makes Buenos Aires its capital.

**EXPORTS AND EXPANSION.** That all began to change in 1776. Responding to the pressure of an increasingly vital Atlantic trade, the growing importance of Buenos Aires, and the meddlesome incursions of outside traders from other countries, Spanish **King Carlos III** named the city the capital of the new **Viceroyalty of the Río de la Plata,** which encompassed much of present day Argentina, Bolivia, Paraguay, and Uruguay. Buenos Aires also became an open port, ending the grossly inefficient days of the Lima system.

# THE 19TH CENTURY

**THE BRITISH ARE ANGRY! THE BRITISH ARE ANGRY!.** The British, however—long the preferred smugglers in the region—did not intend to give up on their profitable enterprises without a fight. In June 1806, an expedition of 1500 men under **General William Beresford** invaded the Río de la Plata region. The viceroy at the time, the **Marquis Rafael de Sobremonte,** lacking reinforcements from Spain, chose to flee. Stiff local resistance to the Brits paved the way to August 1806, when French-born **Santiago Liniers,** in the employ of the Spanish navy, launched the **Reconquista** of Buenos Aires from **Montevideo,** across the Río de la Plata. The British tried to retake the city in 1807 with a new expedition led by **General John Whitelocke,** but faced more resistance from the locals, who pelted the invaders with musket-fire. As if the bullets weren't enough, the *porteños* also fought off the British with **burning hot oil.** The British white flags were eventually raised, the forces of Buenos Aires victorious in an effort known today as **La Defensa.** The surrender flags of the British ships remain in the **Basílica Santo Domingo** (p. 144) in Monserrat.

**¡VIVA LA REVOLUCIÓN!.** In 1808, after deciding he had just about enough of being small, **Napoleon Bonaparte** conquered Spain, and the citizens of Buenos Aires began to rethink their commitments to Europe. After all, they had just scored a major military victory against the world's foremost naval power, Britain, and with the accompanying burst in confidence under their collective belts, the *porteños* started to adopt a "forget Europe" mentality. Things finally came to a head with a **military junta** on May 25, 1810, known as the **May Revolution,** that officially severed ties with Madrid. By 1814, the military actions of General **José de San Martín**—known to this day as **The Liberator** in Argentina and across South America—cleared the way for complete independence. On July 9, 1816, at the **Congress of Tucumán,** Argentina officially declared its independence from Spain. After intermittent rulers led the government, **Bernardino Rivadavia,** a hero of La Defensa, became Argentina's first president in 1825.

**WAIT... WHAT DO WE DO NOW?.** But all was not rosy in the newly formed **United Provinces of Río de la Plata.** The conflicts that had begun over the issue of independence took on new levels of bitterness, as two new political groups split the population: the **Federalists,** who advocated local control, and the **Unitarists,** who wanted a strong central government. Moreover, there was a regional split: BA had become the most powerful force in the area, and the surrounding provinces

**June 1806**
Buenos Aires vs. the British, round one. Britain wins.

**LIFE AND TIMES**

**1806-1807**
Buenos Aires vs. the British, round two. BA wins and then successfully defends the city against a British counterattack with burning hot oil.

**1808**
Napoleon conquers Spain. BA says "screw you, Europe."

**1810**
Argentina officially severs ties with Madrid in the May Revolution.

**1816**
Argentina officially declares independence.

wanted to maintain their influence. The city-country split has remained a recurring theme in Argentine politics since.

**OF ROSES AND CORNCOBS.** With the end of Spanish control came the rise of Argentina's first dictator, **Juan Manuel de Rosas.** A powerful cattle rancher in *la pampa*, Rosas ruled Buenos Aires intermittently from 1829 until 1852 as the first Latin American **caudillo:** an authoritarian military-political leader of high charisma. A federalist dedicated to consolidating power around the city, Rosas created a paramilitary force, **La Mazorca** (the corncob—but also, as was noted, a perfect rhyme to *más horca*, or "more gallows/hangings"), to further this goal by terrorizing BA and its surroundings.

During his first tenure as governor of Buenos Aires, Rosas attempted to expel foreign influences within the new nation, even as European governments attempted to gain greater access, resulting in numerous international conflicts. In the 1820s, Argentines went to **war with Brazil,** and in 1833, the **British took over the Falklands.** Finally, two European **naval blockades** of Buenos Aires by the British and French (1838-40 and 1845-50) after Rosas tried to reincorporate Uruguay and Paraguay as provinces of Argentina took their toll on the city's economy. For the next three years, Rosas left his position as governor and went south to Patagonia, where he began his next project of national unification: the extermination of the southern indigenous tribes. After a campaign of murder and terror—during which time Rosas encountered Charles Darwin, earning himself a mention in the naturalist's *Origin of Species*—he returned to Buenos Aires triumphant in 1835.

**CONSTITUTE THIS.** But his popularity did not last. In 1852, Rosas was overthrown and exiled by **Justo José de Urquiza,** the former governor of **Entre Ríos Province,** and backed by the Uruguayan and Brazilian governments. The **Treaty of San Nicolás** finally called the Constitutional Congress. On May 1, 1853, the Congress enacted a federal Constitution that took centralized power away from the city. With this turn of events, the Buenos Aires Province promptly left the Argentine Confederation. War erupted in 1859, and the Confederation quickly defeated the city's forces. Buenos Aires was officially incorporated into the newly renamed **República Argentina,** with Urquiza as the president.

However, as usual, the fledgling Republic struggled. Buenos Aires—the most powerful, populous, and wealthy nation in the region—rose up yet again in 1861 against the rule of Urquiza's government. Led by **General Bartolomé Mitre,** the rebel army defeated the national army in September, leading to the resignation of President Urquiza. In 1862, a national convention voted Mitre—a prolific writer, founder of the newspaper *La Nación*, and the man whose face appears on the two peso bill—president of the Republic, and moved the nation's capital back to Buenos Aires. Ensuing decades saw Argentina, under the stewardship of war ministers **Adolfo Alsina** and **Julio Argentino Roca,** wage war with Paraguay

**LIFE AND TIMES**

**1829**
Juan Manuel de Rosas takes over as Argentina's first of many dictators.

**1820-1850**
Near continuous international conflict for Argentina with Brazil, Britain, and France.

**1835**
Rosas returns to BA after a war against Patagonia's indigenous tribes.

**1852-1859**
Justo José de Urquiza overthrows Rosas and brings Buenos Aires back into the Argentine fold after the city briefly secedes.

**1862**
After deposing Urquiza, Bartolomé Mitre takes power and moves the Argentine capital to BA.

**1865-1870**
Argentina faces off with Paraguay in the War of the Triple Alliance.

over control of the Río de la Plata region and with the few remaining indigenous tribes of the Patagonian province.

**HEY NOW...YOU'RE AN ECONOMIC ALL-STAR.** Roca eventually ascended to the presidency after his successful Patagonian exploits and the Federalist-Unitarist conflict of the **Revolution of 1880.** Meanwhile, during the last decades of the 19th century, Argentina—with Buenos Aires at its helm—became a dominant force in international trade with its flourishing agricultural economy. During the 1880s, the first mayor of the city, **Torcuato de Alvear,** led an aggressive campaign of modernization, expanding the water and electricity supply, setting up street lights, and—in a tactic that has proven to be a surefire route to popularity for centuries—improving roads. Tall buildings and elegant mansions rose up just as the city's wide avenues and subway systems were established. Roca's predecessor, **Domingo Sarmiento,** also contributed, laying the foundation for one of Buenos Aires' largest parks, **Parque Tres de Febrero.** When the magnificent **Teatro Colón** opened in 1908, its scarlet and gold interior hosted some of the world's best opera singers, and Buenos Aires was hailed as the **"Paris of South America,"** a title it holds to this day.

# THE 20TH CENTURY

**IMMIGRATION, EXPORTATION, AND EXPLOITATION.** The decades surrounding the turn of the century witnessed massive immigration into Argentina, especially from **Italy** and **Spain,** with a smattering of other nationals from Britain, France, Ireland, Portugal, and Russia. While the immigrant population of Buenos Aires had been around a mere 100,000 when the Constitution was adopted in 1853, immigrant numbers soared to over a staggering 1.3 million by the time the Teatro Colón put up its first opera. By **World War I,** BA was the largest and most prosperous city in Latin America, and the envy of the South American world.

Yet the enormous prosperity of the city was concentrated almost entirely in the hands of the wealthy, such that new immigrants were forced into **villas miserias** (shantytowns) around the city's industrial areas. The social inequality of Buenos Aires exploded in 1919, when the military was used to suppress a metalworker's strike in what became known as **La Semana Trágica** (The Tragic Week). Still, the city continued growing at an ever-faster pace, as old buildings were torn down and new streets replaced old alleys.

**IT'S PARTY TIME!** For many years immediately preceding the 1930s, BA continued to be **the hippest place** in Latin America. It had the culture, with galleries and bookstores seemingly on every corner. It had the **tango,** pouring out of the seams of brothels and bars and spreading to countries around the world such as France and Finland. Yes, Finland (when it's extremely cold and dark half of the year, why not

LIFE AND TIMES

**1880**
Roca solidifies his power in the Revolution of 1880.

**1880-1900**
Buenos Aires grows and modernizes during Torcuato de Alvear's mayoralty.

**1908**
BA earns the monicker "Paris of South America." Travel guide companies rejoice at the new, easy-to-use tagline.

**1853-1908**
BA's immigrant population skyrockets from 100,000 to 1.3 million. Argentina's economy reigns as one of the strongest in the world.

**1919**
A military force supresses a labor strike in BA, slowing the era of economc good feelings.

**1920-1928**
Buenos Aires reigns as the place to be in Latin America, with culture and tango aplenty.

LIFE AND TIMES

lighten things up with a little tango?). But dancers weren't the only crowd that created a buzz in Buenos Aires. The city was also a magnet for intellectuals and writers. If you weren't in London, New York, or Paris in the 1920s, Buenos Aires certainly was a respectable alternative.

**THIS PARTY'S OVER (CUE DEPRESSION).** Every party has a crasher, though, and **depression** played the role of spoiler for Buenos Aires. Though it occurred in the United States, the **Wall Street Crash of 1929** had a ripple effect on economies throughout the world, including Argentina's. Incomes plummeted and unemployment skyrocketed. Naturally, the people started to question their leader, President **Hipólito Yrigoyen.** Was he mentally impaired? Why was he so reluctant to appear in public? And why was he so damn **hairy?** Yes, the president was known in some circles as *El puedo* (the mole), due in part to his excessive hairiness. As if economic crisis wasn't bad enough, the man charged with instilling confidence in the people was nicknamed after a blind rodent. Great.

**IT'S COUP TIME.** Clearly, it was time for a change in leadership. A **coup** in 1930, led by **General José Felix Uriburu,** deposed *El puedo* and paved the way for a new era of what everyone hoped would be enlightened and stable politics, economics, and leadership. Naturally, the exact opposite happened. Uriburu's rise to power instead started off the **Infamous Decade,** a time marred by fraud, corruption, and hardship. Ensuing leaders did everything they could to stem the tide of general badness swarming the country. Many paid closer attention to personal grooming, hoping not to be deemed mole-like. For example, **Agustín Pedro Justo,** Uriburu's successor, rarely wore a mustache. Perhaps more importantly, though, new attention was given to the economic strategies guiding the country through the troubled waters of the Depression. Still more figureheads went through the revolving door of the presidency, including **Roberto Ortiz, Ramón Castillo, Arturo Rawson, Pedro Pablo Ramírez,** and **Edelmiro Julián Farrell,** to name some. Finally, in 1946, the baton passed to a new leader who managed to stick around.

**YOU MAY HAVE HEARD OF HIM. Juan Perón** entered the military in 1911 at age 16 and gradually progressed through the ranks, endearing himself to the commoners through massively popular turns as the **Secretary of Labor** and **Secretary of War.** Eventually, by 1945, his peers were so alarmed by his newfound superstardom that they arrested him. This move backfired, though, in large part thanks to his equally popular wife, **Eva Perón,** known widely as **Evita.** Following Juan's imprisonment, Evita took center stage and led, along with the Argentine trade unions, a series of mass protests and demonstrations in the Plaza de Mayo that got Juan out of prison. Perón easily won the next elections in 1946 and Perónmania whipped the country into a frenzy. Whenever Juan and Evita spoke, massive crowds would inevitably follow. The movement, known as **Peronism,** was built on indus-

**1929**
The Wall Street Crash sparks economic collapse in Argentina. The hairy president, Hipólito Yrigoyen, becomes known as "the mole."

**1930**
José Felix Uriburu overthrows Yrigoyen and ushers in the Infamous Decade.

**1930-1946**
In what will become a recurring theme, Argentina goes through a period of instability and hardship.

**1940-1945**
Juan Perón rises through the government ranks but is eventually imprisoned by his fellow leaders.

**1946**
Perón ascends to the presidency following a huge election victory.

trialization and the empowerment of the working class. Evita, in particular, proved to be the endearing face of the movement and a valuable asset to Perón's presidency.

**EVA PERÓN: SUPERSTAR.** After becoming first lady, Eva Perón set to work on a number of endeavors. She maintained critical connections with pro-Perón trade unions and remained a strong advocate for the low-income working class, whom she referred to as the **descamisados** (shirtless ones). She also founded the **Female Peronist Party,** which helped pave the way to **full women's suffrage** by 1946.

The first lady traveled through Europe in 1947 during her **Rainbow Tour,** visiting heads of state as an ambassador for Argentina. She was generally well received, especially in Spain, but the trip proved to be controversial. Dressed head to toe in Dior and Cartier and donning elaborate hairdos, Evita was seen by many Europeans as extravagant and, well, ridiculous. Back at home, jealous elitists derided her as a wannabe. In response, upon her return, Evita took a more conservative approach to appearances in public, hoping to present a more serious persona—she would wear only Dior as opposed to *both* Dior and Cartier.

**DON'T CRY FOR ME, ARGENTINA.** After turning down an opportunity to run for the **vice presidency,** Evita's health rapidly declined as she was stricken with advanced cervical cancer in 1950. For her swan song, she played an integral role in her husband's reelection in 1952 as she rallied the support of women. On July 26th, 1952, a few short weeks after being named the **Spiritual Leader of the Nation,** Eva Perón passed away at the age of 33. Everyday life came to a screeching halt as the country went into mourning. On an unprecedented note for a woman, she was given a state funeral.

**I'LL BE BACK.** Juan Perón's political career seemed to die with his wife. The working class empowerment movement alienated upper-class Argentines, who were angry and summarily left out to dry. As the economy worsened, numerous terrorist attacks rocked Buenos Aires, including two strikes on Perón in the Plaza de Mayo. He survived, but his government was in shambles. In the mid-1950s, the **Catholic Church** joined the anti-Perón party, primarily over a divorce law he enacted. Following excommunication, his once soaring popularity reached a low point. In September of 1955, a coup led by Catholic nationalists in the military, known as the **Revolución Libertadora,** deposed Perón, putting an end to his presidency. With Peronism now effectively banned throughout the country, the embattled former leader fled to exile in Spain.

**INTERLUDE.** A joint military junta, featuring leaders such as **Eduardo Lonardi** and **General Pedro Aramburu,** moved on to rule the country post-Perón, while the radical leftist **Monteneros** guerrilla movement began in force, resisting the new anti-Peronist era of government and calling for the return of Juan. Argentines voiced their support for the exiled president through neutral blank ballots cast in "elections."

**1947**
Eva Perón goes on a Rainbow Tour of Europe.

**1952**
Eva Perón passes away at age 33 from cervical cancer. Despite her wishes to the contrary, Argentina cries.

**1955**
Juan Perón is forced out of office by the Catholic Revolución Libertadora.

**1973**
Following yet another long period of instability, Alejandro Lanusse calls for open elections, paving the way for Perón's return.

LIFE AND TIMES

Eventually, **Alejandro Lanusse,** a military-appointed president, saw the junta as ineffective and called for elections in 1973, legalizing the Peronist party in the process, allowing Juan to return and rule as president once again.

**GUESS WHO'S BACK, BACK AGAIN.** Perón arrived in July of 1973 with his new wife, **Isabel Perón,** and assumed the presidency. Optimism ran high for a renewed era of stability, but any semblance of hope was crushed upon Perón's return at **Ezeiza International Airport.** Millions came out to greet the president, but hidden amongst the crowds were snipers from the far right **death squad, Argentine Anti-Communist Alliance (Triple A).** They clashed with the leftist Peronists, setting off a firefight that killed at least 13 people and injured hundreds more. The bitter aftermath of the attack never lifted and Perón eventually died of a heart attack on July 1st, 1974, just one year into his unsuccessful return. Power passed on to his vice president, his wife Isabel, the first non-royal female head of state in the history of the Western Hemisphere.

Isabel's presidency was very brief, and, unlike Evita, she was highly unpopular. The economy, as usual, continued to do badly, and she was less a ruler and more a figurehead, as most power lay with **José López Rega,** the controversial **Minister of Social Welfare** and the spooky, Rasputin-esque founder of Triple A—a surefire public relations nightmare. Perón eventually agreed to fire him, but the military decided that a change in leadership was necessary to lead the country in a new direction. A bloodless coup deposed Isabel in early 1976 and she fled to everyone's favorite exile destination, Spain.

**THE DIRTY WAR.** The next dictator and de facto president of Argentina was **General Jorge Videla,** who presided over the darkest period of 20th-century Argentine history. His government led the **National Reorganization Process,** or **El Proceso,** the sanitized version of the so-called **Dirty War,** a regime of state-sponsored violence against the citizens of Argentina. Thousands were targeted by government hit squads for **forced disappearance,** including guerrillas, suspected guerrillas, and their families and friends. Other Argentines were subject to disappearance, too, including trade unionists, atheists, students, intellectuals, and journalists. Nearly 30,000 people were sent to the infamous **Navy Mechanics School (ESMA)** in Núñez from 1976 to 1983 to be interrogated, tortured, and executed. The status of these **desaparecidos** remains an issue today, with the Plaza de Mayo as a forum for human rights advocates such as the **Madres de Plaza de Mayo** (p. 140), a group that sought to find out what happened to the *desaparecidos*, many of whom were children of the *madres*.

**FALKLANDS FOLLY.** In April of 1982, in response to deplorable economic conditions and considerable domestic unrest over the Dirty War, the junta, at this point led by **Leopold Galtieri,** chose to invade the British-controlled **Falkland Islands,** an

Atlantic archipelago just off the southeast coast of Argentina. Thanks to the light defenses (who cares about the Falklands, anyway?), the Argentines easily took the islands.

Galtieri was convinced that the British wouldn't bother to launch a counteroffensive, but he was dead wrong. Very wrong. Thanks to superior training and technology, the United Kingdom swooped in and managed to retake the Falklands just two months later. With the defeat, public confidence in the government completely collapsed and the unchallenged supremacy of the junta came to an end.

**DEMOCRACY RETURNS.** In light of their increasing unpopularity, the junta had no choice—the time had come to restore democracy and basic civil liberties. In 1983, the final leader of the junta, **Reynaldo Bignone**, ceded power to the first elected president of the newly democratic Argentina, **Raúl Alfonsín.**

Alfonsín's administration attempted to turn over a new page in Argentine history by starting a **commission** and **tribunal** to investigate the crimes of the Dirty War. However, he was eventually forced to give up these efforts in response to stiff opposition from the still-strong military. Two subsequent laws, the **Law of Due Obedience** and the **Full Stop** law, largely excused all participants in the military junta of any guilt and ended all prosecutions. Meanwhile, the crumbling economy and rampant inflation continued to be unresponsive to any stimulation measures, such as the creation of a new currency to replace the peso, the **austral,** complete with a snazzy new symbol and bank notes. The loans required to create the currency led to huge, unsustainable debts from interest. The economy subsequently collapsed, and inflation continued unabated at ludicrous levels. The country eventually came crawling back to the peso at the end of 1991.

**THE 90S.** After the 1989 elections, new president **Carlos Menem,** a Muslim who converted to Catholicism so he could run for office, succeeded Alfonsín and set out on the same agenda that nearly every president before him pursued—fixing the economy. To help fight inflation, the value of the peso was **pegged** to the United States dollar. Inflation dropped dramatically to nearly 0%, the value of the peso stabilized, and quality of life improved immensely for *porteños.* Menem also managed to decrease federal spending, favoring a free-market system over the Peronist preference for state ownership of most facets of life. The economy responded with healthy GDP growth and Menem was rewarded with re-election in 1995. However, the growth of the 1990s was not without ominous signs for the future. Privatization led to increased unemployment rates, and the gap between rich and poor expanded. Additionally, much of the economic growth of the 1990s was based on loans from the **International Monetary Fund (IMF).** Though the loans helped create an era of prosperity for Argentines, it was highly unlikely that the country would be able to repay its debts. The shaky foundation of the new economy was bound to crumble at some point.

**1982**
Argentina loses the Falklands War to Britain, spelling the end of the military dictatorship.

**1983**
Raúl Alfonsín becomes the first democratically elected president of Argentina in many years.

**1985-1991**
In a failed attempt to jumpstart economic recovery, the austral replaces the peso as the Argentine unit of currency.

**1989**
Carlos Menem becomes president.

**1989-1999**
Argentina enjoys a period of economic growth and prosperity.

# CRISIS AND REBOUND

**LIFE AND TIMES**

**2001**
The Argentine economy collapses, leading to riots and widespread hardship.

**THE ECONOMIC CRISIS.** And crumble it did, in dramatic fashion, in late 2001. If you've taken introductory economics before, this will all make sense to you. If you haven't, bear with us. Here's how it went down. The IMF called upon Argentina to repay its debts, a move that would require **devaluation** of the peso and an abandonment of pegging to the United States dollar. Amid fears of the ensuing devaluation, Argentines rushed to banks to withdraw deposits and started investing overseas to stem losses. In response, the **Minister of Economy, Domingo Cavallo,** placed severe limitations on the number of bank withdrawals one could make, a measure known as the **corallito** (the word for "animal pen" or "corral," appropriately expressive for a move that rounded up and held off panicking Argentines). Those still with pesos at the time, mostly the low- and middle-income brackets of the population, were left defenseless.

What happened next? The economy completely collapsed in December of 2001 and widespread panic and hysteria swept across the nation. Citizens took to the streets in Buenos Aires, calling for the ouster of President **Fernando de la Rúa,** Menem's successor. Mass protests known as **cacerolazo,** in which people banged pots and pans and generally made as much noise as possible, became the norm, with periods of rioting and property destruction. The confrontations became violent on December 20th and 21st, leading to many deaths. Seeing no other way out, de la Rúa acquiesced to the wishes of the people and stepped down as president, fleeing the Casa Rosada by helicopter on the 21st.

**2002-2003**
In an unprecedented turn of events for Argentina, the government never completely collapses during the depression. Ensuing presidents attempt to rebuild the economy.

**WHERE'S THE VICE PRESIDENT?.** There was a slight problem, though—there was no vice president. De la Rúa's former vice president, **Carlos Álvarez,** stepped down in October of 2000, well before the economic crisis was in full force, and a replacement had never been set. Remarkably, in the only positive of the crisis, the military, weakened by budget cuts during Menem's tenure, did not make any move for power. Instead, for a change, the presidential succession procedures outlined in the Constitution were followed, and president of the Senate **Ramón Puerta** took power. He soon resigned, though, and power passed further down the chain of command to other people who never expected to become president, such as the president of the Chamber of Deputies, **Eduardo Camaño.** Eventually, the **Legislative Assembly,** the merged body of both Congressional chambers, convened to select a more permanent interim government. **Eduardo Duhalde,** a former vice president under Menem and governor of Buenos Aires, was given the impossible task of leading the country out of the economic crisis.

He wasted no time. First, he confirmed the default of Argentine debt and devalued the peso by ending the peg to the United States dollar. Rampant inflation ensued, sparking further unrest and driving more Argentines below the poverty line. Though hardship continued, the situation had at least been stabilized. After serving as custodian for a little over a year, Duhalde called for elections in 2003 and passed the baton on to **Néstor Kirchner,** a former provincial governor.

**MEET THE KIRCHNERS.** Kirchner was tasked with rebuilding the economy and bringing Argentina, one of the wealthiest countries in the world at the start of the 20th century, back to respectability. Kirchner largely succeeded, leading a decrease in unemployment and an increase in GDP growth while successfully restructuring the debt with the IMF, paying off a large portion of it in 2005. Successful reforms have also been made in other areas. Laws passed during Alfonsín's tenure that granted amnesty to perpetrators of the Dirty War were repealed, allowing prosecution and investigation to begin anew. High marks also came Kirchner's way for his work restructuring the Supreme Court and the armed forces. Despite strong approval ratings, Kirchner chose not to run for reelection in 2007. Instead, his wife, **Cristina Fernandez de Kirchner,** succeeded him as president with a strong showing in the elections, garnering a whopping 45% of the vote.

**2003**
Néstor Kirchner becomes president and leads a series of successful reforms, rebuilding the country following the collapse.

**2007**
Cristina Kirchner, Néstor's wife, becomes president.

# BUENOS AIRES TODAY

## GOVERNMENT AND POLITICS

### NATIONAL GOVERNMENT

Argentina is a **constitutional republic** with a coup d'etat problem. Since its ratification in 1853, there have been numerous amendments and revisions of the Constitution. Among others, an amendment passed in 1860 incorporated the city of Buenos Aires into the republic of Argentina. Since then, a number of military takeovers have challenged the authority of the Constitution, the last of which took place from 1976 to 1983 and was named the **National Reorganization Process,** better known as the **Dirty War** (p. 60). Today, the most powerful wing of government is the executive, and the president, **Cristina Fernandez de Kirchner,** elected in 2007, is both head of government and chief of state. Since 1947, when women were granted suffrage, the president has been elected by universal popular vote of those 18 and older. Elections are held every four years.

The legislative branch of the Argentine government is made up of the bicameral **Congreso Nacional,** which consists of a 72-seat **Senate,** elected by popular vote for terms of six years, and the 257-seat **Chamber of Deputies,** elected for terms of four years. Not surprisingly, there are a large number of strong political parties in Argentina, most of which are broad coalitions of yet more parties. The most influential party is the **Partido Justicialista** (awkwardly translated as the Justicialist Party, or PJ), the leftist, labor-based party of Juan Perón. It includes current president Kirchner, her husband and former president Néstor Kirchner (elected with only 22% of the vote), and former president Carlos Menem under its auspices, not to mention a majority of seats in both houses of the Congreso Nacional. However, the PJ itself is factionalized, and its most

LIFE AND TIMES

influential faction is the central-leftist **Frente para la Victoria** (Victory Front party, or FPV), which crystallized in order to elect the first Kirchner. Other parties include the century-old social democratic **Unión Cívica Radical** (Radical Civic Union party, or UCR), the leftist **Afirmación para una República Igualitaria** (Support for an Egalitarian Republic, or ARI), and the strong, right-wing **Propuesta Republicana** (Republican Proposal, or PRO). Beyond the party system, at least in theory, is the nine-member **Corte Suprema** (Supreme Court), appointed by the president, and—always to be considered in Argentina—the **military.**

## ECONOMY

A century ago, Argentina was one of the wealthiest countries in the world—the impressive grandeur of BA's embassies and mansions are a testament to the country's successful past. Since then, however, the country and the city have been losing ground to the world's industrialized nations, and have been through repeated **economic crises,** the worst of which shattered the country in 2001. Enormous borrowing during the military dictatorship of 1976-83, during which nearly 500,000 companies went bankrupt, and no efficient plan or repayment over the decades that followed culminated in severe depression, growing debt, and a bank run at the beginning of the new millennium. Interim President **Adolfo Rodriguez** declared the largest default on foreign debt in history, and then resigned only days later. Soon after, the government ended the peso's one-to-one peg with the US dollar, and the economy plummeted, with real GDP 18% smaller than four years earlier, 25% unemployment, and over half of the population in poverty. Argentina, luckily, has a lot going for it, though. With immense natural resources, a highly literate population, and a strong agricultural and industrial export base, the country has seen real GDP bounce back by an average of 9% per year. Inflation, however, reached double-digit levels in 2006, and purchasing power is still minimal, with the Argentine peso worth about one third of the US dollar. But the country is rebounding quickly, and becoming a new hot spot for foreign investment, tourism, and agricultural export.

## ENVIRONMENTAL CONCERNS

There's a big difference in Argentina between environmental law and the reality of its enforcement. On paper, Argentina is a world leader in setting voluntary greenhouse gas targets, and the country ratified the Kyoto Protocol in 2001. However, despite the government's best intentions, Argentina is still subject to enormous environmental degradation common to developing companies. The major problems are split between the land and the water. On land, **deforestation** is running unchecked: over the last hundred years, two-thirds of the nation's native forests have been destroyed, and the burning of forests generates more greenhouse gases than motor vehicles. The soil, too, is in jeopardy, as **pesticide** use has jumped from 40 million liters at the beginning of the 1990s to over 100 million in the 21st century. All of which has created serious problems in Argentina's drinking water. Buenos Aires shares its drinking water, taken from the enormous estuary of the Río de la Plata, with nearly the entire population of Uruguay. The river, however—as its color implies, even if its color has nothing to do with it—is highly **polluted** by unregulated dumping of pesticides, hydrocarbons, and heavy metals, such that about a quarter of Argentine city dwellers and almost two-thirds of rural areas don't have clean drinking water.

# CULTURE

## FOOD

There are two essential things to keep in mind with Argentine cuisine. The first is that Argentina is one of the world's **leading agricultural producers,** and this plays heavily into the kinds of options prevalent on menus. That means there's a lot of **beef** on the table, and a lot of wheat-based **pasta** and **bread.** The second major theme in Argentine—and especially Buenos Aires—cuisine is its **cosmo-politanism.** Argentina is a country of immigrants, and its people have close ties to Spain and Italy. As a result, these cultural influences manifest themselves in Argentine in inventive and tasty ways. Food is an enormous and essential part of Argentine culture, and eating is the country's most important social ritual. Not to mention that Argentine food is just plain awesome.

> **WHERE BEING LATE TO DINNER IS OK.** Jet lag may not be a problem in Buenos Aires, but be ready to adjust your internal hungry clock ahead a couple of hours. Argentines rarely eat dinner before 9pm, and many restaurants often don't open for dinner until at least 8pm. Consider a snack.

## STEAK

Much is said about Argentine beef, and much should be said: it borders on the **divine.** It's no wonder that Argentines consume the greatest quantity of meat per capita (about 68kg per year) of any nation in the world. The secret, according to the foodies and farmers across the country, is **happy cows.** The vast major-ity of Argentina's over 50 million head of cattle graze in the long pastures of **la Pampa,** a region with just enough rainfall for grasslands galore and just about nothing else. Between that and a full-fledged beef culture, Argentina is also the third largest exporter in the world of beef, behind Brazil and Australia.

Cattle were first introduced into Argentina in 1536 by **Pedro de Mendoza,** Span-ish explorer and founder of Buenos Aires. Since then, Argentines have pretty much just been making their menus longer with more and more beef-themed dishes (though they've probably done other stuff, too). It shouldn't come as any surprise, then, that Argentine restaurants reflect the steak-crazed culture of the nation that thinks of a carrot stick as an acceptable substitute for "salad" and red meat as a three-time-a-day joy. A more complete guide to different cuts of beef can be found on p. 130, but here are a few of the main goodies:

**Bife de chorizo:** This is the steak of steak. The go-to guy. The nightly standard of *parrillas* (grills) the city 'round, it's a kind of sirloin or strip steak, akin to NY Strip or a top loin. It's generally served thick, fatty, and cooked such that it's juicy but not hugely rare.

**Lomo:** Another of the most prized Argentine cuts, *lomo* is tenderloin: long, thin cuts of absurdly, um, tender meat. Pork tenderloin is called *lomo de cerdo,* but the beef is just *lomo*—which is short, we've been told, for "joy of the heavens." Really. (Not really. But really.) Also comes in sandwich form—french bread, lettuce, and joy.

**Ojo de bife:** Ribeye—also sometimes known as *bife ancho,* though the two are subtly different—is like a cross between *bife de chorizo* and *lomo:* it's a big ol' chunk of meat, but it's also extra tender, and it has extra serving of flavor. Good with wine, and great with **chimicurri,** a delicious sauce (p. 66).

**Vacio:** This is generally similar to flank steak or hanger steak elsewhere. It's very common in restaurants, somewhat tougher than other cuts, and generally contains a lot of fat and tissue. All of which means it's mind-destroyingly delicious.

**Entraña:** Generally one of the cheaper meats on the menu, entraña is a skirt steak: thin, juicy, and tough. Though it usually comes surrounded by something of a thick membrane or fatty layer, that's how you know it's tasty—and it's easily trimmed off.

# FOOD THAT IS NOT STEAK

**ARGENTINE SPECIALTIES.** Contrary to popular opinion, Argentina does, in fact, cook food that isn't steak. And you'd better believe it's equally life-changing. For instance: **milanesas.** A milanesa, to be sure, is still beef—though it *can* be chicken or veal—but this time, it's dipped into beaten eggs, seasoned, and then breaded and fried. Often, *milanesas* are served *con papas* (french fries), lemon, or, in true *gaucho* form, *a caballo* (with an egg on top). They tend to be cheap and unbearably delicious. **Sandwiches de miga** are small sandwiches made from light, delicate white bread, very thinly sliced meats, and either cheese, lettuce, or tomato. They're generally served as appetizers or snacks, but can also be consumed in large quantities as a (decadent) light meal.

Most important of all, at least for your tastebuds, is the **empanada.** The name for these delightful and varied stuffed pastries comes from the verb *empanar* (to wrap). What is wrapped varies, but the traditional *empanada* is filled with ground beef, onions, green olives, and boiled egg, all spiced with cumin and paprika. The pastry fold is often patterned with an elaborate twisting structure, called a *repulgue*, and the whole thing is either baked or fried. *Empanadas* vary widely, and can be filled with ham and cheese, chicken, fish, sweet corn, spinach, fruit, or any other fun thing you can think of.

**SAUSAGES. Chorizo,** or sausage, is another Argentine staple. Argentine sausage is of a different caliber than North American sausage: thick, soft, and unbelievably flavorful, chorizo—generally prepared from cured pork—is taken seriously in Argentina, even though it is (thankfully) sold at stands and outside nightclubs across the country. Which leads us to say: chorizo-ness is next to godliness. **Morcilla,** on the other hand, is something of an acquired taste. Though it's incredibly rich and tasty, many find the texture of blood sausage somewhat off-putting. For the record, Let's Go endorses *morcilla*.

**CONDIMENTS.** Though Argentines are religious about their steak, one sauce—**chimichurri**—is allowed. Made from parsley, oregano, garlic, salt, pepper, onion, and paprika, all put into an olive oil and vinegar sauce, it is probably the greatest meat marinade and sauce ever created by man. Outside of steak, though, one condiment is everywhere: **mayonnaise.** Generally sold in squeeze bags and sometimes flavored with lemon, it's used in much the same way that ketchup is in North America: on *chorizo* and hamburgers, on french fries, on *milanesas*, or—a true Argentine classic—mixed with ketchup to create **salsa golf.**

**ITALIAN FOOD.** Argentina has a huge population of Italian immigrants, and its cultural character—gastronomically and otherwise—reflects that heritage. It's no surprise, then, that some (non-Italians, of course) describe Argentine pizza and pasta as the best in the world. **Ñoquis** (gnocchi), **ravioles** (ravioli), and **canelones** (cannelloni, rolled pasta filled with cheese or meat) are also made from scratch in Italian restaurants throughout the city.

**ICE CREAM AND RELATED GOODNESS.** Further building on the Italian heritage, Argentine **helado** follows the path of gelato: thick, creamy, and often home-

LIFE AND TIMES

# HOSTEL

## "Making Friends On the Road"

Guapo Hostel was created to welcome you in a friendly and amusing environment to make you feel at home and where you can share experiences and make some good friends. The house was built in the 1930s and it was totally recycled keeping its style and updated to the 21st century. We have a great terrace with grill to enjoy a classic barbecue with a good wine and empanadas, so you'll enjoy in the best argentine way. Our staff is always ready to assist you in every need and make sure your stay with us as comfortable as possible.

Services Included:
Breakfast (coffee, tea, mate with bread toasts and croissants)
TV room with cable and DVD
Free bed linen and towels
Individual lockers inside the rooms
Central heating
Playroom with board games & karaoke
Rooftop terrace with grill and solarium
Fully equipped kitchen
24 hours hot water
Touristic information
Music
24hs reception
Cleaning room service

Don Bosco 3522 - Buenos Aires, Argentina
tel.: +54 11 4860 3117 | e-mail: info@guapohostel.com.ar
http://www.guapohostel.com.ar

made, it's everywhere in BA (p. 122 and p. 129), especially during the hot summer months. Argentines as a whole take their ice cream seriously, such that even chain ice cream is pretty damn good. Even better, though, is **dulce de leche,** a national obsession to rival steak and Maradona. *Dulce de leche* is a sweet, caramel-like paste, and it goes on everything: from cake to ice cream to toast to fruit, it's the sugary goodness *par excellence.* **Flan,** the Spanish caramel custard, is also big in Argentine restaurants and even in grocery store packets-to-go.

**BREAD AND PASTRIES.** The Argentine **panadería** is a central hub of grocery shopping. Based on enormous wheat production and an Italian heritage of tasty fresh bread, bread stores in Buenos Aires are popular and authentic. Bakeries also churn out sweet pastries called **facturas** like there's no tomorrow, and Argentines can't get enough of them. When sweet, they're often layered with *dulce de leche* or doused with powdered sugar; when buttery, they're often in half-moon shape (called **medialunas**) and resemble croissants. Argentines also have a strange fascination with the Mexican-based **pan dulce,** a sweet bread that's often colored, artificial-looking, and highly sugary.

# DRINK

## WINE

In a country obsessed with beef, impressive wine is essential. The first wine, like the first cows, was brought during Spanish colonization, this time by ▧**Juan Cedrón** to **Santiago del Estero** in 1557. Since then, wine culture has exploded: Argentines drink nearly 45 liters a year per capita, ranking it among the top ten wine-consuming countries in the world. Argentina is also the largest wine producer in the world. About 90% of the wine it produces is consumed domestically, leaving the country open to charges of favoring quantity over quality—a charge that is held up by the custom of mixing cheap wine with soda water.

Then again, over the past decade wine export has been growing quickly, and Argentine **Malbecs** rank among the world's best wines. European influences are also widely apparent in Argentine wines, as French immigrants brought the **Auxerrois** grape, and Italians brought **Bonarda** (also known as Charbono). **Torrontés** is another classic Argentine grape, which makes a distinctive white wine. Cabernet Sauvignon, Syrah, and Chardonnay are also planted across the country. The most important wine regions are in the provinces of **Mendoza** (p. 229) and **San Juan,** though it's also made in **La Rioja, Salta, Catamarca** and **Río Negro.** Mendoza produces more than 60% of domestically consumed wine.

## BEER

When it comes to the everyday beer of Argentina, there's really only one brand: **Cerveza Quilmes,** more popularly known as Quilmes. Founded by a German immigrant in Buenos Aires in 1888, the brewery now has over 75% market share in the Argentine beer industry. It's something of a national icon in the country: it has been the beer of choice for nearly a century, it sponsors the national *fútbol* team, and its colors are—like Argentina's—blue and white. Beer is generally sold in one-liter bottles, and is cheap and plentiful, even in restaurants—though imported beer, generally Heineken, can be significantly more expensive.

## NON-ALCOHOLIC DRINKS

**YERBA MATE.** It's not like tea—though yes, it *is* tea—and it's not really like coffee, either. It's more like Maradona, and we mean that with no reference at all to its taste. **Yerba mate** (herb cup) is everybody's drink: more than any *fútbol* star or any political party, this demographic phenom is the single most universally-loved item in Argentina. One study has shown that over 90% of Argentines—regardless of race, region, or socioeconomic class—drink *mate* on a regular basis. All of which is the more remarkable, given that wine producers in Mendoza and vendors on the Calle Florida hardly speak the same language.

A species of holly, the crushed and toasted twigs and leaves of *Ilex paraguariensis* are mixed with hot (but not boiling) water to create an infusion with the caffeine content of coffee and a grassy, albeit delicious, taste. Said to have curative properties, the bitter-flavored tea—often associated with that other loved icon, the **gaucho**—is a cultural phenomenon in Argentina. In a country where political protest is a daily occurrence and where the preparation and consumption of food reaches levels of ritual bordering on the religious, it's strange and almost incredible to see the unifying power of such a simple drink as *mate*, though there are some regional differences in custom. In the North, *mate* is more likely to be sweetened with *azúcar* (sugar), making it more palatable for novices, while in the big city most purists refuse to dilute the bitter, leafy taste. Uruguayans take *mate* to the streets in thermoses and portable gourds; in Paraguay, the beverage is sometimes served cold; *mate cocido* (tea bags) are sometimes sold instead of loose-leave *yerba*. And while drinking rituals also tend to change across regions, the general steps of *mate* consumption—like the drink itself—tend to transcend regional differences. For a quick run-down on how to sip the gourd without looking like a newbie, check out **Friendship of the Drink** (p. 122).

**COFFEE.** Because it's not a cultural thunderstorm, Argentine coffee seems to go under the radar. In fairness, it's not of the Italian-style quality you might hope for, but it's not bad, and it's everywhere. Cafe culture is big in Argentina, and *porteños* like to say that there's a cafe on every street corner. Most offer espresso as their *café*, along with *cortado* (espresso with hot milk), *café con leche* (half coffee, half milk), and hot chocolate (sometimes served as a *submarino:* hot milk covering a bar of dark chocolate).

# HOW TO WORSHIP YOUR FOOD AND DRINK APPROPRIATELY

**RESTAURANTS.** Restaurants don't open for dinner until 9pm at the earliest in Argentina, and if you show up before 10pm, you'll be the first one. Restaurant manners are similar to those in other European and North America countries: Continental silverware positioning (fork in left hand, knife in right), waiters to seat you, and menus that are often in English. If you're lucky or choose well and find somewhere immune to tourists, the menu may be in Spanish only—feel free to point and play Pictionary, or, if you have the skills, bone up on ordering your food and come prepared. See our **Pronunciation Guide,** p. 258.

**DINNER PARTIES.** Beyond the basic etiquette of Argentine social interactions (press on for more details on that), there are only a few things to watch out for when going to dinner at an Argentine household. Don't sit until your host seats you—there might be a seating plan—and wait to eat until you're invited to. Make sure to compliment the chef profusely; as food is such a large part of Argentine culture, good cooking is a highly prized skill.

**BARS.** Like the big bad city it is, BA is home to a ton of bars and nightclubs. While many open their doors early—most by 10pm or so, some as early as 8pm—nearly all stay open late. And "late" in Buenos Aires is a tad later than you'd expect: bars don't get going until about 2am, and trendy clubs will stay hopping until past dawn. Bars in the city are hugely varied, from cosmopolitan, Aussie- and German-packed expat bars to hole-in-the-wall local bars, but most will have a good selection of beer, wine, and liquor. Bars might have dancing, but clubs definitely will; the difference lies in both dress code (fancier in clubs) and in cover (which bars generally don't charge). In general, nightlife is oriented a bit more towards tourists and expats than to locals, who tend to drink (and spend) somewhat less; to escape the ubiquitous British accent, you'll have to do some exploring, or you can just follow our **recommendations** (p. 203).

**GETTING HOME.** With the rise of street crime in BA and the occasional danger of taxis (p. 40), be careful about coming home after a night of drinking or clubbing. Make sure to call a cab yourself, or have the bar call one for you.

# ETIQUETTE

**WHAT TO WEAR.** It's always a good idea, as a traveler, not to look it. So while Argentines dress similarly to citizens of other Western, industrial countries, it pays to ditch the Tevas, fanny pack, and shorts. BA thinks of itself as cosmopolitan, and it dresses the part: women wear amazingly high-heeled shoes, and men tend to dress in solid-colored pants and collared shirts. When entering a church or a cemetery, it's best to wear clean, long-sleeve shirts, pants, and close-toed shoes—and to be respectful about when and how you take pictures.

**THINGS NOT TO SAY.** Argentines are very proud of their country. In general, they are well educated and highly liberal. That said, there are certain subjects to avoid in conversation. Don't bring up *las Malvinas* (the Falkland Islands), or the war with Great Britain; be careful when discussing politics, particularly with the divisive Perón years; and while many may express their opinions about the church in rather strong terms, try to avoid getting involved in religious discussions. In soccer, avoid rooting for Brazil and England.

**GETTING PHYSICAL.** Touch involves relatively complex rules in Argentina. When meeting someone, a handshake is a welcome form of greeting and shows respect; however, for more intimate relationships—more common between women or between a woman and a man, but also sometimes between close male friends or family—an embrace and a kiss on the cheek is expected. Argentines tend to stand somewhat close while speaking, and it's impolite to back away. They also use a significant number of hand gestures—in some circles, the "OK" or thumbs up signs are vulgarities, while in others, hitting the palm of the left hand with the right first means "that's stupid" or "I don't believe you." In some ways, Argentina can also feel like something of a forward country; women may be whistled at, and *piropos* (flirtatious comments) should be taken with a smile and a thank you.

**TIMING IS EVERYTHING.** The pace of life in Argentina—from business to dining—is slower than in Europe, and certainly slower than that of North America. Meetings, both personal and professional, sometimes run far longer than expected, and it's standard procedure to let them run their course and not rush, even if it means being late for another appointment. Social events, for the most part, follow the same basic rule: you are *expected* to arrive half an hour to an hour late to any party. To arrive early is not only unusual, it's impolite. The only exceptions are *fútbol* matches, the theater, and some lunch appointments.

**COURTESIES.** When invited to an Argentine home, it's often polite to bring some small gift of flowers, candy, pastries, chocolates, or imported liquor. Don't make it too expensive, however; Argentines can be quite sensitive to the differences in buying power between themselves and guests. If you are presented with a gift, open it immediately and make sure to express your gratitude. Generally, in small gatherings, wait for a third-party introduction to those you don't know. When leaving, make sure to say goodbye to each person individually—despite the fact that this may take a very long time.

## SPORTS AND RECREATION

### GOOOOOOOOOOOOOOOOOOOOOLLLLL!

The only appropriate title for a passage on a sport with many names. Whether you call it soccer, football, or *fútbol*, this is the ⬛national pastime in Argentina. In fact, it is effectively the state religion. An Argentine will often not identify themselves by creed, nationality, or region; what really matters is the club you support. Are you a **River** fan, or perhaps a devotee of the **Boca Juniors?** Do you bleed **Lanús** garnet, or cheer for **San Lorenzo?** "If you support **Tigre,** I won't be your friend." You get the picture. Of course, Argentina isn't completely fragmented along team lines. During the **FIFA World Cup** or the **Copa América,** everyone roots for the *Albicelestes*—the "white and sky blue" of the **National Team.**

**COPA AMÉRICA 2011.** Argentina fielded a steamroller squad during the **2007 Copa América,** held in Venezuela, dominating the competition through three rounds of play. That is, until the finals, when Brazil stopped the Argentines 3-0 to take the title. In 2011, the Copa, the main international football tournament for South America, will come to Argentina. There are no details yet, but the country is certainly already gearing up for revenge.

### A SHOT OF HISTORY

Although **Brazil** is often seen as the face of Latin American soccer, largely due to their five World Cup titles, Argentina is no joke compared to the traditional superpower, with two Cup championships of their own (1978 and 1986). Brazil's neighbor to the south is just lower profile, perhaps. Certainly nothing to scoff at. The soccer climate is changing today with the current Argentine squad, ranked number one in the world as of early 2008. But standings and distinctions aside, there is one thing Argentina can always hold over Brazil: they started playing soccer **27 years** before the Brazilians. Zing!

OK, so it's not exactly a taunt you'll hear at international friendlies between the two nations, but for a country as in love with soccer as Argentina, a sense of the game's history is worth noting. Maybe you can drop some of these names and dates at a match and elicit a few impressed glances, or bewildered stares.

**STRANGE BEDFELLOWS.** Dateline **1867.** A monumental year in Argentine history. The year soccer arrived in the country through the ports of Buenos Aires. Two English brothers, **Thomas and James Hogg,** established the **Buenos Aires Football Club** in 1867 and played the country's first match that year in Palermo. The Hogg team won 4-0. The opposing side, though having the unfortunate distinction of being the country's **first losers,** at least were defeated by brothers with an easily mockable name. Those pigs.

LIFE AND TIMES

## THE HAND OF GOD

In some ways, it's simple: **Diego Maradona** is the greatest soccer player in history. He was a kid that rose from the slums of Boca to captivate a country that is obsessed with *fútbol*. His epic two goals in a win over **England** in the quarter-finals of the **1986 FIFA World Cup** are downright iconic. FIFA voted them #1 and #3 on the list of greatest goals of all time. He's a near saint (in fact, there's a religion named after him) in a nation that's over 90% Catholic, and his likeness is sold on T-shirts across the world and on prayer candles on the Calle Florida.

In other ways, though, it's a little more complicated. In 1991, Maradona was suspended for failing a **drug test** for cocaine. In 1994, it was ephedrine, and he was sent home from that year's World Cup in the United States. Now, the man who played his first professional game before his sixteenth birthday and whose health is followed as national news, works as a TV show host.

It's almost as if the greater themes and struggles of his life can be brought back to that one great game in 1986. The fierce **rivalary** between Argentina and England on and off the soccer field was at its zenith. It was four years after the United Kingdom and Argentina had fought over the **Falkland Islands.** It was twenty years after a controversial call in the quarterfinals of the **1966 World Cup** sent the Argentine captain off the field, allowing the

For some time following the triumph of the Hoggs, the game remained a British pastime in the city until another Englishman, **Alexander W. Hutton,** brought the sport to the mainstream by introducing it to private schools in 1885. Soccer proved to be a wildly popular sport in the country, mainly due to its simplicity. Got a field? Check. Ball? Check. You're set. Fields are pretty easy to come by in Argentina (see: expansive rural pastures), as are leather balls, thanks to the widespread cattle industry. After all, you have to do something with all of that leather post-beef consumption. Soon after Hutton's expansion of the game, the newfound mass of clubs established the **Argentine Football League Association** in 1893, one of the oldest soccer associations in South America and one of the first outside of the Europe.

**Isaac Newell,** yet another Brit, was the other granddaddy of Argentine football. A secondary school he established in 1884, the **Colegio Anglo-Argentino,** included soccer in the curriculum. Alumni of the school eventually established a squad in honor of their patriarch, the aptly named **Newell's Old Boys,** based in **Rosario,** a city 300km (187mi.) northwest of Buenos Aires. The team has produced many of Argentina's top players, including current national team standouts **Maxi Rodriguez** and **Lionel Messi.**

**RIGGED BALLS.** Cue decades of practice and development. By the 1930s, Argentina had one of the top national squads in the world, and they were ready to flaunt their skills. The **1930 FIFA World Cup,** the first of the now-celebrated international football competition, pitted Argentina against **Uruguay** in the finals, held in Montevideo. The Uruguayans, fresh off a gold medal at the 1928 Summer Olympics in Amsterdam, defeated the *Albicelestes* 4-2.

The match was not without controversy. No one could agree on what ball to use for the game, so FIFA decided to use an Argentine ball in the first half, followed by an Uruguayan alternative for the second half. A recipe for disaster. Sure enough, despite leading 2-1 after the first frame, the *Albicelestes* fell victim to a second half comeback as Uruguay tallied three goals to Argentina's one, sealing the win. Of course, protest immediately erupted, with accusations of **rigged balls** favoring the Uruguayans in the second half. Commentators seemed to forget that the Argentines had to kick the same ball. Nonetheless, in Buenos Aires, angry mobs made their displeasure known by throwing rocks at the Uruguayan consulate.

**THANKS FOR GIVING US SOCCER AND ALL, BUT...** Following the balls fiasco, the Argentine national team fell into 30 years of relative tranquility, until the **1966 FIFA World Cup** in **England.** A quarterfinal match between England and Argentina set off a fierce **rivalry** that lasts to this day. The English took the game 1-0 on a questionable goal. Some thought it was legit, while Argentine supporters believed the scorer, **Geoff Hurst,** was offside. Another alleged travesty of the match for Argentina was the loss of captain **Antonio Rattín,** who was sent off on a disputed call and ultimately escorted from the field by police. The referee, apparently, didn't appreciate the way Rattín looked at him. No rocks were thrown afterwards, but the match left a bitter taste in the mouth for Argentina's fans, who promptly dubbed the match *el robo del siglo* ("the theft of the century").

**TRIUMPH AT LAST.** Finally, after years of scandal, outrage, tampered balls, and supposedly bad calls, Argentina nabbed a championship in the **1978 FIFA World Cup,** held on their home turf, with a 3-1 victory over the Netherlands. The military junta controlling the country at the time, led by dictator **Jorge Videla,** marred the win somewhat by attempting to take credit for the title.

Less than ten years later, the legendary **Diego Maradona** carried Argentina to another championship in the **1986 FIFA World Cup** in Mexico with a 3-2 victory over West Germany in the finals. However, the most memorable game of the tournament was another quarterfinal faceoff with the English. This time, the Argentines exacted revenge for their loss in 1966, albeit through rather controversial means (see **The Hand of God, p. 72**).

**RISE TO THE TOP.** After a fairly uneventful 1990s, Argentina entered the **2002 FIFA World Cup** in Japan and South Korea representing a country racked by economic turmoil. Their performance on the field mirrored the crisis at home as the Argentines failed to advance to the knockout stage of the tournament, registering a loss in the process to the good ol' English. Redemption on the international level came four years later, though, with a **gold medal** at the **2004 Summer Olympics Athens.** Expectations were high for the **2006 FIFA World Cup** in Germany with an Argentine squad headlined by **Juan Román Riquelme, Hernán Crespo, Lionel Messi,** and **Maxi Rodriguez,** but that team, despite being one of the most talented at the tournament, fell short once again, this time to the Germans in overtime penalty kicks. Despite the recent setbacks, the future remains bright for the top ranked *Albicelestes*. Messi, who is only 21 years old as of 2008, has become the face of the team as of late, with a second place finish in the **2007 FIFA**

English to win and advance to the finals, where they won the Cup. Needless to say, the 1986 match was a pretty big deal.

Six minutes into the second half, Maradona played a ball diagonally into the box, too far from his teammate. English defender **Steve Hodge** tried to clear, but the ball hit his foot poorly, heading back towards the goal 6'1" English goalkeeper **Peter Shilton** came out to punch the ball away, but 5'5" Diego Maradona seemed to get the better of him with a header, and the referees called a goal, without quite realizing why the English defenders were so upset. The reason, of course, is that Maradona didn't hit the ball with his head at all, but with his left fist, prompting one of the most famous quotations in sports history: when asked about the legality of his goal, Maradona answered that he scored *"un poco con la cabeza de Maradona y otro poco con* **la mano de Dios"** ("a little with the head of Maradona and a little with the **hand of God"**).

Five minutes after God meddled in things, Maradona broke through five English players, dribbling over half of the field before beating the keeper to make the score 2-0, securing the win. It was voted the **Goal of the Century** in 2002—an all-out run directly into the jaws of the defense. Within the short span of a few minutes, Maradona had scored the most infamous and the most impressive goal in soccer history. His legacy still walks that same, fine line.

**World Player of the Year** award, the highest finish for an Argentine. Maradona, ever present over 20 years after his triumph, has named Messi his "successor." The Argentines nabbed another gold medal at the **2008 Summer Olympics** in **Beijing,** further adding to their long list of accolades.

## THEY HAVE HOW MANY TEAMS?

The Argentine Football Association is divided into two levels. The best, top flight teams play in **Primera A,** while the second tier teams play in **Primera B.** Buenos Aires proper, and Buenos Aires province as a whole, has many Primera A teams, including the so-called **"big five"** clubs: **Club Atlético River Plate,** also known as **River,** based in Núñez; **Club Atlético Boca Juniors,** also known as **Boca,** based in La Boca; **Club Atlético Independiente,** or just **Independiente,** based in Avellaneda; **Racing de Avellaneda,** or simply **Racing,** also based in Avellaneda; and **San Lorenzo de Almagro,** also known as San Lorenzo, based in Boedo *barrio*.

The rivalry between River and Boca, known as the **Superclásico,** is one of the best and most heated rivalries in world soccer. It functions on a geographic level (northern Buenos Aires for River, southern Buenos Aires for Boca) and, much more importantly, on a socioeconomic level—Boca, supposedly, is considered the club for working-class fans, while River is seen as a more elitist team, set in the wealthier northern *barrios*. As of early 2008, the rivalry is remarkably close in record, with 115 wins for Boca and 104 for River.

South America's soccer confederation, **Confederación Sudamericana de Fútbol,** better known as **CONMEBOL,** has two major club championship series. The most important is the **Copa Libertadores de América,** which has traditionally been dominated by Argentine teams. The Boca Juniors won in 2007, while Independiente is the most successful club historically, with seven titles. The other championship is the less prestigious **Copa Sudamericana,** a club series that includes teams from the North American soccer confederation, **CONCACAF,** as well. Argentine teams have done well in the brief history of the Copa Sudamericana, too, taking four of the six titles (two of them for Boca).

Much like many other Latin American leagues, the Argentine soccer year is divided into two seasons. Each season has a champion, leading to twice the fun and twice the glory for fans and clubs around the country. The first season, **Apertura** (opening) plays from August to December, while the second season, **Clausura** (closing) lasts from February to June.

# SPORTS THAT ARE NOT SOCCER

Much as steak isn't the only food in Argentina, soccer isn't the country's only sport. **Basketball** is also immensely popular, with the Argentine national basketball team enjoying great success as of late, taking home the **gold medal** at the **2004 Summer Olympics** in Athens, Greece. Argentina's biggest basketball star, arguably, is **Manu Ginóbili,** a current player for the San Antonio Spurs of the American National Basketball Association (NBA) renowned for his clutch play and ability to slash through opposing defenses with ease.

In a complete about-face, **polo** is also a sport that has found considerable popularity in Argentina. The Argentines dominate the sport today, winning every world championship since 1949 (perhaps the longest streak of uninterrupted dominance in any sport) and producing most of the best players in the world. The **Campeonato Argentino Abierto de Polo,** an international club competition held in Buenos Aires, is one of the world's most important polo tournaments.

**Pato,** the national game of Argentina, is a strange combination of basketball and polo. *Pato* is Spanish for "duck." The name of the game came from its original format on the plains of rural Argentina. Opposing teams on horseback would fight for control of a live duck in a basket. The first team to bring the duck back to their home *estancia* (ranch) would win. Today, the rules are somewhat different. Notably, live ducks are no longer used, a blessing to canards everywhere. Instead, two teams of four riders each must throw a ball through a horizontal hoop. For Harry Potter fans out there, it's like Quidditch, but without magical broomsticks.

# THE ARTS

## ARCHITECTURE

If Argentina was home to a magical mountain of silver, as colonial Spanish explorers originally thought (p. 53), one would expect to find building after building made out of glimmering silver. Unfortunately, the mountain of silver did not exist, and colonial-era buildings in Buenos Aires were unremarkable. This was also due to the fact that BA was, before the 19th century, nothing more than a ramshackle, unimportant town on the Río de la Plata. The few notable colonial buildings that exist are mostly churches.

This all changed when Buenos Aires became the capital of the **Viceroyalty of the Río de la Plata** at the close of the 18th century. For much of the 19th century, architecture was still influenced by the Spanish colonial style. At the close of the century, a distinct **Neo-Baroque** style, heavily influenced by French and Italian architecture, found its way into the city's skyline. Many of Buenos Aires' most striking buildings come from this period. **Vittorio Meano,** an Italian architect, designed several of them, including the **Teatro Colón,** BA's famous opera house, the **Palace of Justice,** and the **Argentine National Congress.** The Neo-Baroque style can also be found in churches throughout the city, such as the **Buenos Aires Metropolitan Cathedral** and the **Cabildo.**

Twentieth-century architecture in Buenos Aires went through two phases. The first was an **Art Nouveau** period, a style marked by highly stylized, non-linear, organic design. More European architects, such as Italians **Francisco Gianotti, Mario Palanti,** and **Virginio Colombo,** dominated this phase. Modernist architecture, inspired by **brutalism** (read: concrete, and lots of it), emerged in the second half of the century, with controversial "landmarks" such as the **Biblioteca National de la República Argentina,** designed by Argentine **Clorindo Testa.**

Perhaps as a response to the mounds of concrete of the 1960s and 1970s, some of BA's newest architectural feats focus on revivals of **Beaux Arts** and **Neo-Baroque** buildings from the late-19th to early-20th centuries. The **Galerías Pacífico,** a major shopping mall on **Calle Florida,** is perhaps the best example of this movement. The contemporary era in Buenos Aires has also seen the rise of many skyscrapers, such as **Torre Fortabat,** designed by **Sánchez Elía,** and Palermo's **Le Parc Tower,** designed by **Mario Álvarez.** Argentine-born architects have also designed major buildings in other areas of the world, such as **César Pelli's** twin **Petronas Towers** in Kuala Lumpur, Malaysia.

## FILM

As the capital of the country, Buenos Aires has long been the center of Argentine film. European photographers, such as the Belgian **Henri Lepage,** the French **Eugene Py,** and the Austrian **Max Glücksmann,** who arrived in Buenos Aires in the late 19th century, were among the country's first film pioneers. Lepage was the first to bring actual filmmaking equipment to Argentina, which he used to create what is believed to be the first Argentine movie, **La Bandera Argentina,** mostly consisting of footage of the Argentine flag billowing in the breeze in the Plaza de Mayo. A German filmmaker, **Federico Figner,** also has a potential claim to the title, with his own footage of landmarks throughout the city.

Argentine filmmaking continued to evolve over the first half of the 20th century, as directors experimented with documentary filmmaking and shorts. Most subject matter came from masterpieces of Argentine literature, such as the poems of **José Hernández.** Tango also became a popular topic for films, particularly those that featured the legendary **Carlos Gardel.** The development of sound expanded horizons for directors, and the first Argentine film with sound, **Adiós Argentina,** was released in 1930. Predictably, the subject matter was tango.

After booming through much of the 1930s and 1940s, the industry hit a slump that coincided with the relatively strict censorship rules of the first Perón presidency. Argentine filmmakers also found it difficult to compete with the ever expanding Hollywood industry, which was slowly but surely coming to dominate the world cinema scene. During the 1960s, in response to the first post-Perón **junta,** filmmakers turned to slapstick comedies. Once dictator **Leopoldo Galtieri** was deposed following the blunder in the Falklands, filmmakers felt free to return to more serious subject matters unhindered. Many of the first films produced after the fall of the junta in 1982 focused on the events of the nightmarish 1970s and early 1980s, especially the Dirty War. **Funny Little Dirty War,** a black comedy, was one such piece emblematic of this era.

Though the Argentine film industry took a major hit during and after the **economic crisis,** with a lack of funds and viewers who couldn't even afford a ticket, the industry has rebounded as of late, in part thanks to government subsidization started by **Néstor Kirchner.** Since then, many films, such as 2002's **El Hijo de la Novia** ("Son of the Bride") have enjoyed success during awards season.

## LITERATURE

There is one truly consistent theme in Argentine culture. At first, most facets were completely European. It wasn't until the 19th century that newly independent Argentina developed a culture of its own. This is the case with Argentine literature. One of the first great Argentine writers of the 19th century was **José Hernández,** a poet best known for his epic work, **Martín Fierro,** a poem set around the *gaucho* rural culture that defines much of Argentine national identity.

The 20th century proved to be a major era for Argentine literature, the true giant of the time being, without a doubt, **Jorge Luis Borges,** a native of BA best known for his short stories, essays, and poetry. Born in 1899, Borges devoted the early years of his professional career to writing essays and poetry for literary journals. However, he would later come to detest these works so much that he attempted to buy all copies of them in existence in order to destroy them. The plot didn't work, but any deficit Borges may have perceived in his early contributions was certainly compensated for by his later brilliance.

One of his most famous early contributions was 1935's **A Universal History of Infamy,** a showcase for Borges' scholarly talent and his trademark touch of fanciful humor. Some pieces blurred the line between non-fiction and short story, while others were in-depth analyses of fabricated texts. Other works that exhibited this magical quality include **The Book of Imaginary Beings** and **The Book of Sand.** Many anthologies of his complete short stories exist, too. Some fairly consistent themes are explored in most of his works, such as the difference between reality and myth, the nature of infinity, mirrors, and, perhaps most famously, **labyrinths.** Curiously, Borges' work was never fully embraced by his compatriots during his lifetime; instead, his work was initially popularized in France, and was only fully appropriated by Latin American audiences after his death. Though Borges was given many honors and awards, such as the

# Analyze This: Buenos Aires on the Couch
## The Porteño Penchant for Psychoanalysis

It was in Wimbledon 2006. Argentine Gastón Gaudio, winner of Roland Garros two years earlier, was not doing well against the little known Georgian Irakli Labadze. You could see it, and then you could hear it, too. After yet another feeble backhand to the net, he suddenly yelled, *"¡Qué mal que la estoy pasando!"* ("I'm having such a horrible time!"). Occasionally, after subsequent errors, he would elaborate: "What am I doing here? I don't get why I didn't stay home"; "They shouldn't have let me in. It's a shame they let me play…"; "Am I going to be any good now here, at 28?"; "Why don't I just leave and stop making a fool of myself?" The tennis cathedral, unaccustomed to confessional speech, was in awe. But what Gaudio was doing was not too different from what *porteños* do all the time: they talk. They talk about their feelings, passions, fears, and they analyze them. True enough, most shy away from televised confessions and do it with friends at a cafe or with psychoanalysts at their offices.

Now, chances are that some of those friends are, in fact, psycholoanalysts. In 1995, almost two of every 400 *porteños* were shrinks. There is even an area of the neighborhood of Palermo known as "Villa Freud" because so many psychoanalysts live and work there. Consider, too, that the "Argentine psychoanalyst" has become a social stereotype in cities like Madrid and Barcelona. But, mind you, the impact of psychoanalysis is not restricted to specialists: psychoanalytic lingo is widely, although sometimes rudimentarily, known and used. Most *porteños* watching TV the day of Gaudio's debacle could have speculated whether he

was engaging in self-sabotage because of some neurosis or repressed desire, or whether he was battling some obscure childhood trauma or engaging in sheer masochism. And then again, maybe he was just having a bad day.

There is no single cause for the ubiquitousness of psychoanalysis in Argentine, and particularly *porteño* culture. Mariano Plotkin enumerates a few possibilities in his *Freud in the Pampas:* "the European background of most of the population and the crisis of identity provoked by its foreign roots; the presence of a large Jewish community; a permanent feeling of disappointment originating in unrealistic expectations; and even the national tradition of the tango and the guitar-strumming *gaucho*." Indeed, most tangos tell stories of middle-aged men who endlessly mourn for lost, and usually long gone, happiness, and *Martín Fierro*, the most emblematic 19th-century narrative of Argentina, is told by a runaway who comforts himself by singing because he cannot rest "from extraordinary pain." The Argentine economy can also leave you with a lot of working through

> ## "In 1995, almost two out of every 400 porteños were shrinks."

to do: it tends to go up and down in erratic cycles, so that being paranoid is a sign of wisdom. Any promising project can become Sisyphean, and in past decades many *porteños* have concluded that the only way out of the crisis is the airport.

One can argue that psychoanalysis had been part of this culture prior to the very existence of psychoanalysis. Before Lacan was explaining the slippage of the signified beneath the signifier, *porteños* knew it somehow. A word can mean many things, even its opposite (Carlos Gardel, the finest tango singer in Argentine history, is praised through his nickname "The mute"; Jorge Luis Borges, the finest writer, wrote that to insult a doctor it comes to cultural production: black humor abounds in newspaper cartoons, the grotesque is the preferred mode in theater, and satire and irony are compulsory in literature. You may wonder how these people, allergic to literality and enamored with hidden, twisted or unconscious meanings, communicate. My hypothesis is that they manage to do so

## "... some porteños actualy need to clarify when they are being serious..."

there was no better way than to call him "doctor" many times.) When it comes to euphemisms, *porteños* are excellent at recognizing them (who is going to buy that "labor flexibilization" and "emerging markets" mean anything but "anti-union laws" and "poor countries"?), and they know that words are only occasionally communicative (in *truco*, the traditional card game, players talk to each other constantly, usually to cause distraction, deceive, or simply as phatic plug-ins.) Rambling speech and irony are so habitual that some *porteños* actually need to clarify when they are being serious— and even when they do, such clarification can be taken as another ironic twist. Really, I mean it. No no, I´m serious, trust me here.

through a common sense of humor. It is of the most corrosive kind, and it has been refined both by socioeconomic circumstances and by the pervasive impact of psychoanalytic lore. Take yourself seriously, sound too serious, and you lose the game out of naïveté. Gaudio lost the match, sure, but at some point he started laughing. At the press conference he explained:

## "... sound too serious, and you lose the game out of naïeveté."

Irony can be detected even in greetings. Classic *porteño* retorts to the question "How are you doing?": "I'm fine, or do you really want to know?"; "If I were doing better it would be obscene"; "Badly, but I´m used to it." You can guess where this leads when

"Oh man, what an embarrassment. I won one point by hitting the ball with I don´t know what part of the racket, and I just got the giggles. I couldn´t help it, and people were laughing along too, you see?" In the end Gaudio knew, like his fellow *porteños*, how to use language to tame unbearable feelings. He knew, too, how to look at the tragedy of losing with an infectious, ironic smirk that can disarm the most painful neurosis.

*Martín L. Gaspar is a doctoral candidate in the Romance Languages and Literatures Department at Harvard University.*

**Cervantes Prize,** the **French Legion of Honor,** and an **Order of the British Empire,** Borges died in 1986 without winning the **Nobel Prize for Literature.**

**Julio Cortázar,** born in 1914, was another 20th-century master who wrote in the tradition of Borges, his predecessor and idol. Though he grew up in Argentina, most of his contributions to literature, mainly novels and short stories, were written in self-imposed exile in France, where he moved in 1951 to protest the presidency of **Juan Perón.** Many of his stories, which, like those of Borges before him, are notable for their fantastic elements, had notable influences on film. **Las Babas del Diablo** (Devil's Spit), a murder story, was adapted into Michelangelo Antonioni's 1966 British-Italian film *Blow-Up,* while **La Autopista del Sur** (The Southern Highway) inspired Jean-Luc Godard to write his 1967 film *Week End.* Cortázar's most famous work, **Rayuela** (Hopscotch), is a novel with a distinctive open-ended structure, featuring "expendable" chapters that the reader can choose or not choose to read. Think of it as an early "Choose Your Own Adventure" story, but much, much better. The other titan of 20th-century Argentine literature was **Manuel Puig,** best known for novels such as 1968's **La traición de Rita Hayworth** (Betrayed by Rita Hayworth) and 1976's **El beso de la mujer araña** (Kiss of the Spider Woman), which was adapted into a movie and a popular Broadway musical.

## TANGO

**WHAT IT'S ALL ABOUT.** Buenos Aires *is* **tango.** When you think tango, you usually think dance and couples shooting across the dance floor, one with a rose in their mouth. However, it's really more appropriate to label it, more generally, as a music form. It combines instruments, which, for tango, is usually a **sextet,** the **orquesta típica,** which includes two violins, a piano, a double bass, and two **bandoneóns,** an instrument similar to the accordion. In addition to the music, tango also involves dance, theatrics, and performance. It is a complete sensory experience that has defined the culture of Buenos Aires for over a century.

Tango is complex, with multiple forms and styles, from traditional **Tango Argentino** to **Ballroom tango** and the peculiar **Finnish tango.** The one thing that remains mostly consistent from style to style is the close, distinguishing embrace, which is used whenever the dancers aren't in a more open stance.

Tango clubs and venues dot the landscape in Buenos Aires. Many are known as **milongas,** which is simply derived from *milonga,* a style of music that often accompanies tango dancing. Often, dancers will openly perform on the street, such as along **El Caminito** in La Boca or at the **Feria de San Telmo,** and most clubs offer plenty of opportunities for amateurs to practice.

**HISTORY.** The origins of tango date back to the late 19th century. As with many facets of Argentine culture, there was a European influence on the evolution of tango music and dance. Many European forms of dance contributed to forming what became tango—Italian tarantella, Polish mazurka, central European polka, and Spanish flamenco, to name a few; even touches of African influence were involved. Immigrants from these regions traveled to Buenos Aires, and, in a rough combination of their musical forms, created early tango.

Eventually, by the early 20th century, tango found its way into the city's **brothels,** a popular entertainment destination for the working class. Strangely, at this time, the population of men in Buenos Aires far outnumbered the women by a whopping 100,000. It comes as no surprise, then, that brothels were a very popular destination. Lines would stretch far out the door, onto the street, and around the corner. Supposedly, tango musicians were employed to entertain those waiting in line. The women, naturally, were preoccupied indoors, so, in another twist, early tango initially involved two men dancing. This, in part, explains why the dance today has an air of aggressive machismo.

As with many popular forms of contemporary music, such as jazz and rock and roll, tango was at first shunned by the higher classes in society, even the middle class. Naturally, a form of music played in brothels offended the senses of the more "sophisticated." Tango did find some popularity in other countries, including the United States, and France, where it became a craze.

The popularized version of tango came back to Argentina in the 1920s and 1930s, where it had newfound success, thanks to the efforts of tango legend **Carlos Gardel,** the "King of Tango." Gardel brought the music to the masses with his sharp, heart throb looks and famous baritone voice, best captured in famous songs such as *Volver*, *Mi Buenos Aires querido* (My Beloved Buenos Aires), and *Soledad*. Gardel died young, only in his mid-40s, in a 1935 plane crash in Colombia. The city celebrates his life with statues and an annual commemoration on the anniversary of his death, June 24th. His tomb in **La Chacarita Cemetery** (p. 164) is also a destination for tango pilgrims and tourists alike.

Thanks in part due to the foundation laid by Gardel, tango entered a **Golden Age** from roughly 1935 to 1952. Orchestra leaders such as **Juan D'Arienzo, Francisco Canaro, Aníbal Troilo,** and **Carlos di Sarli** became the superstar names of this age. Each had their own trademark style. Canaro was known for his slow beats, which were easy to dance to and, thus, popular at parties and other functions. D'Arienzo, on the other hand, set a livelier tone with his fast, persistent beats. Juan Perón's presidency also proved to be a factor that helped tango's popularity reach greater heights. During his tenure, tango was seen as a symbol of national pride. When Perón was deposed by a military coup in 1955, tango briefly died with him under the strict rules of the ensuing junta.

Though it has had varying popularity in recent years, today, tango remains a dominant part of BA's cultural fabric. The music has modernized in many respects, especially with the influence of **rock and roll,** which has led to the addition of **electric guitars** in many tango bands. The dance itself has modernized, too, adopting a more open embrace with fluid motions.

# MEDIA

### NEWSPAPERS

Argentine newspapers are some of the best and most respected in Latin America, but the government and the papers have a rocky relationship. With over 150 daily newspapers, at least two of which are major international news sources, newsstands in Argentina are pretty packed with viable papers. And while there's little formal censorship, the relationship between the media and the government is anything but friendly. President Néstor Kirchner refused to hold press conferences at the presidential palace, and rumors of police brutality and intimidation toward journalists remain prevalent. Provincial governments, reports the censorship watchdog *Reporters Without Borders*, remain the greatest threats to free speech: journalists in the provinces risk being hounded by the police and courts, and the subtle practice of provincial governments buying (or not buying) advertisements in local newspapers has provided sometimes irresistible financial incentive to limit criticism. In Tierra del Fuego, for instance, one source reports that 75% of all ads are paid for by the provincial government—enough to put a stranglehold on small news outlets.

Nevertheless, major Argentine newspapers soldier on, and a few remain international entities, read everywhere from Los Angeles to Madrid to Bogotá.

**La Nación,** a respected conservative daily, and **La Prensa,** Argentina's oldest newspaper, have wide international reputations, while **Clarín** has the largest circulation in Argentina. The **Buenos Aires Herald** is an English-language daily, **Crónica** is a popular tabloid, and **Página 12** is a left-wing daily.

## TELEVISION

Television reaches a huge audience in Buenos Aires, as in other major cities, and Argentine broadcast media is strong and varied. There's a strong news presence, as in other countries, but it's complemented by a strong host of game shows and sports channels. **Canal 7** is the state-run station, while **Canal 11** in Buenos Aires boasts some of the highest ratings and **Canal 13** runs the satellite news channel *Todo Noticias.* Every other channel, it seems, will be a sports channel or a game show—everything from Wheel-of-Fortune style word games to dominoes to rodeos and, of course, *fútbol.*

# HOLIDAYS AND FESTIVALS

It's not so surprising that Argentine holidays and festivals are ridiculously fun, and maybe just a touch dangerous. Holidays mean the best food, the best drink, people getting off of work. In BA, they also mean fireworks going off in every parking lot and backyard, *globos* (paper balloons powered by the hot air of a burning candle) flying through the sky, and an alarming rate of drunk driving. That is to say, holidays can be the best times to visit the city, and especially to get invited to a private home—but as always, be careful.

| DATE IN 2009 | NAME AND LOCATION | DESCRIPTION |
|---|---|---|
| January 1 | Año Nuevo (New Year) | Fireworks—everywhere. |
| March/April | Santo Viernes y Pascua | Good Friday and Easter; a popular vacation time. |
| April 2 | Día de las Malvinas | Commemorates the day Argentina invaded the Falklands. |
| May 1 | Día de los Trabajadores | Labor Day; often a day of social protest. |
| Late May | Arte BA | A huge art fair in La Plaza Italia, Av. Santa Fe, Palermo. |
| May 25 | Revolución de Mayo | Celebrates the 1810 revolution with parades and music. |
| June 20 | Día de la Bandera | Flag day; parades and speeches, blue and white. |
| July 9 | Día de la Independencia | Independence Day; expect more fireworks and food. |
| August 17 | Día de San Martín | The Liberator's death day. |
| October 12 | Día de la Raza | Columbus Day, but with emphasis on Argentine culture. |
| December 25 | Navidad | Christmas; fun times, and lots of food. Parades to follow. |

# BEYOND TOURISM

## A PHILOSOPHY FOR TRAVELERS

**HIGHLIGHTS OF BEYOND TOURISM IN ARGENTINA**

**TEACH ENGLISH** to schoolchildren in poverty-stricken Buenos Aires *barrios* (p. 84).

**COACH SOCCER** to disadvantaged youngsters to Misiones province (p. 85).

**BUILD HOMES** for *porteño* families in need (p. 85).

**FLIP** to our "Giving Back" sidebar features for even more regional Beyond Tourism opportunities (p. 85).

As a tourist, you are always a foreigner. Sure, hostel-hopping and sightseeing can be fun, but connecting with a foreign country through studying, volunteering, or working can extend your travels beyond tourist traps. We don't like to brag, but this is what's different about a *Let's Go* traveler. Instead of feeling like a stranger in a strange land, you can understand Buenos Aires and Argentina like a local. Instead of being that tourist asking for directions, you can be the one who gives them (and correctly!). All the while, you get the satisfaction of leaving Argentina in better shape than you found it (after all, it's being nice enough to let you stay here). It's not wishful thinking—it's Beyond Tourism.

As a **volunteer** in Argentina, you can unleash your inner superhero with projects from saving endangered wildcats in the Argentine wilderness to helping children in disadvantaged Buenos Aires *barrios*. This chapter is chock-full of ideas to get involved, whether you're looking to pitch in for a day or run away from home for a whole new life in Argentine activism.

The powers of **studying** abroad are beyond comprehension: it actually makes you feel sorry for those poor tourists who don't get to do any homework while they're here. Buenos Aires, and other major city centers in Argentina provide excellent opportunities for those looking to study Spanish abroad, and perhaps teach English while learning. There are also many local universities that offer courses in an array of subjects, from the sciences to the humanities.

**Working** abroad immerses you in a new culture and can bring some of the most meaningful relationships and experiences of your life. Yes, we know you're on vacation, but these aren't your normal desk jobs. (Plus, it doesn't hurt that it helps pay for more globetrotting.)

 **SHARE YOUR EXPERIENCE.** Have you had a particularly enjoyable volunteer, study, or work experience that you'd like to share with other travelers? Post it to our website, www.letsgo.com!

# VOLUNTEERING

Volunteering can be a powerful and fulfilling experience, especially when combined with the thrill of traveling in a new place. Most people who volunteer in Argentina do so on a short-term basis at organizations that make use of drop-in or once-a-week volunteers. Most short-term opportunities in Buenos Aires proper focus on community development and serving the homeless and underprivileged. Similar opportunities exist in other large Argentine cities, such as Mendoza and Córdoba. Outside of the city centers, many opportunities exist for environmentally focused work, be it protecting wildlife or farming, but these pursuits are mostly long-term projects. As always, read up on your desired program before heading out.

Those looking for longer, more intensive volunteer opportunities usually choose to go through a parent organization that takes care of logistical details and often provides a group environment and support system—for a fee. There are two main types of organizations—religious and secular—although there are rarely restrictions on participation for either. Websites like **www.volunteerabroad.com, www.servenet.org,** and **www.idealist.org** allow you to search for volunteer openings both in your country and abroad.

**I HAVE TO PAY TO VOLUNTEER?** Many volunteers are surprised to learn that some organizations require large fees or "donations," but don't go calling them scams just yet. While such fees may seem ridiculous at first, they often keep the organization afloat, covering airfare, room, board, and administrative expenses for the volunteers. (Other organizations must rely on private donations and government subsidies.) If you're concerned about how a program spends its fees, request an annual report or finance account. A reputable organization won't refuse to inform you of how volunteer money is spent. Pay-to-volunteer programs might be a good idea for young travelers who are looking for more support and structure (such as pre-arranged transportation and housing) or anyone who would rather not deal with the uncertainty of creating a volunteer experience from scratch.

# URBAN ISSUES

There are two sides to Buenos Aires, and many of Argentina's other large cities—the developed, prosperous neighborhoods, and the *barrios* that are less well off. These volunteer opportunities give travelers a chance to help those areas of urban Argentina most in need. If working closely with locals and helping in a hands-on fashion appeals to you, these options may be the best for you. Many returning travelers report that working among locals was one of their most rewarding experiences while abroad.

**Geovisions,** 101 Sage Hollow Rd., Guilford, CT 06437 (☎203-457-4257; www.geovisions.org). Geovision offers US students and volunteers the opportunity to travel abroad to Buenos Aires and help the impoverished sections of the population. One program in particular, **Make a Difference,** runs a community center in the La Boca *barrio* that provides a safe place for children to learn and play. Volunteers teach English and coordinate activities and workshops with the community, among other tasks. Similar opportunities are also available in other Argentine cities. College education required. Programs last from 1 to 6 months. US$2020-4650.

**Volunteer Adventures,** 915 S. Colorado Blvd., Denver, CO 80246 (☎1-888-825-3454; www.volunteeradventures.com). This organization connects local volunteer organizations and projects on the ground with prospective volunteers around the world. Programs include a community outreach program in Buenos Aires that connects volunteers with local disadvantaged youths and an English teaching program for youths that would otherwise receive no ESL education. Programs last at least 2 weeks. From US$900.

**Habitat for Humanity,** 170 Dardo Rocha, Acassuso, Buenos Aires, Argentina B1641CJD (☎47 93 43 84; www.habitat.org; oficinanacional@hpha.org.ar). A Christian non-profit organization coordinating 9- to 14-day service trips in Buenos Aires, Santa Fe, and Cañada de Gómez. Participants aid local families in constructing future homes. Program costs hover around US$1000-1800, not including airfare.

**Global Crossroad,** 415 East Airport Freeway, Suite 365, Irving, Texas 75062 (☎1-866-387-7816; www.globalcrossroad.com). Global Crossroad supports non-profit organizations in Buenos Aires and Córdoba that provide basic needs, such as food, clothing, and a proper education, for disadvantaged children. Programs last anywhere from 1 week to 3 months. US$1000.

**i-to-i Meaningful Travel** (☎800-985-4864; www.i-to-i.com). In addition to opportunities in ecotourism, i-to-i also offers unique programs directed improving the lives children in impoverished areas of Argentina. One notable project sets up volunteers as sports coaches in Posadas, Misiones province, teaching soccer, basketball, volleyball, and other athletic pursuits to kids. Programs last from 2 to 4 weeks. US$1227 for 2 weeks, plus US$257 for each additional week.

# ECOTOURISM

As more people realize that long-cherished habitats and structures are in danger, diverse programs have stepped in to aid the concerned in lending a hand. There are also opportunities that place volunteers in positions that are not necessarily directed at environmental conservation, but still allow for experiential learning and work on the Argentine frontier.

**World-Wide Opportunities on Organic Farms (WWOOF),** WWOOF Administrator, Moss Peteral, Brampton CA8 7HY, England, UK (www.wwoof.org). Arranges volunteer work with organic and eco-conscious farms around the world. Though Argentina doesn't have a national organization, there are a number of independent hosts within the organization who can arrange volunteer work.

**Foundation for Sustainable Development (FSD),** 517 Potrero Ave., Suite B, San Francisco, CA 94110 (☎415-283-4873; www.fsdinternational.org). This organization, established in 1995, supports the efforts of grassroots environmental groups working to improve sustainability in their communities. Programs in Argentina are directed at running community-awareness workshops,

## GOALS FOR GIRLS

In Recoleta's infamous **Villa 31** slum, girls are kicking up some dirt participating in one of the nation's few **female soccer leagues.** The project began in 2005 when recent American college graduate Allison Lasser moved to BA on a Rotary scholarship and set up a women's *fútbol* club, inspired by a similar group founded in the 1990s in Vicente Lopez, another underprivileged part of the city.

Lasser was driven by the conviction that participating in a team sport teaches discipline and cooperation, in addition to providing structured alternatives to the daily grind in the slum. The group's other goal is to break down the "machismo" of Argentine soccer, which is still mostly a male sport.

Since Lasser returned to the United States in 2007, **Democracia Representativa,** an Argentine nonprofit, has taken the group under its wing and under the leadership of an Argentine coach. The team, about 30 girls who practice twice a week, has gone on to play in national tournaments and travel on field trips with the heads of the female soccer league and the Secretary of Sports for Argentina.

The group subsists primarily on donations, either directly or through **Soccer for Success,** a more global group. For more information, contact Democracia Representativa (www.democraciarepresentativa.org) or check out the group's blog at http://laschicasvilla31.blogspot.com.

measuring greenhouse gas emissions and developing plans to reduce them, and preserving trails used by hikers and bicyclists. Pricing varies from program to program.

**Global Vision International,** Boston, MA 02116 (☎888-653-6028; www.gviusa.com). Expeditions include a trip into the Patagonian Andes Mountains to study the fragile ecosystem of the region while hiking and ice climbing. Other opportunities available. Trips usually last around 5 weeks. From US$2990.

**Earthwatch Institute,** 3 Clock Tower Place, Suite 100, P.O. Box 75, Maynard, MA 01754 USA (☎800-776-0188; www.earthwatch.org). An international nonprofit organization that promotes the conservation of natural resources and cultural heritage around the world. Occasionally offers trips to Argentina. Past trips have focused on studying endangered wildcats in the Argentine wilderness. Expeditions about US$1000 per week.

**LEAPNOW,** 11640 Hwy. 128, Calistoga, CA 94515 (☎707-431-7265; www.leapnow. org). This organization offers volunteer positions on Argentine Patagonian ranches. Available opportunities allow for working while learning about the *gaucho* culture. Programs last from 2 weeks to 6 months. From US$750.

**i-to-i Meaningful Travel** (☎800-985-4864; www.i-to-i.com). Work available in Posadas, Misiones province, home of Iguazú Falls (p. 236), in animal care. Posadas is home to an animal breeding and rehabilitation center that protects the native species of the region's delicate ecosystem. Programs last from 2 to 6 weeks. US$1195 for 2 weeks, plus US$225 for each additional week.

# MEDICAL OUTREACH

Though many areas of Buenos Aires, and Argentina as a whole, are quite well off, several essential institutions, such as hospitals, are still reeling in the wake of the economic crisis. Below are several organizations aimed at serving the medical needs of the city and Argentina as a whole.

**Experimental Learning International (ELI),** 2828 N. Speer Blv., Suite 230, Denver, CO 80211 (☎303-321-8278; www.eliabroad.org). ELI offers a number of work and study abroad opportunities for interns, students, and volunteers. A medical internship program run by the organization allows volunteers, with pre-medical intent or medical school status, to assist in under-equipped and under-staffed hospitals in Buenos Aires' poorest *barrios*. Another program places volunteers in Buenos Aires soup kitchens. Programs last from 2 weeks to 6 months. From US$1000.

**Projects Abroad,** 347 W 36th St., Suite 903, New York, NY 10018 (☎1-888-839-3535; www.projects-abroad.org). Medicine and healthcare volunteers working for Projects Abroad work alongside doctors to treat mentally and physically disabled patients in understaffed hospitals. Programs last from 2 weeks to a year. From US$2695.

**Center for Cultural Interchange (CCI),** 746 N. LaSalle Drive, Chicago, IL 60610, USA (☎866-684-9675; http://cci-exchange.com). CCI offers many medical outreach opportunities in Argentina, from advanced medical volunteer programs to serving as a volunteer at a children's dental clinic or a home for kids infected with HIV in Buenos Aires. Programs start at 4 weeks. US$1490.

**GIC Argentina,** Palacio Barolo, Avenida de Mayo 1370, 3-30, Buenos Aires C1085ABQ (☎54 11 5353 9497; www.gicarg.org). Some volunteer opportunities with GIC assist children with medical needs. Programs focus on feeding and caring for street children in Buenos Aires and assisting doctors in a children's hospital. Programs last from 5 to 8 weeks. Pricing varies depending on the program.

# STUDYING

**VISA INFORMATION.** Citizens of Australia, Canada, Ireland, New Zealand, South Africa, the UK, and the US need a visa for study abroad visits longer than 90 days. Contact the nearest Argentine embassy or consulate for more information and for application forms. Processing time can vary from a few days to several weeks—be sure to start the application process well before your departure date, just in case. A student visa usually costs between US$200-250 and requires a passport, the completed application form, and occasionally a letter of acceptance from an Argentine institution and a medical examination report.

It's hard to dread the first day of school when Buenos Aires is your campus and exotic restaurants are your meal plan. A growing number of students report that studying abroad is the highlight of their learning careers. If you've never studied abroad, you don't know what you're missing—and, if you have studied abroad, you do know what you're missing.

Study-abroad programs range from basic language and culture courses to university-level classes, often for college credit. In order to choose a program that best fits your needs, research as much as you can before making your decision—determine costs and duration as well as what kinds of students participate in the program and what sorts of accommodations are provided. (Since when was back-to-school shopping this fun?)

In programs that have large groups of students who speak the same language, there is a trade-off. You may feel more comfortable in the community, but you will not have the same opportunity to practice a foreign language or to befriend other international students. For accommodations, dorm life provides a better opportunity to mingle with fellow students, but there is less of a chance to experience the local scene. If you live with a family, you could potentially build lifelong friendships with natives and experience day-to-day life in more depth, but you might also get stuck sharing a room with their pet iguana. Conditions can vary greatly from family to family.

## UNIVERSITIES

Most university-level study-abroad programs are conducted in Spanish, although many programs offer classes in English as well as lower-level language courses. Savvy linguists may find it cheaper to enroll directly in a university abroad, although actually receiving college credit may be more difficult. You can search **www.studyabroad.com** for various semester-abroad programs that meet your criteria, including your desired location and focus of study. If you're a college student, your study-abroad office is often the best place to start.

### NORTH AMERICAN PROGRAMS

The following is a list of organizations that can either help place students in university programs abroad or that have their own branch in Buenos Aires.

**American Institute for Foreign Study (AIFS),** College Division, River Plaza, 9 W. Broad St., Stamford, CT 06902, USA (☎+1-800-727-2437; www.aifsabroad.com). Organizes programs for college sophomores, juniors, and seniors at the Pontificia Universidad

Católica Argentina (UCA) in Buenos Aires, with courses in both Spanish and English. Semester-long programs, including tuition, homestay, two meals per day, and cultural excursion US$11,400; discounts for full-year programs. Scholarships available.

**Council on International Educational Exchange (CIEE),** 300 Fore St., Portland, ME 04101, USA (☎+1-207-553-4000 or 800-40-STUDY/407-8839; www.ciee.org). One of the most comprehensive resources for work, academic, and internship programs around the world, including in Argentina. Sponsors study abroad programs in Buenos Aires for around US$11,500 per semester and 7-week public health study programs for around US$5700. Courses are in Spanish.

**School for International Training (SIT) Study Abroad,** 1 Kipling Rd., P.O. Box 676, Brattleboro, VT 05302, USA (☎+1-888-272-7881 or 802-258-3212; www.sit.edu/studyabroad). Semester-long programs in Argentina run approximately US$16,000-18,000. The organization also runs **The Experiment in International Living** (☎+1-800-345-2929; www.usexperiment.org), with 3- to 5-week-long summer programs that offer high-school students cross-cultural homestays, community service, ecological adventures, and language training in Argentina (US$5700).

**American Field Service (AFS),** 71 West 23rd St., 17th fl., New York, NY, 10010 (☎212-807-8686; www.afs.org). AFS has branches in over 50 countries. Summer-, semester-, and year-long homestay exchange programs (US$5000/7500/8600) for high-school students and graduating seniors are available. Study-abroad programs ($7500-9000) are also offered to those 18+.

**Cultural Experiences Abroad (CEA),** 1400 E. Southern Ave., Ste. B-108, Tempe, AZ 85282 (☎800-266-4441; www.gowithcea.com). Operates programs in BA for undergraduates studying in Canada and the US. From US$3900 for a summer course to US$19,000 for the academic year. Classes in both English and Spanish.

**Institute for the International Education of Students (IES),** 33 N. LaSalle St., 15th fl., Chicago, IL 60602 (☎800-995-2300; www.iesabroad.org). Offers year-, semester-, and summer-long study abroad programs in Buenos Aires, with special programs including competitive semester-long internships. All levels of Spanish accepted. US$11,700-12,500 per semester. US$50 application fee.

**International Association for the Exchange of Students for Technical Experience (IAESTE),** 10400 Little Patuxent Pkwy. Ste. 250, Columbia, MD 21044, USA (☎410-997-3068; www.iaeste.org). Offers 8- to 20-week internships in Argentina for college students looking for experience in a particular trade.

**Youth for Understanding International Exchange (YFU),** (☎800-833-6243; www.yfu-usa.org). Places US high- school students and recent graduates with host families in Buenos Aires. Summer-, semester-, and year-long programs: US$6000-8000 per semester. US$75 application fee plus US$500 deposit.

# ARGENTINE PROGRAMS

Below are Argentine-based organizations and schools that offer study-abroad programs in Buenos Aires, Córdoba, Mendoza, and other Argentine cities.

**Universidad de Buenos Aires,** Viamonte 430, Buenos Aires, Argentina (☎54 011 4510 1100; www.uba.ar). Universidad de Buenos Aires is the largest university in Argentina, with 13 faculties and nearly 300,000 students. The university has no central campus, but rather has several centers throughout the city. Enrollment is available for international students in fields from the humanities and sciences.

**Universidad de Belgrano,** Zabala 1837 C1426DQG, Capital Federal, Buenos Aires, Argentina (☎54 11 4788 5400; www.ub.edu. ar). Located in the *barrio* of Belgrano, Universidad de Belgrano is one of the top universities in Argentina. The university has more 14,500 students and welcomes nearly 900 international students every year.

BEYOND TOURISM

# HOSTEL OF **LEISURE**

## **BUENOS AIRES** ARGENTINA

ART & MODERN DAY **CONVENIENCES** IN A 1930s **MANSION**

**SANTO**BAR&LOUNGE

GREAT **LOCATION**
**AMAZING** TERRACE

INFO@SANTOHOSTEL.COM
Phone: (+ 54 - 11) 5031 - 6818

**WWW.SANTOHOSTEL.COM**

**TANGO + SOCCER + SPANISH + FESTIVALS + PARTIES + SHOPPING + RESTAURANTS + CLUBS**

Semester programs begin in Mar. and Aug. and last for 4 months. Classes are offered in both English and Spanish, with placement available in courses taken by Argentine students, language proficiency permitting. US$6900-10,800.

**Universidad de Congreso,** Colón 90 M5500GEN, Mendoza, Argentina (☎54 26 1423 0630; http://www.ucongreso.edu.ar/). Mendoza's top university, Universidad de Congreso offers liberal arts programs in international relations, journalism, business and other fields. Semester programs begin Mar. and Aug. and last for 4 months. Courses only taught in Spanish—intensive Spanish preparatory classes available. US$7600-12,000.

## LANGUAGE SCHOOLS

Enrolling at a language school has two perks: a slightly less rigorous courseload and the ability to learn exactly what those kids in Buenos Aires are calling you under their breath. There can be great variety in language schools—independently run, affiliated with a larger university, local, international—but one thing is constant: they rarely offer college credit. Their programs are also good for younger high-school students who might not feel comfortable with older students in a university program. Some worthwhile organizations include:

**Eurocentres,** 56 Eccleston Sq., London SW1V 1PH, UK (☎+44 20 7963 8450; www.eurocentres.com). Language programs for beginning to advanced students. Though courses in Spanish are available. There are no homestays offered in Argentina.

**Language Immersion Institute,** State University of New York at New Paltz, 1 Hawk Dr., New Paltz, NY 12561, USA (☎+1-845-257-3500; www.newpaltz.edu/lii). Short, intensive summer language courses and some overseas courses in Argentina. Program fees are around US$1000 for a 2-week course, not including accommodations.

## WORKING

Nowhere does money grow on trees (though *Let's Go*'s researchers aren't done looking), but there are still some pretty good opportunities to earn a living and travel at the same time. As with volunteering, work opportunities tend to fall into two categories. Some travelers want long-term jobs that allow them to integrate into a community, while others seek out short-term jobs to finance the next leg of their travels. In Argentina, people who want to work have a variety of opportunities to choose from, from serving as a rancher hand out on the plains or picking grapes on a vineyard near Mendoza. **Transitions Abroad** (www.transitionsabroad.com) also offers updated online listings for work over any time span. Note that working abroad often requires a special work visa.

 **MORE VISA INFORMATION.** Rules and requirements for Argentine work visas are very similar to those for study abroad (p. 87). The application process is lengthy—allow plenty of time for processing. Contact the nearest Argentine embassy or consulate for more information and forms. You must have a passport to apply for a work visa, and you will often have to produce other documentation, including, but not limited to, a medical examination report, a police record, and a letter of introduction from your employer in Argentina. Fees range from US$100-300.

BEYOND TOURISM

# LONG-TERM WORK

If you're planning on spending a substantial amount of time (more than 3 months) working in Argentina, search for a job well in advance. International placement agencies are often the easiest way to find employment abroad, especially for those interested in teaching. Although they are often only available to college students, **Internships** are a good way to ease into working abroad. Many say the interning experience is well worth it, despite low pay (if they're lucky enough to be paid at all). Be wary of advertisements for companies claiming to be able get you a job abroad for a fee—often the same listings are available online or in newspapers Some reputable organizations include:

**Council on International Educational Exchange (CIEE),** 300 Fore St., Portland, ME 04101, USA (☎+1-207-553-4000 or 800-40-STUDY/407-8839; www.ciee.org). CIEE offers an array of study-abroad opportunities in Buenos Aires, ranging from programs on South American politics and economics to public health. Tucked into its study-abroad listings is a resource for international internships. From US$11,300.

**International Association for the Exchange of Students for Technical Experience (IAESTE),** Ave. Cordoba 831 4° P, C1054AAH Ciudad de Buenos Aires, Argentina (☎+54 11 4312 7512/13; www.iaeste.org). Chances are that your home country has a local office, too; contact it to apply for hands-on technical internships in Argentina. You must be a college student studying science, technology, or engineering. "Cost of living allowance" covers most non-travel expenses. Most programs last 8-12 weeks.

**International Cooperative Education,** 15 Spiros Way, Menlo Park, CA 94025, USA (☎+1-650-323-4944; www.icemenlo.com). Finds summer jobs for students in Argentina. Semester- and year-long commitments also available. Costs include a US$250 application fee and a US$700 fee for placement.

# TEACHING ENGLISH

While some elite private American schools offer competitive salaries, let's just say that teaching jobs abroad pay more in personal satisfaction and emotional fulfillment than in actual cash. Perhaps this is why volunteering as a teacher instead of getting paid is a popular option. Even then, teachers often receive some sort of a daily stipend to help with living expenses. Although salaries at private schools may be low compared to those in the US, the relatively low cost of living in Argentina makes it much more profitable. In almost all cases, you must have at least a bachelor's degree to be a full-fledged teacher, although college undergraduates can often get summer positions teaching or tutoring. Many schools require teachers to have a **Teaching English as a Foreign Language (TEFL)** certificate. You may still be able to find a teaching job without one, but certified teachers often find higher-paying jobs.

The Spanish-impaired don't have to give up their dream of teaching, either. Private schools in Argentina usually hire native English speakers for English-immersion classrooms where no Spanish is spoken. (Teachers in public schools will more likely work in both English and Spanish.) Placement agencies or university fellowship programs are the best resources for finding teaching jobs. The alternative is to contact schools directly or to try your luck once you arrive in Argentina. In the latter case, the best time to look is several weeks before the start of the school year. The following organization is extremely helpful in placing teachers in Argentine schools.

**International Schools Services (ISS),** 15 Roszel Rd., P.O. Box 5910, Princeton, NJ 08543, USA (☎+1-609-452-0990; www.iss.edu). Hires teachers for more than 200

BEYOND TOURISM

overseas schools, including in Argentina. Candidates should have teaching experience and a bachelor's degree. 2-year commitment is the norm.

# SHORT-TERM WORK

Believe it or not, traveling for long periods of time can be hard on the wallet. Many travelers try their hand at odd jobs for a few weeks at a time to help pay for another month or two of touring around. Another popular option is to work several hours a day at a hostel in exchange for free or discounted room and/ or board. Most often, these short-term jobs are found by word of mouth or by expressing interest to the owner of a hostel or restaurant. Due to high turnover in the tourism industry, many places are eager for help, even if it is only temporary. *Let's Go* lists temporary jobs of this nature whenever possible. The following resources are good starting points for additional research:

### FURTHER READING ON BEYOND TOURISM

*Alternatives to the Peace Corps: A Guide of Global Volunteer Opportunities,* edited by Paul Backhurst. Food First, 2005 (US$12).

*The Back Door Guide to Short-Term Job Adventures: Internships, Summer Jobs, Seasonal Work, Volunteer Vacations, and Transitions Abroad,* by Michael Landes. Ten Speed Press, 2005 (US$22).

*Green Volunteers: The World Guide to Voluntary Work in Nature Conservation,* by Fabio Ausenda. Universe, 2007 (US$15).

*How to Get a Job in Europe,* by Cheryl Matherly and Robert Sanborn. Planning Communications, 2003 (US$23).

*How to Live Your Dream of Volunteering Overseas,* by Joseph Collins, Stefano DeZerega, and Zahara Heckscher. Penguin Books, 2001 (US$20).

*International Job Finder: Where the Jobs Are Worldwide,* by Daniel Lauber and Kraig Rice. Planning Communications, 2002 (US$20).

*Live and Work Abroad: A Guide for Modern Nomads,* by Huw Francis and Michelyne Callan. Vacation Work Publications, 2001 (US$20).

*Volunteer Vacations: Short-Term Adventures That Will Benefit You and Others,* by Doug Cutchins, Anne Geissinger, and Bill McMillon. Chicago Review Press, 2006 (US$18).

*Work Abroad: The Complete Guide to Finding a Job Overseas,* edited by Clayton A. Hubbs. Transitions Abroad, 2002 (US$16).

*Work Your Way Around the World,* by Susan Griffith. Vacation Work Publications, 2007 (US$22).

# La Murga Argentina

When I brought my trombone with me to Buenos Aires, I only planned to use it to practice occasionally. I had come to Argentina with a study-abroad program to learn Spanish and knew that the best way to do this was to never speak English. This meant avoiding the almost-daily social events my program had scheduled, and I found practicing my trombone in the park to be a useful excuse. One day, three rather ill-kempt teenagers approached me. Surely I was about to lose my trombone—and my wallet.

Turns out I shouldn't have been worried. The kids were members of a neighborhood *murga* and wanted to invite me to join them. February is Carnival month in BA, and every weekend night, *barrio*-sponsored *murgas* (marching bands) travel around the city putting on their shows. My northern *barrio*, Saavedra, had a *murga* called *Los Elegidos del Dios Momo* (The Elect of the God Momo), Momo being, they explained, the god of the *murga*. They had heard me practicing and wanted me to join their horn section.

*Los Elegidos* is about 120 members strong, incorporating a dozen trumpet and trombone players and some thirty drummers—mostly *bombos*, a sort of marching bass drum with a small cymbal on top, but also a few snare drums. All the rest were dancers of all ages. Everyone was decked out in full *murga* regalia, which consists, in our case, of red sequined pants and vests, swathed in red and white tassels and as many logos as you can name, from Puma and Ford to the Chicago Bulls and various cartoon characters.

Our first show was across town. As soon as everyone was off the buses and we were in formation, someone blew a whistle. Then, the *bombos* started to pound, and we were off. We marched, taking up the whole street, with the crowd and our dancers going nuts to the sound of bass drums. At intervals, the horn section would launch, in unison, into one of a half-dozen popular tunes as loud as we could.

After a few blocks, we spilled into an intersection where most of the crowd was waiting. Everyone was cheering and dancing, while kids were running around screaming and shooting silly string at each other. After the mayhem subsided, we boarded the buses and did it two more times in two other *barrios*. The vibe on my bus between shows was, to say the least, ridiculously euphoric. People passed around bottles of beer, beat on the *bombos*, and stuck their heads out the windows to belt out tunes. Several times I took out my trombone and played a song or two.

Three shows, three bus rides, and more than a few brews later, everyone was completely spent. Before staggering home to bed, I exchanged phone numbers with some of the trombone players I met, who in the coming months, would become some of my closest friends in the city. With their

## "These music groups took me places I never would have visited otherwise."

help, I joined two student orchestras, a working big band, and a jazz quintet. These music groups took me places I never would have visited otherwise.

None of the musicians I met spoke any more English than what they could pick up from watching movies. With the musical groups I joined, and the social opportunities they afforded, I was able to gain complete Spanish fluency. No matter where you are in Buenos Aires during Carnival month, keep an ear out for the sounds of whistles, bass drums, and shrieking children—it will inevitably lead you to the nearest *murga*. But only go if you're prepared to be silly-stringed.

*N. Aaron Pancost is an economic research assistant at the Federal Reserve Bank of Boston. He spent time in Argentina learning Spanish while a student at the University of Maryland College Park.*

# PRACTICAL INFORMATION

## TOURIST AND FINANCIAL SERVICES

### TOURIST OFFICES

The government tourist agency, **Turismo de Buenos Aires** (www.bue.gov.ar), operates kiosks throughout the city and at both airports. These handy stations distribute free maps and guides to what's going on around Buenos Aires. In addition to free guided tours (usually on Saturday afternoons, but check the website or a kiosk for more information), the office also offers free audio tours, complete with soothing documentary voiceovers, available for download at www.bue.gov.ar/audioguia. Play the tour on your iPod as you take in the sights. Listed below are tourist office locations in Buenos Aires, some of which focus on tourism within Buenos Aires only, while provincial offices offer recommendations and guidance for the rest of Argentina.

### BUENOS AIRES OFFICES

**Ezeiza International Airport** (☎4480 0224). Open daily 10am-5pm.

**Jorge Newbery Airpark** (☎4771 0104). Open daily 10am-5pm.

**Microcentro,** Florida 100 at Av. Diagonal Rogre Sáenz Peña, one block from the Plaza de Mayo. Open M-F 9am-7pm, Sa 10am-4pm.

**Puerto Madero,** Alicia Moreau De Justo 200 (☎4315 4265), by *Dique* 4 on the western side. Also provides information on Uruguay. Open daily 10am-6pm.

**Recoleta,** Quintana 596 (☎4313 0187), at Ortíz. Open daily 10am-6pm.

**Retiro,** Av. Antártida Argentina Local 83 (☎4311 0528), at the bus station. Open M-Sa 7:30am-1pm. Additional location at the end of Calle Florida on the Plaza San Martín. Open daily 10am-6pm.

### PROVINCIAL OFFICES

**Buenos Aires,** Av. Callao 237, Microcentro (☎4371 7045/47; www.casaprov.gba.gov.ar). Open M-F 9am-7pm.

**Córdoba,** Av. Callao 332, Balvanera (☎4373 4277; www.cba.gov.ar). Open M-F 8am-8pm.

**La Pampa,** Suipacha 346, Microcentro (☎4326 0511/1145/1769; www.turismolapampa.gov.ar). Open M-F 8am-6pm.

**Mar del Plata,** Av. Corrientes 1660 Local 16, Microcentro (☎4384 5658/5722; www.mardelplata.gov.ar). Open M-F 10am-4pm.

**Mendoza,** Av. Callao 445, Microcentro (☎4374 1105; www.mendoza.gov.ar). Open M-F 10am-6pm.

**Salta,** Av. Pte. Roque Saénz Peña 933, 5th fl., Microcentro (☎4326 2456/57/58/59; www.gobiernosalta.gov.ar). Open M-F 9am-6pm.

**Tierra del Fuego,** Sarmiento 745, Microcentro (☎4311 0233; www.tierradelfuego.org.: Open M-F 9am-4pm.

## TOUR AGENCIES

**Eternautas,** Av. Pte. Julio A. Roca 584, 7th fl. (☎5031 9916; www.eternautas.com). Tours for those in search of royal treatment. Launched in 1999 by historians out of the University of Buenos Aires, this agency delivers the city sights with a historical bent. Clients include dignitaries like the Queen of the Netherlands, but it remains affordable, despite its sterling reputation. Walking tours require no advance scheduling and start at AR$10. Bus tours cost about AR$30 and should be reserved beforehand. Check the website for the free tour of the month or to ask about one of the specialized tours, such as "Evita and Peronism," or "Buenos Aires Writers."

**Say Hueque,** Viamonte 749, 6th fl. (☎5199 2517/20; www.sayhueque.com). Targeted at the independent traveler crowd, this agency books tours all over Argentina and Chile starting at AR$159. Price includes a tango show. Excursions to the Pampas and Patagonia also available. Additional location in Palermo Soho at Guatemala 4845, 1st fl. (☎4775 7862).

**OpcionSur,** Juncal 4482 Local 2 (☎4777 9029; www.opcionsur.com.ar). Offers a variety of tours focusing on Buenos Aires and surrounding destinations, such as Tigre, with a personalized, innovative touch.

**Tangol,** Florida 971, ground fl., ste. 31 (☎4312 7276; www.tangol.com). Basic city tours start at AR$55. Tangol also organizes bike tours and soccer excursions. Open M-F 9am-8pm, Sa 10am-6pm.

**Español Andando** (☎5278 9886; www.espanol-andando.com.ar). Interactive Spanish class combines sightseeing with language skills. 4-day, 12hr. group course AR$250.

**Cultour** (☎15 6575 4593/6365 6892; www.cultour.com.ar). Note that the 15 in the contact number indicates that it is a cell phone. Walking tours focus on Argentina's recent past, delving into the details of the military dictatorship, the 2001 economic crisis, and contemporary political trends. Tours run M-F. AR$55. Cash only.

**South American Explorers,** Estados Unidos 577 (☎4307 9625; www.saexplorers.org). A membership fee (from US$50) grants access to clubhouses across South America, discounts, storage, and trip planning resources, among many other services. Open M-F 1-7pm, Sa 1-6pm.

## BIKE TOURS

**Urban Biking,** Moliere 2801, Villa Devoto. (☎4568 4321; www.urbanbiking.com). Tours at 9am and 2pm for AR$100. Helmet, lunch, and *mate* included. The *Porteño* Nightlife tour includes optional "more beer." Since biking in Buenos Aires is always a good idea, it's pretty clear that doing it drunk will be even better (read: extremely dangerous and ill-advised). Let's Go does not recommend drinking and biking at the same time.

**La Bicicleta Naranja,** Pasaje Giufra 306 (☎4362 1104; www.labicicletanaranja.com. ar). Offers standard *barrio* tours, along with a "from the river" package, which includes kayaking on the "picturesque" (read: very brown) Río de la Plata. Bright orange rental bikes. AR$8 per hr., AR$48 per day. Tours M-F 9:30 am and 2pm, Sa and Su 2pm.

**Lan & Kramer Travel Service,** Florida 868 (☎4311 5199; www.biketours.com.ar), in unit H on the 14th fl. of Torre Mauri. Ⓢ San Martín. Runs **Bike Tours** (www.biketours. ~~com ar)~~ which offers a number of bilingual excursions around the city. Tours rendezvous ~~...~~ numento a San Martín in the Plaza San Martín. Rentals also available. ~~...~~ US$100 deposit required. Cash only.

## ~~E~~XCHANGE

~~...ss,~~ Arenales 707, Retiro (☎4312 1661). Ⓢ San Martín. Will exchange ~~...~~ess Travelers Cheques for no commission. Open M-F 9am-5pm.

PRACTICAL INFORMATION

# OSTINATTO
## BUENOS AIRES HOSTEL

Making a difference

Wine cellar / Piano Bar

Microcinema / Rooftop terrace

Mini pool / BBQ place

**Free!** » Tango and yoga

class / Spanish lesson

Walking tour / Theatrical games

Wi-Fi / Breakfast

If you pay one week in advance you get a **10% OFF** and a **PUB CRAWL FOR FREE.**

Chile 680 - San telmo - C1098AAN - Tel.: (5411) 4362 9639
4300 2535 / Info@ostinatto.com - www.ostinatto.com

PRACTICAL INFORMATION

## AIRLINE OFFICES

**Aerolineas Argentinas,** Perú 2, Monserrat (☎4320 2000). Ⓢ Bolívar, Catedral, or Perú. Open M-F 9am-7pm, Sa 9am-1pm.

**Air Canada,** 656 Córdoba, Microcentro (☎4327 3640). Ⓢ Florida or San Martín. Open M-F 9am-1pm and 2-5:30pm.

**Air France,** San Martín 344, 23rd fl., Microcentro (☎4317 4700). Ⓢ Florida. Shared office with **KLM.** Open M-F 9am-5:30pm.

**American Airlines,** Av. Sante Fe 881, Retiro (☎4318 1111). Ⓢ San Martín. Open M-F 9am-7:30pm, Sa 9am-12:30pm.

**British Airways,** Av. Libertador 498, 13th fl., Retiro (☎0800 666 1459). Ⓢ San Martín. The office is occasionally not staffed during regular hours, though a computer and phone is always available. Open M-F 9am-6pm.

**Delta,** Av. Sante Fe 899, Retiro (☎0800 666 0133). Ⓢ San Martín. Open M-F 9am-5pm.

**KLM,** San Martín 344, 23rd fl., Microcentro (☎0800 222 2600). Ⓢ Florida. Shared office with **Air France.** Open M-F 9am-5pm.

**LAN,** Cerrito 866, Retiro (☎4378 2200). Ⓢ Carlos Pellegrini or Tribunales. Open M-F 9am-7pm.

**Lufthansa,** MT de Alvear 590, Retiro (☎4319 0600). Ⓢ San Martín. Open M-F 9am-1pm and 2-6pm.

**United Airlines,** Av. Madero 900, 9th fl., Retiro (☎4316 0777). Ⓢ LN Alem. Open M-F 9:30am-5pm.

# LOCAL SERVICES

## PHARMACIES

There are pharmacies nearly everywhere in the city center—simply look for a **green cross.**

**Farmacity,** Florida 474, Microcentro (☎4322 6559; www.farmacity.com.ar). One of BA's main chains, Farmacity stocks a large variety of foreign and domestic brands. Expect to pay a hefty price for imported products, though not too much more than you'd pay at home. The listed branch on Florida is open 24hr. and will deliver M-Sa 9am-9pm.

## LIBRARIES

In addition to the **Biblioteca Nacional** (p. 155), Buenos Aires runs 26 smaller branches throughout the city. Most are open M-F 10am-5pm. For a list with more specific locations and hours, visit www.bibliotecas.gov.ar.

**Microcentro,** Córdoba 1558 (☎4812 4723). Open M-F 8am-midnight, Sa 10am-2pm.

**Monserrat,** Venezuela 1538 (☎4381 1271). Open M-F 8am-8pm.

**Palermo,** Honduras 3784 (☎4963 2194). Open M-F 11am-6pm.

**Retiro,** Talcahuano 1261 (☎4812 1840). Open M-F 9am-8pm.

## SUPERMARKETS

Supermarkets and grocery stores are not hard to find in Buenos Aires. In residential areas, it seems that there's at least one every three blocks or so. Branches of the following major chains usually have great selections. For each chain, we have listed one of the more central locations.

**Coto,** Viamonte 1571, Microcentro (www.coto.com.ar). Check online for additional locations. Open daily 9am-9:30pm.

**Carrefour,** Santa Fe 1680, Recoleta (www.carrefour.com.ar). Check online for additional locations. Open M-Sa 9am-9:30pm, Su 3-9pm.

## GYMS

The website **www.adondevamos.com** has extensive listings of athletic centers throughout Buenos Aires. Most *barrios* have one or several clubs, which offer classes and facilities for minimal fees.

**Suterh,** Venezuela 330, San Telmo (☎5354 660; www.suterh.org.ar or www.faterhy.com.ar), at the intersection with Balcarse. A large complex with 3 swimming pools and a fully equipped gym. Also offers classes in everything from soccer to belly dancing. Open M-Sa 8am-8pm. Membership fee AR$70 per month.

**Megatlon** (www.megatlon.com). An American-style gym with similar services to Suterh and locations across town. Check the website for addresses.

# EMERGENCY AND COMMUNICATIONS

## EMERGENCY SERVICES

In an emergency, dial ☎911 for **police,** ☎100 for **fire,** and ☎107 for an **ambulance.**

**Tourist Police,** 436 Corrientes, Microcentro (☎4346 5748). Ⓢ Florida. Handles tourist-related crimes, including theft. Dial ☎**101 for emergencies.**

PRACTICAL INFORMATION

## MEDICAL SERVICES

Most medical problems, from the flu to a *fracaso* (disaster) can be treated for free at public hospitals. Private clinics offer improved care and the guarantee of English-speaking doctors, but these bonuses will come at a price.

### PUBLIC HOSPITALS

**Hospital de Clínicas José de San Martín,** Av. Córdoba 2351, Recoleta (☎5950 8000; www.hospitaldeclinicas.uba.ar). Ⓢ Facultad de Medicina. Open 24hr. The information desk (☎5950 8558/5950 8617) is on the ground floor. Open daily 7am-8pm.

### PRIVATE CLINICS

**Hospital Británico,** Perdriel 74, Barracas (☎4309 6400). Open 24hr.

**Hospital Italiano,** Gascón 450, Almagro (☎4959 0200). Open 24hr.

## INTERNET ACCESS

Internet cafes and access points are everywhere in the center, and are particularly highly concentrated along **Avenida de Mayo.** Additionally, most **locutorios** (call centers) have at least a few computers. Access usually ranges from AR$1.50-4, depending on the speed of the connection and the centrality of the cafe. Locations in the city center, for example, will be more expensive.

## POSTAL SERVICES

There are several post office branches throughout Buenos Aires. Most are open 9am-5pm. Look for the **"Correo Argentino"** signs. Many convenience stores, *locutorios*, and kiosks throughout the city center also offer postal services.

**Correo Central,** Gen. Juan D. Perón 300. Ⓢ LN Alem. The temporary main branch of the Argentine postal service. The old building, an epic Beaux Arts masterpiece (p. 145), was closed in March 2008 for renovations that will last until 2011. *Poste Restante* services are on the main floor. Open M-F 8am-8pm, Sa 9am-1am.

# ACCOMMODATIONS

Buenos Aires is a paradise of cheap, yet well-equipped and comfortable, short-term accommodations. Dorms for as cheap as US$10-20 per night? Not a problem. Furthermore, thanks to the favorable exchange rate, hotels that would normally be too expensive for the budget traveler are as pricey as some hostels across the pond in Europe. There's no one hotbed for particularly affordable, top-notch rooms—they're scattered throughout the city, from the center to Palermo and San Telmo. Puerto Madero, Recoleta, and Retiro, though, are often too expensive for penny-pinching globetrotters, while La Boca is too smelly and dangerous. For long-term accommodations, many of BA's hostels offer unbeatable monthly rates, but if you're looking for something more akin to home for even longer stays (hello, study- and work-abroad travelers), there are several resources for searching for inexpensive apartments.

## HOSTELS

Many hostels are laid out dorm-style, often with large single-sex rooms and bunk beds, although private rooms that sleep two to four are becoming more common. They sometimes have kitchens and utensils for your use, bike or moped rentals, storage areas, transportation to airports, breakfast and other meals, laundry facilities, and Internet. However, there can be drawbacks: some hostels close during certain daytime "lockout" hours, have a curfew, don't accept reservations, impose a maximum stay, or, less frequently, require that you do chores. In Buenos Aires, a dorm bed in a hostel will average around AR$20-40 and a private room around AR$80-120.

**A HOSTELER'S BILL OF RIGHTS.** There are certain standard features that we do not include in our hostel listings. Unless we state otherwise, you can expect that every hostel has no lockout, no curfew, free hot showers, some system of secure luggage storage, and no key deposit.

## HOSTELLING INTERNATIONAL

Joining the youth hostel association in your own country (p. 102) grants you membership privileges in **Hostelling International (HI),** a federation of national hosteling associations. Non-HI members may be allowed to stay in some hostels, but will have to pay extra to do so. HI hostels are scattered throughout Buenos Aires, and are typically less expensive than private hostels. HI's umbrella organization's website (www.hihostels.com), which lists the websites and phone numbers of all national associations, is a great place to begin researching BA hosteling. Other comprehensive hosteling websites include www.hostels.com, www.hostelplanet.com, and www.hostelworld.com.

Most HI hostels also honor **guest memberships**—you'll get a blank card with space for six validation stamps. Each night you'll pay a nonmember supplement (one-sixth the membership fee) and earn one guest stamp; six stamps makes you a member. You may need to remind the hostel reception about this. A new membership benefit is the FreeNites program, which allows hostelers to gain points toward free rooms. Most student travel agencies (p. 33) sell HI cards, as do the following national hosteling organizations. All listed prices are valid for one-year memberships, unless otherwise noted.

**Australian Youth Hostels Association (AYHA),** 422 Kent St., Sydney, NSW 200 (☎+61 2 9261 1111; www.yha.com.au). AUS$52, under 18 AUS$19.

**Hostelling International-Canada (HI-C),** 205 Catherine St., Ste. 400, Ottawa, ONT K2P 1C3 (☎+1-613-237-7884; www.hihostels.ca). CDN$35, under 18 free.

**Hostelling International Northern Ireland (HINI),** 22-32 Donegall Rd., Belfast BT12 5JN (☎+44 2890 32 47 33; www.hini.org.uk). UK£15, under 25 UK£10.

**Youth Hostels Association of New Zealand Inc. (YHANZ),** Lvl. 1, 166 Moorhouse Ave., P.O. Box 436, Christchurch (☎+64 3 379 9970, in NZ 0800 278 299; www.yha.org.nz). NZ$40, under 18 free.

**Youth Hostels Association (England and Wales),** Trevelyan House, Dimple Rd., Matlock, Derbyshire DE4 3YH (☎+44 8707 708 868; www.yha.org.uk). UK£16, under 26 UK£10.

**Hostelling International-USA,** 8401 Colesville Rd., Ste. 600, Silver Spring, MD 20910 (☎+1-301-495-1240; www.hiayh.org). US$28, under 18 free.

# HOTELS

Thanks to the relative strength of the American dollar and the euro against the Argentine peso, many BA hotels are affordable options for visitors. Prices can range widely, from AR$40-120 per night for singles to AR$140-200 for doubles. If you make **reservations** in writing, indicate your night of arrival and the number of nights you plan to stay. The hotel will send you a confirmation and may request payment for the first night.

# OTHER TYPES OF ACCOMMODATIONS

## HOME EXCHANGES AND HOSPITALITY CLUBS

Home exchange offers various types of homes (houses, apartments, condominiums, villas) and the opportunity to live like a native. For more information, contact **HomeExchange.com Inc.,** P.O. Box 787, Hermosa Beach, CA 90254, USA (☎+1-310 798 3864 or toll-free 800-877-8723; www.homeexchange.com) or **Intervac International Home Exchange** (☎54 011 4711 3622; www.intervac.com).

**Hospitality clubs** link their members with individuals or families abroad who are willing to host travelers for free or for a small fee to promote cultural exchange and general good karma. In exchange, members usually must be willing to host travelers in their own homes; a small fee may also be required. **The Hospitality Club** (www.hospitalityclub.org) is a good place to start. **Servas** (www.servas.org) is an established, more formal, peace-based organization, and requires a fee and an interview to join. An Internet search will find many similar organizations, some of which cater to special interests (e.g., women, GLBT travelers, or members of certain professions). As always, use common sense when planning to stay with or host someone you do not know.

## LONG-TERM ACCOMMODATIONS

Travelers planning to stay in Buenos Aires for extended periods of time may find it most cost-effective to rent an apartment. The average price for a BA apartment or studio runs around US$500-800 per month. To get your search started, try visiting the following listings websites: www.bytargentina.com, www.inmuebles.clarin.com, and www.segundamano.com.ar.

ACCOMMODATIONS

# ACCOMMODATIONS BY PRICE

**UNDER AR$30 (❶)**

| | |
|---|---|
| ⬛BA Stop (p. 106) | Mic |
| Back in Town - Buenos Aires (p. 112) | PaS |
| Carlos Gardel Hostel (p. 108) | ST |
| Che Hostel (p. 115) | Bal |
| El Hostal de San Telmo (p. 108) | ST |
| ⬛Gecko Hostel (p. 113) | PaH |
| Hostal de Granados (p. 108) | ST |
| Hostel Estoril (p. 104) | Mon |
| ⬛Hostel Tango Suites (p. 107) | ST |
| Hostel-Bar Giramondo (p. 111) | PaS |
| Hotel O'Rei (p. 107) | Mic |
| La Rosada de Belgrano (p. 114) | Bel |
| Limehouse (p. 104) | Mon |
| Palermo House (p. 111) | PaS |
| Recoleta Hostel (HI) (p. 110) | Ret |
| So Hostel (p. 112) | Mon |
| Via Via Hostel (p. 107) | ST |

**AR$30-61 (❷)**

| | |
|---|---|
| Alkimista (p. 105) | Mon |
| Alma Petit Hostel (p. 114) | LC |
| Antico Hostel Boutique (p. 107) | ST |
| Casa Babylon Art Hostel (p. 111) | PaS |
| Casa Esmeralda (p. 114) | PaH |
| Casa Jardín (p. 112) | PaS |
| Che Legarto (p. 104) | Mon |
| ⬛Che Lulu Trendy Hotel (p. 112) | PaS |
| Colonial (p. 106) | Mic |
| El Patio (p. 115) | Bal |
| ⬛Hostel Clan (p. 104) | Mon |
| Hostel Inn (HI) (p. 108) | ST |
| Hostel One (p. 107) | ST |
| Hostel Suites Obelisco (p. 106) | Mic |
| Hostel Suites Palermo (p. 112) | PaS |
| Hotel Carly (p. 109) | ST |

| | |
|---|---|
| Hotel Maipú (p. 107) | Mic |
| La MeNeSuNdA (p. 115) | Boe |
| Milhouse (HI) (p. 104) | Mon |
| Ostinatto (p. 108) | ST |
| Pampa Hostel (p. 114) | Bel |
| Portal del Sur (p. 104) | Mon |
| Sandanzas Hostel (p. 108) | ST |
| St. Nicholas Hostel (HI) (p. 106) | Mic |
| Tango Backpackers (p. 112) | PaS |
| Te Adoro Garcia (p. 114) | LC |
| Telmotango Hostel Suites (HI) (p. 109) | ST |
| V&S Hostel Club (p. 106) | Mic |
| Zentrum Hostel Boutique (p. 112) | PaS |

**AR$62-91 (❸)**

| | |
|---|---|
| Cypress In (p. 113) | PaS |
| Hotel Alcazar (p. 105) | Mon |
| Hotel Gran España (p. 105) | Mon |
| Hotel Lion D'or (p. 110) | Rec |
| Los Tres Reyes (p. 109) | ST |

**AR$92-121 (❹)**

| | |
|---|---|
| Concept Hotel (p. 105) | Mon |
| Goya Hotel (p. 106) | Mic |
| Hotel Avenida (p. 105) | Mon |
| Hotel Central Córdoba (p. 110) | Ret |
| Hotel Chile (p. 105) | Mon |
| Reina Hotel (p. 105) | Mon |
| The Clan House (p. 105) | Mon |

**OVER AR$122 (❺)**

| | |
|---|---|
| Bohemia Buenos Aires Hotel (p. 109) | ST |
| Hotel Castillo (p. 110) | Rec |
| Hotel Europa (p. 106) | Mic |
| Juncal Palace Hotel (p. 111) | Rec |
| La Otra Orilla (p. 113) | PaS |

---

**NEIGHBORHOOD ABBREVIATIONS: Bal** Balvanera **Bel** Belgrano **Boe** Boedo **LC** Las Cañitas **Mic** Microcentro **Mon** Monserrat **PaH** Palermo Hollywood **PaS** Palermo Soho **Rec** Recoleta **Ret** Retiro **ST** San Telmo

**ACCOMMODATIONS**

# ACCOMMODATIONS BY BARRIO

## MONSERRAT

It's not the place to party until dawn, but Monserrat has some excellent accommodations you can come home to *after* partying until dawn. Many prices here have more than doubled in the past few years as the economy has recovered, but the hotels that line **Avenida de Mayo** are still quite affordable and close to the city's central sights. Some of BA's most popular hostels are also here; most provide a variety of services and can give great advice on where to go after sunset. You'll need it—the sheer number of options can get overwhelming at times.

## HOSTELS

 **Hostel Clan,** Adolfo Alsina 912 (☎4334 3401; www.hostelclan.com.ar). $ Lima or Avenida de Mayo. This large, social hostel draws a diverse international crowd. The numerous, brightly colored and well-decorated rooms have high ceilings and no bunk beds. There's also a bar, shared kitchen, pool table, and common room with TV. Spanish lessons offered. Breakfast included. Laundry AR$10. Free Internet. Bike rental free. Reception 24hr. Check-out 11am. Dorms AR$32. Cash only. ❷

**Milhouse (HI),** Hipólito Yrigoyen 959 (☎4345 9604 or 4343 5308; www.milhousehostel.com). $ Lima or Avenida de Mayo. A huge international crowd grabs drinks from the bar and packs the large, brick-walled common room in this hostel. If you want to bypass the party atmosphere downstairs, there's a more relaxing common space with TV upstairs. Tango and Spanish lessons offerred. Shared kitchen. Currency exchange available. Breakfast 8-10:30am (AR$5-9). Security boxes AR$2 per day. Laundry AR$12. Free Internet. Reception 24hr. Check-out 11am. Dorms AR$33, HI members AR$30; singles AR$115; doubles AR$130; triples AR$160; quads AR$180: non-HI members add AR$15. Cash and traveler's checks only. ❷

**Limehouse,** Lima 11 (☎4383 4561; www.limehouse.com.ar). $ Lima or Avenida de Mayo. A social hostel with walls painted in bright colors (including, of course, lime), Limehouse features a pool table, a large common room with TV, its own budget travel agency, and plain, somewhat old, but clean rooms. They also offer free bike and walking tours for guests. Breakfast included. Free Internet. Reception 24hr. Check-out 10am. 4-bed dorms AR$32; 6-bed dorms AR$26; 12-bed dorms AR$20; singles and doubles AR$96, with private bath AR$130. Cash only. ❶

> **A LITTLE TOO FLASHY.** After checking out the websites for accommodations, sights, museums, nightclubs, and other listings, you'll start to notice that nearly every Argentine website is inexplicably laden with tons and tons of flash animation. If you have a slow computer or a lousy internet connection, surfing the web could slow down to a sloth-like pace.

**Portal del Sur,** Hipólito Yrigoyen 855 (☎4342 8788; www.portaldelsurba.com.ar). $ Lima or Avenida de Mayo. This large, colorfully decorated, and sleek hostel sprawls over numerous floors and houses a bar, rooftop terrace, grill, kitchen, and pool table. Portal del Sur is a quieter alternative to Monserrat's rowdier hostels, with reasonably priced dorms and hugely expensive private rooms. Spanish lessons, dance classes, and free walking tours offered. Breakfast included. Free Internet. Reception 24hr. Check-out 11am. Dorms AR$40, with A/C AR$45, with bath AR$50; singles AR$160; doubles AR$180; triples AR$220; quads AR$280. MC/V. ❷

**Hostel Estoril,** Av. de Mayo 1385, 3rd fl. (☎4383 9668; info@hostelestoril.com.ar). $ Sáenz Peña. In an area of the city packed with party hostels, this small accommodation, set in an old townhouse, is much more intimate and very friendly. The hostel has a common room with TV and a shared kitchen, but few other frills. But this, of course, has its benefits—it keeps things quieter. The beds and rooms are simple and small, but the singles and doubles, all with shared bath, are among the cheapest available. Breakfast included 7-11am. Free Internet and Wi-Fi (in the common room). Reception 24hr. Check-out 10am. 6-bed dorms AR$26; 8-bed dorms $26; singles AR$35-45; doubles AR$60; triples AR$96; quads AR$120; 7th day free. Cash only. ❶

**Che Lagarto,** Calle Venezuela 857 (☎4343 4845; www.chelegarto.com). $ Lima or Avenida de Mayo. A smaller hostel that has simple dorms with concrete floors, a shared kitchen, a common room with TV, and "The Madhouse," a restaurant and bar whose walls are lined with modern art. Breakfast included. Free Internet. Reception 24hr. Check-out

ACCOMMODATIONS

noon. Dorms AR$34, with bath AR$40; singles AR$100; doubles and quads AR$160. Discounts on extended stays booked in advance. AmEx/MC/V: 8% surcharge. ❷

**Alkimista,** Av. de Mayo 1385, 2nd fl. "C." (☎4383 2267; www.alkimistahostel.com). [S] Saénz Peña. Mid-sized and relaxed, Alkimista boasts a sunny common room and a centrally located spot close to some of BA's top sights. The rooms tend toward the smaller end of the spectrum and receive varying degrees of light. Breakfast included. Free Internet and Wi-Fi. 5-bed mixed dorms AR$36; 6-bed female dorms AR$32; 8-bed mixed dorms AR$30; singles AR$50; doubles AR$80. Cash only. ❷

## HOTELS

**The Clan House,** Adolfo Alsina 917 (☎4331 4448; www.bedandbreakfastclan.com.ar). [S] Lima or Avenida de Mayo. In a neighborhood filled with relatively generic hotels, this friendly bed and breakfast distinguishes itself with colorful, modern, individually decorated rooms and has a common room with cable TV and a terrace. Spanish lessons offered. Breakfast included. Laundry AR$10. Free Internet and Wi-Fi. Reception 24hr. Check-out 11am. Singles AR$120; doubles AR$130. Cash only. ❹

**Hotel Chile,** Avenida de Mayo 1297 (☎4381 6363; www.hotelchilebsas.com.ar). [S] Lima or Avenida de Mayo or Sáenz Peña. Rooms in this simple hotel are plain but have TVs, A/C, telephones, and some even have large windows and small balconies overlooking the street. There is also a bar downstairs. Breakfast included. Reception 24hr. Singles AR$100; doubles AR$120. AmEx/MC/V. ❹

**Hotel Avenida,** Avenida de Mayo 623 (☎4342 5664; www.hotelav.com.ar). [S] Perú, Catedral, or Bolívar. Very clean, basic rooms with TVs and new, modern furnishings in an excellent location just off Plaza de Mayo. Spotless and recently renovated, with a particularly pleasant breakfast room. Breakfast included. Reception 24hr. Singles AR$120; doubles AR$170; triples AR$190. Cash only. ❹

**Reina Hotel,** Avenida de Mayo 1120 (☎4381 2496; www.reinahotel.com). [S] Lima or Avenida de Mayo. Though it displays signs of wear (cracked mirrors, old rugs), this spacious hotel, with hardwood floors, high ceilings, and a beautifully decorated breakfast room, retains a romantic grandeur. Rooms have TVs and telephones but vary in size, so ask to see a few before deciding; those overlooking the street are worth the few extra pesos. Breakfast included. Singles AR$100, with A/C AR$120; doubles AR$120/140; triples AR$150/170; quads AR$180/200; quints AR$200/230. Cash only. ❹

**Concept Hotel,** Santiago del Estero 186 (☎4384 3473). [S] Lima or Avenida de Mayo. A sleek and modern hotel decorated in bright colors and angular shapes. Their spiffy rooms have telephones and digital panels to control the A/C and TVs. The spacious triples–split over 2 floors–are a great deal. Bar downstairs. Breakfast included. Singles AR$120; doubles AR$170; triples AR$190. Cash only. ❹

**Hotel Alcazar,** Avenida de Mayo 935 (☎4345 0926). [S] Lima or Avenida de Mayo. Though the simple rooms facing an inward balcony can be a bit dark, they are still a great deal given the central location and have TVs and telephones. Reception 24hr. Check-out 10am. Singles AR$90, with A/C AR$110; doubles AR$110/130; triples AR$130/150; quads AR$150/170. Cash only. ❸

**Hotel Gran España,** Tacuarí 80 (☎4343 5541). [S] Lima or Avenida de Mayo. The basic, clean rooms with TVs and telephones are a bit dark but also much quieter than rooms in hotels directly on Avenida de Mayo. Single rooms are priced depending on size, so ask to see a few before you choose. Singles AR$70-90; doubles AR$110. Cash only. ❸

# MICROCENTRO

Staying in Microcentro means you'll be in the middle of the action—and, sometimes, the chaos. In general, it's important to realize that in this *barrio*, rooms with windows overlooking the street are usually bright and airy but sometimes quite noisy during the day. Inner rooms will be much quieter, but will also have less light. Hotel prices here have risen significantly in the past few years, though there still are a few good deals, and the hostel scene—including many that differ significantly both in price and quality—is still going strong.

## HOSTELS

**⊠ BA Stop,** Rivadavia 1194 (☎4382 7406; www.bastop.com). Ⓢ Lima or Avenida de Mayo. This popular hostel has a large common room with TV, ping-pong table, pool table, bar, and spiral staircase. The rooms have hardwood floors and many are decorated with modern, colorful murals. Shared kitchen. Breakfast included. Free Internet and Wi-Fi. Reception 24hr. Check-in 12:30pm. Check-out 11am. 6-bed dorms AR$35 M-Th, AR$37 F-Su; 10-bed dorms AR$30/32; singles with shared bath AR$100/120; doubles with shared bath AR$140/160. Cash only. ❶

**V&S Hostel Club,** Viamonte 887, 3rd fl. (☎4322 0994 or 4327 5131; www.hostel-club.com). Ⓢ Lavalle. A very clean, smaller hostel in a beautiful old building with new, modern furnishings. The bright rooms are carpeted and well maintained, and many have balconies, including the private rooms. There's a common room with TV, a shared kitchen, and a terrace. Looking to brush up your linguistic and dance skills? They also offer free Spanish and tango lessons. Breakfast included. Free Internet. Reception 24hr. Check-out 11am. 6-bed dorms with A/C AR$50; 8-bed dorms AR$40, with A/C AR$47; doubles with private bath and balcony AR$200/236. Cash only. ❷

**St. Nicholas Hostel (HI),** Bartolomé Mitre 1691/93 (☎4373 8841 or 4372 4608; www.snhostel.com). Ⓢ Sáenz Peña. This large hostel has an enormous and well-stocked bar, common room with TV, and a deck with grill. Breakfast included. Free Internet. Reception 24hr. Check-out 11am. Dorms AR$35-45, HI members AR$30-40; singles with shared bath AR$92/80; doubles with shared bath AR$110/98, with private bath AR$120/108. AmEx/MC/V: 10% surcharge. ❷

**Colonial,** Tucumán 509, 1st fl. (☎4312 6417 or 4314 8514; www.hostelcolonial.com. ar). Ⓢ Florida or LN Alem. Though it lacks some services offered by many other hostels, this rather plain but brightly-painted hostel with concrete floors has friendly service, a small common room with TV, and A/C—and may have rooms when others don't. Breakfast included. Free Internet. Reception 24hr. Check-out 11am. Dorms AR$36; singles and doubles AR$96, with private bath AR$120; triples AR$114/165. Cash only. ❷

**Hostel Suites Obelisco,** Corrientes 830 (☎4328 4040; www.hostelsuites.com). Ⓢ Carlos Pellegrini, Florida, Av. 9 de Julio, or Diagonal Norte. A marble staircase and antique elevators are the remains of what was once an elegant apartment building. The hostel is still as nice as its predecessor, with spacious rooms, a large common area with pool table and computers, and staff-organized happy hours, barbecues, and club nights. Breakfast included until 10am. Free Wi-Fi. 6-bed dorms AR$46; singles AR$93; doubles AR$139-153; triples AR$189; quads AR$226. Cash only. ❷

## HOTELS

**Goya Hotel,** Suipacha 748 (☎4322 9269; www.goyahotel.com.ar). Ⓢ Lavalle. Great location, professional service, and very clean, basic rooms with TVs, telephones, and new furnishings. There's relatively little difference between the classes of rooms: "superior" rooms have a shower curtain and remote control, while "presidential" rooms have these features as well as a small sitting area. Breakfast included. Check-in noon. Check-out 10am. Singles "classic" AR$110, "superior" AR$145, "presidential" AR$182; doubles AR$145/182/218; triples AR$182. AmEx/MC/V. ❹

**Hotel Europa,** Bartolomé Mitre 1294 (☎4384 8360; www.eurohotel.com.ar). Ⓢ Lima or Avenida de Mayo. Though it's not in the most beautiful area of the *barrio*, Europa is

ACCOMMODATIONS

still a very good value. The basic rooms are very clean, in great condition, and have TVs, telephones, and A/C. Breakfast included. Free Wi-Fi. Check-in 11am. Check-out 10am. Singles AR$125; doubles AR$158; triples AR$212. Cash only. ❺

**Hotel Maipú**, Maipú 735 (☎4322 5142). [S] Florida. This old building with a grand entryway remains eerily beautiful, if dark and perhaps a little too quiet—a rarity in frantic Microcentro. The furnishings are a bit old, but the rooms are clean, have TVs, and are a great deal for the price. Singles AR$50, with private bath AR$65; doubles AR$70/90; triples AR$100/120; quads AR$140. Cash only. ❷

**Hotel O'Rei**, Lavalle 733 (☎4394 7112; www.hotelorei.com.ar). [S] Lavalle. A longtime backpacker's favorite for its rock-bottom prices, which are among the lowest you'll find in the Microcentro neighborhood. Though the fixtures may be old and the tiles cracking, the rooms are perfectly habitable, and even have TVs. Laundry AR$12. Reception 24hr. Check-out 10am. Singles with shared bath AR$30; doubles with shared bath AR$45, with private bath AR$70; triples AR$60/80. Cash only. ❶

# SAN TELMO

With its narrow, cobblestone streets, quirky shops, and alternative flavor, it's not particularly shocking that San Telmo appeals to the younger traveling set. Much of the *barrio* is packed with hostels, which range from the cheap and simple to the more expensive and sleek; most, however, are not nearly as large as those found in the center. Budget hotels—and, in fact, hotels in general—are harder to come by, though there are still a few good options.

## HOSTELS

🏨 **Hostel Tango Suites**, Chacabuco 747 (☎4300 2420; www.hosteltangosuite.com.ar). [S] Independencia. This beautiful, social hostel, in an old white townhouse, has a large, bright red common room with TV, kitchen access, bar, and grill. Outside, tiled paths lead to a variety of simple, well-kept rooms, all with A/C. Tango and Spanish lessons offered. Breakfast included 7-11am. Laundry AR$10. Free Internet and Wi-Fi. Reception 24hr. Check-out noon. 4-bed dorms AR$40; 6-bed dorms AR$35; 8-bed dorms AR$30, with private bath AR$35; doubles (bunked beds) with private bath AR$100. ❶

**Antico Hostel Boutique**, Bolívar 893 (☎4363 0123; www.anticohostel.com.ar). [S] Independencia. Though the dorm rooms are quiet and simple, the common spaces are extraordinary. The small living rooms, painted in muted colors, are furnished with leather couches and glass coffee tables. The rooftop plant-filled terrace has a small bar and grill. Breakfast included 8:30-11am. Free Internet. Reception 24hr. Check-out noon. 4- to 6-bed dorms AR$40; doubles AR$130, with private bath AR$160. Cash only. ❷

**Via Via Hostel**, Chile 324 (☎4300 7259; www.viaviacafe.com). [S] Independencia. Small, modern hostel with excellent location on one of the *barrio*'s best streets for nightlife. Organizes a variety of tours and daytrips. Rooms upstairs, all with shared bath, are quiet (and usually full), but the cafe and bar downstairs buzz with energy. Private room rates are hard to beat in San Telmo. Breakfast included. Free Internet. Reception 24hr. Check-out 11am. Dorms AR$25; singles AR$45; doubles AR$70. AmEx/MC/V. ❶

**Hostel One**, Bolívar 1291 (☎4300 9322; www.hostelone.com). [S] Independencia. Though a bit far from the action and near a highway overpass in a relatively ugly neighborhood, this simple, airy hostel with high ceilings has a terrace, kitchen, and comfortable, large common room with TV. They also organize an *asado* (barbecue; AR$25) every F. Breakfast included. Free Internet. Reception 24hr. Check-out 11am. 6-bed dorms AR$36; 8-bed dorms AR$32; doubles AR$107, with private bath AR$135; triples AR$161/203; quads AR$214/270. Cash only. 2

**Sandanzas Hostel,** Balcarce 1351 (☎4300 7375 or 4362 1816; www.sandanzas.com.ar). [S] Independencia. Just a few blocks from Parque Lezama, and almost on the border with La Boca, this quiet, relaxed, out-of-the-way hostel draws an alternative, international, 20-something crowd. Winding hallways lead to simple rooms, a shared kitchen, and a common room with TV. Free tango lessons on M and Tu. Breakfast included. Free Internet. Reception 24hr. Check-out 11am. 4-bed dorms AR$40; 6-bed dorms AR$36; singles with shared bath AR$120; doubles with shared bath AR$150. Cash only. ❷

> TIP **KNOCK KNOCK.** Hostels in Argentina have a tendency to blend into their surroundings, the consequence of minimal to nonexistent signage. Fear not. Feel confident in your navigational skills and simply ring the bell. Even if it's the wrong place, at least you'll have a funny story to bring back home.

**Ostinatto,** Chile 680 (☎4300 2535; www.ostinatto.com.ar). [S] Belgrano or Independencia. Located in a converted mansion, Ostinatto has so many services and common spaces that we would call it overkill if it weren't so impressive. The building includes a common room with TV, a large shared kitchen, a sunny terrace on the roof with a tiny pool, and a private bar. Even the dorm rooms, some of which have balconies, are shockingly spacious. M tango classes. Spanish lessons by arrangement. Free walking tours. Bike rental available. Breakfast included. Free Internet and Wi-Fi. Reception 24hr. Check-out 11am. 4-bed dorms AR$42; 6-bed dorms AR40; 8-bed dorms AR$37; 10-bed dorms AR$33; doubles AR$145, with private bath AR$165. Cash only. ❷

**Carlos Gardel Hostel,** Carlos Calvo 579 (☎4307 2606; www.hostelcarlosgardel.com.ar/ingresa.htm). [S] Independencia or Belgrano. The front room in this small, social hostel looks a bit like grandma's living room (sans grandma, with modern touches) but is quite comfy and opens up to a small shared kitchen with TV and some tables. The basic dorm rooms, with bright red floors and brick walls, have enormous lockers and A/C. Open-air terrace upstairs. Breakfast included. Free Internet and Wi-Fi. Reception 24hr. Check-out 11am. 4- or 6-bed dorms AR$30; 10-bed dorms AR$28; doubles with shared bath AR$100, with private bath AR$120. AmEx/V. Cash only for private rooms. ❶

**El Hostal de San Telmo,** Carlos Calvo 614 (☎4300 6899; www.elhostaldesantelmo.com). [S] Independencia. Affordable is the name of the game at El Hostal de San Telmo. Located along a beautiful street, this relaxed, no-frills hostel offers simple rooms, a shared kitchen, a common room with TV, a terrace, and laundry facilities at exceptionally low prices. Breakfast included. Free Internet. Reception 24hr. Check-out noon. 4-bed dorms AR$27; 6- to 8-bed dorms AR$23. Cash only. ❶

**Hostel Inn (HI),** Humberto Primo 820 (☎4300 7992; www.hostel-inn.com). [S] Independencia. This small hostel has simple rooms with bright, plaid bedspreads and shared baths, a tiny common room with TV, a kitchen, and a terrace. The staff arranges a variety of local activities and longer trips, including one to Iguazú Falls (p. 236). Breakfast included. Laundry AR$10. Free Internet and Wi-Fi. Reception 24hr. Check-out 10am. Dorms AR$36, HI members AR$31; singles AR$128; doubles AR$109. Cash only. ❷

**Hostal de Granados,** Chile 374 (☎4362 5600; www.hostaldegranados.com.ar). From the airport, bus #86 arrives directly–otherwise it's a brief walk into San Telmo from the Plaza de Mayo. [S] Catedral. In a quiet San Telmo square, this 1897 house, peach-colored on the inside, opened in 2000 as a quality hostel. The open-air courtyard in the middle and the loft setup in some of the rooms contributes to an airy feel. Space varies significantly from private rooms to dorms, and each extra centimeter factors into the price. Common spaces include two small living rooms and a kitchen on the ground floor. Lockers available. 4-bed dorms AR$40; 6-bed mixed dorms $28-35; 8-bed dorms AR$24-35; doubles with shared bath AR$120, with private bath AR$135-150. V. ❶

**Telmotango Hostel Suites (HI),** Chacabuco 679
(☎4361 5808; www.hostelmotango.com). Ⓢ Belgrano.
A quiet, beautifully restored San Telmo home with pot-
ted plants, a period skylight, and marble and wood
touches. Dorms never have more than two beds, and
with Spanish classes and discounts for longer stays,
the system seems to be set up for students. The common room has large lockers and ample tables, each
with a nifty little reading lamp attached, but the kitchen
could be more spacious. Inquire in advance if you don't
want a bunk bed. 2-bed dorms AR$45; doubles with
shared bath AR$110, with private bath AR$150; triples
with private bath AR$195. Cash only. ❷

## HOTELS

**Bohemia Buenos Aires Hotel,** Perú 845 (☎4115 2561;
www.bohemiabuenosaires.com.ar). Ⓢ Independencia. A bright, modern hotel in the center of San Telmo.
Rooms are simple but clean and bright and have A/C,
TVs, safeboxes, and telephones. The lobby, decorated
with modern art, has a small bar. The rooms may be
more expensive than other options in the *barrio,* but
it's a great deal for what you pay for. Buffet breakfast
included. Free Internet and Wi-Fi. Reception 24hr.
Check-in 1pm. Check-out 11am. Doubles AR$195;
triples AR$255; quads AR$315. AmEx/MC/V. ❺

**Los Tres Reyes,** Brasil 425 (☎4300 9456). Ⓢ San
Juan. Though a bit far from the action, this small hotel
near Parque Lezama is still a good option for those
looking for privacy on a budget. The rooms, all with TVs
and private bath, are very simple; sometimes the only
bit of color is the typical hotel-style bedspread. The
bathrooms are in great shape and the staff is helpful.
Breakfast included 8-10am. Free Wi-Fi. Reception 24hr.
Check-out 10am. Singles AR$100-120; doubles with
"matrimonial" bed AR$120, with twin beds AR$140-
160; triples AR$200; quads AR$260. Cash only. ❸

**Hotel Carly,** Humberto Primo 464-66 (☎4361 7710;
hotelcarly@arnet.com.ar). Ⓢ Independencia. Just off
Plaza Dorrego, this hotel couldn't get much closer to
the center of activity—or much cheaper. The old rooms
are exceptionally basic but still livable, and there's a
shared kitchen. Be forewarned, however: the doors
generally close at midnight. Free Internet. Check-
in 1pm-midnight. Check-out 11am. Singles AR$34,
with private bath AR$46; doubles AR$40/46; triples
AR$46/57; quads AR$57/63. Cash only. ❷

# RETIRO

Considering the fact that real estate in Retiro is some
of the most expensive in Buenos Aires, it's not particularly surprising that budget accommodations

## THE BIG SPLURGE

### PAMPAS PAMPERING

Alright, so BA is an amazing city—
tell us something we don't know.
But let's face it: after weeks of
partying, shopping, wandering,
and sightseeing, even the ultimate
"life in the fast lane" can become
a bit trying. Luckily for those who
are looking for some recuperation,
the expanses of Argentina's pristine **Pampas** lie just beyond the
city's borders, and many of the
nearby **estancias** (ranches) are
opening their doors to tired city
slickers looking to relax.

Just an hour car ride from the
city center is a local favorite, the
**Estancia de los Dos Hermanos.**
The owners, Ana and Pancho
Peña, will pick you up right from
your accommodation and take you
to their massive ranch for a day,
weekend, or even week of relaxing
country life that even clubhopping
urbanites will fall for. The price
of AR$430 per person per night
includes four daily meals, drinks,
accommodations, and two horseback rides. Though those feeling
active can take advantage of the
hiking and fishing, many simply
choose to sit in the private cot-
tages, which include a kitchen,
sitting room, bathroom, and bedroom, to watch the sunset or stare
across the mind boggling vastness
of the *estancia's* fields. Considering the number of services and
the friendliness of the owners, a
one-night stay may not be cheap,
but it's certainly a bargain.

☎4765 4320; www.estancialos-
doshermanos.com.

are very rare in this *barrio*. The streets around **Plaza San Martín** are packed with four- and five-star hotels, and the market has edged out almost everything else. Travelers who do stay in one of the few budget establishments, however, are guaranteed beautiful surroundings, a wide variety of excellent and expensive restaurants, and swarms of businesspeople to keep them company.

 **RETIRE TO RETIRO.** Looking to enjoy the city center without being in the thick of all the traffic and crowds? Consider staying in Retiro, which is close to Microcentro and Monserrat, but far quieter.

## HOSTELS

**Recoleta Hostel (HI),** Libertad 1216 (☎4812 4419; www.hirecoleta.com.ar). Ⓢ San Martín. Despite the name, this accommodation is actually in Retiro. Near Plaza San Martín and just north of Microcentro, this large hostel has an excellent, central location, as well as a small common room with TV and public phone, beautiful and spacious brick atrium, and shared kitchen. Breakfast included 8-10am. Laundry AR$12. Free Internet and Wi-Fi. Reception 24hr. Check-out 10am. 4-bed dorms AR$39, with private bath AR$45; 6-bed dorms AR$36/42; 8-bed dorms AR$33; doubles M-Th AR$102/120, F-Su AR$126/150. HI discount AR$6. Cash only. ❶

## HOTELS

**Hotel Central Córdoba,** San Martín 1021-3 (☎4311 1175; www.hotelcentralcordoba. com.ar). Ⓢ San Martín. A great, affordable hotel with a wonderful location just a block off Plaza San Martín. This is the cheapest hotel you'll find in the area. The rooms are a bit worn but very clean and include TVs, telephones, and A/C. They can, unfortunately, be slightly dim, as many of the windows open up to the walls of the neighboring buildings. Breakfast included. Reception 24hr. Check-out 10am. Singles AR$120; doubles AR$140; suites and triples AR$170. AmEx/MC/V: 10% surcharge. ❹

# RECOLETA

Like Retiro, upscale Recoleta has its share of expensive accommodations, though the *barrio* also offers a good number of budget hotels, usually located south of the cemetery and toward the border with Microcentro. In general, the farther west you go, the more residential and quiet the neighborhood gets; these areas also tend to be less well connected with public transportation and farther away from the central sights, though they are, of course, much closer to **Palermo,** the city's hub for trendy nightlife and restaurants.

## HOTELS

**Hotel Lion D'or,** Pacheco de Melo 2019 (☎4303 8992; www.hotel-liondor.com.ar). Ⓢ Callao. Near Recoleta Cemetery, this hotel offers something for every budget, from small, shared bathrooms to large rooms with balcony, TV, A/C, and fireplace. Rooms are well, if simply, decorated, and there's also a cafe and snack bar in the lobby. The number of room options can be daunting—check out the options online if you're overwhelmed. Reception 24hr. Check-in noon. Check-out 10:30am. Singles AR$70-145; doubles AR$145-250; triples AR$180-300. Cash only. ❸

**Hotel Castillo,** M.T. de Alvear 1893 (☎4815 4561). Ⓢ Callao. It's located just north of the border with Microcentro, so this budget hotel is much better connected with public transportation than most other options in Recoleta. Rooms are simple and clean, and

ACCOMMODATIONS

all include A/C, TV, and telephone—but not breakfast. Reception 24hr. Check-out 10am. Singles AR$150; doubles AR$190; triples AR$250; quads AR$300. Cash only. ❺

**Juncal Palace Hotel,** Juncal 2282 (☎4821 2756; www.juncalpalacehotel.com.ar). Ⓢ Pueyrredón. A smaller hotel in a more residential area, featuring a lovely lobby with carved wood paneling and stained glass. The simple rooms with lime green walls are a bit tacky but have A/C, TV, and telephone. Breakfast included. Reception 24hr. Check-out 10am. Singles AR$145; doubles AR$180; triples AR$215. MC/V. ❺

# PALERMO

After Palermo's explosion of popularity as *the* hot spot in the city for restaurants and nightlife, it was only a matter of time before the city's visitors wanted to sleep here, too. In **Palermo Soho, Palermo Hollywood,** and **Las Cañitas,** new hostels are continually popping up, as are a number of unique B&Bs; both tend to be much smaller and much more relaxed than their counterparts in the center of the city. Though the central sights may be a bit far away, staying in Palermo guarantees easy access to the neighborhood's extensive park system, some of the city's best museums, and, of course, many of the most popular restaurants, bars, clubs, and shops in Buenos Aires.

## PALERMO SOHO

### HOSTELS

**Palermo House,** Thames 1754 (☎4832 1815; www.palermohouse.com.ar). Ⓢ Plaza Italia. Located in a converted townhouse near Plaza Serrano, this clean, relaxed hostel draws a social, international crowd to its large, sprawling common room with TV, shared kitchen, and outdoor terrace. High ceilings compensate for the somewhat cramped dorms, and the hostel's only real drawback is that it's relatively far from the *subte.* Sa night *asado.* Spanish lessons by arrangement. Breakfast included. Free Internet. Reception 24hr. Check-out noon. Dorms AR$30; doubles AR$105, with TV and private bath AR$120; triples AR$135/150; quads AR$180/195. Cash only. ❶

**IN THE THICK OF THINGS.** With the exception of Las Cañitas accommodations, most Palermo hostels are just steps away from the *barrio's* superb dining, boozing, and nightlife scene and are generally not far away from a *subte* stop. Dump those bags at the hostel and get to work!

**Casa Babylon Art Hostel,** Borges 2071 (☎4832 1526; www.casababylonhostel.com. ar). Ⓢ Plaza Italia. Smack dab in the heart of Palermo Soho. Hard to miss—the door is flanked by two blue-and-orange elephant tiles. Chill hostel generally caters to a social, artsy crowd, from average tourists to those studying abroad. Up the staircase, pink walls and the elephant motif continue, giving way to a kitchen, dining area with TV, a patio for grilling. Lockers available. Free Wi-Fi. Check-in 10am-8pm. Confirm reservation 24hr. in advance. Doubles with bath AR$66; 4- and 6-bed dorms AR$45. Cash only. ❷

**Hostel-Bar Giramondo,** Güemes 4802 (☎4772 6740; www.hostelgiramondo.com.ar), at the intersection with Fray Justo Santamaria de Oro. Ⓢ Plaza Italia. This hostel has large, high-ceilinged rooms, some around a charming central atrium, two common rooms with TV, a large patio, and a kitchen. As the name implies, the hostel doubles as a bar, making it sometimes difficult to get a night's sleep. Giramondo also runs **Giramondo Suites,** Fray Justo Santa Maria de Oro 2472 (☎4775 5831), a quieter place up the street with only doubles. Breakfast included. Linens included. Free Internet. Singles and doubles with private bath AR$121; 4-, 6-, and 10-bed dorms AR$27. ❶

ACCOMMODATIONS

**Casa Jardín,** Charcas 4422 (☎4774 8783; www.casajardinba.com.ar). $ Plaza Italia. This small, quiet hostel (which is more like a bed and breakfast) earns its stellar reputation in the details—flowers on the tables in the eating area, a changing screen in the dorm, and excellent bathroom facilities. Wi-Fi access, but only one computer, which guests share with the staff. Doubles AR$100; 4-bed dorms AR$40. Cash only. ❷

**Back in Town - Buenos Aires,** El Salvador 5115 (☎4774 2859; www.baitba.com). $ Plaza Italia. Formerly known as Hostel BAIT, and under renovation as of June 2008, this hip hostel's walls are painted with bright, funky designs. A kitchen and common room with TV surround a brightly lit atrium. Though the dorms are a bit cramped, all beds have curtains, making it a perfect place to sleep late after a long night out. Spanish lessons available. Breakfast included. Free Internet and Wi-Fi. Reception 24hr. Check-out noon. Dorms AR$22; doubles AR$85, with private bath and TV AR$120; triples AR$105/140; quads with private bath AR$160. Cash only. ❶

**Zentrum Hostel Boutique,** Costa Rica 4520 (☎4833 9518; www.zentrumhostel.com. ar), between Malabia and Armenia. $ Scalabrini Ortiz. Zentrum banks on the idea that some backpackers want lodgings as private, quiet, and clean as a hotel, but at accessible prices. They get the job done with their very spacious, well-lit dorms and sturdy beds. Social space includes an upstairs patio that resembles a tropical cabaña. However, there's no Internet access (save for bootleg Wi-Fi) or kitchen. Breakfast included. Linens included. Check-in 8am-10pm. Dorms US$15; doubles US$40. ❷

**So Hostel,** Charcas 4416 (☎4779 2949; www.sohostel.com.ar). $ Plaza Italia. A list of house rules and a beer-stocked fridge by the front desk set the tone for organized fun. Cheerful, full-access kitchen with skylight, and plenty of space for hanging out, from living rooms with TV and DVD to a terrace with grill. Some rooms have balconies (AR$10-20 extra). Breakfast included. Lockers available. Linens included. Free Internet and Wi-Fi. Check-in 2pm. Check-out 11am. All rooms A/C equipped. Singles AR$50; doubles AR$80, with bath AR$110; 6- to 9-bed dorms AR$24. Cash only. ❶

**Hostel Suites Palermo,** Charcas 4752 (☎4773 0806; www.suitespalermo.com), near a quiet corner, set back from the street behind gates. $ Plaza Italia. Uniformed staff (well, ok, so they're only T-shirts) and the well-organized infrastructure give this large, two-story hostel a professional bustle. The dorms are spacious, with large lockers beneath the beds. A small patio with eating area graces the front, while the interior has its own share of services, including a TV room with DVD player. Breakfast included. Linens included. Internet and Wi-Fi access. Reservation confirmation required 24hr. in advance. Doubles with bath AR$155; triples AR$180; 4- to 6-bed dorms AR$39. HI members 5-10% off. All-female dorms available. Cash only. ❷

**Tango Backpackers,** Paraguay 4601 (☎4776 6871; www.tangobp.com), down Thames from the Plaza Italia. $ Plaza Italia. Travelers stream in and out of this party hostel at all hours of the day and night, congregating for drinks and soccer in the large common room or on the barbecue terrace. It offers a range of activities, including the namesake tango lessons, soccer and bike tours, and pub crawls. Bar open 24hr., happy hour 7-9pm. Kitchen available. Breakfast included 8-10am. Lockers available. Linens included. Free Internet and Wi-Fi. Singles with A/C. Check-out 10am. Singles AR$90; doubles AR$125, with bath AR$140; triples AR$150; 4- to 6-bed dorms AR$39. HI members 10-15% off. Cash only (dollars and pesos accepted). ❷

## HOTELS

▧ **Che Lulu Trendy Hotel,** Pasaje Emilio Zolá 5185 (☎4772 0289; www.chelulu.com). $ Palermo. On a small sidestreet between Godoy Cruz and Santa Maria de Oro. A lovely, intimate B&B complete with a comfy common room with TV and bar. The rooms are in great condition and are a top-notch value given the prime location, if relatively small and simple; one has A/C. Breakfast included. Free Internet and Wi-Fi. Laundry AR$15.

A C C O M M O D A T I O N S

**BACK IN TOWN**

buenos aires hostel

(+54 11) 4774 2859

*www.baitba.com - info@baitba.com*
*msn: info@baitba.com - skype: bait_hostel*

BILINGUAL STAFF, SPANISH LESSONS

TANGO, FUTBOL & MORE

KITCHEN, INTERNET, WI-FI

BREAKFAST INCLUDED

the hostel where you belong

**ack In Town**
Buenos Aires

AMAZING LOCATION IN PALERMO VIEJO, TWO BLOCKS FROM PLAZA
SERRANO. INCREDIBLE PRICES FOR DORMS AND PRIVATE ROOMS,
SPECIALS FOR LONGER STAYS. WARM FRIENDLY ATMOSPHERE, ONLY 9
BEDROOMS. ASADO (ARGENTINE BBQ) EVERY THURSDAY FOR ALL GUESTS.

Check-in 3pm. Check-out noon. 5-bed shared room AR$60 per person; private rooms
accommodating 1-2 people AR$121-151, with private bath AR$196. Cash only. ❷

**Cypress In,** Costa Rica 4828 (☎4833 5834; www.cypressin.com). Ⓢ Plaza Italia. In
the heart of Palermo Soho just blocks from Plaza Serrano, this sleek guesthouse is a
great deal for its quality and perfect location. There's a common room with black leather
couches and flat-screen TV, and all the simple rooms, many just renovated and all in
great shape, have comfy, billowy bedspreads along with A/C, TVs, and phones. Breakfast
included. Reception 24hr. Check-out 11am. Singles with private bath AR$151; doubles
AR$193, with private bath AR$227; triples AR$257-287. AmEx/MC/V. ❸

**La Otra Orilla,** Julián Álvarez 1779 (☎4863 7426; www.otraorilla.com.ar). Ⓢ Plaza Italia. It's expensive, and a bit far from the action, but this small, chic B&B is worth the
costs for its stunning common spaces. There's a beautiful garden out back and a classy
Victorian breakfast room straight out of a Jane Austen novel. Each of the 7 themed
rooms has been uniquely decorated, and 5 of the 7 have A/C and TVs. Breakfast and
afternoon tea included. Free Internet and Wi-Fi. Reception 24hr. Check-out 11am.
Single with shared bath and fan AR$127; double with shared bath and A/C AR$145;
doubles with private bath, A/C, and TV AR$257-347; suite AR$402. AmEx/MC/V. ❺

# PALERMO HOLLYWOOD

## HOSTELS

▨ **Gecko Hostel,** Bonpland 2233 (☎4771 0910; www.geckohostel.com.ar). Ⓢ Palermo.
Brand new to Palermo's hostel scene, this relaxed, sprawling accommodation manages to avoid the "party hostel" label while still remaining sociable. It has a bright

ACCOMMODATIONS

terrace, shared kitchen, and comfy common spaces and rooms, but its best feature is its large private bar, where there's live music every Th night. Breakfast included. Free Internet and Wi-Fi. Reception 24hr. Check-out 11am. Dorms AR$30, with private bath AR$45; private rooms accommodating 1-4 people (or more; they'll let you cram in as many as you want, within reason) AR$97/121. Cash only. ❶

**Casa Esmeralda,** Honduras 5765 (☎4772 2446; www.casaesmeralda.com.ar). ⓢ Palermo. Located on a relatively quiet street, this small, chill hostel has simple, colorful rooms, kitchen, small bar, and common room with TV—all of which surround a beautiful, large garden, where there are plenty of wooden tables, benches, and leafy shade. Breakfast included. Laundry AR$12. Internet AR$4 per hr. Reception 24hr. Check-out 11am. Dorms AR$35; doubles AR$100, with private bath AR$110. Cash only. ❷

## LAS CAÑITAS

### HOSTELS

**Alma Petit Hostel,** Jorge Newbery 1708 (☎4771 4345; www.almapetithostel.com), between Arce and Independencia. ⓢ Olleros or Ministerio Carranza. One of the few hostels within walking distance of the Las Cañitas nightlife, this tiny 22-bed accommodation in an old British-style house has hardwood floors and a dark red common room with TV and Internet. The patio with grill and planned nightlife excursions make for ample social opportunities. Alma Petit also organizes tours of the city. Breakfast included 8-11am. Lockers available. Linens included. Free Internet. Check-in noon. Check-out 10am. 4-bed dorms AR$30, with bath AR$45; twins AR$85; doubles with bath and TV AR$118. Discounts for longer stays. Cash only. ❷

**Te Adoro Garcia,** Soldado de la Independencia 1298 (☎4777 2922; www.teadorogarcia.com), at the intersection with Calle Teodoro García. ⓢ Olleros. Though the location has its perks, including nearby Palermo parks and Las Cañitas nightlife, the busy intersection can get noisy. Common room facilities include TV and DVD. Kitchen available. Breakfast included. Linens included. Internet and Wi-Fi access. Will arrange shuttle service to the airport. Doubles AR$99-132; quads AR$148; 4-bed dorms AR$40. Minimum stay two nights. Discounts for stays longer than 10 days. Cash only. ❷

# THE OUTER BARRIOS

Staying in the outer *barrios* may not be one of the more popular options, but for some travelers, that might be part of the appeal.

## BELGRANO

### HOSTELS

**La Rosada de Belgrano,** Av. Cabildo 3041 (☎15 5466 7918 and 15 5028 1514; www.larosadadebelgrano.com.ar), between Iberá and Quesada. ⓢ Congreso de Tucuman. Pink on the outside, blue on the inside, this new hostel draws students planning to stay in Buenos Aires for awhile with its spacious, well-lit dorms without bunk beds and a surprisingly quiet location, despite its spot on Av. Cabildo. Still, it's a few blocks from the last stop on the *subte*, which can be inconvenient. Free Wi-Fi. Triples AR$650 per month per person; 4-bed dorms AR$600 per month. ❶

**Pampa Hostel,** Iberá 2858 (☎4544 2273; www.hostelpampa.com.ar). ⓢ Congreso de Tucuman. Bus 60, 151, 152. Painted in bright colors straight out of Boca's *El Caminito*. Cheerful, friendly hostel has affordable rooms. Ground floor rooms open to a patio, and the setup includes a 2nd-fl. kitchen and third-floor patio. One drawback is the location, which is a bit of a hike from the *subte* and most tourist sights. Breakfast included. Free

ACCOMMODATIONS

Internet and Wi-Fi. 5-bed dorms AR$50; 6-bed dorms AR$45; singles AR$96; doubles AR$77; triples AR$64; quads AR$58. Large discounts for longer stays. MC/V. ❷

# BALVANERA

## HOSTELS

**Che Hostel,** Chile 2017 (☎4942 0807; www.chehostel.com.ar). Ⓢ Pichincha. Though a bit far from the action, this medium-sized hostel makes up for its location with great common spaces and relatively cheap private rooms. Located in a converted townhouse, the simple accommodations sprawl over a number of floors, and there's a shared kitchen as well as a great, airy living room with modern art-adorned orange walls, a TV, and numerous wooden tables. Breakfast included. Free Internet and Wi-Fi. Reception 24hr. Check-out noon. 4-bed dorms AR$30; 6- or 8-bed dorms AR$27; singles AR$55; doubles AR$91; triples AR$110. Cash only. ❶

**El Patio,** Entre Ríos 677 (☎4383 0314; www.elpatiohostel.com). Ⓢ Entre Ríos. Just across from Microcentro, this hostel, frequented by Latin Americans, is much closer to the main sights than most establishments in the outer *barrios*. The dorms aren't particularly attractive, but the hostel has a lovely patio with ping-pong table and bar as well as a shared kitchen and common room with TV. The real reason to stay here, however, are the long-term rates, which are amazingly low. Breakfast included. Free Internet. Reception 24hr. Check-in noon. Check-out 11am. Dorms AR$35; singles with private bath AR$90; doubles AR$120; triples AR$150. Monthly rates AR$330-750. Cash only. ❷

# BOEDO

## HOSTELS

**La MeNeSuNdA,** Av. Boedo 742 (☎4957 0946; www.lamenesundahostel.com.ar). Ⓢ Boedo. Located on Boedo's main strip, this popular hostel draws backpackers looking for an alternative BA experience. The common spaces, including a sun-lit atrium, terrace, and kitchen, are beautiful, and the simple dorms are in great shape. And yes—they actually spell the name of the hostel that way. Breakfast included 8-11am. Free Internet and Wi-Fi. Tango and Spanish classes by arrangement. Reception 24hr. Check-out 11am. 4-bed dorms AR$43; 6-bed dorms AR$33; singles AR$79-91, with private bath AR$137; doubles AR$97-122/152; triples AR$155/192. Cash only. ❷

# FOOD

If you're a steak and wine type person, you came to the right place. Buenos Aires is legendary for its plentiful, shockingly cheap offerings of *bife* and wine fresh from the Argentine fields and vineyards, found at any of the umpteen million *parrillas* and *asados*. Vegetarians need not worry, though—there are also some excellent non-carnivorous options at every eatery, and even some restaurants that are solely devoted to herbivores, though these are harder to come by. Per the European roots of much of the Argentine population, there are also some stellar Italian offerings, particularly in the pizza department, with a wealth of small pizzerias doling out heavenly slices and pitchers of beer. On the fancier end of the spectrum, thanks to the favorable exchange rate with the Argentine peso, BA's top restaurants in chic *barrios* such as Palermo are still happily within reach for the budget traveler's wallet, This, of course, means that establishments considered inexpensive by Argentine standards are ridiculously cheap for visitors. For the crowd just looking for a quick cup of coffee and a pastry, the city's incredible cafe culture is very European in tone, but with some touches that make it distinctively Latin American, such as the occasional tango performance. Did we mention that beef is a pretty big deal?

## FOOD BY TYPE

**ARGENTINE**

| | |
|---|---|
| Anden Restaurant (p. 133) | LC ❷ |
| 🍴Artemisia (p. 130) | PaS ❸ |
| Arturito (p. 121) | Mic ❷ |
| Bar Uriarte (p. 130) | PaS ❸ |
| Boedo Antiguo (p. 136) | Boe ❷ |
| Cabaña Las Lilas (p. 126) | PM ❺ |
| Chiquilín (p. 121) | Mic ❸ |
| Club Eros (p. 131) | PaS ❷ |
| Cuatro Hojas (p. 128) | Rec ❷ |
| El Desnivel (p. 123) | ST ❶ |
| El Español (p. 135) | Bal ❶ |
| El General (p. 135) | Mon ❸ |
| El Obrero (p. 125) | LB ❷ |
| El Patio (p. 121) | Mic ❷ |
| El Pobre Luis (p. 134) | Bel ❷ |
| Freud y Fahler (p. 131) | PaS ❹ |
| Gambrinus (p. 137) | Cha ❸ |
| Gardelito (p. 131) | PaS ❸ |
| 🍴Granix (p. 120) | Mic ❸ |
| 🍴La Cabrera (p. 117) | PaS ❹ |
| La Cupertina (p. 131) | PaS ❷ |
| La Manufactura Papelería (p. 124) | ST ❷ |
| La Peca (p. 132) | PaS ❸ |
| La Taba (p. 119) | Mon ❷ |
| Las Cholas (p. 134) | LC ❷ |
| Miranda (p. 133) | PaH ❸ |
| 🍴Mítico Sur (p. 123) | ST ❷ |

| | |
|---|---|
| Parrilla 1880 (p. 123) | ST ❷ |
| 🍴Parrilla Peña (p. 121) | Mic ❷ |
| Parrilla (p. 132) | PaS ❶ |
| Pekin (p. 132) | PaS ❷ |
| Siga La Vaca (p. 125) | PM ❹ |
| 🍴Status (p. 119) | Mon ❷ |
| Tramezzini (p. 127) | Ret ❷ |

**BAKERY/CHOCOLATIER**

| | |
|---|---|
| Artesano (p. 128) | Rec ❷ |
| Maria de Bambi (p. 128) | Rec ❶ |
| 🍴Mirta Rovagna (p. 129) | Rec ❶ |
| Tikal Chocolates (p. 132) | PaS ❷ |

**CAFE**

| | |
|---|---|
| A222 (p. 122) | Mic ❸ |
| Bar Plaza Dorrego (p. 123) | ST ❷ |
| Cafe Margot (p. 136) | Boe ❷ |
| Cafe Richmond (p. 122) | Mic ❷ |
| Cafe Tortoni (p. 120) | Mon ❷ |
| Clásica y Moderna (p. 129) | Rec ❷ |
| Confitería Ideal (p. 122) | Mic ❶ |
| Confitería La Rambla (p. 129) | Rec ❷ |
| Costumbres Criollas (p. 127) | Ret ❶ |
| La Americana (p. 122) | Mic ❷ |
| 🍴La Biela (p. 128) | Rec ❷ |
| La Paz (p. 122) | Mic ❷ |
| La Puerto Rico (p. 120) | Mon ❷ |
| Las Violetas (p. 136) | Alm ❷ |

FOOD

## CAFE, CON'T.
London City (p. 120)          Mon ❷
Los Angelitos (p. 135)        Bal ❸
M.masamadre es con M (p. 137)  Cha ❸
Meridiano 58 (p. 132)         PaS ❷
Pan y Arte (p. 136)           Boe ❸
Patricia Villobos Deli (p. 134)  PaC ❶
Petit Paris Cafe (p. 127)     Ret ❷
Pride Cafe (p. 124)           ST ❷
Santos Sabores (p. 134)       LC ❶
Tea Connection (p. 126)       PM ❷

## CHINESE
Asia Oriental (p. 135)        Bel ❶
Lai Lai (p. 135)              Bel ❸
Los Chinos (p. 134)           Bel ❷

## CUBAN
Rey Castro (p. 119)           Mon ❶

## DANISH
Club Danés (p. 126)           Ret ❷

## FRENCH
Brasserie Pétanque (p. 119)   Mon ❸
Cluny (p. 132)                PaS ❺
La Bourgogne (p. 128)         Rec ❺
Oui Oui (p. 133)              PaH ❷

## ICE CREAM
Freddo (p. 122)               Mic ❶
Un Altra Volta (p. 129)       Rec ❶

## INDIAN
Bangalore Curry House (p. 132)  PaH ❹
Krishna (p. 131)              PaS ❷

## INTERNATIONAL
Amaranta (p. 128)             Rec ❶
Donata (p. 125)               PM ❺
El Sanjuanino (p. 128)        Rec ❷
Filo (p. 126)                 Ret ❸
MoMo (p. 127)                 Ret ❷
Novecento (p. 134)            LC ❹

## ITALIAN
702 de Gallo Deli Restó (p. 136)  Alm ❷
Bella Italia Cafe-Bar (p. 134)  PaC ❸
Bice (p. 125)                 PM ❺
Cantina Pierino (p. 136)      Alm ❸
Don Carlos (p. 125)           LB ❷
Frodo's (p. 119)              Mon ❷
"i" Fresh Market (p. 125)     PM ❸
Prosciutto's (p. 119)         Mon ❷
Sabot (p. 121)                Mic ❸

## JAPANESE
Comedor Nikkai (p. 120)       Mon ❸
Sake (p. 127)                 Rec ❸

## KOREAN
Bi Won (p. 135)               Bal ❹

## MEXICAN
California Burrito Company (p. 121)  Mic ❷
DF Mexican Restaurante (p. 126)  PM ❸

## MIDDLE EASTERN
Al Andalus (p. 131)           PaS ❹
Bereber (p. 129)              PaS ❹
Club Sirio (p. 127)           Rec ❹
El Chef Iusef (p. 130)        PaS ❷
Sarkis (p. 130)               PaS ❷

## PERUVIAN
Ceviche (p. 133)              PaH ❹
Chan Chan (p. 120)            Mon ❷

## PIZZA
El Cuartito (p. 126)          Ret ❷
La Más Querida (p. 135)       Bel ❷
Los Maestros (p. 128)         Rec ❶
Pizza Güerrin (p. 121)        Mic ❶
San Antonio (p. 136)          Boe ❶
Señor Telmo (p. 123)          ST ❶
Tonno (p. 133)                LC ❷

## POLISH
La Casa Polaca (p. 131)       PaS ❸

## SOUTHEAST ASIAN
Empire Thai (p. 127)          Ret ❸
Green Bamboo (p. 133)         PaH ❺
Sudestada (p. 133)            PaH ❹

## SEAFOOD
La Cancha (p. 124)            LB ❷
Solo Pescado (p. 135)         Bal ❷

## SPANISH
Tancat (p. 126)               Ret ❹

## VEGETARIAN
Abuela Pan (p. 123)           ST ❷
Casa Felix (p. 133)           PaH ❹
La Huerta (p. 121)            Mic ❶
Lotos (p. 127)                Rec ❷
Orígen (p. 123)               ST ❶
Prâna (p. 130)                PaS ❷
Verde Llama (p. 137)          Cha ❷

**NEIGHBORHOOD ABBREVIATIONS: Alm** Almagro **Bal** Balvanera **Bel** Belgrano **Boe** Boedo **Cha** Chacarita **LB** La Boca **LC** Las Cañitas **Mic** Microcentro **Mon** Monserrat **PaC** Palermo Chico **PaH** Palermo Hollywood **PaS** Palermo Soho **PM** Puerto Madero **Rec** Recoleta **Ret** Retiro **ST** San Telmo

FOOD

# FOOD BY BARRIO

## MONSERRAT

Though not known for its restaurants, it's not hard to find a place to grab a bite to eat in Monserrat. Many generic cafes serving pizza and coffee line **Avenida de Mayo** and dot the streets around **Plaza de Mayo** and **Plaza del Congreso.** Some of these are quite good, if slightly overpriced, and they are frequented by *porteños* as well as tourists. A more diverse selection of restaurants can be found lining the southern streets of the *barrio*, just north of **San Telmo.**

### RESTAURANTS

▧ **Status,** Virrey Ceballos 178 (☎4382 8531). Ⓢ Sáenz Peña. Don't let the name fool you; this bright, simple restaurant serves large portions of excellent Argentine and Peruvian cuisine, including a wide range of very fresh fish, at inexpensive prices. The *chupa de mariscos* (seafood soup, AR$17) is particularly delicious. Most entrees AR$7-16. Seafood dishes AR$12-28. Open daily for lunch and dinner. AmEx/MC/V. ❷

**Brasserie Pétanque,** Defensa 596 (☎4342 7930). Ⓢ Plaza de Mayo. This elegant restaurant with high ceilings, wooden detailing, and white tablecloths serves traditional, delicious French cuisine, including rabbit and steak tartare (a.k.a. raw meat). Though dinner can be expensive, especially by local standards, the set lunch *menús* are a great deal at AR$20-28. Entrees AR$20-45. Open M 12:30-3:30pm, Tu-F 12:30-3:30pm and 8:30-midnight, Sa 8:30-midnight. AmEx/MC/V. ❸

**Frodo's,** Balcarce 605 (☎4331 1268). Ⓢ Plaza de Mayo. Frodo's serves mainly Italian cuisine, including vegetable ravioli with cream sauce, and an odd assortment of other dishes that don't really belong, such as chop suey. At lunch, choose from a set *menú* of 6 dishes for AR$15 or 7 for AR$17; a drink and coffee or dessert is included in the price. On weekend nights, the restaurant hosts a dinner show (AR$25) with live music or other entertainment, after which the restaurant transforms into a disco. Go figure. Free Wi-Fi. Open M-Sa 9:30am-8pm, Th-F 9:30am-8pm and 10pm-6am. Cash only. ❷

 **CASH MONEY.** So you have the dinner check and you're ready to pay with your card. But wait! Where's the wait staff? Note that servers will rarely come back after they've given you the bill, unless you pester them about it. Argentines (and tourists in the know) will have cash on hand so they can pay and leave when they're ready.

**Prosciutto's,** Venezuela 1212 (☎4383 8058). Ⓢ Lima. A very ornate yet comfortable restaurant with an impressive carved wood interior that serves classic Italian cuisine to a crowd of tourists and locals. The set *menú* at lunch (AR$25) includes an entree, drink, and dessert. Entrees AR$15-35. Open daily for lunch and dinner. AmEx/MC/V. ❷

**Rey Castro,** Perú 342 (☎4342 9998). Ⓢ Perú or Bolívar. Unsurprisingly, Castro's music provides the (revolutionary) mood in this large restaurant with dim lighting, exposed brick walls, and an arched roof. The menu includes Latin- and Cuban-inspired cuisine. The place is usually subdued throughout the week, but they often host a live band (and boisterous dancing) on weekend nights. Entrees AR$10-20. Happy hour M-F 6-9pm. Open M-Th noon-9pm, F-Sa noon-6am. ❶

**La Taba,** Hipólito Yrigoyen 581 (☎4343 2555; www.lataba.com.ar). Ⓢ Perú or Bolívar. Tucked away just off Plaza de Mayo, this plain and somewhat dimly lit restaurant serves simple Argentine fare, including *empanadas* (AR$2.10) and *chivito* (goat; AR$14-16). Though its tiled floors and plain walls don't have the flair of the cafes along Avenida de

**FOOD**

Mayo, it also doesn't have the high prices. Free Wi-Fi. Sandwiches AR$7.50-10. Pastas AR$9-13. Salads AR$10. Other entrees AR$8-16. Open M-Sa 9am-8pm. Cash only. ❶

**Comedor Nikkai,** Independencia 732 (☎4300 5848), between Piedras and Chacabuco. Ⓢ Belgrano. Tucked inside the Japanese cultural center, this low-key spot is one of the more affordable and authentic sushi places in the city. Don't expect to see a lot of tuna on the menu—as with other BA sushi shops, salmon is the standard fish. Sushi AR$20-50. *Menú* AR$32. Open M-Th noon-3pm and 7-11pm; F noon-3pm and 8pm-midnight; Sa 8pm-midnight. Reservations recommended F and Sa dinner. ❸

**El General,** Av. Belgrano 561 (☎4342 7830; www.restaurantgeneral.com). Ⓢ Belgrano. Though the food here is decent, it's the decor that really draws crowds to this establishment. This traditional *parrilla* is plastered with Perón memorabilia, an experience that restaurateurs suggest feels akin to "poetry." Luckily, support for working classes doesn't mean diners forsake their right to wine glasses and white tablecloths. Entrees AR$20-40. Desserts AR$9-10. Open M-Sa noon-late. AmEx/MC/V. ❸

**Chan Chan,** Hipólito Yrigoyen 1390 (☎4382 8492), between San José and Santiago del Estero. Ⓢ Sáenz Peña. Red and white tablecloths and corny pastoral murals, nevermind the religious icons over the door, give this small Peruvian restaurant a surprisingly authentic feel. Local workers drop in for lunch at this joint known for filling plates of cheap, tasty food. Open Tu-Su noon-4pm and 7:30pm-close. Cash only. ❷

## CAFES

**Cafe Tortoni,** Avenida de Mayo 825/9 (☎4342 4328; www.cafetortoni.com.ar). Ⓢ Lima or Avenida de Mayo. Established in 1858, Tortoni is BA's most famous cafe. Its attractive interior attract hordes of tourists and *porteños* alike—they also draw crowds with their food and delicious desserts. On account of the crowds, service can be a bit slow, and you may even have to wait in line to get in. Still, it's worth a visit, or at least a quick peek. Coffee AR$6. Sandwiches AR$9-25. Entrees AR$8-32. Desserts AR$6-22. Tango shows daily at 9pm AR$60. Reserve in advance. Open daily 8am-late. AmEx/MC/V. ❷

**La Puerto Rico,** Adolfo Alsina 216 (☎4331 2215). Ⓢ Plaza de Mayo. Another one of Buenos Aires' historic cafes, Puerto Rico, founded in 1887, does not boast the stunning interior of Tortoni, but it lacks the mobs of tourists and has lower prices, resulting in a much quieter, relaxing, and wallet-friendly cafe. The cafe also hosts popular dinner and tango shows F nights; reserve in advance. Pastries AR$9-10. Salads AR$10-18. Entrees AR$15-35. Open M-Sa 7am-8pm. AmEx/MC/V: AR$20 min. ❷

**London City,** Avenida de Mayo 599 (☎4342 9057). Ⓢ Perú, Bolívar, or Catedral. This bright, lively cafe is a great place to watch the crowds rushing past on Avenida de Mayo. The pastries and pies (AR$10) here are particularly delicious, as are the breakfast options (AR$10-33). Sandwiches AR$9-28. Open M-Sa 7am-10pm. AmEx/MC/V. ❷

# MICROCENTRO

Microcentro has a huge variety of restaurants, though most serve typical Argentine cuisine; you'll find a bunch of cheap pizza stands, *tenedor libres* (all-you-can-eat buffets), exceptionally elegant (and expensive) *parrillas*, and everything in between. As this is the business district, it's important to keep in mind that many restaurants are only open Monday through Friday for lunch, though quite a few also stay open on weekends.

## RESTAURANTS

▨ **Granix,** in Galeria Güemes, Florida 165, Entrada Mitre, 2nd fl. (☎4343 4020). Ⓢ Florida. It's more expensive than many of Microcentro's other *tenedor libres,* but the food here is also of much better quality. The number of vegetarian entrees served in the bright, pleasant cafeteria is almost overwhelming—and utterly surprising in carnivorous BA—and there's also a well stocked salad bar with fresh fruit. For the price (AR$27), you get unlimited food, drinks, and a dessert. Open M-F 11am-3:30pm. AmEx/MC/V. ❸

**Parrilla Peña,** Rodríguez Peña 682 (☎4471 5643). Ⓢ Callao. It's all about the beef in this tiny, simple *parrilla*, whose prices, despite its popularity and excellent food, remain shockingly low. Try to avoid the lunch rush (1:30-2:30pm), or you may not find a seat; they do not accept reservations. Entrees AR$16-34. Open M-Sa noon-4pm and 8pm-midnight, Su noon-4pm. Cash only. ❷

**El Patio,** in the Convento de San Ramón, Reconquista 269 (☎4343 0290). Ⓢ Florida or LN Alem. Set amid the archways of the convent's cloister, El Patio has a beautiful, airy setting overlooking a lovely patch of grass. Serves simple, inexpensive salads and pastas. Entrees AR$13-32. *Menú del día* AR$35. Open M-F for lunch. Cash only. ❷

**Pizza Güerrin,** Corrientes 1368 (☎4371 8141). Ⓢ Uruguay. Order a piece of cheap, delicious pizza in the dining area or grab an even cheaper slice from the counter at this simple eatery, which many locals maintain is the best pizza joint in the *barrio*. Slices AR$3.50-5. Other entrees AR$12-25. Open daily 7am-2am. Cash only. ❶

**Arturito,** Corrientes 1124 (☎4382 0227). Ⓢ Carlos Pellegrini or Uruguay. Practically a Microcentro institution, this large, simple restaurant with wooden walls and white tablecloths serves excellent *porteño* cuisine and is particularly popular for its beef—which is what you came to Buenos Aires for in the first place, right? Dig in. Entrees AR$10-37. Open daily for lunch and dinner. AmEx/MC/V. ❷

**Sabot,** 25 de Mayo 756 (☎4313 6587). Ⓢ Florida or LN Alem. This quiet, elegant restaurant draws a mainly business crowd with its delicious meat dishes. Apparently, some of them come here to wine and dine their clients. The wooden paneling and waiters in white jackets further contribute to the strangely formal atmosphere, but hey—at least it's affordable. Entrees AR$24-47. Open for lunch M-F. AmEx/MC/V. ❸

---

**COVER: NOT JUST FOR CLUBS.** Many restaurants tack on a *cubierto* (a table charge, or cover) to the bill. This usually runs anywhere from AR$5-10. And you thought a cover charge was only for clubs. Ha.

---

**Broccolino,** Esmeralda 776 (☎4322 7754). Ⓢ Carlos Pellegrini. Though the decor of this restaurant, with its green ceiling and white- and red-tablecloths, suggests that an Italian flag exploded here, it manages to remain classy with its wood paneling and exceptionally friendly service. Popular with both tourists and locals, the restaurant's huge menu includes delicious pizza, salads, and create-your-own-pasta dishes. Entrees AR$12-47. Open daily for lunch and dinner. AmEx/MC/V. ❸

**Chiquilín,** Sarmiento 1599 (☎4373 5166). Ⓢ Uruguay or Callao. This lovely, bright restaurant, with enormous windows and high ceilings, promises huge variety, but the beef is still the main draw for most hungry customers. Free Wi-Fi. Entrees AR$13-45. *Menú del día* AR$35. Open daily for lunch and dinner. AmEx/MC/V. ❸

**La Huerta,** Lavalle 895, 2nd fl. (☎4327 2682). Ⓢ Carlos Pellegrini or Lavalle. Another of Microcentro's vegetarian buffets, La Huerta offers a huge amount of food, as well as unlimited drinks and a dessert, for only AR$15. Though the cafeteria's floor tiles are cracking and the buffet lacks variety, the food is still decent and is a good bargain value for the price. Open daily for lunch. AmEx/MC/V. ❶

**California Burrito Company,** Lavalle 441 (☎4328 3056; www.californiaburritoco.com), between San Martín and Reconquista. Ⓢ Lavalle or Florida. Known to regulars as CBC, this joint is renowned for tasty beef and chicken burritos, accompanied by tacos or salad. Tu 2-for-1 margaritas. *Menú* AR$17-26. Open M-F noon-11pm. Cash only. ❷

**ON THE MENU**

## FRIENDSHIP OF THE DRINK

Sipping **mate** (p. 68) is a holisitc experience—it's a democratic process (everyone drinks from the same gourd), a curative ritual (*mate* is supposed to be good for your health), and it has a strict social protocol. A good rule of thumb to follow in order to not mess up the flow of the tea-passing is to watch what other people are doing and do that. If you're truly at a loss, follow these basic steps and you should be fine:

**1.** The *mate* (gourd; also called a *bomba*) is filled about ¾ with **yerba mate** (the crushed, tea-like plant) covering the **bombilla,** a metal straw with a filter planted deep within the tea. Sometimes, sugar is added lightly on top.

**2.** The **cebador** (server) fills the gourd and hands it off. Each person drinks it to the bottom (until the awesomely acceptable gurgling sound at the end), taking their time—it's impolite to hurry or interrupt anyone.

**3.** After finishing, the *mate* is handed back to the *cebador,* who refills it, and passes it back out. This process continues until the *yerba* leaves are **lavado** (washed out, have lost their flavor). When you're all *mated*-out, simply say *"Gracias,"* and you'll be skipped.

**4.** Be aware: *mate* is **very strong.** A few turns and you'll have all the caffeine you need. It's a perfect way to get wired for BA's notoriously late nightlife.

## CAFES

Cafe culture has been rooted into the fiber of this fast-moving *barrio* since day one, resulting in a huge number of highly diverse and generally great cafes of all styles of interior decor—from old-school columns and wood paneling to slick leather sofas and colored pillows.

**Confitería Ideal,** Suipacha 380 (☎5265 8069). Ⓢ Carlos Pellegrini. Established in 1912, this cavernous cafe has large columns and an intricate ceiling that give the place an old, romantic grandeur. Open tango classes are offered daily, and there are tango shows (p. 184) every evening, usually beginning somewhere between 8pm and 10:30pm. Sandwiches AR$6-17. Breakfast AR$9-15. Entrees AR$8-20. Open M-F 8am-10pm, Sa-Su 9am-9pm. AmEx/MC/V. ❶

**Cafe Richmond,** Florida 468 (☎4322 1653). Ⓢ Florida. This bright, elegant cafe is the perfect place to people-watch on Calle Florida. Maybe Borges did the same when he was a customer here. Sandwiches AR$8-25. Entrees AR$17-30. Desserts AR$6-10. Open M-Sa 7am-10pm. AmEx/MC/V: AR$15 min. ❷

**A222,** Corrientes 222, 19th fl. (☎5199 0222). Ⓢ LN Alem. It may not have the best atmosphere, and the easy-listening music in the background can get a bit grating, but this small cafe and restaurant has one thing most establishments here don't: a hell of a view. Set on the 19th floor, the large windows provide a stunning panorama of the city. The food is not really worth the prices, so you're better off coming for a glass of wine. Entrees AR$25-45. Open M-F for lunch through dinner, Sa for dinner. AmEx/MC/V. ❸

**La Americana,** Callao 83-99 (☎4371 0202). Ⓢ Callao. This large cafe resembles a commercial pizzeria, but the locals don't come here for the atmosphere—they come for the *empanadas* (AR$2.50-5). The pizza (AR$1.50-3 per slice) is also very popular. Entrees AR$16-32. Desserts AR$3.50-10. Open daily. Cash only. ❷

**La Paz,** Corrientes 1593 (☎4373 3647). Ⓢ Uruguay. Once the domain of left-wing intellectuals, this relaxed cafe is still a great place to have a political discussion or to write a revolutionary tract—though now you'll have to share space with businesspeople. It also remains one of the few places in which the smoking section is up front by the windows. Entrees AR$13-34. Desserts AR$7-14. Open daily. AmEx/MC/V. ❷

## HELADERÍAS

**Freddo,** Microcentro: Av. Corrientes and Florida; Palermo: Av. Libertador 5200, Arenales 3360; Recoleta: Puerredon 1894, Sante Fe 1600, Callao 1201, Guido 2000, Quintana 595; San Telmo: Defensa and Estados Unidos (www.

freddo.com.ar). Considered by many locals to be the best ice cream in the city, Freddo's numerous locations dish out dozens of flavors to long lines of customers who haven't been this anxious about waiting for ice cream since they were kids. Each serving (AR$8-15) comes with two flavors, though one of those should probably be their famous *dulce de leche*. ❶

# SAN TELMO

San Telmo has a good number of small, inexpensive restaurants, including several that serve only vegetarian and organic cuisine. Keep in mind that the closer you get to **Defensa** and **Plaza Dorrego,** the more likely it is that hordes of tourists will be your only company, though you shouldn't have trouble finding a table any day but Sunday, when the streets are packed for the **Feria** (p. 147).

## RESTAURANTS

**Origen,** Humberto Primo 599 (☎4362 7979). Ⓢ Independencia. Even carnivores will find it hard to resist the variety of delicious vegetarian and organic sandwiches, salads, pizzas, and pastas at this restaurant. Eat in the dining room or try one of the sidewalk tables in the summer. Try the delectable eggplant sandwiches and realize that great food that is not steak exists in Argentina. Sandwiches AR$10-20. Pastas AR$15-20. Pizzas and salads AR$16-20. Open M-Tu 9am-4pm, W-Su 9am-late. AmEx. ❶

**Mítico Sur,** Pasaje San Lorenzo 389 (☎4362 4750). Ⓢ Independencia. This rustic restaurant and wine bar serves exclusively Patagonian products and wines. The result: excellent cheese plates and fresh, well-prepared salads and tapas. The dining room is tiny, so sidle up to a small barrel table or, if you're lucky, grab one of the tables they set up outside on Su. Salads and sandwiches AR$9-18. Tapas and other entrees AR$10-30. Shared *tablas* AR$38-78. Open M-F 11am-4pm, Su 10am-8pm. AmEx/MC/V. ❷

**Señor Telmo,** Defensa 756 (☎4300 3883). Ⓢ Independencia. The location of this big, airy restaurant guarantees it a large clientele of tourists, though locals also come here for the huge variety of excellent pizzas—which some say are the best in the *barrio*—and good selection of beers (AR$4.50-13). Entrees AR$9-16. Small pizzas AR$14.50-18, large AR$25-34. Open M-Th and Su 10am-12:30am, F-Sa 10am-3am. AmEx/MC/V. ❶

**El Desnivel,** Defensa 855 (☎4300 9081). Ⓢ Independencia. Though you may be among the tourist horde in this exceptionally popular *parrilla*, rest assured that you are here for good reason: the *bife* is not the best in town, but the food is very good, especially for the rock-bottom prices. Be prepared to wait, especially on Su. Entrees AR$8-20. Open M 7:30pm-1am, Tu-Sa noon-4:30pm and 7:30pm-1am, Su noon-1am. AmEx/MC/V. ❶

**Abuela Pan,** Bolívar 707 (☎4361 4936). Ⓢ Independencia. This quiet, out-of-the-way restaurant and cafe, adorned with exposed brick walls covered with old machinery, has good food for cheap prices. Select one of the three rotating vegetarian entrees, or choose from the permanent menu, which includes omelettes, salads, and pastas. Entrees AR$15. Open M-F 8am-7pm. Cash only. ❷

**Bar Plaza Dorrego,** Defensa 1098 (☎4361 0141). Ⓢ Independencia. A *barrio* institution, this long-running bar, cafe, and restaurant occupies prime real estate right on Plaza Dorrego. Decorated with old photos and bottles, it can be a very relaxing spot to grab an excellent hamburger and beer, though on Su and weekend nights, it's bound to be packed with *Feria*-going crowds. Sandwiches and hamburgers AR$10-17. Other entrees AR$15-25. Open M-Th and Su 9am-2am, F-Su 9am-6am. AmEx/MC/V. ❷

**Parrilla 1880,** Defensa 1665 (☎4307 2746). Ⓢ San Juan. Just across from Parque Lezama, the beef at Parrilla 1880 is great and inexpensive, served in a dimly lit dining room decorated with memorabilia. Better yet, it's well removed from the tourist hordes—the crowd here is mostly local *porteños* and their families. Entrees AR$15-25. Open Tu-Su for lunch and dinner. AmEx/MC/V. ❷

F O O D

**La Manufactura Papelería,** Bolívar 1582 (☎6140 4832). [S] San Juan. A block off Parque Lezama, this small restaurant and arts venue, popular with locals, has a great setting in an old paper factory. Just as good as the unique surroundings, however, are the *porteño* cuisine and bargain prices. Arts performances include plays. Entrees AR$10-35. Open Tu-Sa for lunch and dinner. Cash only. ❷

## CAFES

Strangely, there isn't a huge abundance of cafes in this neighborhood, so most restaurants in San Telmo do double duty as coffee shops, too.

**Pride Cafe,** Balcarce 869 (☎4300 6435). [S] Independencia. Tucked away on a quiet side street, this friendly cafe draws a good number of gay men and couples among its mixed crowd. Grab a magazine and relax in the all-white interior, or at one of the tables outside on the sidewalk. Breakfast AR$6.50-12. Sandwiches AR$8.50-12. Other entrees AR$8-25. Open M-F 8am-late, Sa-Su 1pm-late. Cash only. ❷

**La Scala de San Telmo,** Pasaje Giuffra 371 (☎4362 1187; www.lascala.com.ar). [S] Independencia. Home to a beautiful theater with a number of relaxing indoor patios where you'll often see *porteños* sitting around nursing their coffees. Hosts a variety of events, including musicals, operas, jazz, and classical concerts, as well as dance events. Box office open M-F 10am-6pm, Sa-Su 5-10pm. 2

 **A-TIP-ICAL.** If you pay your restaurant or cafe bill with a credit card, you may notice something peculiar on the check—there's no place to write in the tip. Tell the waitstaff in advance how much you would like to add, or better yet, bring some cash and leave it at the table.

**El Federal,** Carlos Calvo 599 (☎4300 4313). [S] Independéncia or San Juan. At the intersection with Perú. In business since 1865, El Federal provides a peak into the city's 19th-century cafe culture, complete with blown glass lampshades and a bar area sunk into the floor. Apparently, the original customers liked to look down on the waitstaff. The menu of pizza, *picadas,* and *parrilla* is classic Argentine. Beer AR$5-8. *Tragos* AR$14-15. Open M-Th 8am-2am, F-Sa 8am-4am. AE/MC/V: AR$20 min. 2

# LA BOCA

Considering the poverty of the neighborhood and the fact that most outsiders only come in during the day, it's not surprising that Boca is not much of an eating destination. You shouldn't have trouble finding a place to eat, however, as the well-touristed streets of **Iberlucea** and **El Caminito** are lined with restaurants, though little distinguishes one from the next. We list a few establishments that merit special attention. A few blocks from here, there are a few options that serve higher quality food, but keep in mind that safety concerns make it unwise to wander any farther afield than our listed establishments.

 **SO... WHERE AM I?** We don't list any *subte* stops in Boca for a reason—there aren't any nearby. There are alternative means, though, and for each listing, we'll provide transportation guidance and some pearls of wisdom. For starters, the easiest way to get into the *barrio* is via the **86 bus from Plaza de Mayo.**

## RESTAURANTS

**La Cancha,** Brandsen 697 (☎4362 2975). Around the corner from the stadium. At this small restaurant, with its white walls and wooden tables, the focus is on the food as opposed to presentation or atmosphere. Customers choose from a variety of excellent seafood dishes, including fish and squid, or opt for the standard beef. Entrees AR$20-32. Open daily for lunch and dinner. AmEx/MC/V. ❷

**Don Carlos,** Brandsen 699 (☎4362 2433). Next door to La Cancha (p. 124). Its bright red brick walls covered with old posters and wine bottles, this Italian restaurant is one of Boca's few eateries also popular with locals. The menu is pretty standard, but there are a few highlights—the pastas, *bife,* and, in particular, the ravioli (AR$25), are delicious. Entrees AR$23-35. Open M-Sa for lunch and dinner. Cash only. ❸

**El Obrero,** Caffarena 64 (☎4362 9912). One of the *barrio's* only popular eateries away from the tourist drag, this long-running restaurant, covered with Boca Juniors memorabilia and photos of past celebrity guests, has been drawing crowds of *porteños* and tourists for years. Tango musicians will occasionally accompany the dining experience. It is, unfortunately, located in a bad area of the neighborhood, so you'll have to take a taxi here and back. Entrees AR$10-22. Open M-Sa for lunch and dinner. Cash only. ❷

# PUERTO MADERO

Most of Puerto Madero's visitors—both local and foreign—come here for one purpose: to eat. Accordingly, the warehouses and buildings on both sides of the four *Diques* are packed with restaurants and cafes, virtually all of which are guaranteed to be sleek, modern, and expensive. That these establishments demand some of the highest prices in the city, however, doesn't necessarily guarantee that they offer the best food in the city, a fact about which some locals regularly complain. Still, there are many excellent restaurants among the pricier establishments, as well as a number of cheaper places where you can get a decent meal and, even better, enjoy an excellent view of the water.

## RESTAURANTS

**▩ "i" Fresh Market,** Azucena Villaflor and Olga Cosentini, on the far side of *Dique 3* (☎5775 0330). Ⓢ Plaza de Mayo. Tucked a block back from the water, this small, refreshingly relaxed restaurant, cafe, and gourmet store has a quieter, less corporate atmosphere than some of the options in the warehouses. Choose from a variety of delicious sandwiches and salads or order a more elegant (and expensive) entree, such as poached salmon (AR$42) or caviar ravioli (AR$43). Sandwiches and salads AR$19-28. Entrees AR$38-43. Open daily 8am-midnight. AmEx/MC/V. ❸

**Donata,** Alicia Moreau de Justo 1110, at the southern end of *Dique 3* (☎4331 5400). Ⓢ Plaza de Mayo. On account of its location, this sleek, glassed-in restaurant can't avoid drawing the business suit crowd, though the high quality of its food brings in other patrons as well. Excellent international cuisine, including a wide range of seafood dishes. Entrees AR$24-90. Open daily noon-late. AmEx/MC/V. ❺

**Bice,** Alicia Moreau de Justo 192, on *Dique 4* (☎4315 6216). Ⓢ LN Alem. One of the best (and most expensive) of Puerto Madero's slew of Italian eateries, this bright restaurant decorated in yellow and brown serves every kind of pasta and pasta-seafood combination your heart could desire. Come early for one of the outdoor tables overlooking the water. Entrees AR$32-90. Open M-Th and Su noon-4pm and 7:30pm-1am, F noon-4pm and 7:30pm-1:30am, Sa noon-4pm and 7:30pm-2am. AmEx/MC/V. ❺

**Siga La Vaca,** Alicia Moreau de Justo 1714, on *Dique 1* (☎4315 6801). Ⓢ Plaza de Mayo or Independencia. In any restaurant called "Follow the Cow," you know that the focus will be on the meat—it's all about the *bife* at this all-you-can-eat *parrilla.* The meat isn't the best in town, especially for the price (AR$45-52), but you get wine and a wide variety of salads. The atmosphere is somewhat lacking, as it looks like a huge, fancy cafeteria, but you'll still be happily full. Open daily noon-late. AmEx/MC/V. ❹

F
O
O
D

**DF Mexican Restaurante,** Olga Cosentini 1611, on the far side of *Dique 2* (☎5787 4004). Ⓢ Plaza de Mayo or Independencia. For those who crave a bit of spice after partaking in the somewhat bland Argentine diet, this simple, inexpensive Mexican restaurant serves up tasty burritos, quesadillas, and other "Tex-Mex" cuisine. Entrees AR$18-60. *Menú del día* AR$20, including appetizer, entree, and drink. Open M-Th and Su noon-1am, F-Sa noon-1:30am. AmEx/MC/V. ❸

**Cabaña Las Lilas,** Alicia Moreau de Justo 516, on *Dique 4* (☎4313 1336; www.laslilas. com.ar). Ⓢ L.N. Alem. Cabaña serves up the best beef in the city, fresh from the *estancia,* but it comes at a price—roughly AR$100 per person, though a comparable meal at home would be more expensive. The wine list is so extensive, it merits its own table of contents. Beef AR$65-97. Other meats AR$64-79. Sides AR$24-29. Wine by the bottle AR$100. Open M-Th and Su noon-12:30am, F-Sa noon-1am. AmEx/V. ❺

## CAFES

▣ **Tea Connection,** Olga Cosentini 1545, on the far side of *Dique 2* (☎4312 7315). Ⓢ Plaza de Mayo or Independencia. Grab a comfy chair by the window in this popular lunchtime spot. The delicious sandwiches and salads (AR$14-28), made only from natural ingredients, complement the huge variety of teas (AR$7.50-9). You can also carry out a sandwich or salad for cheaper and eat it outside by the water. Open M-F 8am-9pm, Sa 9:30am-9:30pm, Su 10:30am-9pm. AmEx/MC/V. ❷

# RETIRO

Located just north of Microcentro, Retiro's ethnic restaurants and trendy cafes draw a massive crowd of businesspeople and tourists, as well as a fair number of the *barrio's* wealthy denizens. Accordingly, establishments here tend to be expensive, and some of them are only open on weekdays for lunch. Still, there are a good number of small, simple establishments that are more affordable, though these will almost certainly be packed during the lunch rush; it's a good idea either to get a seat early—at noon—or to make reservations in advance.

## RESTAURANTS

▣ **Filo,** San Martín 975 (☎4311 0312). Ⓢ San Martín. Always wanted to grab a meal while surrounded by virtually nude mannequins? If your answer is yes, then this popular restaurant is your place. If your head hurts after reading the extensive menu, which includes a dizzying variety of pizza, salads, panini, pastas, and other entrees, you can always take a break in the art space downstairs. Live DJ most nights. Salads and sandwiches AR$22-38. Other entrees AR$32-45. Open daily noon-2am. AmEx/MC/V. ❸

▣ **Tancat,** Paraguay 645 (☎4312 5442). Ⓢ San Martín. This lovely, intimate restaurant and bar serves Spanish cuisine, including a variety of tapas and excellent seafood. The atmosphere can be a bit frantic around lunchtime, when it may be hard to find a seat. Thanks to the red mood lighting and the quaint size, it could be a very romantic date destination. Entrees AR$15-75. Open M-Sa for lunch and dinner. AmEx/MC/V. ❹

**Club Danés,** LN Alem 1074, 12th fl. of the Danish Cultural Center (☎4312 9266). Ⓢ San Martín. Businesspeople and Danish expats who need a break from pasta and *bife* converge at this simple joint, decorated with the requisite Danish flags and sentimental pictures of Denmark. The fixed lunch *menú* (AR$23-26) includes a drink, coffee or tea, and your choice of four or five excellent and relatively authentic entrees, such as fried salmon or herring spiced with dill and caraway. If you'd like a seat by the window with excellent views of the city, reserve in advance. Open M-F for lunch. V. ❷

**El Cuartito,** Talcahuano 937 (☎4816 1758). Ⓢ Tribunales. El Cuartito is *the* place to be for pizza in Retiro. Serves up delicious slices to take away or to enjoy in the large, bright

FOOD

dining room covered with various pieces of Argentine memorabilia. Slices AR$3.50-5. Small pizzas AR$16-28, large AR$25-50. Open daily noon-late. Cash only. ❷

**MoMo,** Esmeralda 943 (☎4312 7369). Ⓢ San Martín. Choose from the many well-loved salads, pastas, and sandwiches on the inexpensive fixed daily lunch *menú* (AR$20-23, including a drink) in this small, chic restaurant that serves a laid-back clientele of businesspeople. Open M-F for lunch. Cash only. ❷

**Tramezzini,** Sante Fe 975 (☎4393 9950). Ⓢ San Martín. One of the long line of popular establishments along Sante Fe, this large restaurant serves tasty Argentine cuisine, including *bife* and a variety of pastas. Not the best place for an outdoor meal, as hordes of people are usually wandering by, but still lovely in good weather. Entrees AR$19-34. Open M-F 9am-7pm, Sa 9am-5pm. AmEx/MC/V. ❷

**Empire Thai,** Tres Sargentos 427 (☎4312 5706). Ⓢ San Martín. Tucked away on a quiet pedestrian street, this hip and popular restaurant serves Thai cuisine that is of questionable authenticity but still tasty. Come early to get a seat at one of the outdoor tables, or eat in the comfy dining room with leather booths and gold decor. Lunch entrees AR$24-28, dinner AR$25-45. Open M-F noon-late, Sa 7:30pm-late. AmEx/MC/V. ❸

## CAFES

**Petit Paris Cafe,** Santa Fe 774 (☎4312 5885). Ⓢ San Martín. This large, bright cafe has the perfect location right on the edge of Plaza San Martín. Enjoy a cup of coffee next to one of the large windows that provide excellent views of the green expanse across the street as well as the business crowds rushing by (they're probably late). Salads and pastas AR$11-25. Open daily 8am-10pm. Cash only. ❷

**Costumbres Criollas,** Libertador 308 (☎4393 3202). Ⓢ San Martín. Unlike many other cafes in the city, this small, out-of-the-way joint is a great place for drinks *and* food. Relax with a cup of coffee and choose from its beloved menu of regional cuisine, including *empanadas* (AR$2.50-3) and *tamales* (AR$7.50). Other entrees AR$11-18. Open daily 11am-4pm and 7pm-midnight. Cash only. ❶

# RECOLETA

Because it's not quite as popular or fashionable an eating destination as its neighbors, many of Recoleta's restaurants, bakeries, and cafes tend to be less expensive than Retiro's and more intimate and relaxed than Palermo's. There are, of course, a number of upscale options, particularly in the region of Recoleta that borders Palermo—an area sometimes referred to as **Barrio Norte.** It's also important to note that though the streets around the cemetery are packed with flashy restaurants, these are usually overpriced and serve mainly tourists; even just a few blocks away, establishments tend to be quieter and cheaper.

## RESTAURANTS

▩ **Sake,** Beruti 2640 (☎4822 9100). Ⓢ Pueyrredón. Located in Recoleta's upscale *Barrio Norte* region, this classy Japanese restaurant serves delicious sushi and other entrees. Tend to be full by 10:30pm, so it's a good idea to get here early or reserve in advance. Sushi and maki AR$22-36. Other entrees AR$17-46. Open daily for dinner. MC/V. ❸

**Lotos,** Córdoba 1577 (☎4812 4552). Ⓢ Callao. Right on the border with Microcentro, this bright, modern vegetarian restaurant offers a small rotating menu of salads and hot and cold vegetarian entrees, including delicious stews and tarts, all served cafeteria-style. A full meal, including entree and dessert, should only set you back AR$20-25. Entrees AR$10-17. Open M-F 11:30am-6pm, Sa 11:30am-4pm. Cash only. ❷

**Club Sirio,** Ayacucho 1496 (☎4806 5764). Ⓢ Callao. Walk up the intricate double staircase to reach this classy, beautiful restaurant with hardwood floors and wood-paneled

FOOD

walls. The buffet (M-Th AR$45, F-Sa AR$50) offers delicious versions of traditional Middle Eastern cuisine, including tabbouleh, hummus, grape leaves, and kebabs. There's even a belly dancer on weekends. Open M-Sa 8:30pm-1:30am. AmEx/MC/V. ❹

**Maria de Bambi,** Ayacucho 1821 (☎4804 9800). **S** Callao. This relaxed cafe and restaurant is well loved for its pastries and cakes. For those who can't survive on chocolate alone, it also has a variety of Argentine and Italian standbys, including lasagna and *milanesas*. Breakfast AR$6-11. Entrees AR$11-22. Open M-Sa 8am-9:30pm. AmEx/V. ❶

**Amaranta,** Junín 1559 (☎4803 9755). **S** Callao. Though just around the corner from the cemetery, this small, American-style deli still manages to avoid the tourist hordes. Grab a seat at one of the tables early in the morning for pancakes and waffles or later in the day for excellent salads and sandwiches. Free Wi-Fi. Breakfasts AR$10-18. Salads and sandwiches AR$10-17. Desserts AR$8-10. Open M-Sa 8am-8pm. Cash only. ❶

**CAN I HAVE SOME WI-FI WITH THAT, PLEASE?** Cafes in Buenos Aires have jumped aboard the information superhighway—many now provide Wi-Fi access for their patrons. If you brought your laptop with you, you should be able to find a viable hot spot as a nice alternative to *locutorios*.

**Los Maestros,** Uriburu 1305 (☎4821 4658). **S** Facultad de Medicina. Thought delicious pizza could not be had at dirt cheap prices? Los Maestros will prove you wrong. The masters of pizza here serve up mind-numbingly good, yet inexpensive, pies. Slices AR$3-5.20. Pizzas AR$9-40. Open daily for lunch and dinner. Cash only. ❶

**El Sanjuanino,** Posadas 1515 (☎4804 2909). **S** Callao. One of the cheapest restaurants near the cemetery; remarkably, most of the Italian, Argentine, and Mexican entrees served here are under AR$20. Recoleta's beautiful parks are just a few blocks away, so it's also a top-notch carry-out place. The *tamales*, in particular, are exceptional. Entrees AR$7-40. Open Tu-Su for lunch and dinner. AmEx/MC/V: AR$18 min. ❷

**Artesano,** Mansilla 2748 (☎4963 1513). **S** Pueyrredón. Located near Recoleta's border with Palermo, this cafe and restaurant is best known for its delicious, fresh-baked breads and desserts. Given its proximity, it's a great place to settle down before or after a visit to the Museo Xul Solar (p. 175). They also, somewhat randomly, offer yoga classes. Entrees AR$14-22. Open M-Sa 9am-8pm. AmEx/MC/V. ❷

**Cuatro Hojas,** Junín 1155 (☎4827 9546). **S** Facultad de Medicina. This simple, *tenedor libre* restaurant is a great option for those who are feeling very hungry. Pack in all the pasta, salad, and *bife* you can for AR$18-28. Unlike standard all-you-can-eat establishments, this place doesn't use a buffet—you just keep ordering until you're done. Sign us up. Lunch M-F AR$18, Sa AR$24, Su AR$28. Dinner M-Th and Su AR$24, F-Sa AR$28. Open daily noon-3:30pm and 8pm-12:30am. Cash only. ❷

**La Bourgogne,** Alvear Palace Hotel, Av. Alvear 1891 (☎4804 2100; www.alvearpalace. com), with an entrance on Ayacucho. **S** Callao. A discussion of Buenos Aires' restaurants that doesn't include Le Bourgogne is a bit like a dinner conversation that ignores the elephant in the room—a bright, white, glittery elephant. Located in the ritziest hotel in town, a French dinner at Le Bourgogne comes out as an AR$480-plus affair. Lunch, with a slightly less exciting and extravagant menu, is a bit more affordable, with a *prix fixe* of AR$118. Backpackers will rarely have the dough, or the duds, on hand to make the cut, but we had to mention it as a potential shoot-for-the-moon splurge. Open daily noon-3pm and 8pm-midnight. AmEx/MC/V. ❺

## CAFES

🞰 **La Biela,** Quintana 600 (☎4804 0449). **S** Callao. Founded in 1850, this popular, bright cafe just across from the cemetery is a Recoleta institution. Its beautiful patio

**FOOD**

(where menu items are slightly more expensive) is shaded by one of the neighborhood's enormous gum trees. Breakfast AR$25-48. Pastries AR$12-17. Salads and sandwiches AR$10-39. Other entrees AR$17-48. Open daily 8am-10pm. V. [3]

**Confitería La Rambla,** Posadas 1602 (☎4804 6958). [S] Callao. For a local experience without venturing too far from tourist sights, head to this beautiful cafe, popular for its sandwiches. Enjoy the elegant interior or survey the lovely surrounding architecture from the shaded sidewalk. Breakfast AR$10-30. Pastries AR$2-9. Salads and sandwiches AR$7-28. Other entrees AR$9-30. Open 9am-10pm. AmEx/MC/V: AR$30 min. [2]

**Clásica y Moderna,** Callao 892 (☎4812 8707). [S] Callao. The food here is pretty generic, but this small cafe, with exposed brick walls and dim lighting, still has a wonderfully romantic atmosphere—and serves an excellent cup of coffee (AR$5). There's a book shop in the back with a selection of English-language titles. Salads and sandwiches AR$14-23. Entrees AR$24-38. Open daily 8am-3am. AmEx/MC/V. [2]

### HELADERÍAS

**Un Altra Volta,** Recoleta: Callao and A. Pacheco de Melo, Quintana and Ayacucho, Sante Fe 1826; Belgrano: Echeverria 2302; Palermo: Av. Libertador 3060; (☎4783 4048; www.unaltravolta.com.ar). Freddo's (p. 122) main, smaller rival shuns the standard ice cream parlor look for a sleek, borderline futuristic style. What's most important, of course, is the ice cream, and they get the job done, dishing out serving after serving of heavenly gelato. And for those who can't survive on ice cream alone, Volta also serves a wide variety of mouth-watering pastries and snacks. [1]

### SHOPS

👍 **Mirta Rovagna,** Rodríguez Peña 1714 (☎4816 3215; www.mirtarovagna.com.ar). A catering agency with an alternate identity as the city's best *patisserie.* The baked delicacies aren't cheap, but they're so good, you'll have to start eating while you're walking down the street. Brownie AR$6. Bag of cookies AR$8. Open daily 10am-9pm. Additional location in Belgrano, Virrey del Pino 2615 (☎4785-2155). AmEx/MC/V. [1]

# PALERMO

If you're looking for dirt cheap nourishment, turn around. Diners don't go to Palermo to penny pinch on food—they go to eat well, although the prices are, of course, remarkably affordable. Close to 1000 cafes and restaurants compete for customers here, and the result has been an explosion of offerings that venture well beyond traditional pizza and *parrilla* fare. Even the most jaded globetrotter will have difficulty picking a place from the astounding variety. Cuisines run the gamut from Peruvian *ceviche* to Polish sauerkraut. Shockingly, you can even find vegetarian fare, though spicy food is slightly more difficult to come by. With few exceptions, restaurants maintain a uniform sleek and trendy feel (read: lounge areas of questionable comfort in the front, dining room in the back), though they rarely devolve into outright fancy. Expect to pay around AR$30-50 per person, and you can anticipate getting slammed with *cubierto* (cover charge), which will be roughly AR$3-30. But don't worry too much about prices—just get ready to eat. A lot.



## PALERMO SOHO

### RESTAURANTS

👍 **Bereber,** Armenia 1880 (☎4833 5662), on the Plaza Viejo. There's North African food fit for a king in this aqua-colored building, decorated with mosaics and vaguely Moorish flair.

Menu highlights include melt-in-your-mouth cous cous del rey (lamb in a stew of honey and chickpeas), well-spiced stuffed pumpkin with a salad of beansprouts, and a sizeable chocolate and mint parfait. Entrees AR$37-47. Desserts AR$20. Open M-W 8:30pm-close, Th-Su 12:30-4pm and 8:30pm-close. AmEx/MC/V. [4]

✎ **La Cabrera,** Cabrera 5099 (☎4831 7002), at the intersection with Thames. La Cabrera is another one of those "best beef in the city" joints, and deservedly so. Its enormous portions proved so popular that the owners opened a second location down the street at Cabrera 5127. Everything on the menu comes with side dishes, like sweet potatoes, cinnamon-infused beets, and applesauce. Incessant Celine Dion and Whitney Houston top off the experience. Entrees AR$30-60. Open T-Su 11am-close. AmEx/MC/V. [4]

✎ **Pråna,** El Salvador 5101 (☎4773 2538). [S] Plaza Italia. Several blocks from Plaza Serrano, this small vegetarian eatery serves up delicious salads, sandwiches, soups, pastas, and curries. The menu is constantly changing, but whatever you get is guaranteed to be fresh. If the veggie ravioli is on the menu, give it a whirl. Breakfast AR$7-20. Soups AR$8. Salads, sandwiches, and entrees usually AR$15-24. Open M-F 9:30am-7:30pm, Sa 11:30am-6pm. Cash only. [2]

✎ **Artemisia,** Cabrera 3877 (☎4863 4242; www.artemisiaresto.com.ar). This mainly vegetarian restaurant definitely qualifies as bohemian chic; though above ground, the whole place has the feel of a medieval refectory, albeit with modern touches. Service is a little slow, but the fish and vegetarian creations, including a *croque de calabaza* (AR$25) and a salmon ravioli (AR$35), are worth waiting for. Appetizers AR$14-19. Salads AR$18-21. Entrees AR$24-38. Open Tu-Th 8:30pm-midnight, F-Sa 8:30pm-1am. Cash only. [3]

**Bar Uriarte,** Uriarte 1572 (☎4834 6004). [S] Plaza Italia. Relaxed music and low lighting set a chill mood at this popular bar and restaurant. Serves standard Argentine fare, such as *ojo de bife* (ribeye steak; AR$42) and spinach, tomato, and onion gnocchi (AR$33), as well as more unique dishes, like stuffed figs (AR$25). Entrees AR$28-42. Desserts AR$15-21. Open daily noon-late. AmEx/MC/V. [3]

**Sarkis,** Thames 1101 (☎4772 4911). [S] Plaza Italia. This large, boisterous Armenian/Middle Eastern restaurant is packed for dinner every night. The ambience is nothing special, but the food has a deservedly high reputation. However, vegetarians should take notice: virtually every dish has meat—including the vegetables. Entrees AR$8-25. *Parrilla* AR$11-25. Desserts AR$7-13. Open daily noon-3pm and 8pm-1am. Cash only. [2]

**El Chef Iusef,** Malabia 1378 (☎4773 0450). Find Middle Eastern classics without any frou frou trappings

## KNOW YER' ARGENTINE MEATS

✎**Steak** is life in Argentina, and much like life, it can get a little complicated. Everyone needs a little advice when it comes to life, so, in turn, everyone could use some steak pointers here and there. Here's a quick guide:

1. **Bife de chorizo:** The world's best sirloin steak. Period.
2. **Bife de ojo:** Ribeye. Really, *really* good ribeye.
3. **Entraña:** Skirt steak. Same commentary as above.
4. **Lomo:** Tender tenderloin. Also look for these between slices of bread; they will destroy your conception of the sandwich.
5. **Vacio:** Flank steak, or the like.
6. **Chorizo:** Really, really good sausage, sold everywhere from street corners to fancy restaurants. Eat plain or in a bun with some light mayo. Not as gross as it sounds.
7. **Bife de angosto:** Porterhouse and strip steak. Mind-blowing.
8. **Bife de costilla:** T-bone steak. T-bone included. T-asty.
9. **Chinchulin:** Lower intestine. *Delicious* lower intestines.
10. **Cuadril:** Rump roast. Availible in both large and small cuts, but go for the gold and get the large.
11. **Matambre:** A super-thin cut of *vacio*, or flank steak, sometimes rolled and stuffed.
12. **Mollejas:** Sweetbreads.
13. **Rinones:** Kidneys.
14. **Tira de asado:** Short ribs—sometimes bones are attached, sometimes removed.

at this hidden budget gem. Serves a deliciously garlicky hummus that would keep vampires at bay—or just other people, once they smell your breath. For the price (AR$8 for 3 rounds of falafel), it's possibly the best bang-for-your-buck food Palermo has to offer. The half portions are perfectly sufficient. Starters AR$8-15. Grill AR$9-30. Open daily noon-2:30pm and 8-11:30pm. AmEx/MC/V. ❷

**Al Andalus,** Godoy Cruz 1823 (☎4832 9286; www.al-andalus.com.ar). Ⓢ Palermo. Though undeniably chic, this "Eastern fusion" restaurant manages a more relaxed and romantic atmosphere than many of its ritzier competitors. The dining room is spacious and airy—there's even a small garden out back. The menu constantly changing, but whatever is available—usually curry, cous cous, and fish—is bound to be delicious. Entrees AR$38-50. Occasional set *menú* AR$80. Open Tu-Su for dinner. AmEx/MC/V. ❹

**Gardelito,** Thames 1914 (☎4777 8338). Ⓢ Plaza Italia. Though it may not be the best *bife* in the city, Gardelito is a great value. With its simple, traditional decor, this relaxed and attentive *parrilla* serves up good quality meats as well as tasty pastas, chicken dishes, and *milanesas;* the mushroom ravioli (AR$28) is particularly good. *Parrilla* AR$10-23. Pastas and other entrees AR$12-40. Open daily for lunch and dinner. V. ❸

**HEY! WHERE'S THE BEEF?** Jet lag may not be a problem in Buenos Aires, but be ready to adjust your internal "I'm hungry" clock ahead at least a couple of hours. Argentines rarely eat dinner before 9pm, and many restaurants often don't open for dinner until at least 8pm. Consider a snack.

**Krishna,** Malabia 1833 (☎4833 4618). Ⓢ Plaza Italia. The only word for this place, complete with a disco ball, is eclectic—or maybe relaxed bohemian, whatever that means. The entrees, including soy, squash, and beet dishes, may not be exactly what you've come to expect from an "Indian" restaurant, but are nonetheless delicious. Don't miss the ginger juice (AR$5) and the Thali platter (AR$25). Entrees AR$17-25. Desserts AR$4-10. No alcohol served. Open Tu-Su for lunch and dinner. Cash only. ❷

**La Cupertina,** Cabrera 5296 (☎4777 3711). Ⓢ Palermo. The decor, with its Argentine flags and chairs with hearts cut out of the backs, can be a bit kitschy, but this small restaurant is still a great place to go for affordable, traditional Argentine food, including a variety of *locros* (stews; AR$14-19) and *empanadas* (AR$3-5); the unique zucchini *empanadota* (AR$5.50) is especially tasty. Other entrees AR$13-20. Open Tu-Su 11:30am-3:30pm and 8-11:30pm. Cash only. ❷

**Freud y Fahler,** Gurruchaga 1750 (☎4833 2153). Ⓢ Plaza Italia. Considering the name, the decor here isn't too shocking: white walls, white tablecloths, a few antique touches, and a number of psychoanalytical drawings on the walls (and on the menu). Classy and simple, the restaurant can be a splurge or a mid-priced meal (for Palermo). At dinner, the menu includes well-spiced, subtle meat, fish, and pasta dishes; the tender *pollo patagónico* (Patagonian chicken, AR$44) is phenomenal. Lunch set *menús* AR$34-48. Mains AR$40-67. Open M-Sa for lunch and dinner. AmEx/MC/V. ❹

**La Casa Polaca,** Jorge Luis Borges 2076 (☎4899 0514; www.casapolaca.com.ar), between Soler and Guatemala. Behind the dark steel gates of the Polish immigrant center, this humming basement restaurant dishes out authentic Eastern European food for reasonable prices. Eight different kinds of pierogi, healthy plates of sauerkraut and pork, and, last but not least, goulash. The only thing that's missing are drafts of Polish beer. Entrees AR$24-30. Wine by the glass AR$7. Open Tu-Sa 8pm-12:30am. Closed Jan. Reservations recommended on weekends. AmEx/MC/V. ❸

**Club Eros,** Uriarte 1609 (☎4832 1313). Founded in 1941, Club Eros is a holdover from pre-posh Palermo. The food is fine, but you're really there to ogle *porteños* in their native clime. Serves *agnelotti* (similar to ravioli) as doughy and large as *empanadas*.

*Parrilla* AR$14-16. Pastas AR$8-15. Salads AR$7. Wine by the glass AR$5. Open daily noon-3:30pm and 8:30pm-midnight. Cash only. ❷

**Parrilla,** 2476 Thames. The name pretty much says it all. An all-you-can-eat bonanza at a somewhat down-at-the-heels establishment, with appropriately fluorescent lighting and mustard colored tablecloths. Pick up your meat from the grill-man at the back, then fill your plate with side dishes as varied as sweet potatoes and egg rolls. It might not be the best food you've ever had, but for AR$14, it's a steal. On weekends, the price bumps up AR$2. Open daily 1-5pm and 8pm-12:30am. Cash only. ❶

**La Peca,** Gascón 1493 (☎4867 4280; www.lapecarestaurant.com.ar). Ⓢ Scalabrini-Ortiz or Bulnes. Wobbly tables and chairs—and some of the only beer nuts in BA—make cheerful, relaxed La Peca (the freckle) an appealing neighborhood pub. The house specialty is the *barcos* (boats)—a sandwich that really does look like a ship. M-Tu all-you-can-eat pizza AR$16 per person. Entrees AR$19-35. Appetizers AR$15-27. Mixed drinks AR$15. Tequila shots AR$6. Happy hour daily 6-9pm. Open daily 11:30pm-2:30am. ❸

**Cluny,** El Salvador 4618 (☎4831 7176; www.cluny.com.ar), between Malabia and Armenia. Ⓢ Scalabrini Ortíz. It's not a budget-friendly destination, but when in BA, you might as well take advantage of some affordable splurge opportunities. French-inspired dishes include the *risotto al azafran,* packed with shrimp and squid in a butter sauce (AR$45) and chicken stuffed with mushrooms, potatoes, and sweet potatoes with herbs, baby vegetables, and spinach (AR$42). Appetizers AR$25-32. Entrees AR$37-60. Desserts AR$17-24. Open M-Sa noon-1am. AmEx/MC/V. ❺

## CAFES

**Meridiano 58,** Jorge Luis Borges 1689 (☎4833 3443). Ⓢ Plaza Italia. Grab a comfy, leather seat inside the dining room or outside on the sidewalk for some excellent people-watching at this small cafe near Plaza Serrano. The spot is relaxing in summer with its classic BA surroundings—cobblestone streets and European-style buildings. Catch some sun while sipping on a milkshake or *licuado* (smoothie; AR$12). Sandwiches AR$10-28. Cakes and desserts AR$10-15. Open daily noon-late. AmEx/MC/V. ❷

## SHOPS

**Tikal Chocolates,** Honduras 4890 (☎4831 2242/2208; www.chocolatestikal.com). To give a box of chocolates from anywhere else somehow just wouldn't feel right. It's that good. Flavors like lemon-mint, "Tía Maria" truffle, and the ever-present *dulce de leche,* (AR$5 for 2). Bar of chocolate AR$8. Additional locations at Florida 165 and Galería Güemes. Open M-Sa 2-8pm. AmEx/MC/V. ❷

**Pekin,** Honduras 5301 (☎4833 9600). This shop does a bustling trade in late-night *empanadas.* Grab a seat at the bar or get your goodies to go. All the standard flavors, along with some exotic ones, including roquefort and garlic. *Empanadas* AR$2.50-3. Pizzas AR$15-30. Open Tu-Su 11am-midnight, F-Sa 11am-6am. Cash only. ❷

# PALERMO HOLLYWOOD

## RESTAURANTS

🍴 **Bangalore Pub & Curry House,** Humboldt 1416 (☎4779 2621). Ⓢ Palermo. Part pub, part restaurant, Bangalore is the perfect place to begin, continue, or end a night out. Serves plenty of fried pub grub and relatively cheap pitchers of beer (AR$12). Upstairs, the restaurant section serves delicious versions of Indian staples. Get here early on weekends if you want to eat upstairs. If you just want a drink, no need to worry about crowds. Beer AR$8-15. Mixed drinks AR$22-48. Entrees AR$40-58. Open M-Th and Su 6pm-3am, F-Sa 6pm-6am. Kitchen open 9pm-1:30am. Cash only. ❹

FOOD

**Oui Oui,** Nicaragua 6068 (☎4778 9614; www.ouioui.com.ar). Though a hike from just about everywhere, Oui Oui's picnic tables still burst with people during weekend brunch. The menu includes bagels with smoked salmon, scrambled eggs on brioche, and less traditional fare, like spinach crepes. Expect crowds. Entrees AR$20-25. *Menú ejecutivo* M-Th AR$28, F-Su AR$30. Open M-F 8am-8pm, Sa-Su 10am-8pm. Cash only. ❷

**Ceviche,** Costa Rica 5644 (☎4776 7373). Ⓢ Palermo. This chic seafood establishment doles out delicious versions of traditional Peruvian cuisine, including a variety of creative *ceviches* (raw seafood salad), as well as a range of fish and shellfish; try the melt-in-your-mouth *salmón rosado* with quinoa risotto. Entrees AR$34-46. Desserts AR$16-22. Open M-Sa 8pm-1am. Reservations recommended. AmEx/MC/V. ❹

**Sudestada,** Guatemala 5602 (☎4776 3777), at the intersection with Fitzroy. With the minimalist decor, food is the focus at this South Asian eatery. Though it's a bit pricey for dinner, the lunch *menú* (AR$27) is entirely affordable and delicious. Appetizers AR$18-21. Entrees AR$30-50. Desserts AR$16-18. Open M-Th noon-3:30pm and 8pm-midnight, F-Sa 8pm-1am. Reservations recommended. AmEx/V. ❹

**Green Bamboo,** Costa Rica 5802 (☎4775 7050). Ⓢ Palermo. Grab a seat on the surprisingly comfy floor, at the massive wraparound bar, or just at a regular table, and peruse the kitschy-turned-chic decor, as well as the menu. The list of creative Vietnamese dishes includes citrus and ginger chicken with rice and vegetables (AR$42) and beef tenderloin with lemongrass, black pepper, honey, and chili (AR$51). If you're worried about your wallet, just go for the heavenly dessert. Entrees AR$43-65. Desserts AR$21-26. Open M-Th and Su 8:30pm-midnight, F-Sa 8:30pm-1am. AmEx/MC/V. ❺

**Casa Felix,** Av. Dorrego (☎4555 1882; www.diegofelix.com). The five-course vegetarian *menú* at this restaurant focuses on South American ingredients that vary weekly. One of the most popular of the city's many *puertas cerradas* (closed door) restaurants—you must reserve in advance. Open Th-Sa for dinner. Cash only. ❹

 **AT HOME IN BA.** Casa Felix is just one example of the rising *puertas cerradas* (closed doors) restaurant phenomenon. These restaurants are usually just the home of the chef opened to customers looking for a more a personal dining experience. Reservations are usually strictly limited—Casa Felix, for example, only takes 12 reservations per night.

**Miranda,** Costa Rica 5602 (☎4771 4255), at the intersection with Fitzroy. Miranda might bill itself as a *parrilla,* but its real treasures are the leafy fresh salads, which come with rounds of warm squash and sunflower seeds. Expect enormous portions. Appetizers AR$6-18. Pasta AR$18-28. Salads AR$15-27. Grill AR$30-44. Wine AR$25-160. Open M-Th and Su 9am-1am, F-Sa 9am-2am. AmEx/MC/V. ❸

# LAS CAÑITAS

## RESTAURANTS

**Anden Restaurant,** Av. Santa Fe 5302 (☎4773 0707). Ⓢ Ministro Carranza. This restaurant, near the *subte* stop, retains the hustle and bustle of a railway cafe, with efficient service and patrons more likely to scarf their food than linger. The place rumbles with conversation at lunchtime, or whenever the train rolls past—it's difficult to tell the two apart. The menu is extensive, with all the basics from pork chops and fries to pasta (AR$15-30). *Café con leche* AR$6.50. Open daily, from early to late. AmEx/MC/V. ❷

**Tonno,** Arce 401 (☎4776 0360). Cozy, low-key Tonno is a cross between a bar and a coffee shop, but their real specialty is the pizza. Try the individual pies, like the classic

Argentine *fugazetta* (AR$13-25). Alternative music videos and soccer games usually play on the TV. Free Wi-Fi. Open M-F 8am-1am, Sa 10am-2am, Su noon-1am. Additional location at Thames 4400. AmEx/MC/V. ❷

**Las Cholas,** Arce 306 (☎4899 0094). A popular Las Cañitas *parrilla*, with a vaguely Mexican twist, good for a decent, affordable meal whenever those pangs of hunger strike. Crayons allow you to access your inner child (the temptation is hard to resist) while you wait for the food. Don't skip the bread—it's salty and delicious. Grill AR$20-25. Sandwiches AR$6-15. Dessert AR$8. Open daily noon-late. Cash only. ❷

**Novecento,** Báez 199 (☎4778 1900; www.bistronovecento.com), at the intersection with Arguibel. Ⓢ Ministro Carranza. Novecento, a small bistro, is not a bad restaurant—in fact, it's reputed to be one of the best ones in the city. It's just not that exciting, though it brings fancy dining formality at a relatively affordable price. Appetizers AR$20-35. Entrees AR$30-50. Open daily 12:30pm-12:30am. AmEx/MC/V. ❹

## CAFES

**Santos Sabores,** Aguilar 2104 (☎4783 3672). Ⓢ Olleros. Set in a quiet, residential area near Belgrano, this lovely, tiny cafe with patio is a great place for a relaxing afternoon break with the locals. Though the coffee is good, the focus here is definitely the tea; the menu describes the blends in detail, including the best time of day to enjoy each one. Also offers a tantalizing variety of tortes, cakes, and pies (AR$10-14). Sandwiches and salads AR$6-20. Breakfast AR$12. Open Tu-Su 8:30am-8:30pm. Cash only. ❶

# PALERMO CHICO

## RESTAURANTS

🌠 **Bella Italia Cafe-Bar,** República Árabe Siria 3330 (☎4807 5120; www.bellaitalia-gourmet.com.ar). This affordable Italian cafe rightfully makes the list of Palermo favorites. The chef adds seasonal specialties (like crepes stuffed with mushroom and ricotta, drizzled with a sweet cream sauce; AR$25), but that doesn't stop regulars from ordering their favorites without looking at the menu. The salads, as well as an Italianate tandoori chicken, are popular. Entrees AR$20-30. Open M-Sa 8pm-close. AmEx/MC/V. ❸

## CAFES

**Patricia Villobos Delicatessen,** Castex 3317 (☎4801-1867/4804-0636). A tiny hole-in-the-wall jam-packed with pastries, this branch serves as the base for a much broader catering and delivery service. Specializes in "diet" (and non-diet) sweets, but also serves baked goods, such as quiches and *empanadas*. One *cordobesito* with as much *manjar* as the cook can muster; AR$3. Open M-F 8am-10:30pm, Sa-Su 9am-10:30pm. ❶

# THE OUTER BARRIOS

## BELGRANO

### RESTAURANTS

**Los Chinos,** Av. Frederico Lacroze 2121 (☎4777 6789, 4776-0229, or 4778-9688), between 11 de Septiembre and Arribeños. Ⓢ Olleros. Set in an old mansion, Los Chinos is the place to go for tasty Chinese food, even though it's not in Chinatown. Appetizers AR$7-18. Noodles AR$9-15. Entrees AR$18-26. Open daily noon-3pm and 8pm-midnight. Closed Tu lunch. Delivery also available. AmEx/MC/V: min. AR$25. ❷

**El Pobre Luis,** Arribeños 2393 (☎4780 5847), at the intersection with Blanco Encalada. Ⓢ Juramento. This lively two-story *parrilla* was once a favorite spot of *fútbol* legend

Diego Maradona. The house specialty is the Uruguayan *pamplona de lomo,* which is meat stuffed with cheese, peppers, and ham (AR$33). *Parrilla* AR$28-45. Sides AR$10-12. Beer AR$8-10. Open M-Sa 8pm-midnight. AmEx/MC/V. ❷

**Asia Oriental,** Mendoza 1661, just past Arribeños. Ⓢ Juramento. Forget the Arribeños strip—locals say the place to eat real Chinese is a supermarket. This stand, inside one of Belgrano's bigger Chinese shops, serves heaping bowls of rice and noodles hot and ready to slurp. Entrees AR$5-14. Open Tu-Su 11am-6pm. ❶

**La Más Querida,** Echeverría 1618 (☎4788 1455). Ⓢ Juramento. The perfect pizzeria for the gourmet palate. The eponymous pizza consists of smoked salmon, mushrooms, arugula, and mozzarella. Large pizzas AR$25-35, small AR$17-25. Open Tu-Su 8pm-midnight. Delivery also available. Cash only. ❷

## SHOPS

**Lai Lai,** Arribeños 2168 (☎4780 4900). Ⓢ Juramento. This small, friendly shop stands out along the Chinatown strip for its inventive menu, with specialties like cashew shrimp. Appetizers AR$6-12. Entrees AR$22-32. Desserts AR$5-8. Beer AR$6-14. Min. consumption AR$18. Open M-F 11am-3:30pm and 8pm-midnight, Sa-Su 11am-midnight. Closed W lunch. Delivery also available. Cash only. ❸

# BALVANERA

## RESTAURANTS

**Bi Won,** Junín 548 (☎4372 1146). Ⓢ Facultad de Medicina. For those who can't make it all the way down to BA's Korean neighborhood in Parque Chacabuco, this more central restaurant, just blocks from Recoleta, is a great alternative. The classic and authentic Korean cuisine, including a variety of soups, seafood, dumplings, and stews, is very well-prepared and well-spiced; try the classic *dolsot bibim bap* (rice with beef, hot pepper, and grilled vegetables, AR$35). Can get very busy at lunch. Entrees AR$32-50. Open M-F noon-3pm and 7-11pm, Sa 8pm-midnight. Cash only. ❹

**Solo Pescado,** Anchorena 533 (☎4861 0997). Ⓢ Carlos Gardel. Hungry after a day of shopping at Abasto (p. 201)? Head across the street to this small, diner-style restaurant that serves mainly fish, but also pasta, *bife,* and chicken. A glass counter displays the variety of fish on offer, most of which can be ordered to taste, and includes a choice of sauces, from roquefort to mushroom; the salmon with *mariscos* (AR$31) is top-notch. Entrees AR$12-35. Open Tu-Sa 9am-3pm and 6-11pm, Su noon-4pm. Cash only. ❷

**El Español,** Rincón 196 (☎4951 4722). Ⓢ Pasco. Four blocks west of the Palacio del Congreso, this cafeteria-style joint, a local favorite, is a great place to get a quality, filling meal for cheap. Serves Argentine entrees, like *milanesas* and *bife,* as well as several set *menús* (AR$15-16), which include a meat dish, a pasta dish, a side, bread, and a drink. Entrees AR$7-21. Open daily 8am-4pm and 8pm-1am. AmEx/MC/V. ❶

 **HAVE A SANDWICH.** While in BA, try a lomito. It's a small piece of heaven that consists of a slice of beef, ham, cheese, lettuce, tomato, a fried egg, and mayonaise, sandwiched between two pieces of bread. All other sandwiches will forever pail in comparison once you've had this.

## CAFES

**Los Angelitos,** Rivadavia 2100 (☎4952 2320). Ⓢ Pasco. A large, historic cafe just far enough from the tourist drag to guarantee a local clientele of *porteños.* The stunning interior includes crystal chandeliers and stained-glass embellishments, as well as portraits of famous tango personalities. Also hosts nightly tango shows that are a little on the expensive side (AR$170-450), but otherwise enjoyable. Breakfast AR$22. Cakes and tortes AR$8-12. Salads and sandwiches AR$7-27. Other entrees AR$20-39. Open daily 10am-10pm. AmEx/MC/V: AR$30 min. ❸

# ALMAGRO

## RESTAURANTS

**702 de Gallo Deli Restó,** Gallo 702 (☎4861 0472). Ⓢ Carlos Gardel. This *barrio* institution serves huge, great value breakfasts and basic Italian dishes to a hungry clientele of locals and businesspeople. Breakfast AR$7-21. Sandwiches and salads AR$6-21. Pizza AR$11-41. Pastas and risottos AR$15-24. Open M-Th 9am-midnight, F 9am-2am, Sa 10am-2am, Su 6pm-midnight. MC/V. ❷

**Cantina Pierino,** Lavalle 3499 (☎4864 5715). Ⓢ Carlos Gardel. From Almagro's slew of Italian restaurants, Cantina Pierino, founded in 1909, is likely the local favorite. The decor is pretty run-of-the-mill, but the classic Italian dishes are as delicious as ever. Entrees AR$20-40. Open Tu-Sa for lunch and dinner. AmEx/V. ❸

## CAFES

**Las Violetas,** Rivadavia 3899 (☎4958 7387; www.lasvioletas.com). A relaxing oasis of a cafe in a bustling, commercial *barrio*. Waiters in tuxes deliver coffee and tea to a classy, older crowd in the beautiful, Parisian-style interior. Breakfast AR$28-31. Tortes and cakes AR$13. Sandwiches AR$12-25. Open M-F and Su 10am-11pm. AmEx/V. ❷

# BOEDO

## RESTAURANTS

**Boedo Antiguo,** José Mármol 1692 (☎4921 3500; www.boedoantiguo.com.ar). Ⓢ La Plata. A romantic, relaxed restaurant that draws local couples and families with simple entrees including pastas, chicken dishes, and *bife*. Those planning on going out afterwards, beware: the quiet live music in the background can rapidly induce sleep. Entrees AR$18-25. Open F-Sa 8pm-late. AmEx/MC/V. ❷

**San Antonio,** Av. Juan de Garay (☎4921 4118). Ⓢ Boedo. This popular joint is as straightforward as they come—cheap, delicious pizzas in the usual cafeteria environment. Slices AR$2-4.50. Pizzas AR$13-40. Open daily 11am-midnight. Cash only. ❶

## CAFES

**Cafe Margot,** Boedo 857 (☎4957 0001). Ⓢ Boedo. Founded in 1904, Cafe Margot, one of the original bohemian haunts in Boedo, is in the middle of a comeback. A newer, younger crowd carries on the left-leaning tradition over coffee, beer, and inexpensive food. Snacks AR$3-9. Sandwiches AR$6-19. Salads AR$14. Pizzas AR$9-13. Other entrees AR$11-40. Beer AR$8-12. Mixed drinks AR$12-15. Open M-Th and Su 7am-2am, F-Sa 7am-4am. MC/V. AR$20 min. ❷

**Pan y Arte,** Av. Boedo 876-880 (☎4957 6922). Ⓢ Boedo. A lovely cafe which, with its comfy couches, and requisite art exhibitions on the walls, is a wonderful cross between modern and rustic. Also home to a small theater that hosts modern productions on weekends (p. 190). Salads and sandwiches AR$9-22. Other entrees AR$20-40. Free Wi-Fi. Open M-Sa 9am-late. AmEx/MC/V. ❸

# CHACARITA

## RESTAURANTS

▨ **Verde Llama,** Jorge Newbery 3623 (☎4554 7467), between Charlone and Roseti. **S** Federico Lacroze or Olleros. After the umpteenth night of beef and Quilmes, Verde Llama's raw-food selections hit you with a shot of healthy living. Devour pizzas, spinach fettuccini, wraps, and salads, while washing it all down with a citrus-ginger *licuado*. Try the salad with radishes, sunflower seeds, and blueberry mousse. Cooking classes also available. Appetizers AR$10-15. Entrees AR$18-25. Open daily for lunch, Th-Sa for dinner. Additional branch at Av. Santa Fe 1670, *Barrio Norte*. Open 11am-8pm. ❷

**Gambrinus,** Av. Frederico Lacroze 3779 (☎4553 2139). Waiters in tuxes and Art Nouveau lamps give Gambrinus a classic old school feel. The menu is standard Argentine fare (meat and pasta), with the exception of fish, which is unusually well-represented and far cheaper than at other places. Nonetheless, you'd think a restaurant named for the "patron saint of beer" would offer a more extensive selection of brews. Open daily noon-3:30pm, 8pm-11:30pm. AmEx/MC/V. ❸

## CAFES

**M.masamadre es con M,** Olleros 3891 (☎4554 4555). This quiet, low-key cafe on the corner of Olleros and Fraga dishes out reinvented old staples. Try the Caesar salad, which has dark meat chicken on top. Free newspapers. Salads AR$17-20. Entrees AR$23-28. Desserts AR$8-14. Wine by the bottle AR$35. Beer AR$8-15. Open M-Th and Su 9am-midnight, F-Sa, and holidays 9-1am. Cash only. ❸

# SIGHTS

Like any world city, and a national capital, at that, Buenos Aires has the usual collection of traditional sights beckoning to backpackers looking for Kodak moments to bring home—grand opera houses, beautiful palaces, tree-lined avenues, and the like. What sets BA's landmarks apart, though, is their consistent ability to surprise with neverending, uniquely Argentine quirkiness. A strangely pink presidential mansion? Check. A gigantic metal flower? They've got one. A humongous animatronic Jesus, complete with hourly resurrections? What, you've never seen one before? Mixed in are the vestiges of a distant Spanish colonial past and the city's attempts to assert its own identity in response, through streets with brightly colored homes to cemeteries larger than towns.

## MONSERRAT

Buenos Aires' historic heart, Monserrat encompasses the city's most famous sights and its most important plazas and avenues. Bounded by **Avenida de Mayo** to the north and **Avenida de Independencia** to the south, the *barrio* provides a transition from hectic **Microcentro** to bohemian **San Telmo**. There are a variety of architectural styles, flitting from 19th-century French to Art Nouveau to modern. The buildings lining the blocks directly south of **Plaza de Mayo** and along all of Avenida de Mayo are particularly beautiful and merit a **walking tour** (p. 142). Other parts of the neighborhood, however, are in states of disrepair.

## PLAZA DE MAYO AND SURROUNDINGS

**PLAZA DE MAYO.** The Plaza de Mayo has long been a hotbed of political activity. In the 16th century, Juan de Garay (p. 54) first began mapping out Buenos Aires here in the Spanish style grid style. Later, in 1945, Eva Perón ascended to superstardom here as she rallied the masses and called for the release of her husband, Juan Perón, from prison. Massive crowds of *porteños* continued to gather in the Plaza through the late 1940s, assembling to hear the speeches of the beloved Evita and Juan. The rallies also became bombing targets for anti-Peronists. For thirty years, the Madres (see Los Madres, p. 140) protested the murders of the military dictatorship of 1976-83 during the Dirty War (p. 60). Most recently, droves of citizens banging pots and pans gathered in the square during the Argentine economic crisis in late 2001, forcing then-President Fernando de la Rúa out of office. Today, political activists still congregate in its center, and there's some kind of protest nearly every day—often attended by interested, albeit somewhat oblivious, tourists. At the center of the Plaza is a small obelisk, the **Pirámide de Mayo,** erected in 1811 in honor of the 1810 May Revolution (for which the Plaza is named; p. 55) that ultimately culminated in independence in 1816. We know—that's a lot of dates to remember, but don't worry, there's no pop quiz on any of this stuff. French sculptor Joseph Dubourdieu designed the monument, which has been renovated and moved around the square multiple times since. **Azucena Villaflor,** the founder of the Madres de la Plaza, is buried at the base of the obelisk. (Ⓢ *Plaza de Mayo.)*

**CASA DE GOBIERNO (CASA ROSADA).** At the Plaza's eastern end stands Buenos Aires' very pink presidential palace. Originally the city's fort, the edifice was remodeled as a palace over the course of the 18th and 19th centuries, when painting stately buildings pink was more common, and when ox blood was used to create the color. Oxes everywhere, breathe a sigh of relief: we're pretty sure that blood isn't used for new coats of paint today. So why pink? Some maintain that President Domingo Faustino Sarmiento (p. 57), the fellow who named it Casa Rosada in the first place, painted it that color as a symbolic union of the country's warring political parties, the **Reds (Federalists)** and **Whites (Unitarios).** Others believe that he just liked pink, long before it was metrosexually popular. Regardless, since Sarmiento, numerous presidents and political figures, including Juan and Eva Perón, have given speeches from the building's balconies. Recently, the Casa Rosada has been opened to the public, though as of 2008, it was closed indefinitely for renovation; the building's small **museum** (p. 171), however, remains open. *([S] Plaza de Mayo.)*

**CABILDO.** Across from the Casa Rosada, the 18th-century Cabildo is the only remaining building of its period in Monserrat. Construction started in 1725, but went through various stages of remodeling and further construction until 1810. Surrounded by more imposing buildings, it seems out of place, though the contrast is an interesting sight to behold. Originally extending the length of the Plaza de Mayo, the Cabildo housed the city council and city jail from its establishment until 1822. Today, the interior holds a small **museum** (p. 171). Parts of the original structure were demolished twice in the name of progress, most recently in the 1880s when the Avenida de Mayo was widened after the example of Paris' grand avenue, Champs d'Élysées. Oh, BA—eternally attempting to be like Paris, and succeeding in doing so. *([S] Plaza de Mayo.)*

**CATEDRAL METROPOLITANA.** Though it's not the most beautiful in Buenos Aires, this cathedral, BA's main Catholic church, is nevertheless an imposing and important historical sight. While a church has occupied this spot since the 16th century, the cathedral in its current incarnation was not completed until 1827. The building is a smorgasbord of different architectural styles. Some of the interior details are Baroque and rococo, while the distinctive feature of the exterior is its massive Neoclassical facade. Though the interior shows a few signs of wear, the intricate silver-plated altar is worth a look, as is the **tomb** of Argentine independence superhero **General José de San Martín,** which is guarded by statues representing Argentina, Peru, and Chile. Though the general died in exile in Europe in 1850, his body was

### THE LOCAL STORY

## LOS MADRES

Every visitor to BA will stop at the **Plaza de Mayo** expecting the shockingly pink facade of the **Casa Rosada**—but not, perhaps, the hordes of protestors. Practically every day, a different group arrives, setting up huge placards in the very center of the square. For nearly thirty years, the most well-known protest group in the square was *Los Madres de la Plaza de Mayo.*

During the **Dirty War** of 1976-1983, the military dictatorship arrested, tortured, and executed its opponents, many of whom were young dissidents; most were kidnapped suddenly and quietly, never to be heard from again. In 1976, a few of the mothers of these dissidents started gathering in the Plaza de Mayo, ostensibly not to accuse the government of any wrongdoing, but to "request" information about the whereabouts of their loved ones.

Even after the demise of the dictatorship in 1983, the movement continued to grow as the new governments refused to investigate the former regime. Recent leaders have pledged to launch inquiries, though, and in 2006, in support of the new government, the *Madres* picked up and left. Many, however, continue to work in activism and have taken up a variety of causes. The **white headscarves** they wore have become a symbol of dissidence in Buenos Aires, sported on T-shirts and even painted on the cement at the center of the Plaza de Mayo, the epicenter of protest.

brought back to Buenos Aires in 1880. The tomb of the **Unknown Soldier of the Independence** is also nearby. *([S] Plaza de Mayo. ☎4345 3369. Open M-F 8am-7pm, Sa-Su 9am-7:30pm. Guided tours of the cathedral and crypt M-F 11am. Free.)*

## SOUTH OF PLAZA DE MAYO

Head just south of Buenos Aires' main square and you'll encounter some of the most beautiful sections of the city, complete with culturally and historically significant churches and other stone buildings. There's not much to see at **Casa Rivadavia** today (it's a parking garage), but it's where Argentina's first president, Bernardino Rivadavia, lived in the early 19th century. Sure, it's an unglamorous finish for a building of such historical significance, but extra parking is always welcome in the city center. *(Defensa 360.)* Nearby, **Casa Liniers** is simply a white, colonial-looking building where Santiago Liniers lived. He was one of the last viceroys before Argentine independence and leader of the invasion force that recaptured the city from the British in the early 19th century. *(Venezuela 469.)* Behind its imposing Neoclassical front, **Centro Nacional de la Música** holds concerts and practice rooms, but, as the facade says, it was originally the Biblioteca Nacional before it moved to the concrete mushroom cloud in Recoleta (p. 155). Borges was the director here for some time. *(México 564.)*

**COMPLEJO FRANCISCANO.** The site of a church since 1582, this large, ornate, stone complex has long been one of BA's most important cultural and religious centers. As you walk up the stone steps and through the gate, one of the city's least visited churches, the **Basílica de San Francisco,** is immediately in front of you. Built in 1726, the single long nave is lovely, if eerily quiet, with beautiful tiled floors, wooden side chapels, magnificent tapestries, and a lack of visitors; the crypt, which contains obscure Argentine patricians and politicians, can only be visited on a guided tour. Across the patio, the **Capilla de San Roque,** also built in 1726, is a smaller, if similarly Neo-Baroque, version of the basílica. Next door, the small **Museo Monseñor Fray José María Bottaro** explores the relationship between the Franciscan order and national culture, and includes a collection of religious paintings, icons, and liturgical garments in three lovely galleries.

For those who plan well in advance, one Saturday each month, the monks open up the doors of the **Convento Santa Úrsula** for a guided tour of its stone cloisters, cells, and refectory. This tour is also the only way to see the city's oldest **library,** which includes a 16th-century Bible. *(Adolfo Alsina 380. [S] Plaza de Mayo. ☎4331 0625; www.complejofranciscano.com.ar. Basílica and capilla open M-Sa 10am-6pm. Free. Museum open M-Sa 10am-5pm. AR$7, students AR$3.50. Guided tours of the basílica and crypt every hour W-Su 11am-5pm. AR$5. Guided tours of the capilla every hour W-Su noon-3pm. AR$5. Guided tours of the museum every hour W-Su 10am-4pm. Free with admission. Guided tours of the monastery and library 1st Sa of every month 5pm. AR$10.)*

**MANZANA DE LAS LUCES (BLOCK OF ENLIGHTENMENT).** They certainly set high expectations with a name like the "Block of Enlightenment." Since this small slice of the city is the historical center of culture and learning in Buenos Aires, consider the expectations met. The Block of Enlightenment was originally the domain of the Jesuits, who founded the city's oldest church, **Iglesia San Ignacio,** here in the mid-17th century. Since then, the block has hosted a variety of educational and political institutions, most recently part of the Universidad de Buenos Aires. On account of numerous reconstructions and remodelings, however, only pieces of many of the original buildings remain, including just one of San Ignacio's cloisters. If you want to get inside the block's massive walls, you'll have to take one of the **guided tours,** which visit a few original halls, a reconstruction of Buenos Aires' first legislature, and a small section of a tunnel system that once connected the churches. You won't get to see a whole lot,

**TIME:** Roughly 3-4 hours.
**SEASON:** Year-round.

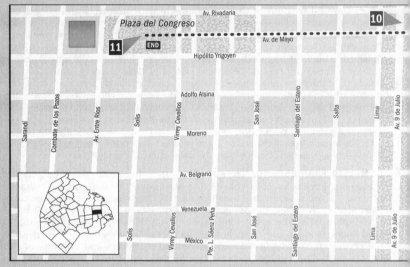

# THE HISTORY TEXTBOOK

**1.** Begin at the center of the **Plaza de Mayo** (p. 139), where Buenos Aires was founded in the 16th century. You won't be able to miss the bright pink **Presidential Palace,** or **Casa Rosada,** at the eastern end of the Plaza, the epicenter of virtually every famous protest and speech in Argentine history. Continue counter-clockwise around the Plaza to the **Catedral Metropolitana.** Duck inside for a peek at the beautiful altar and the tomb of **San Martín,** Argentina's independence hero. Just across from the cathedral, check out the stark white **Cabildo** (p. 140), the seat of the Argentine government from the 16th century until 1822, and one of the only colonial buildings left in this part of the city. If you choose, pop into the **museum** (p. 171), which isn't particularly interesting, but it's the only way to get inside the walls.

**2.** Continue around the plaza for one block and turn right on Defensa to enter the historic district south of the **Plaza de Mayo** (p. 141). After one block, at Defensa's corner with Alsina, on your right will be the **Complejo Franciscano,** which houses one of the city's oldest churches, the tranquil, beautiful **Basílica Franciscano,** as well as the city's oldest library. Continue down Defensa for another block, and, if you're up for history of a different sort, dodge a half block left to Moreno 350 for the excellent **Museo Etnográfico** (p. 171). Back on Defensa, a half block south on the left, is the **Casa Rivadavia,** the home of the first president of Argentina. There really isn't anything to see except a plaque.

**3.** Continue for another half block to the intersection with Belgrano, where there's the imposing stone **Basílica de Santo Domingo** (p. 144), still marred by shrapnel from the British invasions. The building also houses the gigantic **mausoleum of General Belgrano.**

**4.** Continue one block more along Defensa, then turn right on Venezuela. Three-quarters of a block down, on the right, you'll see the plain white walls of the **Casa Liniers** (p. 141), the home of the one of the last Viceroys, **Santiago de Liniers.** Now it's the **Estrada Editorial.**

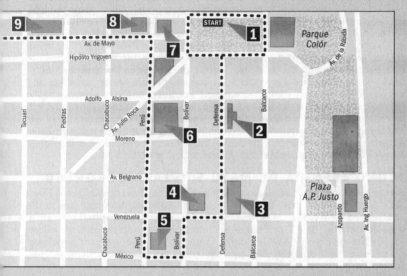

**5.** Hang an immediate left on Bolívar, and after one block, turn right on Mexico. Three-quarters of a block down on the left is the stunning and imposing Neoclassical façade of the former **Biblioteca Nacional** (before it was moved to the awful concrete-mushroom-cloud in Recoleta). Borges was once a director here, and it's now the **Centro Nacional de la Música** (p. 141).

**6.** Take an immediate right on Perú, and on your right, after three blocks, you'll see the **Manzana de Las Luces** (p. 141), the center of culture and learning in Buenos Aires for several centuries. The only way to get inside, though, is to take one of the tours.

**7.** Continue north on Perú until Av. de Mayo. Cross the street and take a right to number 575, one-quarter of a block down, the former headquarters of **La Prensa** (p. 144), one of the city's major newspapers during the 19th century. The building is now owned by the government.

**8.** Turn around and head west on Av. de Mayo. If you choose, pay the AR$0.90 necessary to enter the **Perú Station,** which has been recreated in early 20th-century style.

**9.** At number 878 is **Cafe Tortoni** (p. 120), one of the city's most beautiful and historic cafes. If you're willing to wait in line, grab a cup of coffee, or, alternatively, head next door for the history of tango at the **Museo Mundial del Tango** (p. 171) at 833.

**10.** A few blocks later down Av. de Mayo, you'll cross the massive **Avenida 9 de Julio.** Unless you're Superman, you won't be able to cross it in one go—pause at the central traffic island for an excellent view of the **Obelisco** (p. 146), the city's number one phallic symbol.

**11.** Continue to the end of Av. de Mayo, cross the numerous green plazas, and you'll end up at the **Plaza del Congreso** (p. 144), home to the **Palacio del Congreso,** the seat of both houses of the Argentine government. There will likely be many protestors here, as usual in Argentina.

but the Spanish-language tours are still packed with information. *(Perú 272.* **S** *Perú or Bolívar.* ☎ *4342 3964. Guided 1hr. tours M-F 3pm, Sa-Su 3, 4:30, and 6pm. AR$5.)*

**BASÍLICA DE SANTO DOMINGO.** At the corner of Belgrano and Venezuela is the striking 18th-century Basílica de Santo Domingo, also called the Basílica de Nuestra Señora del Rosario. The facade boasts little decoration, though replicated shrapnel on the eastern tower serves as a reminder of attacks on the British, who took the cathedral in 1806. For more on what they were doing there, see p. 55. A small accompanying museum, the **Museo de la Basílica del Rosario,** displays some relics of the conflict, including captured British flags. The building was put under siege again in 1955 and was partially gutted by fire during the military uprising that deposed Juan Perón, the **Revolución Libertadora.** Conflict aside, the basílica also served as a secularized natural history museum and astronomy observatory during the early 19th century, only to be returned to the Dominican order a few decades later. Step outside into the courtyard and it will be difficult to miss the massive **tomb of General Manuel Belgrano,** creator of the Argentine flag and an important commander during the independence struggle. At the time of publication, the basílica's ornate interior was closed to the public for renovation. *(Belgrano and Defensa.* **S** *Plaza de Mayo.* ☎ *4331 1668.)*

# ALONG AVENIDA DE MAYO TO PLAZA CONGRESO

Avenida de Mayo, the cafe-lined axis that connects Plaza de Mayo and Plaza del Congreso to the west, is one of the most important thoroughfares in the city. Named for the 1810 May Revolution, the avenue was inspired by equivalents across the Atlantic in Europe, such as Madrid's Gran Vía and, of course, Paris' Champs-Élysées. The buildings, largely in Neo-Baroque and Neoclassical style, are appropriately European in spirit, too. One distinctive example, **La Prensa,** a gorgeous, massive ornate building with wrought-iron lamps, doors, and stone carvings, was once the headquarters of the prominent newspaper of the same name. It's a government building today. *(Av. de Mayo 575.)* Another standout is the Art Nouveau **Cafe Tortoni,** one of the city's most famous spots for coffee, tea, and relaxation (p. 120) and a magnet for tourists and locals strolling along the Avenida de Mayo strip. *(Av. de Mayo 829.)*

**PLAZA DEL CONGRESO.** At the very western edge of Monserrat, Avenida de Mayo terminates at the Plaza del Congreso, a long, grassy square that hosts a playground and a variety of monuments, pigeons, and tourists. At the heart of the Plaza is the **Monumento a los dos Congresos,** a large, statue-covered monument erected for the founding of the Republic of Argentina. Inspired by the Capitol Building in Washington, D.C. and completed in 1906 after eight years of construction, the classical **Palacio del Congreso,** which looms over the Plaza and sports an 85m green dome, is headquarters for Argentina's legislative branch, the **Congreso de la Nación Argentina.** The bicameral body is divided into the 72-member Senate and the 257-seat Argentine Chamber of Deputies. For those interested in the workings of Argentine politics, guided English-language **tours** visit the building's upper and lower chambers. *(Hipólito Yrigoyen 1846.* **S** *Sáenz Peña. Tours M-Tu and Th-F 11am and 4pm. Free.)*

**PALACIO BAROLO.** Halfway between the Casa Rosada and Congreso, this eclectic, 22-story office building is an homage to Dante's *Divine Comedy* designed by Italian architect **Mario Palanti.** Textile magnate and Freemason **Luis Barolo** commissioned the building in 1918 to house the remains of Dante. With the carnage of WWI still raging, he hoped to transport the poet's remains across the ocean for safe-keeping. And what better place than Buenos Aires? Unsurprisingly, the Italian government put a wrench in the works of that plan, but the building itself, the tallest in Latin America upon completion, renders quite adequate—and elaborate—homage to Dante's epic masterpiece. Its height, in meters, corresponds to the number of verses in the poem, the rows of 11 windows allude to the 11 lines in each verse (there can also be 22 in some verses, which explains the number of stories). Ever wondered what **Hell** looks like? Stepping into the ground floor of the building gives you a glimpse of the burning abyss in a surprisingly white and cathedral-like approach, though there are ◼dragons grinning down from the sides and the floor tiles resemble flames. The nine domes represent the nine areas of Hell (they really took this whole Dantesque homage thing quite seriously) and the colors—red, white, and green—honor the Italian flag. It comes as no surprise that the offices in **Heaven** (floors 15-22, capped off with a shining lighthouse; God, anyone?) come with more prestige than those in **Purgatory** (floors 1-14), which have a decidedly blah view. Barolo himself had offices on the first two floors, connected by a secret elevator. The top provides great views of Congreso and the Av. de Mayo below. *(Av. de Mayo 1370.* S *Saez Peña.* ☎ *4383 1063; www.pbarolo.com. ar. Guided tours M and Th 2pm; includes a visit to the top of the building. AR$20.)*

# MICROCENTRO

At once hectic, chaotic, and thrilling, Buenos Aires' business district buzzes with astounding energy. Tourists, businesspeople, and shoppers crowd along its often narrow avenues, vying with the continual stream of traffic for walking space. Just north of **Plaza de Mayo** in Microcentro's southeastern half lies **La City,** the city's banking and financial district, once known as **Barrio Inglés** for the numerous British immigrants who set up shop there. If you manage to look up, you'll notice the beautiful, intricate, and imposing facades of some of the city's oldest banks and financial institutions. To the west of La City runs **Calle Florida,** a crowded pedestrian street that is also a popular tourist shopping area. Located even farther west, the enormous **Avenida 9 de Julio** bisects Microcentro. At its intersection with **Avenida Corrientes,** the *barrio's* east-west artery, stands the **Obelisco,** which commemorates the city's multiple foundings, its christening, and its declaration as capital.

## LA CITY AND SURROUNDINGS

### GALERÍAS PACÍFICO. The designers of this huge shopping center envisioned a grand artcade modeled on Paris' Bon Marché department store. They succeeded. Begun in 1889, the glitzy complex includes relaxing, modern cafes and upscale stores with intricate facades, not to mention a great place to escape the heat. Spread throughout the shopping center are numerous colorful murals, painted in both modern and classical styles. On the ground floor is the **Centro Cultural Borges,** which has a space for photography and modern art exhibitions and offers both tango shows and lessons. *(On the 700 block of Florida.* S *Florida.* ☎ *5555 5110. Open M-Sa 10am-9pm, Su noon-9pm. 30min. guided tours twice daily. Free.)*

### CORREO CENTRAL (MAIN POST OFFICE). Modeled on New York City's post office, the James A. Farley Building, construction on this imposing, intricately carved stone edifice started in the early 20th century. Its grand steps overlook a large grassy square, while inside, beautifully maintained wooden furnishings sweep up to the vaulted ceiling high overhead. In the front entryway, there's a small museum (closed at publication) dedicated to the post in Argentina. As of March 2008, the building is closed for renovation and will not reopen until 2011. The main branch of the postal service has since been moved to a new location (p. 99) a few blocks away. *(Sarmiento 151.* S *LN Alem.)*

**CONVENTO DE SAN RAMÓN.** Though the white arcades of this small convent are themselves attractive, the main draw of the complex is the lovely courtyard at its heart. In the early afternoon, *porteños* converge here to sit, chat, or eat lunch among the manicured paths, trees, and flowers—one the few patches of green in Microcentro's concrete jungle. On your way out, be sure to drop by the beautiful **Basílica de Nuestra Señora de la Merced** next door and glance up at the towering **Banco Francés** building—not that you'll be able to miss it. *(Reconquista 269. [S] Florida or LN Alem. Open M-F 10:30am-5pm. Guided tours Th 4pm. Free.)*

## PLAZA LAVALLE AND SURROUNDINGS

Just west of Avenida 9 de Julio lies the beautiful **Plaza Lavalle,** a three-block long park dotted with trees. With so many fewer tourists than the Plaza de Mayo, it's a great place to relax. At its southern end stands the imposing Neoclassical Supreme Court building, or **Justicia,** with which the Plaza is often associated.

**SINAGOGA CENTRAL DE LA CONGREGACIÓN ISRAELITA DE LA REPÚBLICA ARGENTINA.** The center of Judaism in Argentina, this synagogue is also one of the country's oldest and most active. The beautiful carved facade gives way to an even more stunning sanctuary, decorated with gilt detailing, stained glass windows, and brasswork. There's also a **museum,** with a small but high-quality collection of artifacts, as well as photos and records of Argentina's Jewish community. Unless you come for a service, the only way to visit the building is with a guided tour. Security is very, very strict, so be prepared to show your passport and answer questions about your background and reasons for visiting. The synagogue also distributes a **kosher map** of Buenos Aires. *(Libertad 785. [S] Tribunales. ☎4123 0102. Guided English- and Spanish-language tours Tu and Th 3-5:30pm; call ahead for tours in German, French, or Hebrew. AR$15.)*

**TEATRO COLÓN.** The country's main performance center, Teatro Colón occupies a beautiful, seven-story Italian Renaissance building at the eastern end of Plaza Lavalle. Since it opened in 1908, it has been one of the world's major venues for opera, ballet, and classical music, and many of the "greats" have performed here, including **Callas, Nijinsky,** and **Rubinstein.** Highlights of the interior include the **entrance hall,** adorned in marble and stucco and capped off with a dome, and the magnificent mirrored and gilded **Salón Dorado** (Golden Hall), a venue used for small concerts and lectures that closely resembles the halls of Versailles in France. The traditional horseshoe-shaped **auditorium,** with a capacity of nearly 3000 and world-renowned acoustics, has three tiers of seats rising to a domed ceiling complete with an enormous bronze chandelier that surely makes spectators below somewhat nervous. The dome itself, decorated with frescoes of dancers and musicians, was painted by Argentine artist **Raúl Soldi.** The theater was closed in 2006 for renovations with a planned reopening on May 25, 2008 to celebrate the opera house's centennial with a performance of Verdi's *Aïda*, the first production that was staged there. However, construction delays have pushed back the reopening to sometime in 2010. At that time, the theater will resume its **guided backstage tours,** which visit the costume and set workshops as well as the rehearsal and dressing rooms. *(Libertad 621. [S] Tribunales. ☎4378 7344; www.teatrocolon.org.ar.* *See p. 184 for box office information.)*

**OBELISCO.** Technically called the **Obelisco de Buenos Aires,** this obelisk sits in the **Plaza de la República** at the intersection of Avenida Corrientes, the mammoth Avenida 9 de Julio, and Roque Saenz Peña. Erected in 1936 in honor of the city's 400th anniversary, and to mark the spot where the Argentine flag was first flown, the monument was quickly weighted with political baggage. Its initial construction was pushed through in 31 days to forestall the building of a monument meant to honor the populist **Hipólito Yrigoyen** (p. 58)—like many of Argentina's other famous figures, he was commemorated with a nearby street name instead. In the 1970s, at the beginning of the **Dirty War,** a giant sign urging drivers to cut down on the use of horns gave a mal á propos warning, *"el silencio es salud"* ("silence is health"). Apparently, the military dictatorship did not realize that the sign also carried a negative connotation of censorship. The obelisk is also the center of many celebrations in the city, including rallies following wins for the Argentine national soccer team. Despite these moments, though, it seems pretty clear what the long white column represents. Shortly after the monument was built, feminist groups called for it to be chopped in half, saying they found the masculine symbol oppressive. In 2005, the entire shaft was wreathed in a giant pink condom in honor of World AIDS Day. *([S] 9 de Julio, Carlos Pellegrini, or Diagonal Norte.)*

## SAN TELMO

Though located only 10 minutes' walk from Microcentro, San Telmo seems years away—around 140 years, to be exact. Once the city's upper-class district, most of its original denizens left in 1871 to escape a **yellow fever epidemic.** Soon after, newly arrived immigrants and laborers moved into the abandoned mansions and converted them into tenements, giving the *barrio* a new, working-class character that later made it popular among bohemians, artists, and students. Since the change in ownership, little has been changed architecturally, and this results in a strange and strangely compelling mix. The vibe of the neighborhood is uneven, to say the least. Some of the streets are beautiful, adorable even, and have great atmosphere, while other areas have become so industrial and covered with graffiti that they're just plain ugly. The *barrio* remains functional, though, and the decaying, grand mansions lining the cobblestone streets house a range of shops and restaurants. San Telmo's new popularity among tourists is finally bringing about some changes, including the arrival of high-end boutiques, the restoration of some of the mansions, and a general increase in prices. These effects are most apparent along **Defensa,** the *barrio*'s main north-south artery, and around **Plaza Dorrego,** its central square at the intersection of Defensa and **Humberto Primo.** Though most days the area is pleasantly quiet, Sundays bring a deluge of tourists and locals for the very popular (and very enjoyable) weekly **feria,** or flea market, which centers on Plaza Dorrego and spills out into the surrounding streets.

**✓PLAZA DORREGO AND THE FERIA.** Surrounded by antique shops, bars, and restaurants, Plaza Dorrego is the center of action in San Telmo. Most days, it hosts a variety of artisans peddling their wares around the tables set up by nearby restaurants. Klezmer and tango bands will occasionally set up shop, while at other times, the square will be filled with the sound of a solitary guitarist strumming everything from Bob Dylan to Sublime. The Plaza is best known, however, as the focus of the boisterous **✓Feria de San Telmo.** Every Sunday, the surrounding streets are blocked to traffic to make way for numerous street musicians and stalls, which start setting up around mid-morning and sell everything from souvenirs and T-shirts to local art, antiques, and old costume jewelry. Given its popularity with both locals and tourists, prices here are not particularly low, but almost everyone will find something unique to take home. At around 5pm, the stalls in the Plaza itself are torn down to make way for an informal **milonga.** Things start off with old *porteños* dressed to the nines and younger ones flashing their moves, but if you wait and watch long enough, it's likely that professional dancers will show up at some point to strut their stuff, a great way to catch a high-quality tango show for **free.** *([S] Independencia.)*

**IGLESIA DE SAN PEDRO TELMO.** Just a block from Plaza Dorrego lies the lovely, ornate, blue-and-white facade of the Iglesia de San Pedro Telmo, founded by the Jesuits in 1734. Some parts of the church's interior shows signs of wear, but the numerous gilded altars are certainly worth a look. To the left, just before the entrance, is a one-room **museum** devoted to the church's history. The collection of relics, paintings, and documents is small, but of a very high quality. *(Humberto Primo 340. [S] Independencia. ☎4361 1168. Open Sa 10am-3pm, Su 3:30-6:30pm. Captions in Spanish. Voluntary contribution AR$2. Guided tours Su 4pm. Free.)*

**CASA MÍNIMA.** Just off Defensa, about four blocks north of Plaza Dorrego, is one of San Telmo's most appealing and well-restored streets, the **Pasaje de San Lorenzo.** Near the corner, on the right-hand side of the street, keep a sharp eye out for the Casa Mínima, which, at just over two meters wide, is Buenos Aires' narrowest building, barely accommodating a doorway and a small balcony. Liberated slaves built the house on a tiny plot given to them by their former masters. It's impossible to escape the irony of a charitable gift of land this small. You can't go inside, but there probably wouldn't be much to see anyway, given the minuscule size of the rooms. *([S] Independencia.)*

**EL ZANJÓN.** Only recently renovated, this pretty building recreates the classic San Telmo transformation of a mid-19th-century mansion into a tenement building. Guided tours visit the building's foundations, a section of the underground tunnels that once held the city's water, and a number of restored rooms. Considering the relatively high price of a tour, however, this sight may only be worthwhile for those interested in mansions turned tenements. There has to be one of you out there. *(Defensa 755. [S] Independencia. ☎4361 3002. 1hr. English-language guided tours M-F 11am-2pm. AR$30. 30min. guided tours Su 2-6pm. AR$12.)*

**PARQUE LEZAMA.** On San Telmo's border with Boca, Parque Lezama provides a great spot to relax along with the *porteños* away from the bustle of Plaza Dorrego. Though it doesn't have much in the way of grass, the palm-dotted expanse is nonetheless lovely and draws a good number of locals who come here to walk, chat, and play. At the park's northwest corner stands a large concrete monument to **Pedro de Mendoza,** who reputedly founded the city on this spot in 1536 (p. 54). Across the street from the park's northern end, at Brasil 315, the sight of the ornate facade of the **Russian Orthodox Church** among the more sedate surrounding buildings can come as quite a shock. Built in 1904 in 17th-century Muscovite style, the frescoes and onion domes of the church are wonderfully incongruous and quite beautiful, though the church itself is only open for services on Saturdays at 6pm and Sundays at 10am. *([S] San Juan.)*



## LA BOCA

Though not far south of the city center, gritty, blue-collar Boca seems miles away from the sleeker northern *barrios,* and its residents revel in their individuality, often referring to themselves as **La República de la Boca.** Once the city's main port on the **Riachuelo,** the neighborhood was settled in the 19th century mainly by Italian immigrants, who painted their houses with the leftover paint from boats, a practice that gave the *barrio* the brightly colored houses along **El Caminito** for which it is now famous—and so very popular among tourists. At times, it can feel like an amusement park. Along with its unique architecture, the neighborhood also identifies itself heavily with its resident soccer team, the **Boca Juniors,** Argentina's most famous club and another big tourist draw.

Despite the *barrio*'s popularity, visitors should be aware that it is still very poor, and should avoid wandering in quiet areas away from the main sights, as there have been a number of muggings in recent years. There is no *subte* stop in Boca; the easiest way to get here is to catch bus #86 from Plaza de Mayo, which passes right in front of the soccer stadium, or to walk from **Parque Lezama** in San Telmo along **Avenida Almirante Brown.**

 **SAFETY IN LA BOCA.** The *barrio*'s non-touristed districts can be unsafe by day and night and are best avoided. If you must travel through these areas, exercise caution or consider taking a taxi.

**LA BOMBONERA AND EL MUSEO DE LA PASIÓN BOQUENSE.** Located just a few blocks from the waterfront, the **Boca Juniors'** stadium is, in many ways, the center of the neighborhood, as well as its most important symbol. Built in 1940, La Bombonera, or "the chocolate box," seats only 40,000—a number which is shockingly small considering the team's popularity. The entire exterior is painted in the squad's colors, an equally shocking **blue and yellow.** According to the local story, the group of kids who founded the club in 1904 couldn't figure out what colors to adopt and therefore agreed to accept the colors of the flag of the next ship that entered the harbor, which turned out to be **Swedish.** If you don't make it to a game, you can also catch one of the **official stadium tours,** which visit the stands, the field, the press room, and the locker rooms, complete with hot tubs and icons of the Virgin. La Bombonera also houses a high-tech, interactive **museum** devoted to the Boca Juniors. Here, you can catch up on your stats, watch famous historic goals and footage from the team's championship matches, and get your fill of team memorabilia. Though the exhibits themselves may not be particularly fascinating to non-soccer fans, the complex's enthusiasm for both the sport and the team is infectious—and may convince you to attend a match (p. 190) after all, especially after hearing the recording of announcers screaming "goooollllllllllllllllllll" on loop. *(Brandsen 805. ☎4362 1100. Stadium and museum open daily 10am-7pm; box office closes at 6pm. Museum AR$14. Stadium tour AR$14. Combined ticket AR$22.)*

**LA VUELTA DE ROCHA AND EL CAMINITO.** On Boca's southern edge lies La Vuelta de Rocha, a small inlet of the Riachuelo that once formed the center of the *barrio*'s port. From the walkway

## TOP TEN LIST

### WAYS TO CELEBRATE YOUR SOCCER TEAM'S VICTORY

**1.** Gorge on large amounts of **beef,** and come to regret it later.

**2. Streak** from the stadium to the city center. Never mind that all stadiums are outside of the city center, or that it's illegal.

**3.** Name your **firstborn child** after the team. I mean, who doesn't want a kid named **Club Atlético San Lorenzo de Almagro?** It could be Clubby for short.

**4.** Stage a **mini-milonga** and show off your skills... or lack thereof.

**5.** Rally at the **Obelisk** (p. 46) and attempt to **scale** the monolith. After failing, say "well, that was a pretty 'Obel-risky' move there."

**6.** After pissing off your peers with the lame joke, **dart across** the **Avenida 9 de Julio,** a human game of Frogger, for the thrill of it.

**7.** Proceed to **streak** down said avenue. There are 16 lanes; surely there's room for streaking traffic.

**8.** Antagonize the **barrabranas** (hooligans) of the opposing team and, to defend yourself, stage a reenactment of the 1806-1807 **defense of the city** against the British (p. 55)... without using **burning hot oil,** which is illegal.

**9.** Head to a pick-up soccer game, claim to be **Maradona's successor,** and leap into the air and handball the ball into the net (p. 72). While leaping, say "now that's some *good air!*" (Buenos Aires is Spanish for "good air")

**10. Flee again,** following yet another lame joke gone awry.

that lines the banks, you can see a number of colorful ships (and shipwrecks) still docked here, though you may have to hold your nose while doing so; the stench this close to the river is intense. If you look to your left, you'll see the ugly iron bridges **Puente Transbordador** and **Puente Nicolás Avellaneda,** both built in the first half of the 20th century to connect Boca with the suburb of Avellaneda. Branching off diagonally from the center of La Vuelta is one of Boca's main sights, **El Caminito,** an open-air museum named after a tango song and devoted to showcasing pristine examples of Boca's colorfully painted houses. In the early 1800s, a small stream branch of the Riachuelo flowed on the site of the modern city's streets. The creek eventually dried up, and was replaced by a railroad and then an unattractive landfill and road in 1954. Then **Benito Quinquela Martín,** an artist, came along and forever changed the neighborhood from dump to tourist mecca. He painted a series of murals on daily life across the *barrio* and, per an old Genoese custom, encouraged the residents to paint their homes in bright colors using leftover paint from boats in the port. Thus, El Caminito was born. As soon as you enter the street, it becomes clear that no one actually lives here anymore. Lined with cafes offering free tango shows and, on weekends, stalls selling local artwork, the street is sometimes so packed with tourists taking pictures that it's nearly impossible to see the buildings themselves. Depending on your tastes, El Caminito can either be a fun place for a stroll and a meal, or the biggest tourist trap in the city.

# PUERTO MADERO

Occupying a thin strip of land east of the city center, Buenos Aires' newest *barrio* is also one of its ritziest. Originally developed in the 1880s to replace Boca as the city's main port, Puerto Madero quickly proved too small to handle the city's massive cargo traffic and had to be abandoned just 10 years after completion. The new port, Puerto Nuevo, was built farther north up the river in Retiro (p. 151). The area sat unused for decades, but in the last 20 years it has undergone a transformation. Today, real estate prices here are among the highest in the city, and the converted warehouses and developments that surround the four *diques* (docks) at its center are packed with sleek and expensive restaurants and lofts. **Puerto Madero Este,** located east of the docks, is undergoing even more massive development, and new high-rise apartment and office buildings are continually being added. Though a bit corporate, the *barrio* is great place to wander, if only for the sense of space lacking in many other crowded parts of the city and the mercifully stench-free waterfront walkways.

**🖾RESERVA ECOLÓGICA COSTANERA SUR.** Less than a mile from the city center lies one of Puerto Madero's most surprising sights: a fully protected ecological reserve right on the banks of the Río de la Plata. Though this small area of land had long been clear of wildlife, a landfill once located here was abandoned in the early 1980s, leaving Mother Nature to her own devices. A wide variety of plants and animals, particularly waterfowl, quickly took over, and the area was declared a reserve in 1986. Now the several well-maintained **trails** that wind through the expanse of marshy grassland provide hikers and bikers with an excellent escape from the noise, pollution, and frantic pace of the city—you can see skyscrapers nearby, but they seem a world away. Neither of the reserve's two entrances are particularly convenient or served by public transportation, but it's not too difficult to walk here. The **northern entrance** is located east of *Dique 4.* To get to the **southern entrance,** the more easily accessible one, walk down Vera Peñazola, the eastern extension of Estados Unidos, wedged between *Diques 1* and *2,* and keep heading east for 1km. On some, unpredictable days, the trails are closed to bikers—call ahead for more information. *(Reserve office Tristán Achával Rodríguez 1550. ☎ 4315 1320/4129. Open Tu-Su Apr.-Oct. 8am-6pm, Nov.-Mar. 8am-7pm. Guided tours Sa-Sa 10:30am and 4pm. Free.)*

**PUENTA DE LA MUJER (WOMEN'S BRIDGE).** This beautiful, modern pedestrian bridge, which spans *Dique 3*, was designed by **Santiago Calatrava** and unveiled in 2001. The span is in a characteristic Calatrava bridge style, technically referred to as a **cantilever spar cable-stayed bridge.** We'll put on our architect hat and try to explain it for you: the bridge has a single, tall beam on one end from which several support cables run. Most cable-stayed bridges have two beams on each end, so this crossing seems to defy gravity. With its phallic, solitary point jutting up into the air, it can be a fun game to try and guess why the bridge has its name; it looks more like an unfinished harp to us.

# RETIRO

Once the retreat, or *retiro*, of a hermit, monks, and, later, a Spanish governor, Retiro has become one of Buenos Aires' wealthiest and most beautiful *barrios*. At the beginning of the 20th century, the city's most influential, richest families began building lavish, Parisian-style palaces here, several of which are open to the public. Today, these grand edifices rub shoulders with ritzy hotels, upscale apartment buildings, and expensive restaurants, most of which are around the lovely **Plaza San Martín**, located just a few blocks north of Microcentro. Nearby are the decaying **Estación Retiro**, the city's main train station, and the main bus terminal, **Terminal de Omnibus.** Though the neighborhood's relaxing squares and grand architecture make it a great place for aimless wandering, the area north of the stations has long held a dangerous shantytown that is best avoided.

## PLAZA SAN MARTÍN AND SURROUNDINGS

The heart of Retiro, beautiful Plaza San Martín draws tourists and *porteños* to its palm tree-shaded paths and grassy expanses for relaxing strolls, romantic rendezvous, and picnics. Designed, like everything else in the city, by **Carlos Thays** (p. 157), the Plaza focuses on a bronze equestrian statue of **General José de San Martín,** the liberator, Argentina's most important independence hero. Downhill, on the northern side of the Plaza, is the less obtrusive **Monumento a los Héroes de las Malvinas,** a monument dedicated to the soldiers who died in the Falklands War against Britain (p. 60). For **Jorge Luis Borges** fanatics, just a block from the park's southern side, at Maipú 974, is the author's **last residence,** though there isn't much to see; look for a commemorativeplaque on the wall of the nondescript apartment building. (**S** *San Martín.*)

**🖾PALACIO PAZ.** On the southern edge of the Plaza is one of BA's most spectacular palaces. Built between 1902 and 1914 for **José Paz,** a wealthy sugar baron and founder of the newspaper **La Prensa,** it would be the country's largest residence—alas, it shed its residence status long ago due to prohibitive living expense. Paz, who had been promised Argentina's presidency, wanted a grand edifice whose exterior resembled Paris' Louvre. Unfortunately, he died in 1912, before he could see the building finished or become president. By the end of the 1930s, Paz's family could no longer afford to keep the house and sold it to the **Círculo Militar,** which keeps a portion of the palace open to the public. Tours visit a selection of the palace's impressively lavish rooms, which are decorated in artistic styles ranging from breathtaking Gothic to Baroque to Empire and even include a small version of Versailles' Hall of Mirrors. The roster of ridiculously opulent rooms also includes a hunting-themed dining hall and the epic **Hall of Honor,** which is decked out in eight kinds of marble and topped off by

**THE LOCAL STORY**

### ANCHORENA WHO?

There are certain names you encounter a lot in this guide. The Peróns are a pretty big deal, as is the liberator, San Martín. So is Carlos Thays, who, apparently, designed every park and public square... ever. Then there's the **Anchorena family.**

In Buenos Aires' wealthy northern *barrios,* it's hard to miss this name, which is attached to nearly every home, palace, and church. Even decades after they lost their fortune, the one-time wealth of this Spanish family that immigrated to Argentina in the 18th century is legendary; indeed, they were likely the richest family in the country from 1860-1930.

Surprisingly enough, from this long line of rich landowners, the most recognizable name of all is **Mercedes Castellanos de Anchorena** (1840-1920), who actually married into the family in 1863. Daughter of landowner **Aaron Castellanos,** Mercedes quickly became the social matriarch of the Anchorena family, spending the family's money on lavish palaces and churches, such as the **Palacio San Martín** and the **Basílica del Santísimo Sacramento.** The progenitor of wealthy *porteño* society, Anchorena gave birth to a whopping 11 children, though only five survived childhood. The family eventually faded away, though their footprints–their very *luxurious* footprints–remain.

a large dome. The building also hosts the Círculo Militar's **Museo de Armas** (p. 174), a museum focusing on the history of weapons. *([S] San Martín. Sante Fe 750. ☎4311 1071. Guided Spanish-language tours Tu and F 11am and 3pm, W-Th 11am, 3, 4pm, Sa 11am. AR$15. Guided English-language tours Tu 4pm, Th 4:15pm. AR$25.)*

**PALACIO SAN MARTÍN.** Built between 1905 and 1909 for **Mercedes Castellanos de Anchorea,** a leading member of one of Argentina's wealthiest and most influential families, Palacio San Martín, located just off the western edge of Plaza San Martín, is not quite as impressive as Palacio Paz—but it's just as beautiful and in even better condition. When the family lost its fortune in the Great Depression, they sold the palace to the government, which now uses the building for state functions and boring offices. Fortunately, much of the palace, which is actually composed of three separate buildings joined by a grand courtyard and entryway, remains open to the public. Tours visit the extravagant interior, including a variety of massive rooms decorated with stunning draperies, stained glass, ironwork, and even some of the original furniture. There's even a small **museum** that displays a variety of pre-Columbian artifacts, though the axe heads, ceramics, and stone figures seem slightly out of place with the rest of the palace. *([S] San Martín. Arenales 761. ☎4819 8092. Tours in English and Spanish Tu and Th 2:30pm. Free.)*

**BASÍLICA DEL SANTÍSIMO SACRAMENTO AND EDIFICIO KAVANAGH.** Hidden almost completely from sight by the surrounding skyscrapers, the beautiful **Basílica del Santísimo Sacramento** was built between 1908 and 1916 by the wealthy **Mercedes Castellanos de Anchorena.** Inspired by Parisian churches, the lavish, sometimes colorful, interior incorporates several types of marble and stone as well as delicate stained glass, intricate tile floors, carved wood, and beautiful glass lighting. Though the massive marble **altarpiece** is likely the church's most captivating feature, every bit of the interior seems to be decorated; even the **crypt,** where Anchorena is entombed, is almost as lavish as the sanctuary. It's a simply stunning example of Buenos Aires architecture. *(San Martín 1039. [S] San Martín. ☎4311 0391. Open daily 6:30am-8pm. Free.)* At Florida 1065 and directly in front of the basílica is the **Edificio Kavanagh,** a concrete, Art Deco eyesore built by **Corina Kavanagh,** a wealthy rival of Anchorena. When the fashionable residence was constructed in 1935, it was the tallest in South America. There's a little history behind the building connected to the Kavanagh-Anchorena rivalry with a *Romeo and Juliet* twist (minus the tragic deaths at the conclusion). Supposedly, back in the day, one of Corina's daughters fell in love with one of the Anchorena sons. However, the Anchorena family disapproved of the relationship. As revenge, Corina supposedly built the Edificio Kavanagh to block the Anchorena's view of the Basílica del Santísimo Sacramento from their home, **Palacio San Martín** (p. 152), on the opposite side of the Plaza. Of course, a large fence would have worked, but Kavanagh had no interest in cutting corners.

**TORRE DE LOS INGLESES.** Just north of Plaza San Martín lies the rather desolate **Plaza Fuerza Aérea Argentina** (Argentine Air Force Plaza), once known as the **Plaza Británica,** but renamed following the Falklands War with Britain. From the surrounding area it's hard to miss the Torre de Los Ingleses, a 76m-high "miniature" of London's Big Ben which stands in the middle of the Plaza and was a gift from Buenos Aires' British community in 1916. Ironically, the tower was also a target of their bombs in 1982, when the Argentine government futilely attempted to rename it. Though closed at the time of writing, it is usually possible to climb to the top of the tower, which offers excellent views of the city that fortunately overlook the trash and graffiti at the base. *([S] San Martín.)*

## RECOLETA

When a massive yellow fever epidemic struck San Telmo in the 1870s, its wealthy denizens chose Recoleta as their new home, probably because it was as far removed from San Telmo as possible. Since then, the *barrio* has remained one of Buenos Aires' most elite residential areas, its streets lined with upscale apartment buildings. Recoleta is perhaps best known for its eponymous **cemetery,** one of the city's most fascinating (and least expensive) sights. It isn't the *barrio*'s only draw; Recoleta also hosts several of the city's most impressive arts centers and museums, as well as a beautiful system of **parks.**

**[✓] LA RECOLETA CEMETERY.** Ironically, one of Buenos Aires' liveliest and most exciting sights is a place where dead people hang out. Through a set of gates, flanked by large white Neoclassical Greek columns, lies this cemetery in the heart of Recoleta. Established in the mid-19th century in the former gardens of a group of Franciscan monks known as the **Recoletos** (the root of the *barrio*'s name), the cemetery has been the final resting place for the city's rich and well-connected ever since. Walking the stone pathways is almost like looking at a map of Buenos Aires: all the Alems, Mitres, Pellegrinis, and Sarmientos of Argentine history are here and buried in style amidst the city-like network of streets. The massive, lavish, and often intricately carved tombs represent nearly every architectural period imaginable; miniature Gothic cathedrals and Neoclassical temples stand next to modernist blocks of black marble and Art Deco shrines. One of the simplest, however, belongs to the cemetery's most famous resident, **Eva Perón.** Partly due to a classism that still reigns over who makes it into the cemetery, the black tomb is only marked **"Duarte,"** Evita's maiden name, and isn't signposted. To get here, simply follow the tourist hordes, or, if they happen to be absent, follow the signs to the left of the entrance toward **President Sarmiento's** grave and continue along that avenue for four or five "blocks"; the tomb is on the left. For a more detailed tour of the plot, consider Robert Wright's color map, with highlights of tombs and mausoleums that merit special attention (AR$20). See www.urbex.com.ar for more information. *(Junín 1790. [S] Callao. ☎ 4804 7040. Open daily 7am-6pm. Guided Spanish-language tours Tu-Su 11am and 3pm. Guided English-language tours Tu and Th 11am. Free.)*

**BASÍLICA NUESTRA SEÑORA DEL PILAR.** Immediately north of the cemetery stands this elegant, bright white church, one of the few colonial buildings left in the city (the other being **Cabildo,** p. 140). Built by monks in the early 18th cen-

## La Recoleta Cemetery

| 1 | Juan Manuel de Rosas | 8 | Domingo Faustino Sarmiento | 13 | Doctor Valentín Alsina |
| 2 | Eva Duarte (Eva Perón) | 9 | Bartolomé Mitre | 14 | Juan Bautista Alberdi |
| 3 | Adolfo Alsina | 10 | José de San Martín's parents | 15 | Teniente General Julio Argentina |
| 4 | Eduardo Lunardi | 11 | Cemetery of the Three Friends | | Roca |
| 5 | Leandro N. Alem | | Adolfo Mitre | 16 | Doctor Carlos Pellegrini |
| | Hipólito Yrigoyen | | Alberto Navarro Viola | | |
| | Arturo U. Illia | | Benigno Baldomeno | | |
| 6 | José Hernández | | Lugones | | |
| 7 | Enrique Larreta | 12 | Central Jesus Christ | | |

tury, the simple exterior hides a beautiful interior lined with colorful side chapels of carved wood. Head up the stairs to the left of the sanctuary to reach the church's small **museum,** located in the monastery's original cloisters. Though the collection is quite small, it includes a wide variety of high-quality religious paintings, images, icons, embroidery, wooden carvings, and silverwork. Be sure to look out the windows for great views of the cemetery. *(Junín 1904.* S *Callao.* ☎ *4803 2209. Open M-Sa 10:30am-6:15pm, Su 2:30-6:15pm. Captions in Spanish and English. Call ahead for guided tours. Church free. Museum AR$3.)*

**PLAZA SAN MARTÍN DE TOURS AND SURROUNDINGS.** In front of the cemetery and church, a system of parks stretches north toward **Avenida Libertador** and includes Plaza San Martín de Tours, a small grassy area dominated by huge, beautifully contorted gum trees with a spectacular network of exposed roots perfect for tourist Kodak moments. Despite the flashing bulbs, *porteños* still frequent the spot. Nearby, **Plaza Francia** hosts the **Feria Artesanal** (Craft Fair) every Friday, Saturday, and Sunday, when the city's artisans set up booths along the pathways and sell a variety of arts and crafts. Though it's unlikely that you will find a masterpiece here, it's still a great place to pick up interesting souvenirs, including scores of carved *mate* gourds, leather goods, jewelry, photography, paintings, and clothing. *(*S *Callao.)*

SIGHTS

**AVENIDA ALVEAR.** Running from **Plaza San Martín de Tours** to **Plaza Carlos Pellegrini** in Retiro, Avenida Alvear is one of the city's ritziest streets. Lined with upscale hotels, apartment buildings, art galleries, and stores such as Louis Vuitton and Cartier, it's a great place to shop—for the select few who can afford it. For everyone else, it's still a fine place to wander and watch said wealthy people as you stroll past early 20th-century palaces and **Plaza Carlos Pellegrini.** On the corner with **Ayacucho,** keep an eye out for the **Alvear Palace,** an Art Deco building that is now an exclusive hotel. Farther along, on the corner with **Rodríguez Peña** stands the **Palacio Hume,** a monstrous Art Nouveau creation built for engineer **Alexander Hume.** Located just next door, the French-inspired **Palacio Duhau** was built for the wealthy Duhau family and is now another hotel. *([S] Callao.)*

**BIBLIOTECA NACIONAL.** With a collection of nearly five million books, including a 15th-century **Gutenberg Bible** and a first edition of **Don Quixote,** Argentina's Biblioteca Nacional is one of the largest libraries in Latin America. Though only opened in 1992 after 21 years of construction, the building, which resembles a geometric, concrete mushroom-cloud, is already showing some signs of wear, including cracks and stains. Unsurprisingly, the monstrosity was actually designed in the 60s, a decade after the building that once occupied its spot—the **palace** where Eva and Juan Perón lived (and where Evita died)—was razed by the government, who feared the building would become a shrine to Evita. Today, the library, which is open to the public, hosts dry exhibits showcasing the library's collections, as well as lectures by major authors. Head up to the top floor for excellent views over BA or to the cafe on the second floor for a snack. The inside, happily, is one of the few places around where you can't see the exterior of the building. The surrounding grounds and parks, officially named **Plaza del Lector** and **Plaza Evita,** feature gardens, a terrace, and statues of Eva Perón and Pope John Paul II—an odd pairing. *(Agüero 2502. [S] Facultad de Medicina. ☎4808 6000; www.bn.gov.ar. Open M-F 9am-9pm, Sa-Su noon-7pm. Free.)*

**FLORALIS GENÉRICA.** If you happen to be near the **Plaza de las Naciones Unidos,** located at the northern end of Recoleta, it's hard to miss this gigantic "generic" metal flower sculpture, designed by Argentine architect **Eduardo Catalano** to represent all flowers. Blooming daily at 8am, its petals close at sunset, though they remain open four nights a year: May 25 (anniversary of the 1810 **May Revolution,** p. 55), September 21 (the first day of spring), and December 24 and 31. The **park** around the sculpture is a pleasant enough place for a stroll any day, but the flower is at its most impressive at night, when it's bathed in bright red light. It's as beautiful as a gigantic, metallic red flower can possibly be. *([S] Callao.)*

# PALERMO

## PALERMO CHICO AND BARRIO PARQUE

Just across Palermo's northern border with Recoleta, tiny Palermo Chico, one of the city's wealthiest neighborhoods, centers on **Plaza Chile** and hosts many of the city's embassies, as well as the excellent **Museo de Arto Decorativo** (p. 177). Stretching north from here, the layout of the winding, leafy streets of **Barrio Parque** was designed by **Carlos Thays** (p. 157); beautiful mansions and villas line the streets and provide a stunning, if imposing, place to wander.

**PLAZA CHILE.** Like most of Palermo's string of beautiful green spaces, Plaza Chile is an excellent refuge from the frantic traffic of Av. Libertador. Bordered on one side by the Chilean embassy, the Plaza is also surrounded by some of the striking mansions of the wealthy *porteño* elite, as well as the **Casa Grand**

**Bourg** (see below). In the Plaza's northwest corner, a semicircle of statues, all erected in 1950, commemorate a number of the heroes of the **Chilean War of Independence** (1810-1818), as well as several Chilean authors. The Plaza focuses on a statue of **Bernardo O'Higgins,** who—despite his Irish-sounding name (his father was born in Ireland)—was the Chilean equivalent of José de San Martín, the liberator of Argentina himself. After leading the independence effort, O'Higgins became the first leader of free Chile and launched several radical reforms, such as the establishment of democracy and the abolition of titles of nobility. He would later participate, along with San Martín, in independence efforts elsewhere in South America in countries like Peru. (**S** *Agüero.*)

**INSTITUTO NACIONAL SANMARTINIANO.** Located just across the street from Plaza Chile, this beautiful white mansion, known as the **Casa Grand Bourg,** houses a cultural center mainly devoted to José de San Martín, Argentina's most famous independence hero. A reproduction of Martín's villa near Paris, where he lived in exile for over a decade later in his life, the house is only open to the public for readings and lectures during the hours listed below; see the website for the current schedule. *(Mariscal Carilla and Alejandro Aguado.* **S** *Agüero.* ☎ *4801 0848; www.sanmartiniano.com. Open M-F 10am-6pm.)*

---

**PARKING PROBLEMS.** The people who wave cars into parking spaces along Palermo's streets are called *cuidacoches*. These workers typically charge between AR$7-8 per car, earning an average of AR$300 per night. However, a 2004 law illegalized their activity, enforcing a punishment of AR$200-400 or up to two days of volunteer work. Recently, tensions between Palermo residents and the *cuidacoches* have run high over their "rental" of parking spaces for AR$8-10 per night. Finding a parking spot back at home doesn't seem like such a hassle anymore.

---

# NORTHERN PALERMO

**PARQUE TRES DE FEBRERO.** No person can (or should) cover every inch of the Parque Tres de Febrero, 25 hectares of grassy splendor in the north of Palermo that end at the Jorge Newbery Airpark. Filled with joggers and amorous couples, the park has been the retreat for BA's rich and famous since its opening at the turn of the century. Then-president **Domingo Faustino Sarmiento** (p. 57), a classic 19th-century liberal who championed democracy and had an obsession with Europe, commissioned it in 1875 as part of his mission to civilize the country. He named it for the day in 1852 when his archnemesis, Argentine *caudillo* **Juan Manuel de Rosas** was bloodily defeated. The marble **Monumento de los Españoles,** at the intersection of Avenida del Libertador and Avenida Sarmiento, is at the heart of the park. A gift from Spaniards living in Buenos Aires, the bronze figures at the base of the monument represent four areas of Argentina: the **Andes** (look for the condor), the **Chaco,** the **Río de la Plata,** and the **Pampa,** represented by a voluptuous reclining woman.

If you enter from **Monumento de los Españoles,** the park's most beautiful section is a diagonal left just across the street. Though you'll never really escape the hum of the highway, this is as tranquil as it gets. This area is known as the **Parque de las Poetas,** with benches and sculptures of the major figures of poetry. Dante, by the trellised walkway, and Shakespeare, up the center path, round out the roster of greats. Ironically, the statue of Borges, Argentina's most famous poet, is considerably harder to find, to the right of the second rectangular fountain. A lovely patio with blue tiles, the **Patio**

S I G H T S

Andaluz graces the right of the statue, along with a pergola. The **Rosedal,** a rose garden designed by our old friend **Carlos Thays,** opened in 1914. It blooms throughout the year, even in winter, but is at its most glorious in November. Nearby, next to the boating pond, is one of the many statues of **Sarmiento,** this one in Art Nouveau style. The other statue, a marble and bronze **Rodin** piece, is at the corner of **Plaza Sicilia.** Across the marble bridge from the Art Nouveau statue is the **Museo de Artes Plásticas Eduardo Sívori** (p. 177), an excellent Argentine art museum. You can also rent **paddle- and row-boats** by the half hour. *(www.parquetresdefebrero.gov.ar. Rosedal open daily summer 8am-8pm, winter 8am-6pm. Boat pond rentals AR$20-30 per 30min.)*

**PLANETARIO GALILEO GALILEI.** At the eastern end of **Parque Tres de Febrero** is Buenos Aires' very spherical and very 1960s (read: ugly and concrete) planetarium. Though it sporadically hosts interactive exhibits on various topics, such as meteorites, the planetarium is usually dedicated to shows that deal with astronomy and astrological phenomena. The presentations rotate frequently and are aimed at a number of audiences: adults, children, and English-speaking, to name a few. Check the website for information on the planetarium's current offerings. *(Av. Sarmiento and Figueros Alcorta.* S *Plaza Italia.* ☎ *4771 9393; www.planetario.gov.ar. Shows AR$4.)*

**PLAZA ITALIA AND SURROUNDINGS.** If you're heading to one of Palermo's many parks or into Palermo Soho, chances are good that you'll travel through Plaza Italia, yet another landscaped space designed by **Carlos Thays** (p. 157). Once known as the **Plaza de Portones,** its name was changed to Plaza Italia after the statue of **Giuseppe Garibaldi,** a hero of both Italian unification and Uruguayan independence, was erected here in 1904. Just across the roundabout from the Plaza Italia, it's hard to miss the massive **Sociedad Rural Argentina,** located in the **Predio la Rural** building, founded in the beginning of the 20th century by a group of advocates of traditional farming practices. Now the massive conglomeration of halls and pavilions that stretches along Av. Sarmiento hosts a wide variety of exhibitions and events, including everything from industrial equipment and furniture to cultural activities. It is also the venue for **Opera Pampa,** a massive dinner event showcasing traditional *gaucho* dancing and herding skills. *(Av. Sante Fe 4363.* S *Plaza Italia. Societad Rural Argentina:* ☎ *4777 5500; www.la-rural.com.ar. Opera Pampa:* ☎ *4777 5557; www. operapampa.com.ar. Event runs Th-Sa 8pm. AR$140-220.)*

**THE LOCAL STORY**

### THAYS' BA

Predictably, it's a Frenchman's fault, that a city populated by Spanish and Italian immigrants is habitually called (mostly by guidebooks more inclined towards such cheese) the "Paris of South America." **Charles Thays**—a French landscaper better known today as **Carlos Thays**—landed in a city that had, by 1889, been Argentina's capital city for less than a decade. Thays fell in love with the fast-growing nation, resolving, so the story goes, to live out his life in the City of Fair Winds.

More than that, Thays quickly and ambitiously set out to remake and beautify his adopted town. By 1891, he had become **Director of Parks and Walkways,** and petitioned the government to set aside nearly 8 hectares of land for his greatest projects. When his request was granted, Thays set to work designing the **Jardín Botánico** (p. 158) that now bears his name, creating a personal stake in the beauty and success of the gardens by building his home on the grounds.

During the 6-year construction period, Thays also designed the **Parque San Martín** and the enormous **Bosques de Palermo.** His other handiwork, including **Plaza de Mayo,** and virtually every other park in the city, shows the indelible mark Thays left on BA. Later in his life, he branched out beyond BA; his largest-scale project was the 1911 landscaping of **Parque Nacional Iguazú** (p. 239). No, he didn't make the falls.

THE LOCAL STORY

## CALL HIM "CHE"

In life, and in death, **Ernesto "Che" Guevara** has been called both a hero and a butcher. There's little variance, even among those who disagree over his legacy, when it comes to the man himself: he was a great writer, a powerful persuader, and a scary enemy. He was an executioner, a diplomat, and a doctor. He was Che.

Now he is a T-shirt. There's a fine line between iconic and ironic, and the well-known face of the Argentine revolutionary treads that line with no visible discomfort.

Before he was "Che," Ernesto Guevara was the oldest of five children in a wealthy family. During medical school, he took a year off to tour Latin America, a trip recounted in the novel-turned-movie *The Motorcycle Diaries.* He became a ☭commie, he went to Guatemala to overthrow President Guzmám, and in June of 1955, in Mexico City, he met **Fidel Castro.**

During the next five years, he became a prominent member of the **26th of July Movement,** eventually becoming a commander in the **revolution** to overthrow Cuban dictator **Fulgencio Batista.** He arrived a medic, became a military leader, and, after the revolution, held many high government positions. The first and most notorious post was as **supreme prosecutor** for the revolutionary tribunals. There, he presided over the executions of several hundred people convicted of treason, earning the nickname **"Fidel's executioner."** From there, he became

**JARDÍN BOTÁNICO CARLOS THAYS.** The Jardín Botánico, with 5500 plant species (and nearly as many cats), is a leafy, botanical garden refuge at the edge of the Palermo park system. Declared a national historical monument in 1996, the sculpture-dotted, seven-hectare plot was built between 1892 and 1914 under the direction of French landscaper **Carlos Thays** (see p. 157).

Thays designed the park to have several different sections, including **French** and **Italian gardens,** which are kept up today by a staff of more than 80 custodians. Walk in via the **Plaza Italia** entrance, heading up the path past the fountain. The brick building straight ahead, originally the palace of a Polish military man (which may explain the fortress-like towers), displays contemporary and historical maps of the park, and hosts rotating art exhibits. Thays lived here with his family while the park was being built, giving the building its name, **Casona Carlos Thays.** Just to the left, you can see the 20th-century **Saturnalia,** a sculpture by Aldredo Bizatti depicting a Roman orgy. The Dirty War military dictatorship (p. 60) deemed it so scandalous, they hid it in one of the garden sheds. *(Santa Fe 3951. ☎4831 4527; www.jardinbotanico.gov.ar. Weekend music and entertainment, often directed at children. Open daily summer 8am-7pm, winter 8am-6pm. Guided tours Sa-Su and holidays 10:30am; English-language F noon. To reserve a night tour, call ☎4831 4614 M-F 9am-4pm. Free.)*

**JARDÍN ZOOLÓGICO.** Popular with young couples, and foreign tourists, BA's zoo is surprisingly large considering its location in the middle of busy Palermo. The zoo showcases several thousand animals from all over the world, and all the usual suspects are here: hippos, lions, snakes, spiders, zebras, and so forth. Along with an **aquarium, reptile house,** and **mini-tropical forest,** the complex also features a small temple, mosque, and pagoda, though, surprisingly enough, no particular exhibits on the fauna of Argentina. Designed by the omnipresent **Carlos Thays** (p. 157), the cages and buildings are beginning to show some signs of wear, and the quality of the habitats a bit uneven. *(Av. Sarmiento 2827.* [S] *Plaza Italia. ☎4011 9900; www.zoobuenosaires.com.ar. Open Jan.-Feb. daily 10am-6pm; Mar.-Dec. Tu-Su 10am-5:30pm. General admission AR$8. "Pasaporte Ahorro," including the reptile house, aquarium, and tropical forest house, AR$15.)*

**JARDÍN JAPONÉS.** Set in the middle of Palermo's already extensive park system, this garden-within-a-garden was designed—and is still run—by Buenos Aires' Japanese community. With its winding pathways, lacquered bridges, and flowering trees, the park's landscaping is certainly beautiful, but it can be difficult to reach any state of mental relaxation with the constant screeching of traffic just outside. Still, it's a fine place for a leisurely walk and a cup of tea, which is sold from a bright red **cafe** within the park. Just next door to the cafe is a **Japanese cultural center,** which hosts demonstrations and classes on everything from origami and natural medicine to martial arts and shiatsu massage; see the website or visit the garden for the current schedule. *(Av. Casares 2966.* Ⓢ *Plaza Italia.* ☎ *4804 9141; www.jardinjapones.org.ar. Open daily 10am-6pm. AR$5.)*

# SOUTHERN PALERMO

South from Av. Sante Fe, narrow cobblestone streets and low-slung townhouses comprise the residential sub-neighborhoods of **Palermo Viejo,** once popular among the city's immigrant communities and home to both **Borges** and **Che Guevara.** Nowadays, though Palermo Soho, Palermo Hollywood, and Villa Freud boast few sights, they are the city's most popular entertainment areas, rife with places to shop, eat, drink, and dance.

## PALERMO SOHO

The region of Palermo Viejo bounded by Av. Sante Fe to the north, Av. Córdoba to the south, Av. B. Justo to the west, and Av. Scalabrini Ortiz to the east is affectionately known as Palermo Soho for the high concentration of alternative boutiques, bars, cafes, and restaurants that line its streets. Centering on **Plaza Cortázar** (usually called **Plaza Serrano**), the beautifully crumbling houses and shops definitely have a bohemian flair, though the neighborhood has become exceptionally popular among the city's upper-middle-class youth and is by no means down-and-out.

**PLAZA SERRANO.** Surrounded by numerous cafes, restaurants, bars, and boutiques, Plaza Serrano is Palermo Soho's shopping and nightlife hub, as well as its geographical center. While the Plaza itself is nondescript, it usually hosts lines of craft stalls that sell a variety of colorful, often kitschy, souvenirs, T-shirts, photos, jewelry, and knick-knacks. On summer weekend days, the number of vendors increases and some of the Plaza's bars host temporary "boutiques," where budding designers show off their (usually inexpensive) wares. Though almost never used, the Plaza's official title is **Plaza Cortázar,** after the important Argentine author **Julio Cortázar** (p. 79), who set his most famous novel, *Rayuela* (Hopscotch), in Palermo Soho. Grab a copy and plop down on a bench. *(*Ⓢ *Plaza Italia.)*

head of the **National Bank,** where he encouraged diversification and nationalization, becoming one of Cuba's most admired leaders— and quickly rivaling Castro. For that reason, Castro sent him off as an ambassador, where he spread communist ideology and designed the friendly relationship between the **Soviet Union** and Cuba.

In 1965, he left Cuba to spread revolution in the **Congo.** After a failed pair of years, he returned to Latin America in secret, where he started training a **guerrilla** unit in **Bolivia.** In 1967, with the aid of the **CIA,** the Bolivian Army wounded, captured, and quickly executed Che. Legend has it that, just before his death, his executioner asked if he was thinking of his immortality. "No," he answered. "I'm thinking about the immortality of the revolution."

Since his death, Che—or, more specifically, his face—has become a symbol of enormous power and, ironically, marketability. A 1960 **Alberto Korda** photograph of him wearing a beret and sporting long hair and a weedy mustache, entitled **Guerillero Heróico** (Heroic Guerrilla) is among the most reproduced images in the world. Since his death, his face has become a symbol of left-wing ideology, its exploitation, and the silliness of a culture—or, well, many cultures—that buy into the empty idealizations of a man whose complexities, deep and fatal flaws, and whose courage are flattened and misrepresented by the very commercial world he fought to destroy.

**CASA BORGES.** Flanked by two high-rises, this small, well-kept brick building rests on the former site of a small two-story villa, complete with mill, where **Jorge Luis Borges** (p. 76) lived from 1901-1914. Borges described his home as "two patios, a garden with a tall windmill pump and, on the other side of the garden, an empty lot." You'll have to take his word for it. *(Jorge Luis Borges 2135.)*

**IF YOU'RE IN THE NEIGHBORHOOD.** The two plaques outside of 2366 Fray Justo Santamaria de Oro don't merit a detour, but are worth checking out if you're in the area. Installed in the pavement, they commemorate two of the *desaparecidos* that "vanished" during the Dirty War (p. 60).

## PALERMO HOLLYWOOD

In the 1990s, many TV and radio producers moved their operations to the area of Palermo Viejo just west of Palermo Soho, and the area consequently became known as Palermo Hollywood. Full of businesspeople in suits at lunchtime, a much younger—though almost as wealthy—crowd packs the area on weekend nights and spills out of its countless bars, clubs, and restaurants.

### VILLA FREUD AND SURROUNDINGS

**PARQUE LAS HERAS.** For a rolling green park popular among massive numbers of happy lovers, sunbathers, dog owners, and families, Parque Las Heras has a sad past. Until 1962, these few square blocks were actually the site of one of the city's most important jails, infamous as the location where members of a failed rebellion against the military government of the 1950s were executed. If you search hard enough, you might be able to find the plaque marking the spot where the rebellion's leader, **Juan José Valle**, was shot. History aside, the park is yet another great place to sit down and relax in Palermo. *(S Bulnes.)*

# THE OUTER BARRIOS

## THE NORTH

### BELGRANO

Belgrano, once the summer retreat of the city elite, has retained its suburban, upscale feel over the years. It's what Palermo used to be like before it became Palermo: prosperous, but not yet overrun with tourists). Established in 1855, the *barrio* found itself at the center of political life for two weeks in 1880, when the capital was briefly relocated there during one of the many tussles between centralists and federalists (p. 55). Things have quieted down since then. A stroll through the neighborhood is like singing your ABCs. Belgrano **R** (a.k.a. residential) is marked by wide, tree-lined avenues and some of the largest houses in the city. **Avenida Cabildo** (an extension of Av. Santa Fe) is the area's main thoroughfare, and cuts through the middle to form Belgrano **C**, the commercial center. Most of the *barrio*'s museums, the picturesque **Plaza de Belgrano**, which is packed with ice cream parlors, and the **Barrancas de Belgrano**, a park with weekend tango, can be found in C, an easy walk from the Juramento *subte* station. Down around the train tracks, there is a bit more hustle and bustle, marking BA's one-block **Chinatown** and a wealth of other restaurants. Plan to budget one day to fully explore Belgrano's sights.

SIGHTS

**PLAZA BELGRANO AND SURROUNDINGS.** Smack dab in the middle of commercial Belgrano, the Plaza Belgrano, bordered by cafes and ice cream shops, honors (who else?) **Manuel Belgrano,** creator of the Argentine flag. The **Parroquía Inmaculada Concepción Belgrano,** known as "La Redonda" for its circular shape, is at the western side of the Plaza. Though the church was not completed until 1878 due to a lack of funding, the site has been the home of a house of worship since the arrival of the Franciscans in the 18th century. *(Open daily 7am-9pm.)*

Most of Belgrano's museums either surround the Plaza or are nearby. The (pleasant?) smell of fresh fish welcomes visitors to **Mercado Modelo de Belgrano,** at the intersection of Juramento and Ciudad de la Paz, a covered market that sells fresh produce, cheese, and other foods. *(Open M-Sa 8am-1pm and 5-8:30pm.)* A few blocks south lies the Carlos Thays-planned **Barrancas of Belgrano.** Though it's grittier than parks in the more touristy parts of town, the gentle slopes, grafitti-strewn statues, and lampposts point to its original beauty. Belgrano's one-block **Chinatown,** on Arribeños at the base of the hill and just across the train tracks, has a series of restaurants and shops selling all the kitschy Hello Kitty socks you'll ever need. The local **Buddhist temple,** really just a converted conference room with a couple of statues, is nearby at 2175 Montañeses. *(Open M-F and Su 2-6pm.)* A bit farther down Arribeños, the geography and culture changes again with **Pasaje Andaluz,** which replicates the look of a southern Spanish village.

**TIERRA SANTA.** Christ rises once an hour at this intensely kitschy (and that's an understatement) "religious theme park," a seven acre, plaster mini-Jerusalem Since its opening in 1999, the park has attracted more than 3 million visitors, many of whom come with entirely earnest intentions. The main circuit traces the Bible story from the Creation to the Resurrection. Interspersed are four performances, the first of which, Creation, is a trippy light show (if it's going to take seven days, might as well have lasers) with a menagerie of questionably Biblical creatures, dancers, and bad music. Next up, the Resurrection, starring a giant 14-meter tall Christ, complete with 20 different animatronic movements, is topped off by rendition of Handel's "Hallelujah Chorus" from the *Messiah.* Other represented spiritual leaders range from Martin Luther to Mahatma Gandhi, but Jesus Christ is the superstar. As is appropriate for a park with utopic intentions, the devil seems remarkably absent, though it is possible to find a snake somewhere near the Last Supper. *(Costanera Norte. Colectivos 28, 33, 37, 42, 45, 107, 160.* ☎ *4784 9551; www.tierrasanta-bsas.com.ar. Open winter M-F 9am-9pm (ticket office closes 7pm), Sa-Su and holidays noon-10pm (ticket office closes 8pm); summer F-Su 4pm-midnight (ticket office closes 10pm). AR$20.)*

**PARQUE DE LA MEMORIA.** Nominally a park, this concrete wasteland at the edge of the city is the official monument to those who disappeared or were assassinated during the **Dirty War** (p. 60). Begun in 1998, the location of the memorial was chosen for its proximity to the airport used by the military to fly planes that dropped the bodies into the Río de la Plata. It's quite a trek from the city center, so a visit may not be worth the time for visitors who are in BA only for a short while. *(Av. Intendente Güiraldes and Av. Costanera Rafael Obligado. Bus # 33, 37, 42, 45, 107, and 160; look for buses heading to the Ciudad Universitaria. www.parquedelamemoria.org.ar. Wall open W-Th noon-4pm, Sa 10am-2pm. Sculpture park open daily 10am-6pm.)*

# CHACARITA AND COLEGIALES

Identified by the sprawling **cemetery** that takes up most of the *barrio,* and the small but booming flower industry it supports, the tranquility of **Chacarita's** streets seems well suited to a neighborhood defined by death. Just west of

**TIME:** Roughly 6-8 hours.

**SEASON:** Year-round.

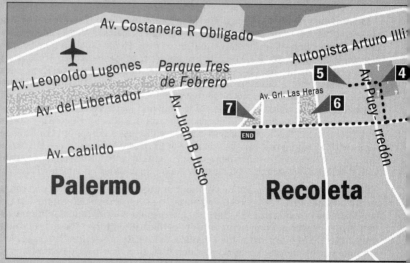

Av. Costanera R Obligado

Autopista Arturo Illi

Av. Leopoldo Lugones

*Parque Tres de Febrero*

**5**

**4**

Av. del Libertador

Av. Grl. Las Heras

Av. Puey rredón

**7**

**6**

Av. Juan B Justo

END

Av. Cabildo

## Palermo

## Recoleta

# DEAD AND LOVING IT

**1. PALACIO BAROLO.** Go to Hell. Not really. But you can, in theory, at this 22-story office building (p. 144) on Av. de Mayo, designed by Italian Mario Palanti. The tower, a hodgepodge of multiple architectural styles (Art Nouveu, neo-Gothic, neo-Romantic...you name it, it has it), is inspired by Dante's epic poem, *The Divine Comedy*. The basement and the ground floor, replete with grotesque figures, dragons, and a floor pattern that resembles fire, represent Hell. Floors 1-14 are Purgatory, and are, appropriately, blah. The top, floors 15-22 are—you guessed it—Heaven, capped off by a shining rooftop lighthouse meant to embody God and salvation. It was the tallest building in the city upon completion in 1923, until 1935, that is, when another tower on our tour, Edificio Kavanagh, rose to the north.

**2. CAFE RICHMOND.** So what if Jorge Luis Borges, Argentina's most famous writer, is buried in Switzerland? That doesn't mean you can't commune with him at this elegant Calle Florida cafe (p. 122), which he used to frequent back in the day as a customer. Take a midday break on your jaunt through the city and grab a cup of coffee.

**3. PLAZA SAN MARTÍN.** Grudges during one's lifetime can quietly go to the grave—or they can be forever immortalized with massive, ugly, concrete skyscrapers. Filthy rich Corina Kavanagh chose the latter option. Kavanagh was a rival of the similarly wealthy Anchorena family, who lived in an opulent palace on the western side of the Plaza, the Palacio San Martín (p. 152). As the story goes, one of Corina's daughters fell in love with one of the Anchorena sons, but in a well-known twist of fate, the Anchorena family disapproved of the relationship. Kavanagh's revenge? Build a humongous Art Deco skyscraper, Edificio Kavanagh (p. 152), on the eastern side of the Plaza that would block the Anchorena's view of their beautiful church and family tomb, the Basílica del Santisimo Sacramento (p. 152) from the Palacio San Martín. While you're in the neighborhood, don't forget to check out the magnificent Palacio Paz on the western side of the Plaza San Martín—a building that is refreshingly grudge-free.

**4. RECOLETA CEMETERY.** Strangely enough, this city of the dead (p. 153) buzzes with lively bunches of tourists strolling down its narrow, catacomb-lined corridors. Each of the tombs are like mini-cathedrals, complete with stained glass, altars, and steeples. Most of the famous names you see on Buenos Aires' street signs are buried here, along with many other notable luminaries of Argentine history. The cemetery's most famous inhabitant, by far, is Eva Duarte, better known to the world as Eva Perón, or simply, Evita.

**5. BIBLIOTECA NACIONAL.** After checking out her tomb, take a stroll north to see one of the city's statues dedicated to Eva at this colossally ugly library (p. 155). The monstrosity was built on the location of Juan and Eva Perón's former home. The government bulldozed the mansion in the 1960s, fearing that it would become a shrine to the former president's wife. Now the site is merely a shrine to misguided 1960s brutalist architecture.

**6. PARQUE LAS HERAS.** One of Palermo's many beautiful leafy greens, Parque Las Heras (p. 160) is a big hit with sunbathers, dog walkers, and those just looking to chill for an afternoon. The park has a surprisingly depressing past, though. Until 1962, the green was the site of one of the city's prisons, where many members of a failed 1950s rebellion against the government were executed, including the ringleader of said uprising, Juan José Valle. Hidden somewhere in the park is a commemorative plaque in Valle's name.

**7. JARDÍN BOTÁNICO CARLOS THAYS.** This beautiful, leafy refuge at the heart of Palermo's park system (p. 158), designed by French landscaper extraordinaire Carlos Thays (p. 157), was recently embroiled in controversy when it was discovered that some of the gardeners and custodians had been taking kick backs in exchange for letting *porteños* use the park as a burial ground. Somehow, we don't think that's what Thay's originally had in mind when he envisioned the park's use.

Palermo across **Avenida Dorrego,** this dusty gathering of small, short houses was originally settled by Jesuits, who founded the *chacras* (farms) from which the *barrio* acquired its name. After expropriation by the crown in 1767, the land became a kind of summer retreat for students, known as the **Chacarita de los Colegiales.** It was only when immigrants flooded the northern area around the turn of the century that the neighborhood officially split in two, with Chacarita to the south and **Colegiales** to the north. Squished between Palermo and Belgrano, Colegiales, once a similarly middle-class *barrio*, is beginning to feel the bite of gentrification. Though it remains largely residential, more upscale restaurants and shops are starting to make the migration over.

**LA CHACARITA CEMETERY.** Both less ritzy and less touristed than its counterpart in Recoleta, La Chacarita Cemetery distinguishes itself instead with its size—97 hectares, covering most of Chacarita *barrio*, with dimensions large enough to support its own *colectivo* system. It first opened in 1871 to hold victims of the yellow fever epidemic that swept through San Telmo and southern Buenos Aires. Today, it's known as the *cemeterio popular* (the people's cemetery), where everyone—from anonymous bodies on the street to tango legend **Carlos Gardel**—ends up in even ground.

Surrounded by walls, the cemetery is divided into three different sections. The **bovedas,** closest to the entrance, are large family or associational crypts as large as houses. No new space is allocated to *bovedas* today, but it's still possible to buy the rights to one, provided the original owners are willing to sell. Most people are buried beyond the *bovedas* in the green fields dotted with white wooden crosses provided by the municipality. The graves are good for six years; after this time, relatives or friends must pay a fee to keep the site. If they fail to do so, the city sends the body to the crematorium, located within the cemetery, and allocates the spot to someone new. The final options are the massive, concrete galleries built in the 1970s and connected via underground passageways. Famous "residents" include early 20th-century aviator **Jorge Newbery,** namesake of BA's regional airport, and the **Recinto de Personalidades,** a sort of collective shrine to Argentine entertainment greats, from movie stars and racecar drivers to poets. Until 2006, Chacarita also held the bones of **Juan Perón.** That year, his supporters moved the remains to a mausoleum in San Vicente, where the general and Evita had a summer home, to keep them safe from defacement. Raiders chopped off his hands in 1987, and in 2006 his bones were the subject of a negative DNA test, due to a lawsuit brought by a woman claiming to be his illegitimate daughter. *(Guzman 680.* S *Frederico Lacroze.* ☎ *4553 9338. Guided tours 2nd and 4th Sa of each month 3pm, weather permitting. Free.)*

# NÚÑEZ AND SAAVEDRA

At the end of the 19th century, Buenos Aires' elite, many of them fleeing the yellow fever epidemic to the south, began its push to settle the outlying areas of the city, stretching to present-day **Núñez** and **Saavedra,** the northern tip of Capital Federal. The *barrios*, which are largely residential, with a mix of prosperous and more depressed parts, have some sights and have experienced their fair share of history, despite their relatively brief existence. During the Dirty War, the military used the **Escuela de Mecánica de Armada (ESMA),** the naval school, as a holding pen for prisoners. A museum at the site is still in the works. If you're one of those people that enjoyed the United States' Four Corners and places where you can excitedly say "I've been in several places at once," **Parque Saavedra,** at the edge of the map, is right on the city limits.

SIGHTS

# THE WEST

## ALMAGRO

Like Balvanera, Almagro is a grey, commercial *barrio,* and the region of **Abasto** (p. 165) spills over its borders. Though it has no major sights to speak of, the section of Abasto that falls within Almagro is well-known as the **"off-Corrientes" theater district** (p. 189) and a great place to go for alternative productions.

## BALVANERA

Sprawling out west of Microcentro and Monserrat, Balvanera is a commercially important, if unattractive and cramped, *barrio.* Locals rarely call it by its official name, instead referring to its three main sub-neighborhoods. On Balvanera's eastern fringes, **Congreso** bustles with office workers on lunch from the center, though it can also be painfully quiet the farther you get from Congreso. There's little reason beyond curiosity to linger here, unless you head up north to the border with Recoleta and to the fascinating **Palacio de las Aguas Corrientes. Abasto,** however, does draw a number of tourists to its enormous, eponymous **shopping center** (p. 201) and to the **Museo Carlos Gardel** (p. 181). And, though true of the entire *barrio,* it's in **Once** that Balvanera's immigrant population is most apparent. Centered around a massive train station, this sub-*barrio* hosts a hectic market that may remind you that you are, after all, in Latin America.

**PALACIO DE LAS AGUAS CORRIENTES.** Walking down Av. Córdoba, it's hard to miss this massive building, the "Palace of the Running Waters." It looks, indeed, like a palace. Strangely enough, it was never a residence, but the city's water-storage facility. Constructed by British and Swedish engineers during 1887-1894, the building is a mix of architectural styles and is strangely colorful; the entire exterior is covered by glazed ceramic tiles and embellishments in yellows, blues, and greens. The interior skeleton of the structure couldn't be more different; the building houses 12 enormous tanks that once held up to 72 million liters of water, as well as a huge number of offices. The only way for tourists to get inside is to visit the small **museum** on the second floor, which has exhibits on the history and architecture of the building, as well as a not-so-interesting collection of toilets, urinals, bidets, faucets, and pipes. Though the museum is absorbing for those interested in the building's background, it's best to come during one of the **guided tours,** when visitors are also allowed to see some of the Palacio's inner industrial skeleton and a few of the impressive original water tanks. *(On Córdoba, between Ayacucho and Riobamba. Museum entrance: Riobamba 750l. [S] Facultad de Medicina. ☎6319 1104; www.aysa.com.ar. Open M-F 9am-1pm. Guided Spanish-language tours M, W, F at 11am. Free.)*

### ABASTO

Abasto teems with activity around **Avenida Corrientes** and around the shopping center. Head off into the backstreets to the **Museo Carlos Gardel** (p. 181), however, and you'll find it surprisingly low-key and relaxed, if a bit run-down.

**SHOPPING ABASTO.** Walking down Av. Corrientes, it's hard to miss the massive Abasto shopping center, which towers over Balvanera. Finished in 1893 and renovated in the 1930s, this beautiful Art-Deco building housed the city's central fruit and vegetable market until 1984, when the market was moved out of the city center and the building was left empty. In the 1990s, new buyers successfully transformed the building into the city's largest shopping complex. It now draws a mainly middle-class clientele and includes several banks, kiosks, a food court, a cinema, and even a miniature theme park. *(Av. Corrientes 3247.* **S** *Carlos Gardel.* ☎ *4959 3400; www.abasto-shopping.com.ar. Open daily 10am-10pm.)*

## ONCE

For those tired of the expensive, "chic" *porteño* shopping experience, Once is a hectic, oh-so-Latin-American haven. Centered on the Once train station, this sub-neighborhood is a great place to go for 60-peso jeans, 20-peso tops, and even 100-peso suits. Outlet stores, cheap shops, and street vendors line the streets surrounding the station and continue up Av. Pueyrredón toward Recoleta. With Spanish pop and reggaeton playing in the background, there are also plenty of food vendors selling *tamales* and other snacks. This immigrant neighborhood draws people from all over Latin America and Asia. Historically, it has also been home to one of Buenos Aires' numerous Jewish communities; it was here that the AMIA Jewish community center was bombed in 1994 (p. 27) in one of the deadliest terrorist attacks on Argentine soil, though there are few outward signs of tension here today. If you're up for a frenzied, energetic experience, hold tightly to your valuables and dive into the crowds.

**ESTACIÓN ONCE.** Officially known as the **Estación Once de Septiembre** (Station Eleventh of September), Balvanera's gigantic train station is named after the date of Buenos Aires' 1852 rebellion against the federal government (p. 56). Local and long-distance trains depart from the grand stone building for Lobos, Lujan, and some of the city's suburbs. *(***S** *Once.)*

**PLAZA MISERERE.** Right next to the station, this large, tree-shaded square, more commonly known as **Plaza Once,** is always packed with locals lounging on benches or waiting in huge lines for the buses. Consistent with its long political history—armies clashed here during the British invasions of 1806—don't be too surprised to see a minister or revolutionary here ranting about God or the government. At the center of the square is a massive monument, created by **Rogelio Yrurtia** (p. 179) to **Bernardino Rivadavia** (p. 55) Argentina's first president, depicting him in classical style (think toga) mostly naked. *(***S** *Once.)*

## CABALLITO

South of Chacarita and west of Almagro, the middle-class and rambling *barrio* of Caballito centers on the unremarkable **Plaza Primera Junta** and is bisected by the very commercial **Avenida Rivadavia.** South of Rivadavia, there's very little to see, though the area can be a beautiful place to wander. More upscale than the rest of the neighborhood, the tree-lined cobblestone streets host beautiful townhouses and an unnecessary historic tram. In the northeast, two pleasant **parks** offer great spaces for rest and relaxation, and one, **Parque del Centenario,** is home to the city's **natural sciences museum.**

**PARQUE DEL CENTENARIO.** In Caballito's far northeastern corner, the circular Parque del Centenario, recently revamped by the city, draws crowds of locals to its small pond, complete with a fountain and miniature botanical island. On weekends, vendors set up stands around the park's outer fences and hawk everything from clothes to crafts to CDs. The park's biggest draw is the **Museo Argentino de Ciencias Naturales** (Argentine Museum of Natural Sciences, p. 181) in its northwestern corner. *(***S** *Angel Gallardo. Open daily 8am-8pm.)*

**PARQUE RIVADAVIA.** Located in Caballito's center is the beautifully maintained and landscaped Parque Rivadavia. Green throughout the year, it's especially popular with families and loving couples. At the center of the park is an imposing stone monument to **Simón Bolívar,** the Latin American statesman, and namesake of Bolivia, as well as a tiled fountain from the 1930s. The park also hosts a daily book market, where you can pick up the odd English novel or Spanish coffee-table book, as well as CDs, DVDs, vinyl, and magazines. On Sunday mornings, there's the random **Feria del Ombú,** a collectibles market that surrounds the remaining pieces of a once-massive gum tree. (§ *Acoyte.*)

**TRANVÍA HISTÓRICO (HISTORICAL TRAM).** About six blocks south of Plaza Primera Junta, a "historic" tram departs from a graffiti-covered station and makes a twenty-minute loop around the southwest corner of Caballito. The tram, however, isn't particularly historic; it's simply a plain, 1950s car that had to be brought over to Buenos Aires from Portugal, as the city had already gotten rid of all of its own. Though it does go through a beautiful section of the neighborhood, the tram probably won't be of much interest to most travelers, except those who happen to be in the area and are really, really interested in trams—we know you're out there. *(Emilio Mitre 500, on the corner with José Bonifacio.* § *Primera Junta.* ☎ *4431 1073; www.tranvia.org.ar. Runs Dec.-Feb. Sa 5-8:30pm, Su 10am-1pm and 5-8:30pm; Mar.-Nov. Sa 4-7:30pm, Su 10am-1pm and 4-7:30pm. Free.)*

# MATADEROS

**FERIA DE MATADEROS.** On Sundays, a six-block stretch of Mataderos, a *barrio* in far southwestern Buenos Aires packed with *porteños*, becomes a mecca for those looking to go *gaucho* while still in the city. The BA equivalent of a state fair, the **Feria de Mataderos** celebrates traditional rural Argentina through a combination of music, *mate,* and caramel apples trimmed with popcorn. Smoke from the many grills fills the porticos of the restored pink **Antiguo Edificio de la Administración de Mataderos,** which surrounds a plaza at the intersection of Lisandro de la Torre and Av. de los Corrales. Look for **El Resero,** the "working

SAY HUEQUE
Tours in Argentina & Chile

the **travel** agency for
**independent**
travellers

New
Office in
Palermo
Soho

Dowtown: Viamonte 749 6º of. "1" – Tel/ Fax: (+5411) 5199 2517/20
Palermo Soho: Guatemala 4845 1º of "4" – Tel /Fax: (+5411) 4775 7862
Buenos Aires – Argentina
info@sayhueque.com - www.sayhueque.com

*gaucho*" statue, which overlooks a stage where groups—from professional to amateur to impromptu tourist—perform traditional dances, while food and *artesanía* (crafts) stalls spoke off from the plaza. Around 3pm, farther east on Lisandro de la Torre, young *gauchos* can be found competing on horseback to enter a pen-shaped lance through a ring not much larger than a finger. Yes, it's actually as difficult as it sounds. *(Mataderos is about a 45min. bus ride to the southwest of the center. Bus 55 will take you directly there from the Plaza Italia, dropping you at the corner of Lisandro de la Torre and Av. Directorio, just before a Petrobras station. The Feria is to your left, down the street that borders the park. To take the bus back, walk one block west from the fair to Av. Jose Rodo. Other buses that will get you to the Feria include 63, 80, 92, 103, 117, 141, 155, and 180. ☎ 4323 9400, ext. 2830, on Su 4687 5602; www.feriademataderos.com.ar. Runs Su 11am-6pm; sometimes moves to Sa in the summer., check website for details. )*

# THE SOUTH

## BOEDO AND SAN CRISTÓBAL

Though in some ways as working-class as the neighborhoods that surround it, Boedo is a *barrio* on the rise—again. In the 1920s, an artsy, leftist crowd, led by a group of important Argentine and Uruguayan writers known as the **Boedo Literary Group,** settled here. Boedo was also closely associated with **tango,** and famous lyricist **Homero Manzi** lived in and sang about the area. Twenty years later, however, a new generation failed to arise and little was heard from the neighborhood for the next half-century. Nowadays, the alternative, artistic side of the *barrio* is slowly reappearing. Disheveled 20-somethings carrying messenger bags mingle with the neighborhood's elderly denizens, and many of its famous cafes, including **Cafe Margot** (p. 136), are once again becoming bohemian haunts. Boedo has also become a center for alternative theater—a number of its restaurants host live shows. Successfully marketing themselves as alternatives to the commercialized center, hostels are sprouting up throughout the neighborhood, granting visitors access to the new scene. The same is partly true of neighboring **San Cristóbal,** which is often considered part of Boedo.

Though there are few sights *per se* in the neighborhood, it can be a great place to wander. Mixed among the ugly modern buildings are romantically crumbling turn-of-the-century houses with beautiful embellishments. And Boedo is all about atmosphere anyway; this is the place to grab a cup of coffee at a historic cafe, catch a cutting-edge theatrical production, or enjoy a beer at a relaxed bar. Still, for those who are looking for official sights, there's always the small **Museo del Banco Ciudad "Monte de Piedad"** (p. 181).

## CONSTITUCIÓN

Just west of San Telmo and south of Monserrat, Constitución marks a definite transition to the *other* south—a part of the city that is grittier, poorer, and, let's face it, uglier than the northern and western neighborhoods. The *barrio* itself centers on the massive **Estación Constitución,** a tribute to the color pink, which sends trains to areas south of the city. Otherwise, with the exception of a historic convent, there aren't really any sights to speak of in this both residential and commercial working-class neighborhood. Despite the proximity of some of the major tourist *barrios,* you might feel remarkably out of place.

**ESTACIÓN CONSTITUCIÓN AND SURROUNDINGS.** Constitución's focal point is without a doubt its namesake train station. Construction on the huge building began in 1925, when the then Prince of Wales, on an official state visit, laid the foundation stone. More recently, on May 16, 2007, the station was the site of a violent riot when passengers protested being held on a broken-down—25 were injured in the melee. Across from the station is the sprawling **Plaza Constitución,** which, despite lacking decent grass, is a popular relaxation spot among locals and an important hub for many of the city's buses. It was also the site of a number of bloody clashes between Perón's supporters and opponents during the 1950s. On the side of the Plaza opposite the station, the strangely Neo-Gothic spires of the **Parroquia Corazón de María** tower over the neighborhood and can even be seen from various points in the city center. (**S** *Constitución.*)

**SANTA CASA DE EJERCICIOS ESPIRITUALES.** Just across the border from Monserrat is the city's oldest building to be preserved in its original form, the Santa Casa de Ejercicios Espirituales. Occupying most of a city block, the plain colonial exterior conceals a maze of beautiful galleries, cloisters, patios, and chapels. Founded as a convent in 1795, the same order of nuns occupy the building today and run one monthly, two-hour tour of the complex, which visits one of the chapels, galleries displaying religious art and relics, beautiful white stucco patios, and the cloisters. (*Independencia 1190, at the intersection with Salta.* **S** *Independencia.* ☎ *4304 0984. Tours 3rd Sa of the month at 3pm. AR$5.*)

# MUSEUMS

To be blunt, Buenos Aires is hit or miss when it comes to museums. Some collections are magnificent, and rival, or surpass, those of the world's greatest museums with a fascinating blend of indigenous Argentine works and items from the Old World. On the other end of the spectrum are some downright bizarre museums, complete with sickeningly large collections of weapons and wax models showing gruesome snake wounds. Such displays are, of course, enjoyable in their own right (especially if you happen to enjoy viper bites and guns). There are also the standard museum offerings any tourist would expect from BA, from shrines to Evita and tango crooners to collections solely devoted to Argentina's never-ending love affair with soccer.

## MONSERRAT

**MUSEO ETNOGRÁFICO JUAN BAUTISTA AMBROSETTI.** Just off Plaza de Mayo, this small but excellent museum displays a variety of ethnographic exhibits from around the world. The most fascinating and impressive displays are those that focus on the pre-Columbian indigenous peoples of South America and, in particular, of Argentina. Though the captions are in Spanish only, the artifacts themselves—including ceramics, jewelry, tools, and clothing—are stunning and engrossing even without the explanations. Make sure to head upstairs to check out the native costumes, including one made to resemble a jaguar. (Moreno 350. S Plaza de Mayo. ☎4331 7788. Open Tu-F 1-7pm, Sa-Su 3-7pm. AR$2 suggested contribution. Guided tours Sa-Su 4pm. Free.)

**MUSEO MUNDIAL DEL TANGO.** Housed in the Academia Nacional del Tango, this small, new museum painstakingly traces the historical development of tango through chronologically ordered displays packed with memorabilia, including old photos, records, playbills, and even shoes. There are also a few tango costumes and, not surprisingly, tango music in the background. (Avenida de Mayo 833. S Avenida de Mayo or Lima. Captions in Spanish. Open M-F 2:30-7:30pm. AR$5.)

**MUSEO DE LA CIUDAD (MUSEUM OF THE CITY).** Devoted to an exploration of porteño life and culture, the city's museum displays a somewhat boring collection of toys, furniture, and old photos. It also hosts often amusing rotating exhibits on a variety of topics, including, for example, an exploration of the city's garden gnomes, of which there are many, apparently, in various scenes. We're sure you've been dying to see them. (Adolfo Alsina 412. S Plaza de Mayo. ☎4331 9855. Captions in Spanish. Open M-F 11am-7pm, Sa-Su 3-7pm. AR$3.)

**MUSEO DE LA CASA ROSADA.** On the south side of the Casa Gobierno is a small museum devoted to the palace's former inhabitants, starting in the early 19th century. The exhibits, which include an array of presidential memorabilia—such as medals, sashes, and canes—provide a good refresher course on the past two centuries of Argentine politics, if little else. (Hipólito Yrigoyen 219. S Plaza de Mayo. ☎4344 3802. ID required. Captions in English and Spanish. Open M-F 10am-6pm, Su 2-6pm. Guided tours M-F 11am and 3pm, Su 4pm. Free.)

**MUSEO DEL CABILDO.** Though the museum itself is not particularly exciting, visiting it is the only way to get behind the stark white facade of the Cabildo (p. 140)—the seat of the city's government until 1822—and see its bright patios

**MUSEUMS**

and refurbished colonial rooms. The museum contains a collection of 18th- and 19th-century period pieces, including portraits and ornate furniture that might have been in the building at the time, as well as the requisite historical documents and standards. *(Bolívar 65. S Plaza de Mayo. ☎ 4343 4387. Open Tu-Su noon-6pm. AR$3. Spanish-language guided tours F 3:30pm, Sa-Su 12:30, 2, 3:30pm. Free.)*

# MICROCENTRO

**MUSEO MITRE.** This small museum was once the home of **Bartolomé Mitre,** who was the president of Argentina from 1862 to 1868 and founder of the important newspaper *La Nación.* The rooms on display, which include a study, bedroom, and library, retain many of the original furnishings and provide interesting insight into the lifestyle of the upper-crust gentry during the 19th century. Objects on display include selections from Mitre's extensive library and historical manuscripts. At the time of publication, the museum was closed indefinitely for renovation. *(San Martín 336. S Florida. ☎ 4394 8240; www. museomitre.gov.ar. Open Tu-Su 10am-6pm. Suggested contribution AR$2.)*

**MUSEO DE LA POLICÍA FEDERAL.** Located on the 7th and 8th floors of a nondescript building, this museum seems dedicated as much to the people who oppose the law as to those who enforce it. The bottom, rather uninteresting, floor—devoted to the latter—seems a jumble of (often unlabeled) uniforms, medals, banners, and police equipment. The upper floor, however, is a veritable lesson in drug smuggling, illegal gambling, and counterfeiting, showcasing a variety of generally law-breaking devices. Those with a weak stomach beware, however: the forensics exhibit at the end of the floor is infamously explicit, complete with gruesome photos and mutilated wax corpses. Now that's just unnecessary. *(San Martín 353. S Florida. Some English captions. Open Tu-Sa 3-7pm. Free.)*

**MUSEO HISTÓRICO ARTURO JÁURETCHE.** This sleek museum explains the intricacies of Argentina's economic history in a chronological series of Spanish captions, beginning in the early 19th century and ending in the 1990s. Aside from old photos and a huge amount of paper money, the displays include 19th-century printing machines and antique furniture from the city's most powerful banks. *(Sarmiento 362. S Florida or LN Alem. Open M-F 10am-6pm. Free.)*

# SAN TELMO

**MUSEO DEL TRAJE.** This small but entertaining museum hosts rotating exhibits of period clothing from the 17th century to the present. Past exhibits have covered, well, pretty much everything—indigenous clothing, military uniforms, hippie garb, children's fashion, you name it. Though you can't try any of it on, you can get your picture taken behind one of the wooden cut-outs that can. *(Chile 832. S Independencia. ☎ 4343 8427. Open M-F and Su 3-7pm. Free.)*

**MUSEO PENITENCIARIO.** Built in the 18th century, the building that houses this museum once served as a convent and a women's prison. Though some rooms, including the chapel and the director's office, have been preserved in their original state, many of the others now contain bland exhibits on the history of the Argentine penal system. More interesting are the two reconstructed cells: a "modern" version, complete with graffiti (featuring an overrepresentation of Homer Simpson), and a 19th-century recreation. Strangely enough, the museum also offers tango classes every Sunday at 5pm. (*Humberto Primo 378.* S *Independencia.* ☎ *4361 0917. Captions in Spanish. Open W-F 2:30-5:30pm, Su 1-7pm. AR$1.*)

**MUSEO DE ARTE MODERNO DE BUENOS AIRES (MAMBA) AND MUSEO DEL CINE.** Housed in a former tobacco factory, this museum displays the works of 20th-century Argentine modernists and hosts a variety of temporary exhibits. The Museo del Cine, which has an important collection of film and objects related to Argentine cinema, is nearby. As of summer 2008, both museums are closed indefinitely for a renovation that will combine them into a single cultural center, the **Complejo Polo Sur Cultural.** The old **Correo Central** (p. 145), originally used as a temporary exhibition space, is now also under renovation, like much of BA. For the time being, there is no space designated for future showing of the museums' collections. (*San Juan 350.* S *San Juan.* ☎ *4361 1121.*)

**MUSEO HISTÓRICO NACIONAL.** Located on the western edge of Parque Lezama, a beautiful—if slightly out of place—red and white colonial building houses the large Museo Histórico Nacional. Exhibits move chronologically through Argentine history, paying particular attention to the 19th century and British invasions of 1806 and 1807. Though as of June 2008, most of the museum was closed for renovation, certain pieces remain on display, including many of the collection's numerous portraits of major national figures, from the conquistadors to the fighters for Argentine independence. (*Defensa 1600.* S *San Juan.* ☎ *4307 1182. Captions in Spanish. Open Tu-Su 11am-7pm. AR$3.*)

# LA BOCA

**⊠FUNDACIÓN PROA.** This large, remodeled mansion is widely regarded as one of Buenos Aires' best art museums for the caliber of its temporary exhibits. Though the museum, which expanded in 2008, usually displays Latin American works, ranging from pre-Columbian to contemporary, it also hosts exhibits on major international artists such as Marcel Duchamp. Many locals will claim that it's the one of the few reasons to visit Boca. They might just be right. (*Don Pedro de Mendoza 1929.* ☎ *4104 1000; www.proa.org. Open Tu-Su 11am-7pm. AR$3.*)

**MUSEO DE BELLAS ARTES DE LA BOCA.** This long-running museum has a solid collection of late 19th- and early 20th-century Argentine artists, but its real star is **Benito Quinquela Martín.** He's kind of a big deal in Boca, and in Argentina as a whole—so much so that they decided to recreate his bathroom and turn it into an exhibit. Now *that's* fame. Born and raised in Boca, Martín devoted his career to portraying the sights and people of the neighborhood, from its brightly colored houses to the ships that docked in the harbor. Martín founded the museum himself on the site of his studio in 1938, and the third floor is devoted to some of his best works, as well as his personal effects. After perusing his paintings, be sure to head out to the series of rooftop terraces, which function as sculpture gardens and provide excellent views of the neighborhood and the harbor. (*Don Pedro de Mendoza 1935.* ☎ *4301 1080; www.mbqm.com.ar. Open Tu-F 10am-6pm, Sa-Su 11am-6pm. Guided tours Tu-F 10am and 2:30pm. Voluntary contribution AR$3-5.*)

**MUSEO HISTÓRICO DE CERA.** This tiny museum has a short series of exhibits portraying historical scenes and figures as well as a creepy, grisly collection of snake bites and wounds—all in wax. Unless you really love wax museums and snake bites, this one is probably not worth the rather steep entrance fee. (*Dr. Enrique del Valle Iberlucea 1261.* ☎ *4303 0563; www.museodecera.com.ar. Captions in English and Spanish. Open M-F 10am-6pm, Sa-Su 11am-8pm. AR$15.*)

# PUERTO MADERO

**MUSEO FRAGATA SARMIENTO.** Docked in *Dique 3*, this perfectly maintained museum ship was built in England in 1897 and served as one of the Argentine navy's most important vessels at the beginning of the 20th century. Though it never saw combat (Argentina didn't have too many naval conflicts then), it did serve as a major training ship and sailed around the world numerous times between 1899 and 1938. Onboard, you can view the ship's holds and engine rooms and peruse exhibits on its past voyages and residents. *(Dique 3. [S] Plaza de Mayo. ☎4334 9386. Open daily 9am-5pm. Voluntary contribution AR$2.)*

**BUQUE MUSEO CORBETA ARA URUGUAY.** North of Fragata Sarmiento in *Dique 4* is this similar, though smaller, museum ship. Built in 1874, also in Britain, it's the oldest vessel in the Argentine fleet and, much like the Fragata Sarmiento, has taken several spins around the global block. It also served as a training vessel for the Argentine navy and was used in many of the country's expeditions to Antarctica, where Argentina, strangely enough, has a large land claim. *(Dique 4. [S] LN Alem. ☎4314 1090. Open M-F 2-7pm, Sa-Su 10am-7pm. Voluntary contribution AR$1.)*

# RETIRO

**★MUSEO MUNICIPAL DE ARTE HISPANOAMERICANO ISAAC FERNÁNDEZ BLANCO.** Say that name five times fast. Located in the **Palacio Noel,** this gorgeous museum, with a name sadly too long for a reasonable acronym, boasts a setting as spectacular as its collection. The palace itself is named after its architect, **Martín Noel**, who designed the simple, white building in 18th-century, Neocolonial Peruvian style as a protest against the copying of Parisian palaces so common at the time. He later donated the building to the city, which, fittingly, turned it into a museum of colonial artwork. The most stunning pieces of the diverse ensemble are found on the main floor, which displays mostly religious artwork, including oil paintings, carved wooden statuary, and elaborate silver devotional pieces, in rooms with beautifully painted ceilings and carved doorways. The upper floor contains a library and temporary exhibits, while the basement showcases a huge variety of silver and recreated rooms incorporating colonial furniture. Outside are relatively extensive and attractive—if somewhat poorly maintained—gardens. In 1992, the building was damaged during the bombing of the Israeli embassy next door (p. 146), though it has since been repaired. The former location of the Israeli embassy has been left empty as a memorial to the thirty people who lost their lives in the bombing. *(Suipacha 1422. [S] San Martín. ☎4326 3396. Captions in Spanish. Open Tu-Su 2-7pm. AR$3.)*

**MUSEO DE ARMAS DE LA NACIÓN.** Get trigger happy (or slightly ill) in this meandering museum in the Palacio Paz (p. 151), which showcases a dizzyingly enormous collection of the ways people have used to kill each other in war. Displaying 12th-century German pikes, 20th-century machine guns, and everything in between, the collection focuses in particular on the development of the sword, revolver, rifle, and pistol, of which there are seemingly numberless examples. There's also a small room of Asian armor and weapons as well as a room of missiles and cannon. *(Sante Fe 702, in Palacio Paz. [S] San Martín. ☎4311 1071; www.circulomilitar.org. Open M-F 1-7pm. AR$5. Guided visits available by arrangement.)*

**MUSEO NACIONAL DE INMIGRACIÓN.** Located in the rather decrepit former **Gran Hotel de los Inmigrantes,** the entry point for many Argentine immigrants at the beginning of the 20th century, this small museum explains the history

MUSEUMS

of Argentine immigration and the Hotel itself. The somewhat bland displays include photographs, personal effects, maps, and immigration cards. Though it's not particularly difficult to get here from Plaza San Martín, it can be a bit like crossing an industrial wasteland; if you don't fancy traversing what seem like fifty lanes of traffic, it might be wise to take a taxi. The museum is technically in **Puerto Madero,** but is much closer to Retiro. *(Antártida Argentina 1355.* S *San Martín.* ☎ *4317 0285. Captions in Spanish. Open M-F 9am-5pm, Su 11am-7pm. Free.)*

**MUSEO NACIONAL DEL TEATRO.** Housed in the slightly worn but still beautiful **Teatro Nacional Cervantes** (p. 187), this very small museum has exhibits on the history of Argentine theater, ranging from costumes to instruments to photographs. As you can imagine, it's only for those really interested in the subject. *(Córdoba 1199.* S *Uruguay.* ☎ *4815 8883. Captions in Spanish. Open M-F 10am-7pm. Free.)*

# RECOLETA

☒**CENTRO CULTURAL RECOLETA.** In a bright red edifice neighboring Recoleta's cemetery and basílica is one of Buenos Aires' best cultural centers, built in the early 17th century for a group of Franciscan monks. The extensive arched hallways now host up to, if not more than, eight fantastic rotating photography, sculpture, and art exhibits at once displayed in an innovative fashion. Fortunately, the exhibits here lack the institutional quality present in many museums and are a great way to get a feel for what's going on in Argentine art at this very moment. The center also contains the small **Museo Participativo de Ciencias** (Interactive Science Museum), intended for children, and hosts a variety of lecture series, classes, movies, and small theater productions. *(Junín 1930.* S *Callao.* ☎ *4803 1040; www.centroculturalrecoleta.org. Center open daily 10am-9pm. Art exhibits open M-F 2-9pm, Sa-Su 10am-9pm. Science museum open M-F 9am-5pm, Sa-Su 2:30-7:30pm. Art exhibits free. Science museum AR$10.)*

**MUSEO XUL SOLAR.** Located near Recoleta's border with Palermo, this small, manageable, excellent museum is devoted to the life and work of early 20th-century *porteño* painter **Xul Solar** (p. 176). Solar devoted much of his youth to traveling Europe, and many of his colorful, modernist paintings have been compared to those of the Symbolists and Surrealists, as well as certain works by Klee. Scattered throughout the museum, however, are some of Solar's other, perhaps more fascinating pieces, including his highly original Tarot cards, masks, belts, and several impressive pianos with color- and texture-coded keys originally designed to be played by the blind, but also emphasizing the relationship between color and music. There are also small, wooden altars devoted to his "universal religion"—Solar invented universal languages and had an affinity for symbols such as the sun. His name, after all, is a tribute to our celestial neighbor, as well as a replacement for his actual, longer name, **Oscar Agustín Alejandro Schulz Solari,** which would have been a pain in the ass to sign on a canvas. While perusing the collection, be sure to look around at the building's design; housed in the **Fundación Pan Klub,** where Solar spent the last 20 years of his life, the museum's winding staircases and geometric forms might as well have come directly from his abstract paintings. *(Laprida 1212.* S *Agüero.* ☎ *4824 3302; www.xulsolar.org.ar. Some captions in English. Open Tu-F noon-8pm, Sa noon-7pm. AR$6, local students AR$2. Guided tours Tu and Th 4pm, Sa 3:30pm.)*

**MUSEO NACIONAL DE BELLAS ARTES.** Located in a simple red building directly north of the cemetery, Argentina's foremost art museum boasts a constantly rotating collection of over 10,000 pieces, though the number of works on display at one time is surprisingly modest. The first floor offers a whirlwind tour

MUSEUMS

of **European art** from the 13th century to the present. Few periods are explored in depth, but what is on display is certainly impressive and usually includes at least one work from artists ranging from Tintoretto, Rubens, Rembrandt, and El Greco to Rodin, Monet, Klee, and Rothko. Those for whom all of this is old hat, however, can head straight upstairs to the second floor, where **Argentine art** is on display. Though little seems to distinguish the smallish collection of 19th-century works from their European inspirations, the subject matter of a number of paintings is certainly original; keep an eye out, for example, for Cesáreo Quiros' dramatic series **"Los Gauchos."** Still more original and interesting, however, is the massive hall of contemporary Argentine art, including a number of politically dissident works from the 60s and 70s. *(Av. Libertador 1473.* S *Callao.* ☎ *4803 0802; www.mnba.org.ar. Open Tu-F 12:30-7:30pm, Sa-Su 9:30am-7:30pm. Free.)*

**PALAIS DE GLACE.** Across Plaza San Martín de Tours from Centro Cultural Recoleta, this large beige "palace" was actually built to house an ice rink, though it later hosted some of the first "high society" dances that served to make tango mainstream acceptable. Today, it's an art space, drawing a wide variety of temporary exhibits, often one month in duration and usually devoted to a particular contemporary artist. Drop by or check online to see what's currently being offered. *(Posadas 1725.* S *Callao.* ☎ *4804 1163; www.palaisdeglace.org. Open Tu-F noon-8pm, Sa-Su 10am-8pm. Free. Guided English-language tours Sa-Su 5pm. AR$10.)*

**MUSEO DE LA DEUDA EXTERNA (MUSEUM OF EXTERNAL DEBT).** This museum opened its doors in 2006, just a few years after the 2001 climax of Argentina's economic crisis, with the mission of explaining how the financial collapse could have happened. It does so by tracing the country's economic history—and specifically its relationship to foreign debt—from 1810 to the present through a series of fairly technical labels. The displays are drawn from a work of economic history by a father-son team of economists, **Alfredo Eric Calcagno** and **Eric Calcagno,** the former and elder an ex-member of the United Nations Economic Commission for Latin America (ECLA), and the son a sociologist and minister in the Cristina Kirchner government. Needless to say, if you can't read Spanish, and economics doesn't get your juices flowing, the museum won't hold much appeal. If so, however, the museum is a fascinating window into Argentina's perspective on its own financial situation. Perhaps unsurprisingly, the museum has little to say in favor of the IMF's recommendations from the 1980s on; it approaches the country's own dealings, and possible missteps, with its money less thoroughly. Don't miss the powerful **Boda de Oro** exhibit, one of the few times the museum uses a medium other than words. The argument is fairly polemical, so background knowledge is useful, and makes the exhibits that much more interesting. *(Pte. J. E. Uriburu 763, in the basement.* S *Facultad de Medicina.* ☎ *4370 6105; www.econ.uba.ar. Open M-F noon-8pm. Free.)*

# PALERMO

**🖼MUSEO DE ARTE LATINOAMERICANO DE BUENOS AIRES (MALBA).** Housed in a beautiful, airy building in northern Palermo, the MALBA is undoubtedly one of Buenos Aires' best art museums, and unlike many of the city's other major collections, the MALBA's focuses solely on **Latin American art.** The museum's permanent collection, which is refreshingly manageable in scope, located on the second floor, is named after Eduardo Costantini, the museum's patron, and moves chronologically through the 20th century. Though some of the works, including those by **Frida Kahlo** and **Diego Rivera,** will be recognizable to most visitors, the collection provides an excellent introduction to lesser-known artists,

MUSEUMS

including Argentines **Xul Solar** (p. 175) and **Antonio Berni**. The museum also hosts a variety of temporary exhibits, usually held on the third floor and in the basement, on contemporary Latin American artists or quirky themes, as well as an art cinema. *(Av. Presidente Figueroa Alcorta 3415.* $\boxed{S}$ *Agüero.* ☎ *4808 6500; www.malba.org. ar. Open M and Th-Su noon-8pm, W noon-9pm. AR$15, W free.)*

**MUSEO EVITA.** This mecca for all things Eva Perón (p. 59), inaugurated in 2002 on the 50th anniversary of her death, serves the purpose of preserving (and, to some degree, whitewashing) her legacy. Located in a building she converted into a girls' home, the exhibit labels spend much of their time quoting from Evita's own biography and dismissing all critics as cruel, simply accusing them of sharing the sentiment *"viva el cáncer!"* (the cult-like figure died of cervical cancer at a young age). Suspicions of bias become less surprising once you learn that Evita's grandniece was the president of the group responsible for establishing the museum. Though it is more of a touristy shrine, complete with sultry background tango music, than a museum, the Museo Evita does have highlights. Unlike most Argentine museums, this one has attempted to provide labels in English. Additionally, the displayed video footage, with clips from one of Evita's early movies, as well as scenes from the masses in the streets on the day of her funeral, and the day her husband, Juan Perón, first assumed power, merit a visit in their own right. Other pieces in the collection include the first lady's dresses and suits (these articles alone could fill a massive museum) and editions of her propaganda materials. The ground floor room includes a video from the museum's opening, but the main draw of the lobby is, surely, the delicious smells wafting from the **cafe**, technically a separate entity, but a welcome distraction, nonetheless. *(Lafinur 2988.* $\boxed{S}$ *Plaza Italia. Buses 10, 15, 37, 38, 41, 59, 60, 64, 93, 118, 128, and 161 will drop you off nearby on Av. Las Heras.* ☎ *4807 0306/4809 3168; www.museoevita.org or info@museoevita.org. Open Tu-Su and holidays May-Oct. 1-7pm; Nov.-Apr. 11am-7pm. AR$10. Cafe has a separate entrance at Gutiérrez 3926. Open daily 9am-1am.)*

**MUSEO NACIONAL DE ARTO DECORATIVO.** Set in the turn-of-the-century **Palacio Errázuriz**, this museum's setting is just as impressive as its collection. Designed by French architect René Sergent and built in 1911 for the Chilean diplomat Matías Errázuriz and his wealthy Argentine wife Josefina de Alvear, the palace's grand halls and decadent rooms showcase the couple's extravagant art collection, which encompasses numerous centuries as well as styles. Everything from 18th-century Bohemian cut glass to 16th-century Flemish tapestries to 17th-century Russian portraits are on display, and many well-known artists are represented, including El Greco and Manet. Though periods and styles are jumbled together, the collection's lack of organization only serves to grant the palace the more relaxed feeling of a home—albeit it an uncommonly luxurious one—as opposed to that of a museum. If you do start to feel comfortable here and choose to stay a bit longer, by night, the museum's grand hall also serves as a venue for literary and classical **music events,** ranging in price from free to AR$50; see the website for the current schedule. *(Av. del Libertador 1902.* $\boxed{S}$ *Agüero.* ☎ *4801 8248; www.mnad.org. Open Jan.-Feb. Tu-Sa 2-7pm; Mar.-Dec. Tu-Su 2-7pm. AR$2. Guided English-language tours Tu-Su 2:30pm. AR$8.)*

**MUSEO DE ARTES PLÁSTICAS EDUARDO SÍVORI.** The Rosedal's (p. 156) white **Puente Principal** (main bridge) spits you out at the door of this colorful eight-room museum, filled with canvases by Argentine artists from the first six decades of the 20th century. The collection boasts more than 3000 works, though only a handful are actually displayed. Opened in 1938, the museum takes its name from Eduardo Sívori (1918-47), famous as the "painter of the Pampa" and a founder of the Argentine National Academy of Fine Art. Originally a businessman, Sívori visited Europe at the age of 27 to take up painting. The rest is history. Just inside the first door you can see one of his pieces, the delicate *Pampa* (c. 1902), Paintings are grouped by school, with many of the museum's most famous works coming from the so-called Boca School, here represented by Benito Quinquela Martín (1890-1977) and Emilio Pettouruti (1892-1971), a Cubist and friend of Xul Solar (p. 175), another famed Argentine artist. The museum's most important piece is *Chacareros* (c. 1952), or *Farmhands*, a work by Antonio Berni (1905-1981), the painter responsible for some of the frescoes at the Galerías Pacífico (p. 196) downtown. Berni briefly dabbled in Communist Party politics, his paintings reflecting personal concerns about the lower classes in society. The exhibit signs, all in Spanish, seem primarily to be an exercise in name-dropping more artistic figures. The back of the museum features a patio with cafe and sculpture garden. *(Av. Infanta Isabel 555.* S *Plaza Italia, Palermo, and Ministro Carranza.* ☎ *4775 7093; www.museosivori.org. Museum and cafe open Tu-F noon-6pm, Sa-Su and holidays 10am-6pm. AR$1, W and Su free.)*

**CASA MUSEO RICARDO ROJAS.** Opened as a museum in 1958, this elegant stone building was formerly the home of **Ricardo Rojas** (1992-1957), a prominent writer and teacher. Rojas, born into a wealthy family in the province of Santiago de Estero (his father was governor of the province), served as the rector of the University of Buenos Aires from 1926-1930 and founded the Institute of Argentine Literature and Folklore. Like many members of the early 20th-century BA intelligentsia, Rojas was preoccupied with the development of "cultural nationalism"—something Argentina, a country mostly composed of European immigrants, lacked for many years. Unlike Sarmiento, who hoped to "civilize" the country, Rojas believed that indigenous influences played a large role in making up Argentine identity. The other two ingredients were Spanish heritage and the soil itself. His home, designed by Angel Guido, reflects this philosophy—it combines Spanish architecture with more native touches. Fervent nationalism eventually contributed to the spark of a 1930 military coup. The coup prompted Rojas to join the Radical Party, though his activities led to four months of incarceration in Tierra del Fuego in 1934. His most popular work, *El Santo de la Espada*, told the biography of San Martín and was an attempt to distance Argentina's mythic founding father from militaristic influences. The museum collection includes more than 30,000 books from Rojas's personal library. *(Charcas 2837. Closed for renovation at the time of publication. If the guard is around, you can still poke your head around the patio, arguably the house's best feature.)*

**MUSEO NACIONAL DEL HOMBRE.** This tiny museum, housed in the mouthful **Instituto Nacional de Antropología y Pensamiento Latinoamericano** (National Institute of Latin American Anthropology and Thought), displays both Argentine archaeological finds as well as modern indigenous crafts. The pieces on display, including a number of the Stone Age ceramics and colorful, modern textiles, basketwork, and jewelry, are of exceptional quality and beauty, but the exhibits are poorly put together and the information is only in Spanish. For those who do understand Spanish and have a specific interest, however, this museum is a great introduction to Argentina's past and present indigenous cultures. *(Tres de Febrero 1378.* S *Olleros.* ☎ *4782 7251; www.inapl.gov.ar. Open M-F 10am-7pm. Free.)*

**MUSEO DE ARTE POPULAR JOSÉ HERNÁNDEZ.** This small, somewhat boring museum, dedicated to preserving the relics of traditional Argentine life on the *Pampas*, was named for **José Hernández** (1834-1886), the poet who authored *El Gaucho Martín Fierro* (1872), a 2316-line epic poem about military campaigns in the Argentine provinces. The permanent collection showcases Argentine and indigenous arts and crafts, including local silverware, the gaudy sequined costumes worn in honor of *carnaval*, and a display on the poncho. The most interesting part of the museum is a small laminated booklet in the last room with 1930s newspaper clippings documenting the life and death of Argentine sportsman **Felix Bunge** (1894-1935), the original owner of museum's house. Before his *mucamo* (servant) murdered him, Bunge ran his aristocratic Argentine circles during the boom years of the 1920s as a part-time supporter of reactionary politics and the trainer of world-class boxing legend Luis Ángel Firpo (look for the picture of the two of them together, with Firpo towering over Bunge). The exhibit labels are only in Spanish, leaving much to the imagination. The museum itself is located in four rooms in the complex's second building, which you access by passing through a pleasant interior courtyard. The museum also offers classes and workshops—see the website for more details on enrollment. *(Av. del Libertador 2373.* S *Scalabrini Ortiz. Buses 10, 37, 38, 41, 59, 60, 67, 92, 93, 95, 102, 108, 110, 118, 128, and 130.* ☎ *4803 2384/4802 7294; www.museohernandez.org.ar. Open Tu-F 1-7pm, Sa-Su and holidays 10am-8pm. AR$3, residents AR$1, Su free. Spanish guided tours Tu-F 2:30-6pm and Su 2-7pm.)*

**MUSEO METROPOLITANO.** Despite its name, this museum well off the beaten path is more of an art gallery than anything, home to rotating exhibits by contemporary artists. The building, the **Palacio Anchorena,** represents one of the fine turn-of-the-century Palermo Chico mansions, one of many that has since passed on to the government. Built in 1906 by Alejandro Christophersen (1866-1945) for the Mesquita Luro family, it was eventually sold to the Anchorena family (p. 152). Before its turn as a museum, the mansion played host to the Ministry of International Relations and Culture. An elegant stone courtyard, complete with cafe and antique shop, complements the wood-paneled interior. Though the art collection is nothing special, a trip here is worth it for the opportunity to see a classic Palermo mansion. *(Castex 3211.* ☎ *4802 1911 and 4803 4458; museo@museomet.org.ar. Open M-Sa 2-8pm. Free.)*

# THE OUTER BARRIOS

## BELGRANO

**CASA DE YRURTIA.** This madhouse of a museum is packed with works by early 20th-century Argentine sculptor **Rogelio Yrurtia** and his second wife, the daughter of his mentor, painter **Lía Correa Morales.** After studying in Europe, where he came under the

## THE LOCAL STORY

### CROONING CARLOS

Without a doubt, there's no one figure more emblematic of tango than the legendary **Carlos Gardel.** For many, his melodic voice and bright personality are the perfect embodiment of tango style and culture. Virtually every singer in BA's popular shows tries to imitate him, people from all over the world have seen his movies, and Argentines claim he sings better every day—despite the fact that he's been dead for over 70 years.

Born in France (a fact hotly contested by both Argentina and Uruguay), he claimed Buenos Aires as his home town and spent much of his life in the city's **Abasto** neighborhood, where a small **museum** devoted to him has been opened in his former house (p. 181). Though he started his career in 1925 singing folk songs—randomly, a decade after some claim he was wounded in a bar fight with Che Guevara's (p. 158) father Ernesto—it was the tango hit *Mi Noche Triste* that catapulted him to fame. After this, he began touring the world and starring in a number of major films. But his career was cut tragically short at its peak when he was killed in a plane crash in 1935. Such a dramatic death, of course, only served to heighten his popularity. A huge number of visitors still visit his grave in **La Chacarita Cemetery** (p. 164) to place a cigarette between the outstretched fingers of his statue.

MUSEUMS

influence of Rodin and acquired the Picasso painting hanging in the first room, Yrurtia returned to Buenos Aires to begin his career as an artist and settled in this building with Morales for nearly twenty years. The mustard-trimmed house was converted into a museum in 1949, though with all of the naked bodies lunging out at odd angles, it feels like walking into a studio that could still be in use today. Frequently commissioned to produce works for the city, Yrurtia's museum displays the models he used to create the sculpture of **Bernardino Rivadavia** in Plaza Miserere, **Justicia** in the Palacia de la Justicia, and **Monumento a Manuel Dorrego**, at Suipacha and Viamonte. In the back, there is a small garden with a fine sculpture of two boxers frozen in time. *(O'Higgins 290.* S *Juramento. Bus 60, 107, 114.* ☎ *4781 0385; www.casadeyrurtia.gov.ar. Captions in Spanish. Open Tu-F 1-7pm, Su 3-7pm. Guided tours Tu-F 3pm, Su 4pm. AR$3.)*

**BANCO FUNDACIÓN FRANCÉS.** This neocolonial building, built on a plot of land expropriated from Juan Manuel de Rosas (p. 56), one of Argentina's first (of many) military dictators, was the home of Belgrano's founder, Valentín Alsina, in the early 19th century. After passing through other hands, it most notably became a small **museum,** located on the first floor of a restored mansion, which houses a collection of works by one of Argentina's foremost contemporary artists, 20th-century sculptor and painter **Libero Badii.** Italian-born, Badii moved to Argentina at the age of 11 and eventually started his career as a sculptor, using the stone-cutting techniques he picked up from his father, who was a funerary carver. The young artist quickly won international acclaim (even in the United States, where his 1965 bronze sculpture, *Phoenix,* now sits in the Kennedy Center in Washington, D.C.). In the 1980s, Badii turned his focus to painting, producing a series of colorful pieces featuring angled figures and popping eyes. While the works are well-displayed, labels are scarce. The museum is perfect for a quick stop if you're in the neighborhood, but it isn't worth a significant detour. The front door is often locked, so ring the bell and see if anyone is around. Even if you come during the supposed "opening hours," there's a chance it will be closed—try calling ahead to double check or to arrange a visit. *(11 de Septiembre 1990.* ☎ *4784 8650 or 4783 3819. Open M-F 10am-6pm. Free.)*

**MUSEO HISTÓRICO SARMIENTO.** Though it pales in comparison to the Casa Rosada, this beige, Neo-Renaissance building on the Plaza Belgrano also served as the headquarters of the national government—if only for two short weeks more than a century ago. Now it houses a museum devoted to the legacy of thick-jowled **Domingo Sarmiento** (p. 57), a political and intellectual giant whose shadow continues to hover over Argentina today. His list of accomplishments is long and varied. He led the resistance against Juan Manuel de Rosas, one of Argentina's early *caudillos* (military dictators), in part through his famous work of creative non-fiction, *Facundo: Civilization and Barbarism,* a book that critiqued the dictator. As the seventh president of Argentina (1868-1874), Sarmiento also supported public education and the expansion of parks as means of civilizing Latin American society, which he considered backward after a trip to the United States. Among his other achievements, Sarmiento wrote a biography of Abraham Lincoln and conducted Argentina's first national census. Talk about a modern day Renaissance Man. Exhibits include old photographs, some of his belongings, including furniture and china, and the first editions of some of his books, including *Facundo.* Though the captions are mostly in Spanish, they are more extensive than those found in other museums. Fortunately, Sarmiento's life was fascinating enough to speak for itself. *(Juramento 2180.* S *Juramento.* ☎ *4782 2354 or 4781 2989; www.museosarmiento.gov.ar. Open M-F and Su 1-5:30pm; Dec.-Mar. closed Su. AR$1, Th free. Guided tours Su 4pm.)*

# BALVANERA

**MUSEO CASA CARLOS GARDEL.** Just blocks from the Abasto shopping center is the former residence of Argentina's (and perhaps the world's) most famous tango crooner, **Carlos Gardel** (p. 79). The townhouse, which Gardel purchased in 1927 for himself and his mother, has been lovingly restored and now hosts exhibits on Gardel and his life as well as photos of the building as it was when Gardel lived there. The displays, composed mainly of old photos, tango memorabilia, musical scores, and Gardel's personal effects, receive little explanation, however, and may only interest diehard tango fans and the interested aspiring crooner. *(Jean Jaures 735.* S *Carlos Gardel.* ☎ *4964 2015. Some English captions. Open M and W-F 11am-6pm, Sa-Su 10am-7pm. AR$3, local residents AR$1, W free.)*

# CABALLITO

**MUSEO ARGENTINO DE CIENCIAS NATURALES** (NATURAL SCIENCES MUSEUM OF ARGENTINA). In the northwestern corner of the Parque del Centenario (p. 166), Argentina's natural sciences museum draws people of all ages to its exhibits on the past and current flora and fauna of Argentina. Receiving a much-needed facelift at the time of publication, many of the older, mustier exhibits are being replaced by sleeker, educational displays aimed mainly at children, though there is plenty here to tempt the interested adult (or child-at-heart) as well. The first floor houses a miniature aquarium, but the real draw is the paleontology exhibit, which includes a number of mid-sized dinosaur skeletons discovered in Argentina. Still, you should at least walk through the other rooms; don't miss the giant clam in the mollusks exhibit or massive shell of the extinct giant armadillo in the high-quality ancient mammal exhibit. Upstairs, the focus is mainly on the current flora and fauna of Argentina (and elsewhere), including plenty of stuffed mammals and preserved spiders. Be forewarned, however; the captions (in Spanish) are very limited, and you probably won't learn much about what you're seeing, impressive as some of it is. *(Ángel Gallardo 480.* S *Ángel Gallardo.* ☎ *4982 4791; www.macn.gov.ar. Open daily 2-7pm. AR$6.)*

# BOEDO AND SAN CRISTÓBAL

**MUSEO DEL BANCO CIUDAD "MONTE DE PIEDAD".** Perhaps Boedo's only official sight, this museum chronicles the history of the Banco Ciudad. Founded as the "Monte de Piedad" in 1878, the bank originally aimed to lend money at fair rates to Buenos Aires' exploding immigrant population, and, along with the requisite, somewhat boring collection of old bank documents and teller windows, the museum also hosts small exhibits on immigrant life, including a recreated *conventillo*, or tenement. There's also a recreation of the leftist Cafe Biarritz that once held the spot the bank now occupies and that drew a number of famous Argentine artists. On the way out, be sure to check out the bank bannister smashed during the 2001 economic crash, or the photos of the subsequent riots. Everyone who visits (and there aren't too many) is given a personalized tour in Spanish, which makes it easy to see whatever particularly interests you. *(Av. Boedo 870, 2nd fl.* S *Boedo.* ☎ *4931 8204. Open M-F 10am-5pm. Free.)*

# ENTERTAINMENT

Ah, Buenos Aires. Where else can you tango two-step and scream yourself silly at a soccer game in the same day? The city boasts a phenomenal array of unique Argentine entertainment options, along with everything else you would expect from a major metropolitan center. The art galleries display works by internationally renowned masters and lesser-known Argentines, the opera houses and theaters, some of the most beautiful in the world, stage epic productions, and clubs hum with world class tango crooners, flamenco dancers, and jazz musicians. There's something for every taste, and the only time you'll find yourself idle is just when you're struggling to pick a soccer club to root for.

## MONSERRAT

### ART GALLERIES

**Wussman,** Venezuela 570 (☎4331 1887). Ⓢ Belgrano. Though in reality a very expensive paper shop, most of the space in Wussman is actually taken up by a cutting-edge art gallery in front displaying works by edgy, modern Argentine artists. The art supplies, paper goods, gifts, antique books, and beautifully bound journals in back are, unfortunately, way overpriced. Open M-F 10:30am-8pm, Sa 10:30am-2pm. AmEx/V.

### CLASSICAL MUSIC AND OPERA

**Teatro Avenida,** Avenida de Mayo 1222 (☎4342 7650; www.balirica.org.ar). Ⓢ Lima or Avenida de Mayo. This large, opulent theater mostly hosts Argentine lyrical opera. Tickets vary in price, from AR$180 for prime real estate to AR$25 for distant standing room.

### LIVE MUSIC AND CONCERTS

**La Trastienda,** Balcarce 460 (☎4342 7650; www.latrastienda.com). Ⓢ Plaza de Mayo. National and international groups play a variety of music here—pop, rock, electronica, reggae, tango—usually on F nights in a large hall behind the store and outdoor restaurant. Tickets AR$35-100; purchase online or at the box office. AmEx/MC/V.

### TANGO

**Cafe Tortoni,** Avenida de Mayo 825/9 (☎4342 4328; www.cafetortoni.com.ar). Ⓢ Lima or Avenida de Mayo. Buenos Aires' most famous cafe (p. 120) puts on a laid-back, yet lively tango show. The performance also often includes comedy bits, tap dancers, string quartets, and drummers. Sandwiches AR$9-25. Entrees AR$8-32. Wine by the bottle AR$16-105. Shows nightly at 9pm AR$60. Reserve in advance. AmEx/MC/V.

**El Queradí,** Perú 302 (☎5199 1770; www.querandi.com.ar). Ⓢ Perú or Bolívar. Housed in a lovely 1920s building, El Queradí offers traditional tango/dinner shows nightly beginning around 8pm. Tickets AR$250. AmEx/MC/V.

## MICROCENTRO

### ART GALLERIES

🖼 **Praxis,** Arenales 1311 (☎4813 8639; www.praxis-art.com). With branches in New York and Miami, Praxis has worked since the 1970s to take Argentine art to the international arena. The gallery has four floors in a futuristic, minimalist set-up, with exhibits from furniture to etchings. Open M-F 10:30am-8pm, Sa 10:30am-2pm.

**Galería Rubbers,** Av. Alvear 1595 (☎4816 1864; www.rubbers.com.ar). [S] Callao. Rubbers opened in 1957 with an exposition of works by Xul Solar (p. 175) and continues to display big-name artists, like Colombian painter Roberto Botano, and the first exhibition of Andy Warhol in Latin America. Open M-F 11am-8pm, Sa 11am-2pm.

## CLASSICAL MUSIC AND OPERA

👍 **Teatro Colón,** Libertad 621 (☎4378 7344; www.teatrocolon.com.ar). [S] Tribunales. Argentina's premier opera house offers world-class opera and ballet productions and the Buenos Aires Philharmonic Orchestra. The theater is currently under renovation as of summer 2008, with reopening targeted for the 2010 season. Tickets must be purchased at the box office. Foreigners are usually charged a much higher price than Argentines. Bring an Argentine friend! Box office open M-F 9am-5pm. Tickets AR$15-70.

## LIVE MUSIC AND CONCERTS

**Teatro Gran Rex,** Corrientes 857 (☎4322 8000). [S] Carlos Pellegrini. This large venue seating over 3000 shows musicals, theater, and national and international bands such as Coldplay and Interpol. Tickets are usually purchased online through Ticketex.

**Estadio Luna Park,** Bouchard 465 (☎5279 5279; www.lunapark.com.ar). [S] LN Alem. This massive venue on the edge of Microcentro puts on Disney ice shows, concerts, boxing matches, and other spectacles, including major Argentine bands, like the Babasonics, and popular international acts such as Joss Stone and Dream Theater. Tickets AR$30-400. Box office open M-Sa 10am-7:30pm.

## TANGO

👍 **Confitería Ideal,** Suipacha 384 (☎4322 1653). [S] Carlos Pellegrini. Offers a wide range of tango events on the cafe's 2nd fl. (p. 122). Excellent classes for beginners through advanced students are offered daily, usually starting in the early afternoon. After the classes, experienced dancers take over, turning the space into a *milonga.* There are then dinner and tango shows virtually every evening beginning sometime between 8 and 10:30pm. Check the stands in the front of the cafe for the week's schedule.

[TIP] **T-A-NGO.** Having trouble picking up the steps? Since the most basic tango involves two slow steps followed by three faster ones, repeating T A NGO as you do the steps can help you keep the rhythm. Or at least distract you from your maladroit jerkings.

## THEATER

**Teatro General San Martín,** Corrientes 1530 (☎0800 333 5254; www.teatrosanmartin.com.ar). [S] Uruguay. This large theater has numerous auditoriums showing dance and music performances, as well as contemporary and traditional theater. The building also hosts art and photography exhibits. Box office open 10am-10pm, or buy tickets online.

**Teatro Opera,** Corrientes 860 (☎4326 1335). [S] Carlos Pellegrini. A beautiful old Art Deco theater with a wide variety of productions from tango and modern dance to classical and contemporary music. Box office open daily 10am-8pm.

**Teatro Presidente Alvear,** Corrientes 1654 (☎4373 4245; www.teatrosanmartin.com.ar). [S] Callao or Uruguay. A variety of theatrical and musical productions at this theater with one large auditorium. Box office times variable; check online for times and tickets.

**Teatro la Plaza,** Corrientes 1660 (☎6320 5300). S Callao or Uruguay. A small theater that puts on comedic productions and contemporary and traditional theater. Also shares a building with several art galleries.

**Teatro el Vitral,** Rodríguez Peña 344 (☎4371 0948). S Callao. This small independent theater focuses on contemporary productions and alternative theater, including musical comedies and improv. Tickets from AR$20.

**Teatro del Pueblo,** Roque Sáenz Peña 943 (☎4326 3606; www.teatrodelpueblo.org.ar). S Carlos Pellegrini. One of the first independent theaters in Argentina and South America. Hosts small, modern productions.

# SAN TELMO

## CLASSICAL MUSIC AND OPERA

**La Scala de San Telmo,** Pasaje Giuffra 371 (☎4362 1187; www.lascala.com.ar). S Independencia. Home to a beautiful theater and cafe. Events include musicals, operas, jazz, classical concerts, and dance. Box office open M-F 10am-6pm, Sa-Su 5-10pm.

**Teatro Margarita Xirgu,** Chacabuco 875 (☎4300 8817; www.mxirgu.com.ar). S Independencia. A plain stone facade, complete with neon sign, conceals this sleek, beautifully renovated theater, which shows both operas and classical music events.

## LIVE MUSIC AND CONCERTS

■ **Mitos Argentinos,** Humberto Primo 489 (☎4362 7810; www.mitosargentinos.com.ar). S Independencia. Just off Plaza Dorrego, this alternative venue hosts a variety of talented local underground groups, as well as tribute acts to major Latin American bands, such as the Heroes del Silencio. Open Th-Sa until late. Cover AR$10-15.

## TANGO

San Telmo is, by most accounts, *the* center of tango in the city. Though most *barrios* these days have great tango bars, no other neighborhood has as many popular, traditional, and fun places.

**Bar Sur,** Estados Unidos 299 (☎4362 6086; www.bar-sur.com.ar). S Independencia. This small, intimate venue offers traditional tango shows nightly 8pm-3am. Though audience members are never far from the action, they are usually invited to participate by the end of the evening. Get ready. Tickets from AR$125.

**El Viejo Almacén,** Balcarce 799 (☎4307 6689; www.viejo-almacen.com.ar). S Independencia. Housed in an old mansion, El Viejo Almacén has long been one of the city's most popular, and famous, tango venues,

**THE HIDDEN DEAL**

### LET'S GO: TANGO

Tango, *bife,* nightlife—some of the main reasons BA is the world's hottest destination. While we wish you luck getting steak and drinks for free, there's no need to pay to see dance moves. At the following venues, you can see some excellent tango action for just a few pesos—and maybe without even touching your wallet at all.

**La Feriá de San Telmo (p. 147):** On Su at 6pm, after the booths have been torn down, **Plaza Dorrego** hosts an informal *milonga.* If you hang around long enough, a professional couple will usually take over the floor for a (free!) 1hr. tango performance.

**El Balcón, San Telmo (p. 205):** On F and Sa nights and Su afternoons, this colorful, modern bar hosts folk and tango dancing, crooning, and guitar. But while the shows are free, it's good form to order something off the menu.

**El Caminito, La Boca (p. 149):** Tango dancers are everywhere in this tourist trap; they might even prevent you from walking down the street. For a more formal experience, head indoors to **Caminito Tango Show (p. 186),** which is still free, though you should get lunch.

**Calle Florida, Microcentro (p. 195):** Every evening, several couples manage to carve out some space on the city center's busiest street for some romantic tango. Heading north from Florida's intersection with Av. Corrientes, you're bound to run into one eventually. We usually did.

offering nightly shows that are traditional, sleek, high-quality, and well attended. Dinner 8pm Show 10pm. Tickets from AR$175.

**Taconeando,** Balcarce 725 (☎4307 6696; www.taconeando.com). Ⓢ Independencia. Offers traditional tango shows Th-Sa at 9pm. A relaxed atmosphere in an old, out-of-the-way mansion in San Telmo. The 25% advance online booking discount makes it one of BA's most affordable shows. Cocktail hour show AR$140, dinner show AR$180.

**El Balcón,** Humberto Primo 461, 2nd fl. (☎4362 2354; www.elbalcondelaplaza.com. ar). Ⓢ Independencia. Tango shows are on F and Sa nights starting at 10pm and Su afternoons from 1-7pm at this brightly painted bar. The shows themselves are free, a welcome break from the high prices at other venues, though it's good form to order a meal while you're there. Food AR$15-35. Drinks AR$10-25. Cash only.

**El Tasso,** Defensa 1575 (☎4307 6506). Ⓢ San Juan. Located just across the street from Parque Lezama, this small, relaxed *milonga* draws a crowd of locals who come to dance to a small orchestra on Su nights. Free.

# LA BOCA

## LIVE MUSIC AND CONCERTS

**Blues Special Club,** Almirante Brown 102 (☎4362 7052). This popular club hosts bands playing jazz, blues, rock, and reggae. There's usually a jam session on F nights and major shows on Th, Sa, and Su. The neighborhood is dangerous, so take a taxi. Cover varies.

## TANGO

Tango is everywhere on the streets in La Boca. If you stick around long enough, you're guaranteed to run into a random exhibition happening somewhere. Some establishments also run official shows.

**Caminito Tango Show,** Dr. Enrique del Valle Iberlucea 1151 (☎4301 1520). Though many of the restaurants that line El Caminito and Del Valle Iberlucea regularly put on tango shows to entertain the crowds, this daily indoor show is more formal than most. It's still free, but you're expected to buy lunch. Entrees AR$8-25.

# RETIRO

## ART GALLERIES

🏛 **Fundación Federico Jorge Klemm,** M.T. de Alvear 626 (☎4312 3334/4443; www. fundacionfjklemm.org), between Maipú and Florida, in the basement of the mall just opposite the Plaza San Martín. Ⓢ San Martín. This small, well-established gallery shows works by contemporary artists and a permanent collection that includes works by Max Ernst, Picasso, and Warhol. Open M-F 11am-8pm.

**Galería Arroyo,** Arroyo 830 (☎4325 0947; www.galarroyo.com). Ⓢ San Martín. Opened in 1989 with an eye toward reinvigorating interest in out-of-fashion Argentine painters. Since 1997, the gallery has also hosted *subastas* (auctions). Open M-F 11am-8pm.

**Palatina,** Arroyo 821 (☎4327 0620; www.galeriapalatina.com.ar), across from Galería Arroyo. Another quality Arroyo gallery. Open M-F 10:30am-8pm, Sa 10am-1pm.

## CLASSICAL MUSIC AND OPERA

**Teatro Coliseo,** M.T. de Alvear 1125 (☎4816 3789). Ⓢ San Martín. This large venue, originally a circus site, shows ballet, classical music, theater, and musicals. It also has a little bit of history—in 1920, Wagner's opera *Parsifal* was broadcast by radio from here, making it one of the first operas to be sent over the airwaves. Only 20 homes in BA had receivers at the time, so not many got to hear it. Talk about a special engagement.

### LIVE MUSIC AND CONCERTS

**ND/Ateneo,** Paraguay 918 (☎4328 2888; www.ndateneo.com.ar). [S] San Martín. Large theater hosts a huge variety of shows, concerts, and plays. Acts range from improv groups to schmaltzy tango singers and classical pianists. Box office open M-Sa noon-8pm.

### THEATER

**Teatro Nacional Cervantes,** Libertad 815 (☎4816 4224; www.teatrocervantes.gov.ar). [S] Uruguay or Carlos Pellegrini. This opulent theater presents musicals, theater productions (many Spanish plays, in particular), and dance. At the time of publication, the theater was partially closed for a much-needed face lift.



## RECOLETA

### ART GALLERIES

**Ruth Benzacar,** Florida 1000 (☎4313 8480; www.ruthbenzacar.com). The entrance to Ruth Benzacar may look like it leads into a parking lot, but the gallery's white walls and blonde wood floor actually make up one of the sleekest contemporary art galleries around. Open M-F 11:30am-8pm, Sa 10:30am-1:30pm.

**Aguilar,** Florida 950 (☎4313 0225/8080 or 4312 8242; www.galeriamuseoaguilar.com). Two stories with walls chock-a-block 2500 Argentine paintings. The works on display include mostly 20th-century artists, from well-known masters like Antonio Berni to lesser-known painters. Open daily 8am-9pm.

### LIVE MUSIC AND CONCERTS

👍 **Notorious,** Av. Callao 966 (☎4813 6888; www.notorious.com.ar). [S] Callao. Though it looks like a basic music store from the street, the racks of CDs—all of which you can listen to before you buy—actually conceal a hip restaurant, bar, and garden out back frequented by BA's younger crowd. By night, hosts a wide variety of concerts, readings, and local acts and is particularly well known as a jazz venue. Tickets usually run AR$10-25. Breakfast AR$6-19. Salads and sandwiches AR$6-22. Other entrees AR$25-39.

## PALERMO

### FLAMENCO

**Tiempo de Gitanos,** El Salvador 5575 (☎4776 6143; www.tiempodegitanos.com.ar). [S] Palermo. A small, intimate restaurant in Palermo Hollywood that puts on flashy flamenco shows W-Su. The price (AR$35) W-Th includes delicious *tapas,* but F-Su, expect a more traditional, and filling, Argentine *menú.* Reserve ahead.

### LIVE MUSIC AND CONCERTS

👍 **Thelonious,** Salguero 1884 (☎4829 1562; www.theloniousclub.com.ar). [S] Bulnes or Scalabrini Ortiz. This small, New York-style jazz club is well loved for its intimate and relaxed atmosphere. Hosts some of the country's best jazz musicians, as well as inter-

## WEEKENDS:
## NOW STARRING MONDAY

After a week of solid partying, you're probably thinking to yourself—does this city ever sleep? **No.** Usually Not. Some nightlife spots take a break on Monday, but that's about it. This changed in 2006, though, when the weekend took over Monday for many young *porteños* who frequent the popular, cool, and alternative *La Bomba de Tiempo* show.

West of the city center in Balvanera, a small group of musicians have turned a massive, open-air converted warehouse known as the **Konex Center** into the place to be on Monday night. Twelve of the country's most accomplished percussionists huddle on a small stage, pounding out rhythms that draw from all musical styles—from Brazilian and Indian beats to Jazz and Bop. Everything is improvised, and there are no repeats. The group seems to be successful, drawing around 400 beer-fueled (AR$10) stomping dancers. By the time the show ends at 10pm, most are ready for another long night on the town.

Before you head to the warehouse, note that this event is no secret. It's a good idea to arrive early, especially in the summer.

*Konex Center, Sarmiento 3131. S Carlos Gardel. ☎4864 3200; www.labombadetiempo.com. Shows M 7-10pm. AR$10. Box office opens at 6pm.*

national acts, for jam sessions, swing, and hard bop. Check the website for the current schedule. Beer AR$8-11. Mixed drinks AR$11-19. *Pizzetas* AR$14-16. Desserts AR$13. Cover free-AR$20. Open W-Su, usually starting at 9:30pm. AmEx/MC/V.

**La Peña del Colorado,** Güemes 3657 (☎4822 1038; www.delcolorado.com.ar). S Bulnes. Even some members of the younger set flock to this rustic, restaurant-style venue, where a new Argentine folk act (usually guitar trios and quartets) plays every night Tu-Su. Grab a seat, chow down on some inexpensive *parrilla* fare (AR$14-25), and enjoy the music, which has a good chance of becoming participatory—you may want to bring a guitar if you have one. Shows AR$12-25.

**Virasoro,** Guatemala 4328 (☎4831 8918; www.virasorobar.com.ar), between Scalabrini Ortiz and Araóz. S Scalabrini Ortiz. A tiny jazz club that hosts some of the most intimate acts around. The house serves food, but stick with its simpler options. Salads AR$18-22. Burgers AR$12-28. Wine AR$22-26. Minimum consumption AR$10. Cover varies depending on the act, usually AR$10-20. W-Su nights starting at 9:30pm.

## TANGO

**La Virutá,** Armenia 1366 (☎4774 6357; www.lavirutatango.com.ar). S Scalabrini Ortiz. In the Armenian Cultural Center. One of the city's biggest and most popular venues, offering lessons, *milongas,* and shows. Tango lessons W-Su AR$13-25. Rock lessons Sa-Su. Salsa lessons Tu and Th-F. Popular *milongas* (AR$7-10) W-Th and Su midnight-3:30am, F-Sa midnight-6am. As if that weren't enough, on Th and F, the dancing stops briefly for performances, when tables are set up for a late dinner. Entrees AR$23-45.

**Salón Canning,** Scalabrini Ortiz 1331 (☎4832 6753). S Scalabrini Ortiz. This venue has various shows, classes, and *milongas*. Bilingual lessons F-Sa 8pm (AR$10). A *milonga* (AR$5) begins afterwards and ends at 4am on F and 3am on Sa. If you're feeling rusty and need more practice, there's also a *milonga* W 4-11pm.

# COLEGIALES

### THEATER

**The Roxy Teatro,** Frederico Lacroze 3455 (www.elteatroonline.com.ar), at the intersection with Alvarez Thomas. Though mainly based in Palermo, the Roxy conglomerate (p. 213) still manages to reach out to the nearby Colegiales crowd with this entertainment venue, home to live music, dance, and theater. Check the website for details and schedules.

# BALVANERA

## THEATER

**Ciudad Cultural Konex,** Sarmiento 3131 (☎4864 3200; www.ciudadculturalkonex.org). [S] Carlos Cardel. This converted warehouse shows major musicals, like *Rent,* modernist theater, and opera in its numerous concrete patios and art spaces. There's a bar downstairs serving cheap drinks, and the venue is especially popular on M for its weekly *La Bomba de Tiempo* percussion shows (see feature, p. 188). Tickets AR$10-70.

# ALMAGRO

## LIVE MUSIC AND CONCERTS

**Club de Amigos de la Vaca Profana,** Lavalle 3683 (☎4867 0934; www.vacaprofana.com.ar). Two floors of tables face the stage in this alternative venue, which looks like a black box theater and whose motto is *"De cerca nadie está normal"* ("around here, nothing is normal"). Mainly shows live music events, usually folk or neo-ethnic, beginning 8:30-10pm, but also stages small theater productions and readings. Drinks AR$7-22. Pizzas AR$25-30. *Picadas* AR$35-62. Cover AR$12-25, sometimes free. Cash only.

## TANGO

**La Catedral,** Sarmiento 4006 (☎15 5325 1630). Bilingual instructors conduct daily tango classes—and one weekly folk dancing class—in a small, funky hall. Sporadic, energetic *milongas* draw a younger, diverse crowd. Admission AR$5-10.

**Bien Bohemio,** Sanchez de Loria 745 (☎4957 1895; www.bienbohemiobar.com.ar). [S] Loria. Just a few blocks from the border with Boedo, this small, lovely tango hall hosts *milongas* as well as tango and theater classes, poetry readings, and a tango show on Sa night; check out the website for current offerings. Open daily from 5pm.

## THEATER

👍 **El Camarín de las Musas,** Mario Bravo 956-60 (☎4862 0655). [S] Carlos Gardel. Part theater, part gallery, part restaurant, this small off-Corrientes venue is popular for its cutting-edge theater and dance and free art exhibitions. Buy tickets (AR$15-30) at the restaurant (entrees AR$20-25). Open daily 11am-10pm. AmEx/MC/V.

**Teatro Anfitrion,** Venezuela 3340 (☎4931 2124; www.anfitrionteatro.com.ar). [S] Loria. A group of young actors, authors, and directors stages small alternative productions in this small, modern theater. There's also a bar downstairs. Tickets usually AR$15-25.

**Actor's Studio,** Díaz Vélez 3842 (☎4958 8268; www.actors-studio.org). [S] Castro Barros. Puts on alternative theatrical productions, ranging from local works to Chekhov interpretations. Box office usually open 3hr. before showtime. Tickets free-AR$30.

# BOEDO

## TANGO

**La Esquina de Homero Manzi,** Av. San Juan 3601 (☎4957 8488; www.esquinahomeromanzi.com.ar). [S] Boedo. After famous tango lyricist Homero Manzi sang about the corner of Av. Boedo and Av. San Juan, it didn't take too long for someone to found a tango establishment in this historic cafe. The daily shows at 10pm are, unsurprisingly,

### WHO'S A HOOLIGAN?

Coming from a country derided around the world for its lack of enthusiasm for the sport, I could not have been more excited by the hype surrounding Argentine soccer. Like every other tourist, I'd heard stories about crazed fans, riots, fights, and outright insanity. Naturally, I was looking forward to throwing myself into the melee and was preparing myself for the worst (best). I was completely unaware, however, to what lengths the authorities would go to oppose that same insanity I was just getting revved up for.

After arriving at a match between **River** and **Racing** and taking my seat, I did the first thing I could think of—I looked around for a beer. I quickly discovered, though[redacted]hat the stadium no longer sold alcohol. Apparently it was thought to contribute to drunken fights. Go figure. Slightly disappointed, I went for a Coke instead, only to find that it was served heavily watered down in paper cups. Apparently, the whizzes upstairs had also determined that glass bottles were excellent projectiles for throwing at players and other fans.

Trying to internalize how sensible such measures were, I settled down with my soda and waited, at least, for the soccer-crazed fans. Surely they would show up and sweep away the beer-deprived crowd in their mayhem. However, I was unable find them anywhere.

Then[redacted]ight before the game began, my friend pointed out a

a flashy affair; get here an hour early if you'd like to have dinner. From AR$50.

### THEATER

**Pan y Arte,** Av. Boedo 876-880 (☎4957 6922). [S] Boedo. A small theater that shows modern productions on weekends (tickets from AR$15). Next door, there's a lovely cafe (p. 136) which is a wonderful cross between modern and rustic atmosphere. Salads and sandwiches AR$9-22. Other entrees AR$20-40. Free Wi-Fi. Open M-Sa 9am-late. AmEx/MC/V.

**Timbre 4,** Av. Boedo 640 (☎4932 4395; www.timbre4.com). [S] Boedo. An alternative theater that has hosted the very popular *La Omisión de la Familia Coleman* F-Su in the evenings for the last 4-5 years. Tickets AR$30.

**Boedo XXI,** Av. Boedo 853 (☎4957 1400). [S] Boedo. Yet another small, cutting-edge theater, which stages productions on weekends. Tickets AR$10-20.

## SAN CRISTÓBAL

### TANGO

**Club Gricel,** La Rioja 1180 (☎4957 7157). [S] Urquiza. An energetic, local crowd dances among the flashing lights at this popular neighborhood *milonga,* where daily tango classes are also held for those looking to make their own moves. *Milonga* F-Sa from 11pm, Su from 9pm (AR$10-15). Classes AR$15-18.

## FLORES

### THEATER

**Teatro Flores,** Av. Rivadavia 7806 (www.elteatroonline.com.ar), at the intersection with Campaña. Yet another Roxy theater venue (p. 188), this time way out in western BA, but with a twist this time—on Sa nights, Teatro Flores turns into a disco. Check the website for details and schedules. Shows usually W-Sa.

## SPORTS

### SOCCER

Whether you're a diehard fan or a relative novice, no trip to BA is complete without attending a *fútbol* game. Many hostels lead somewhat expensive soccer tours that include tickets and transportation to and from the stadium. Tickets are typically in the *platea* section, where you have seats, as opposed to the standing-room-only area. For **Boca Juniors** and **River Plate** games, you can also contact **Ticketek** (☎5237 7200; www.ticketek.com).

**Boca Juniors,** Estadio Alberto J. Armando Bransden 805 (www.bocajuniors.com.ar). Based in the working class south of the city, the Boca Juniors are one of Argentina's top teams, having won a record 17 international titles. Their 1940 stadium, known as *La Bombonera* (chocolate box), is wreathed in the yellow and blue colors of the home team and seats 60,000 fans. To buy tickets on match day, head for the box office on Wenceslao Villafañe or the **Casa Amarilla.** Beware of people trying to sell you fake tickets—just because they're wearing a Boca jersey doesn't mean they're an official. Ushers will scan the tickets just before you enter the stadium to make sure they are the real deal. Tickets in the standing-room-only *popular* section, which exposes you to fans lighting blue flares, start at a dirt cheap AR$24.

**River Plate,** Estadio Monumental Núñez (www.cariverplate. com.ar). Boca's greatest rival, the red and white squad of River Plate, plays in the 67,000-seat *El Monumental* in the wealthier northern area of the city. The ticket windows are on Av. Figueroa Alcorta, close to the intersection with Almte. Solier. *Popular* seats AR$27 (yes, more expensive than Boca, but River is the higher class team, after all).

After Boca and River, the rest of the teams in the city can be lumped together into an "everyone else" category. **Independiente,** based in Avellaneda, just due southeast of Boca, historically finishes third behind Boca and River. (www.caindependiente. com.) The same applies for Independiente's chief rival, **Racing,** which is also based in Avellaneda. (www.racingclub.com.) In addition to these two clubs, the city's top soccer league boasts three other teams—**Huracán** (www.clubahuracan.com.ar), their Boedo rivals **San Lorenzo** (www.sanlorenzo.com.ar), and the **Argentinos Juniors** (www.argentinosjuniors. com.ar), former team of the beloved, and somewhat controversial, Diego Maradona.

## POLO

Strangely enough, Argentina dominates in polo. The majority of the top 50 players in the world are from Argentina, and since 1949, the country has held the first place position in the world polo rankings. As if that weren't impressive enough, in addition to players, its *"petiseros"* polo horses have a reputation for being some of the most well-bred. Just across from the Hipodrómo Argentino (p. 192) is BA's polo field, the only one in the world located in a metropolitan center. The season runs September to December, and the most important event, the **Campeonato Argentino Abierto,** takes place every November. (Av. del Libertador

small area in the upper stands. The *barrabranas*, the official "hooligans" for the teams (yes—they have official mischief makers), were finally entering the stadium. There was no doubt about their enthusiasm, but they seemed distant. I soon realized why: they were being funneled into an enclosed area completely surrounded by high fences. As if that weren't enough, the fences were also topped with stretches of barbed wire—in other words, the section was completely mayhem-proof and prepared for World War I.

After seeing all of this, I settled in for a much calmer experience than I had expected. Though enthusiastic, the fans never really went ballistic, and I never had to use that right hook I'd been practicing. Once the game ended, I stood up to leave, only to find that I couldn't. For fifteen minutes after the finish, we were held in the stands until the opposing team left—I assume in one piece.

Exiting the stadium, I suppose I was happy that all had ended well and without violence. But still, I couldn't help but sigh to myself. I wouldn't have minded a little bit of harmless insanity to stave off the blues of watching American soccer back at home, starring comparatively zombified fans.

*—Ingrid Gustafson*

4300 and Dorrego. ☎4777 6444; www.aapolo.com. Tickets can be bought the day of the match or via Ticketek; ☎5237 7200.)

## HORSE RACING

**Hipodrómo Argentino,** Avenida del Libertador 4101, Palermo (☎4778 2800; www. palermo.com.ar). Ⓢ Ministro Carranza or Palermo. Buses 10, 34, 64, 130, 160 and 166. Founded in 1876, the Hipodrómo Argentino, a track that plays host to 120 horse races per year, provides a distinctly pastoral scene in the heart of bustling Buenos Aires. For the best seats, head away from the Dorrega entrance and up into the stands. For a look at the horses themselves, pay a visit to the stables, which are located near the Dorrega entrance. Races usually take place in the early afternoon or evening. The horses are hardly the hippodrome's primary draw, though—slot machines, housed incongruously in buildings dating from 1908, are open 24hr. per day, 365 days per year, drawing around 20,000 people per day. The hippodrome also has a cafe, albeit an overpriced one. Races M, F, Su 2:30-10:30pm. AR$3.

**COLOR CODED.** Informed travelers to Buenos Aires, even those not formerly obsessed with soccer, should know the basics of the game and the nuanced local rivalries. If you're overwhelmed by the multitude of teams, just learn them by color: Boca Juniors are blue and yellow, River Plate are red and white, San Lorenzo are blue and red, Independiente are red....and the list goes on. Forever and ever. At least it's a start.

## RUGBY

As with soccer, Brits brought rugby to Argentina in the late 19th century and the Argentines promptly adopted and embraced the sport. The national team, **Los Pumas** (named for the jaguar on their crest), finished third in the 2007 Rugby World Cup. Though the country ranks in the top tier, it has been tussling with the International Rugby Board to admit it into an international league with more regular competitions, as it does not face off regularly against neighboring nations. The two most prestigious local teams, **Club Atlético de San Isidro** and the **San Isidro Club,** compete just outside the city in San Isidro (p. 217).

# CINEMAS

There's no shortage of cinemas in Buenos Aires, from art house establishments to smaller independent theaters and massive megaplexes. Many of the city's older theaters can be found on the section of **Avenida Corrientes** in Microcentro, though the newer, flashier complexes tend to be in more residential areas. Still, a number of the city's major shopping centers, including **Patio Bullrich** (p. 199), **Galerías Pacífico** (p. 196), and **Abasto** (p. 201) house sleek cinemas. Throughout the city, Hollywood blockbusters are by far the easiest to find, though the larger theaters will also show Argentine and foreign films, as will the smaller, independent theaters; the **MALBA** (p. 176), for example, runs an excellent series of art films. Most foreign films will be in the original language with Spanish subtitles, though this is not always the case; check beforehand to avoid bad dubbing. We've listed a selection of centrally located cinemas below, though there are many, many more; check out www.infobae.com/cartelera/destacadas_cine.html for a complete listing of theaters, movies, and showtimes.

ENTERTAINMENT

**Arteplex,** Av. Cabildo (☎4781 6500), between Congreso and Ugarte. Arteplex is an art-house cinema with 4 theaters named after movie greats. Tickets M-W AR$12, Th-Su AR$16 after the first showing. Discounts for seniors and children under 11.

**Cine Cosmos,** Av. Corrientes 2046, Balvanera (☎4953 5405; www.cinecosmos.com). Ⓢ Callao. This small theater shows independent and foreign films, including some Hollywood blockbusters, on 2 screens. Tickets AR$10-15.

**Cine Lorca,** Corrientes 1428, Microcentro (☎4371 5077). Ⓢ Uruguay. A small, central theater that shows anything ranging from Hollywood flicks to foreign and independent films on 2 screens. Tickets AR$12-18.

**Cinemark Palermo,** Beruti 3399, at Bulnes, Palermo (☎0800 222 2463). Ⓢ Bulnes. This large complex shows 6-7 films, usually all Hollywood pictures. Tickets AR$15-20.

**Compleja Tita Morello,** Suipacha 442, Microcentro (☎4322 1195). Ⓢ Carlos Pellegrini. Having sworn off the Hollywood blockbuster, this older theater shows 4-6 Argentine movies, as well as 2-3 foreign films. Tickets AR$7, students AR$5.

**Espacio INCAA (Instituto Nacional de Arte Audiovisuales): Cine Gaumont,** Av. Rivadavia 1635, Microcentro (☎4371 3050). Ⓢ Congreso. Usually screens 3-4 Argentine new releases and independent films. Tickets AR$4, students AR$2.50.

**Gen. Paz,** Av. Cabildo 2702 (☎4781 1412). This cinema has 6 theaters that show mainstream Hollywood movies. Tickets sold outside. Tickets M-W AR$12, Th-Su AR$16 after the first showing. Discounts for seniors and children under 11.

**Sala Leopoldo Lugones,** Corrientes 1530, 10th fl., Microcentro (☎0800 333 5254; www.teatrosanmartin.com.ar/cine). Ⓢ Uruguay. Located in the Complejo Teatral San Martín, this small cinema usually shows 1-2 arthouse flicks; check the website for what's currently playing. Tickets AR$7, students AR$4.

**Showcase Cinemas,** Av. Monroe 1655 (☎4786 3232 or 4780 3349). This megacomplex includes a 10-theater cinema, McDonald's, fast-food *parrilla*, and a bookstore. As if that's not enough, there's even a bowling alley, **Paloko Bowling.** Perfect for catching that blockbuster you'll miss back at home. Bowling M-Th AR$12 per person, F-Su and holidays AR$14. Theater open M-Th and 10am-midnight F-Sa 10am-3am.

**Village Recoleta,** at Junín and Lopez, Recoleta (☎0810 810 2463; www.villagecines.com). Ⓢ Pueyrredón. A massive, ultra-modern complex that houses several restaurants, cafes, and stores, as well as over a dozen screens. Shows a wide variety of Hollywood blockbusters, Argentine and foreign pictures, and independent films. Tickets AR$15-20. Additional locations listed on their website.

ENTERTAINMENT

# SHOPPING

A walk down Calle Florida, BA's most famous (and expensive) shopping thoroughfare, offers a one-sided glimpse of the offerings available for dishing out pesos—one dominated by malls and chain stores. Beyond the crowded Microcentro street are glamorous boutiques in Palermo, kitschy houseware shops in San Telmo, huge bookstores set in former theaters, and the classic Buenos Aires flea markets that take over plazas on Sunday afternoons. Not everything is affordable for the budget traveler—it's a big city, after all—but there's something for everyone, from the window shopper to the bargain hunter.

**ANTIQUES**

| | |
|---|---|
| Gil Antigüedades (p. 197) | ST |
| HB Antiquedades (p. 197) | ST |

**BOOKSTORES**

| | |
|---|---|
| ◪Ateneo Grand Splendid (p. 198) | Rec |
| Boutique del Libro (p. 199) | Pal |
| Eterna Cadencia (p. 199) | Pal |
| Kel Ediciones (p. 198) | Ret |
| Libreria Hernandez (p. 196) | Cen |
| Walrus (p. 197) | ST |

**CLOTHES AND ACCESSORIES**

| | |
|---|---|
| Amor Latino (p. 199) | Pal |
| Condimentos (p. 200) | Pal |
| Diseño Argentino (p. 200) | Pal |
| ◪El Buen Orden (p. 197) | ST |
| Gabriell Capricci (p. 198) | Ret |
| ◪Galería 5ta Avenida (p. 198) | Ret |
| Hoy Como Ayer (p. 200) | Pal |
| Keak (p. 200) | Pal |
| Los Vados del Isen (p. 198) | Rec |
| Maria Allô (p. 200) | Pal |
| ◪Palacio de las Artes (p. 201) | Bel |
| Rapsodía (p. 200) | Pal |
| Salsipuedes (p. 200) | Pal |
| Seco (p. 200) | Pal |
| Tinta China (p. 198) | Ret |
| Un Lugar en el Mundo (p. 197) | ST |
| Verbo (p. 200) | Pal |

**CRAFTS AND SOUVENIRS**

| | |
|---|---|
| Arte Indígena (p. 196) | Cen |

**HOUSEWARES**

| | |
|---|---|
| Calma Chicha (p. 200) | Pal |
| L'ago (p. 198) | ST |
| Papelera Palermo (p. 200) | Pal |

**MARKETS**

| | |
|---|---|
| ◪Feria de San Telmo (p. 197) | ST |
| Las Pulgas Antigüedades (p. 200) | Pal |

**MUSIC**

| | |
|---|---|
| Miles Discos (p. 200) | Pal |
| Musimundo (p. 196) | Cen |
| Zival's (p. 196) | Cen |

**SHOPPING CENTERS**

| | |
|---|---|
| Alto Palermo (p. 200) | Pal |
| Bond Street Galería (p. 199) | Rec |
| Buenos Aires Design (p. 199) | Rec |
| Galerías Pacífico (p. 196) | Cen |
| Paseo Alcorta (p. 201) | Pal |
| Patio Bullrich (p. 199) | Ret |
| Shopping Abasto (p. 201) | Bal |

**SPORTS AND OUTDOORS**

| | |
|---|---|
| Buenos Aires Sport (p. 197) | Cen |
| Camping Center (p. 199) | Ret |
| Canaglia Bicicletas (p. 196) | Cen |
| Depor Camping (p. 201) | Pal |
| ◪Wildlife (p. 196) | Cen |

**TANGO**

| | |
|---|---|
| ◪Flabella (p. 197) | Cen |

---

**NEIGHBORHOOD ABBREVIATIONS: Bal** Balvanera **Bel** Belgrano **Cen** The Center (Monserrat, Microcentro) **Pal** Palermo **Rec** Recoleta **Ret** Retiro **ST** San Telmo

## THE CENTER

Though there is certainly no lack of stores in Microcentro or Monserrat, few travelers will find either location to be an interesting shopping destination. The types of stores you'll find here are exemplified by those along **Calle Florida**, Microcentro's main north-south artery. Florida has long been one of the city's prime shopping destinations, and every day, thousands of people elbow their way through the crowds and into the shops that line both sides of the street, making a trip down Florida an experience in itself. Many of the buildings still sport the charming, intricate stone facades they've had since the beginning of the twentieth century, but visitors will find that the street's heyday is, unfortunately, over. Nowadays, the shoe, clothing, music, and bookshops that line the street are generic and touristy. This is especially true of Florida's northern end, where the crowds thin out and a huge mess of shops press foreigners to purchase their pricey, often beautiful, leather goods. It is possible to find excellent deals on Florida, but the likelihood of finding something unique here is slim. The same is true of **Avenida Corrientes** and **Avenida Córdoba;** though less touristy, you'll usually run into chains or generic shops. On the other hand, if you have a favorite brand you're looking for (like Puma or Zara), they'll have a store here. And there are exceptions; we've listed some of them below.

## BOOKSTORES

**Libreria Hernandez,** Av. Corrientes 1436 (☎4372 7845; www.libreriahernandez.com.ar). A Corrientes bookstore with a slightly more imaginative selection of novels than usual (read: including titles other than the classics). Open M-Sa 9am-11pm. AmEx/MC/V.

## CRAFTS AND SOUVENIRS

**Arte Indígena,** Balcarce 234 (☎4343 1455). [S] Plaza de Mayo. Considering its location in tourist territory, the wares at this small, non-profit store, including arts and crafts and jewelry, are surprisingly affordable (AR$20-50). Open M-F 9am-7pm. AmEx/MC/V.

## MUSIC

**Zival's,** Callao 395 (☎4371 7500). [S] Callao. Zival's has the best selection of the many music stores in the area. Every genre is represented here, from classical and tango to metal and jazz. The store also stocks local bands as well as a variety of books, setting itself apart from other generic music emporiums. Open M-Sa 10am-9pm. AmEx/MC/V.

**Musimundo,** Florida 267, Microcentro (☎4322 9298; www.musimundo.com). [S] Florida. The city's largest chain of music stores, Musimundo stocks a variety of books, CDs, and DVDs, as well as an excellent selection of music-related equipment (new headphones, iPod gadgets, etc.) Check the website for other branches throughout the city. Open M-Sa 9:30am-9:30pm, Su 11am-9:30pm. AmEx/M-C/V.

## SHOPPING CENTERS

**Galerías Pacífico,** Florida 750, Microcentro (☎5555 5110; www.galeriaspacifico.com.ar). [S] Florida. The shops in this large, flashy mall may not be unique, but the building itself is certainly one of the city's most beautiful. Painted murals and intricate facades front clothing and shoe stores, small boutiques, and book shops. The mall also has the added benefit of being exceptionally central. Open M-Sa 10am-9pm, Su noon-9pm.

## SPORTS AND OUTDOORS

👍 **Wildlife,** Hipólito Yrigoyen 1133, Monserrat (☎4381 1040). [S] Lima. Sells everything you need for that next climbing/camping/trekking/skiing trip or military excursion you've always wanted to do. The variety and volume of gadgets and gear is impressive, and they also sell some cheaper secondhand items. Ideal for anyone planning to visit the Andes or Patagonia. Open M-F 10am-8pm, Sa 10am-1pm. AmEx/MC/V.

**Canaglia Bicicletas,** Suipacha 625, Microcentro (☎4322 3426; www.canaglia.com). This shop sells everything for the cyclist crazy enough to bike around BA. Air pump out-

SHOPPING

side. Open M-F 9:30am-6:30pm. Additional location at Salguero 3066 (☎4803 9477). Open M-F 9:30am-1pm and 3-7:30pm, Sa 9:30am-2pm and 3-5pm. AmEx/MC/V.

**Buenos Aires Sport,** Av. Corrientes 301 (☎4508 6740). This Microcentro shop is the place to go for everything from quick dry clothing to tennis racquets and backpacks. Open M-F 9am-8pm. Additional locations throughout the city.

## TANGO

◾ **Flabella,** Suipacha 263, Microcentro (☎4322 6036). Ⓢ Carlos Pellegrini. One of six or seven tango supply stores in this half-block of Suipacha, Flabella sells a range of glittering, sexy tango shoes and outfits for both women and men at some of the lowest prices in the area (AR$200). Open M-Sa 10am-10pm. AmEx/MC/V. For a wider variety of (slightly more expensive) shoes, head across the street to **Suipacha 256 Tango,** and for a wider variety of tango costumes, to **La Tienda de Tango,** next door at 259.

# SAN TELMO

San Telmo is the place to go in BA for antiques. From Av. Independencía to Av. San Juan, **Defensa** is lined almost solely by flashy stores, hawking urns, statuary, and furniture. Most are well out of the price range of budget travelers, but it can still be entertaining to drop by and ogle a few of them. Alternatively, the ◾Feria de San Telmo (p. 147) is the perfect opportunity to find cheaper, and usually more random, goods, along with vintage jewelry and clothes, used books, art, and souvenirs. If antiquities aren't your thing, San Telmo does have a few excellent boutiques and vintage clothing stores to tempt a younger crowd.

## ANTIQUES

**Gil Antigüedades,** Humberto Primo 412 (☎4361 5019). Ⓢ Independencia. This large store, right on Plaza Dorrego, is crammed chock full of 19th-century collectibles and antiques. Among other things, the Victorian vintage clothing and jewelry are particularly drool-worthy. Open Tu-Su 11am-7pm. AmEx/MC/V.

**HB Antiquedades,** Defensa 1016 (☎4361 3325). Ⓢ Independencia. Few mortals can afford what's on display in this massive antiques store. Still, it can be the ultimate "window-shopping" experience. Gaze at the stunning inlaid tables, Italian marble statues, and massive crystal chandeliers. Open M-F 10am-7pm, Su 11am-5pm. Cash only.

## BOOKSTORES

**Walrus,** Estados Unidos 617 (☎4300 7135). Identifiable by the quaint lamppost outside, this San Telmo neighborhood staple is devoted exclusively to used English-language books. Open T-Su 10am-8pm. AmEx/MC/V.

## CLOTHES AND ACCESSORIES

◾ **El Buen Orden,** Defensa 894 (☎5936 2820). Ⓢ Belgrano or Independencia. It's amazing how much desirable, affordable stuff is packed into this tiny store. Crammed into every corner, there's funky vintage jewelry, including a great selection of earrings (most AR$25-50) and chains, as well as vintage sunglasses, shoes, clothes, and bags (AR$40-150). Open daily 11am-7pm. Cash only.

**Un Lugar en el Mundo,** Defensa 891 (☎4362 3836). Ⓢ Belgrano or Independencia. Right in the heart of antique territory, this sleek boutique showcases the clothes and accessories of several new, up-and-coming Argentine designers. It's affordable, but not cheap; the simplest T-shirt is AR$70, and most items are AR$120-250. MC/V.

### HOUSEWARES

**L'ago,** Defensa 919 and 970 (☎4362 3641). [S] Belgrano or Independencia. An ultra-modern housewares store in the middle of the antiques district. The Pac-Man ghost pillows, Petit Prince *mate* gourds, Roy Lichtenstein prints, and funky lamps are perfect for the BA apartment. Even a flower lamp will set you back AR$200, though. Ignoring prices, the place is still worth checking out. Open daily 10am-8pm. AmEx/MC/V.

## RETIRO AND RECOLETA

If Palermo is the center for relatively expensive, yet independent stores, Retiro and Recoleta have a slew of even more upscale options and are peppered with pricey shops and boutiques. **Avenida Alvear** (p. 155), which stretches into Recoleta from the border with Retiro, is the city's ritziest street for shopping and is the place to go for designers like Hermes, Cartier, and Louis Vuitton. To the south, **Avenida Sante Fe** hosts more affordable chains, as well as smaller *galerías* that sell cheaper clothing. One of the best of these is the relatively large **Bond Street Galería** (p. 199), where shops sell used clothes as well as edgier styles for the punk within, including a variety of great sneakers, jackets, and T-shirts. Though many of the shops within the neighborhood are out of the price range of the average backpacker, we've included a few of our favorite exceptions.

### BOOKSTORES

👍 **Ateneo Grand Splendid,** Av. Santa Fe 1860, Recoleta (☎4811 6104), between Callao and Riobamba. Even if you hate to read (unlikely, since you're reading this book), this store is worth a visit. Located inside a restored 1919 theater, the box seats have been converted into reading areas and the stage is now a cafe (*menú del día* AR$28-30). English-language section. Open M-Th 9am-10pm, F-Sa 9am-midnight, Su noon-10pm. Additional, less beautiful locations sprinkled throughout the city. AmEx/MC/V.

**Kel Ediciones,** M.T. Alvear 1369, Retiro (☎4814 3788; www.kelediciones.com). This small, one-room English shop is packed with a variety of titles. Their selection of English-language titles is nearly unbeatable in BA. Additional location in Belgrano, Conde 1990 (☎4555 4005) and Caballito. Open M-F 9am-7pm, Sa 9:30am-9:30pm. Cash only.

### CLOTHING AND ACCESSORIES

👍 **Galería 5ta Avenida,** Av. Santa Fe 1270, Retiro (☎4816 0451; www.galeria5taavenida.com.ar). [S] San Martín. Packed with vintage stores, cheap shops, and even the odd tattoo parlor, this is a haven of unique, oh-so-inexpensive finds—in particular, great jackets—in otherwise pricey Retiro. Open M-Sa 10am-9pm.

**Gabriell Capricci,** Av. Alvear 1477, Retiro (☎4815 3636). [S] San Martín. On a street dominated by high-end designers, this small shop is unique. The clothes and great jewelry are all bright, flashy, and retro. And considering the location, the prices are quite reasonable—think AR$80-200 for a purse. Open M-Sa 10:30am-8pm. AmEx/MC/V.

**Tinta China,** Talcahuano 1291, Retiro (☎4813 7275; www.tinta-china.com.ar). [S] Callao. This boutique sells great, simple, yet trendy clothes at affordable prices. Shirts AR$50. Jackets AR$150. Open M-F 11am-8pm, Sa 11am-2pm. AmEx/MC/V.

**Los Vados del Isen,** Guido 1699, Recoleta (☎4802 8969). [S] Pueyrredón. As colorful as its pink exterior, this small shop sells fun and bright jewelry from bangles to chunky necklaces at reasonable prices. Open M-F 10am-8pm, Sa 10am-4pm. AmEx/MC/V.

## SHOPPING CENTERS

**Patio Bullrich,** Av. Libertador 750, Retiro (☎4814 7400; www.shoppingbullrich.com.ar). Ⓢ San Martín. This exclusive, slightly snobby mall hosts designer boutiques as well as major international chains, including Zara, Diesel, and Christian Lacroix. For those who need a break from unaffordable clothing, there's a cinema on the top floor that usually features three or more American films. Tickets AR$14-18. Open daily 10am-9pm.

**Bond Street Galería,** Sante Fe 1670, Recoleta (www.xbondstreet.com.ar). Ⓢ Callao. If you're feeling the need for some tattoos and piercings, this "alternative" mall, strangely placed in upscale Recoleta, is the place for you. Even for those not particularly into body art, the *galería* has enough funky clothes and accessories to spice up any wardrobe. You'll never see goths, skaters, and hipsters hanging out together anywhere else, either, so it has a nice unity theme, too. Open M-Sa 11am-8pm.

**Buenos Aires Design,** Pueyrredón 2501, Recoleta (☎5777 6000; www.designrecoleta. com.ar). Ⓢ Agüero. A home decoration emporium, this large mall sells home furnishings, fixtures, rugs, and that designer ashtray you've been dying to get. Perfect for the study- and work-abroad-er in a new apartment. Open M-Sa 10am-9pm, Su noon-9pm.

## SPORTS AND OUTDOORS

**Camping Center,** Esmeralda 945, Retiro (☎4314 0305). Ⓢ San Martín. If you're missing some of your favorite brands from home, including Gore-Tex and Columbia, come to this small store, which stocks a variety of high-quality camping, hiking, and climbing gear. Open M-F 10am-6:30pm, Sa 10am-5pm. AmEx/MC/V.

# PALERMO

Expensive shops line the streets in Palermo, especially around **Plaza Serrano,** but the quiet streets and occasional cafe make ducking in and out of stores here one of the more pleasant shopping experiences around. Those in search of bargains will want to head a bit further afield. A list of some of the more interesting—but by no means cheap—stores follows.

## BOOKSTORES

**Eterna Cadencia,** Honduras 5574 (☎4774 4100; www.eternacadencia.com), between Humboldt and Fitzroy. This bookstore and cafe, set beneath sunny skylights, is the Palermo retreat for BA intellectuals. Though most of the selection is in Spanish, there's a small, varied collection of English-language books next to the cash register. Also offers monthly courses on authors like Borges and Jung (AR$100). Cafe *menú* AR$20-30. Open M-F 10am-9pm, Sa-Su and holidays 11:30am-8pm.

**Boutique del Libro,** Thames 1762 (☎4717 4873; www.boutiquedellibro.com.ar). Loaded bookshelves line the walls of this cushy Palermo shop, whose motto is *"libros pase lo que pase"* (books are with you no matter what). Small selection of music and English-language books. Free Wi-Fi. Cafe with *menú del día* AR$22. Open M-Th 10am-10pm, F 10am-11pm, Sa 11am-11pm, Su and holidays 2-10pm.

## CLOTHES AND ACCESSORIES

**Amor Latino,** El Salvador 4813 (☎4813 6787; www.amor-latino.com.ar). Looking to get decked out for *amor Latino* (Latin love) in Amor Latino? This is your place. Funky lingerie available at a range of prices, along with a *Kama Sutra* kit to get things going. Red leather handcuffs AR$160. See-through black bra AR$20. Chocolate-scented body candle AR$120. Open M-Sa 10:30am-8pm, Su 2-7pm. AmEx/MC/V.

SHOPPING

SHOPPING

**Verbo,** Serrano 1545 (☎4831 2634). Verbo carries everything from punk to prep at prices that are surprisingly affordable, given the neighborhood. Hawks wearable clothes by local designers. Accessories also available. Open Tu-Su 1-9pm. AmEx/MC/V.

**Diseño Argentino,** Honduras 5033 (☎4832 2006; www.mujermilenio.com.ar). A collection of clothes from several up-and-coming designers who will probably be in the shop when you visit. Reasonable prices. Open Tu-Su 2-8pm. V.

**Salsipuedes,** Honduras 4814 (☎4831 8467). This shop's perfect concoctions of satin, lace, and sequins come at a steep price (AR$750). Additional location in Recoleta. Open M-F 10:30am-9pm, Sa 10:30am-8pm. Accepts US$. AmEx/MC/V.

**Hoy Como Ayer,** Thames 1925 (☎4771 1986; www.hoycomoayervintage.com). This glittery secondhand shop offers some vintage steals mixed in with pricier duds—be prepared to hunt for a bargain. Open M-Sa 1-8pm. Cash only.

**Condimentos,** Honduras 4874 (☎4833 9403). Literally means "condiments," but don't expect to find ketchup—this is a place for the accessories of the fashion world. Open M-Sa 10:30am-8pm, Su 3-7pm. AmEx/MC/V.

**Rapsodía,** El Salvador 4757 (☎4832 5363; www.rapsodia.com.ar), at the intersection with Arce. Launched in 1999, this clothing store sells supremely soft sweaters and other trendy clothes (AR$100 and up). Open M-Sa 10am-10pm, Su 10am-9pm. AmEx/V.

**Maria Allô,** Armenia 1647 (☎4831 3773). The pricey clothes at this shop take their inspiration from 1980s glam—think big shoulder pads and ruffles. Open M-Sa 10am-8:30pm, Su 4-8:30pm. AmEx/MC/V.

**Seco,** Armenia 1646 (☎4833 1166). An entire store devoted to rain gear is just about as cutesy as it sounds. The selection includes red and white polka dot trench coats and floral rainboots. Open M-Sa 10:30am-8pm, Su 2-7pm. AmEx/MC/V.

**Keak,** Costa Rica 5758 (☎4772 2189), one block north from Bonpland. A vintage clothing store with tweed jackets and Jackie O. glasses. Open M-Sa noon-8:30pm.

## HOUSEWARES

**Calma Chicha,** Honduras 4909 (☎4831 1818; www.calmachicha.com). Cowhide totes, cowhide rugs, cowhide butterfly chairs—you get the point. Open M-Sa 10am-8pm, Su 2-8pm. Additional location in San Telmo at Defensa 856 (☎4361 0489). AmEx/MC/V.

**Papelera Palermo,** Honduras 4945 (☎4833 3081/3672; www.papelerapalermo.com.ar). This store sells handmade journals, boxes, and fancy cards. They also offer courses and workshops M-F 1-7pm. Open M-Sa 10am-8pm, Su 2-8pm. AmEx/MC/V.

## MARKETS

**Las Pulgas Antiguedades,** at the corner of Dorrego and Cabrera. Most of the stalls at this flea market buy and sell furniture. It's technically in Colegiales, but the official border with Palermo is across the street. Open Tu-Su 10am-5pm. Cash only.

## MUSIC

**Miles Discos,** Honduras 4912 (☎4832 0466; www.milesdiscos.com.ar). A stock of CDs that runs the full gamut of musical tastes, from classical to classic rock, and of course Argentine tango. AR$10 and up. Open M-Sa 10am-10pm, Su 1-9pm. AmEx/MC/V.

## SHOPPING CENTERS

**Alto Palermo,** Sante Fe 3253 (☎5777 8000; www.altopalermo.com.ar). Ⓢ Bulnes. In a *barrio* filled with pricey boutiques, this large shopping center is surprisingly low key. Families, youngsters, and other regular ol' people actually come to the stores here. Contains many of the major Argentine and a number of foreign brands, including North Face, Sony, and Ayres, among others. Open daily 10am-10pm.

**Paseo Alcorta,** Salguero 3172 (☎5777 6500; www.paseoalcorta.com.ar). **S** Scalabrini Ortiz. Though located a bit far north of the center, this shopping mall is the place to go for those sleek, modern Argentine designs. Stores range from mid-priced to very expensive, and include Ayres and Rapsodia. Open daily 10am-10pm.

## SPORTS AND OUTDOORS

**Depor Camping,** Sante Fe 4830 (☎4772 0534/0674; www.deporcamping.com.ar), between Humboldt and Fitzroy. Fleeces aplenty in classic brands like Columbia and Northland. Stocks other outdoor gear as well for those wilderness excursions you're planning. Open M-Sa 9:30am-8:30pm. Additional location in Microcentro at Carlos Pellegrini 737 (☎4328 6100). AmEx/MC/V.

# BELGRANO

## CLOTHES AND ACCESSORIES

■ **Palacio de las Artes,** Zapiola 2196 (☎4542 7904; www.palaciodelasartes.com.ar). **S** Juramento. In 1997, this stately 1912 mansion opened its doors as a private cultural center. In addition to an art gallery, which offers classes, it houses a boutique selling affordable clothes by local designers, the **Diseño Club** (☎4542 3528; www.disenio-club.com.ar), on the 3rd fl. Most items AR$50-170. Open M-F 2-6:30pm. AmEx/MC/V.

# BALVANERA

## ONCE AND ABASTO

For bargain-hunters, this is the perfect alternative to shopping in the city center. One of the sub-neighborhoods of Balvanera, **Once** (p. 166), really just a system of streets around a train station, hosts a slew of outlet stores and cheap shops where 20 to 50 pesos will buy you pretty much anything from jeans and jackets to that fake Boca Juniors shirt you've always wanted. Heading down Avenida Pueyrredón from Recoleta into Balvanera, both sides of the street are lined with shops, and once you reach the train station, the street turns into a virtual outdoor market. The clothes may not be of the best quality, but that can't really be expected at these low prices.

## SHOPPING CENTERS

**Shopping Abasto,** Av. Corrientes 3247 (☎4959 3400; www.abasto-shopping.com.ar). **S** Carlos Gardel. This massive 19th-century Art-Deco shopping center housed one of the city's produce markets until 1984, when the market was moved out of the city center and the building was left vacated. In the 1990s, new buyers transformed the market into the city's largest shopping complex, complete with a miniature theme park called Neverland. Yes, Neverland. We will not make the obvious joke. Open daily 10am-10pm.

# NIGHTLIFE

Buenos Aires is truly a city that *never* sleeps. Ever. What would be considered normal nightlife hours in other towns is merely pregame time in BA, or even early dinner. Most bars and clubs don't really get going until well after midnight, and they continue hopping into the early morning hours, sometimes into the following afternoon, blasting every type of music imaginable. Electronica, techno, salsa, and 80s is merely the beginning of the story. There's something to do every night of the week, from the popular tourist haunts and neon lights of the center to chic, trendy offerings in Palermo. The only norms, for the most part, are strobe lights and crazy affordability. Bottoms up.

## BARS

| | |
|---|---|
| 878 (p. 213) | VC |
| 🎵AcaBar (p. 211) | PaH |
| 🎵Antares (p. 209) | PaS |
| 🎵Bangalore Curry House (p. 211) | PaH |
| Bar Británico (p. 206) | ST |
| Bar Seddon (p. 204) | Mon |
| Bar Taller (p. 210) | PaS |
| Bárbaro (p. 207) | Ret |
| Buller (p. 208) | Rec |
| Bulnes Class (p. 210) | PaS |
| Carnal (p. 211) | PaH |
| Celta Bar (p. 205) | Mic |
| Congo (p. 210) | PaS |
| Contramano (p. 208) | Rec |
| Cossab (p. 214) | Boe |
| CRÓNICO (p. 209) | PaS |
| 🎵Dadá (p. 206) | Ret |
| DE Bar (p. 205) | Mic |
| Deep Blue (p. 207) | Ret |
| Downtown Mathias (p. 205) | Mic |
| Drink Gallery (p. 212) | LC |
| Druid Inn (p. 207) | Ret |
| 🎵El Balcón (p. 205) | ST |
| El Living (p. 208) | Rec |
| Gibraltar (p. 206) | ST |
| Gran Bar Danzón (p. 206) | Ret |
| Granados Bar (p. 206) | ST |
| Jackie O. (p. 212) | LC |
| Kilkenny (p. 207) | Ret |
| Kim y Novak Bar! (p. 210) | PaS |
| 🎵La Cigale (p. 204) | Mic |
| La Puerta Roja (p. 206) | ST |
| Le Bar (p. 205) | Mic |
| Malasartes (p. 209) | PaS |
| Milión (p. 208) | Rec |
| Mundo Bizarro (p. 210) | PaS |
| Post (p. 210) | PaS |
| 🎵Puerta Uno (p. 213) | Bel |
| Shamrock (p. 208) | Rec |
| Sitges (p. 208) | Rec |
| Sugar (p. 210) | PaS |
| The Roxy Resto Bar (p. 211) | PaH |
| Unico (p. 211) | PaH |
| Van Koning (p. 212) | LC |
| Zanzibar (p. 207) | Ret |

## CLUBS

| | |
|---|---|
| Azúcar (p. 213) | Bal |
| Bahrein (p. 205) | Mic |
| Big One (p. 204) | Mon |
| Caix (p. 212) | CN |
| Club Araóz (p. 211) | PaS |
| Cocoliche (p. 204) | Mon |
| Crobar (p. 212) | CN |
| El Especial (p. 210) | PaS |
| Kika (p. 211) | PaS |
| Klub Killer (p. 214) | Boe |
| Maluco Beleza (p. 205) | Mic |
| Moliere (p. 206) | ST |
| Museum (p. 204) | Mon |
| Niceto (p. 211) | PaH |
| Pachá (p. 213) | CN |
| Podestá Súper Club (p. 210) | PaS |
| Rumi (p. 213) | CN |
| The Roxy Disco (p. 213) | CN |
| Verona (p. 204) | Mon |

## GLBT

| | |
|---|---|
| Alsina (p. 215) | Mon |
| Amerika (p. 215) | Alm |
| Angels (p. 214) | Rec |
| 🎵Bach Bar (p. 214) | PaS |
| Flux (p. 214) | Ret |
| 🎵Glam (p. 214) | Rec |

**NEIGHBORHOOD ABBREVIATIONS: Alm** Almagro **Bal** Balvanera **Bel** Belgrano **Boe** Boedo **CN** Costanera Norte **LC** Las Cañitas **Mic** Microcentro **Mon** Monserrat **PaH** Palermo Hollywood **PaS** Palermo Soho **Rec** Recoleta **Ret** Retiro **ST** San Telmo **VC** Villa Crespo

# MONSERRAT

Monserrat is by no means a hopping place at night. Most people who stay in the area past sunset end up in so-called "resto-bars"—restaurants or cafes that turn into discos on weekend nights. Most others, though, venture across into San Telmo or one of the livelier nighttime hot spots around the city.

## BARS

**Bar Seddon,** Defensa 695 (☎4342 3700). Ⓢ Plaza de Mayo or Independencia. Just north of Monserrat's border with San Telmo, Bar Seddon, with its black-and-white-tiled floor and antique furnishings, seems like more of a cafe than a bar. But come here on Sa and you'll find the place packed for one of the live bands that play a huge variety of music most nights. Open M-F and Su 6pm-late, Sa 8pm-late. Cash only.

## CLUBS

**Museum,** Perú 535 (☎4543 3894). Ⓢ Perú or Bolívar. This three-story club—one of the hottest in the city—draws a raucous crowd of fashionable youth from all over BA to its massive dance floor with a mix of 80s, 90s, and Latin. Especially popular and lively are the Tu and W night after-office parties, when professionals pour in from the business district and let loose. Sa cover men only AR$20. Open W, F, Sa until late. AmEx/MC/V.

**NEVER TOO LATE TO PAR-TAY.** Just like how Argentines like to eat late, they also have no qualms about partying late. Clubs don't hit peak capacity until around 3am.

**Cocoliche,** Rivadavia 878 (☎4331 6413; www.cocoliche.net). Ⓢ Piedras. Located in an old converted townhouse just across the border with Microcentro, this surprisingly small club draws a local, early-20s, alternative crowd. DJs come from all over the world to pound out various forms of electronica for the packed basement dance floor, which, with running neon lights on the ceiling, is much less epileptic than most other clubs in the city. Mixed drinks AR$18-25. Cover AR$20. Open F-Sa 1am-late. Cash only.

**Big One,** Adolfo Alsina 940 (☎4334 0997; www.bigone.com.ar). Ⓢ Piedras. Alsina, one of the city's most popular gay clubs (p. 214), transforms itself every Sa night for one of BA's renowned electronica nights. DJs come to spin music for a massive, mixed crowd dancing away in this former mansion. Those who need a break can head upstairs to relax on one of the couches and peer down upon the sweating masses below. Beer AR$12-14. Mixed drinks AR$15-25. Cover AR$40. Open Sa 1-8am. AmEx/MC/V.

**Verona,** Hipólito Yrigoyen 968 (☎15 5427 2962). Ⓢ Av. de Mayo. Between Tacuarí and Pellegrini. With two dance floors, Verona is perfect for the indecisive partygoer. Salsa, reggaeton, and *cumbia* play upstairs, while downstairs, people perform what amounts to step aerobics to electronica. Cover F women free until 2am, men AR$15-20; Sa women only AR$20. Beer $10-12. Mixed drinks AR$12-15. Open F-Sa 1am-late.

# MICROCENTRO

Not surprisingly for a business-oriented district, Microcentro doesn't offer much in the way of a night scene. Most cafes and restaurants have some kind of bar seating, but there are few true nightspots and even fewer clubs. That said, people still seem to find a way to have fun at night in this *barrio*.

## BARS

🏛 **La Cigale,** 25 de Mayo 222 (☎4312 8275). Ⓢ LN Alem. An alternative, student haven in the midst of the business district, this large, modern bar glows with colorful lights. Occa-

NIGHTLIFE

sional live music, and almost always a live DJ pounding out various forms of electronica. Tu nights, when French cocktails are the special, are especially popular. Happy hour M-F 6-10pm, Sa 8pm-midnight. Open M-F 6pm-late, Sa 8pm-late. AmEx/MC/V.

**Downtown Mathias,** Reconquista 701 (☎4312 9844). S LN Alem. This pub and restaurant is a bit too big to achieve the intimate feel of a real pub, but is nevertheless a great place to stop and relax over a drink. For an Argentine bar, it has a wide selection of beer, including, of course, Guinness. Live music on some Th, F, and Sa nights. Drinks AR$8-30. Food AR$18-35. Open M-F and Su 7am-3am, Sa 7am-6am. AmEx/MC/V.

**Celta Bar,** Sarmiento 1701 (☎4371 7338). S Callao. With its wooden tables, bright paintings, and unique light fixtures, this bar is better for a relaxing few glasses of wine than a raucous night out. It can seem a little far away from the action, but it is decidedly chill. On some weekend evenings the basement hosts a live rock band. Draws a crowd of all ages. Drinks AR$6-20. Open daily noon-2am. AmEx/MC/V.

**DE Bar,** Rivadavia 1132 (☎4381 6876). S Lima or Avenida de Mayo. This tiny bar painted in black with bright, green neon lights draws a mixed crowd, as well as groups of young people from the nearby hostels, which organize frequent drunky-time excursions to this locale. Open M-F 6pm-late, Sa-Su 8pm-late. Cash only.

**Le Bar,** Tucúman 422 (☎5219 0858), between Reconquista and San Martín. S Florida. A chic after-office bar in the heart of downtown Microcentro, Le Bar plays non-intrusive, trendy music and serves up delicious, modern fusion food. Tapas AR$8-10. Entrees AR$24-29. Drinks AR$14-25. 2-for-1 happy hour 6-10pm; requires you to get the same drink twice. Open M-F noon-2am, Sa 9pm-2am. AmEx/MC/V.

## CLUBS

**Maluco Beleza,** Sarmiento 1728 (☎4372 1737; www.malucobeleza.com.ar). S Callao. DJs mixing samba and reggae draw crowds to this Brazilian club, one of the most popular nightlife spots in the city. The exposed brick walls and neon lights create a more relaxing mood upstairs. Be sure to stop by on W nights, when Brazilian music and snacks are the name of the game. Open W and F-Su 1:30am-late. Cash only.

**HOW TO BOOZE EFFICIENTLY.** Ordering drinks can always be a tricky process when the bar is crowded—this is especially the case in Buenos Aires. In most clubs, you should first head for the cashier to exchange your money for a drink card. Elbow, vigorously if necessary, your way over to the bartender with the card in hand to actually get served.

**Bahrein,** Lavalle 345 (www.bahreinba.com). S LN Alem. Located in an old mansion, this new, hip club is the ultimate one-stop nightlife emporium, with a main-floor (pricey) restaurant, a chill bar upstairs, and a dim, smoky club downstairs. Weekday crowds are mostly tourists, but that comes as no surprise. Music ranges from funk and hip-hop to house and techno, but the club is especially popular on Tu nights, when it's all about drum n' bass. Cover women AR$15, men AR$20. Open Tu-Sa 6pm-late.

# SAN TELMO

San Telmo is no mecca for clubbing, save for Moliere, but what it lacks in dance floors and DJs it makes up for with an excellent array of relaxing bars around the **Plaza Dorrego** perfect for drinks and conversation.

## BARS

**El Balcón,** Humberto Primo 461, 2nd fl. (☎4362 2354; www.elbalcondelaplaza.com.ar). S Independencia. This hip venue hosts many events, including tango shows on F and Sa nights at 10pm and Su afternoons 1-7pm. After the shows are over, a young crowd takes over and stays until long after the 2-for-1 happy hour ends at 3am. Get here early on weekends for a seat on the balcony, which has views over Plaza Dorrego, or on the rooftop terrace. Drinks AR$10-25. Reggae Nights W 11pm and Th 12:30am. Open M-Th 10pm-4am, F-Sa 10pm-6pm, Su 1-7pm. Cash only.

**La Puerta Roja,** Chacabuco 733 (☎4362 5649; www.lapuertaroja.com.ar). [S] Independencia. Though it's unmarked, go right on up to the door and head up the stairs. A refreshingly un-self-conscious local crowd hangs out at the bar, or huddles around the pool table in back. There's a smoking room in front covered, strangely enough, by *Animal House* quotes. Good selection of beer AR$7-10. Mixed drinks AR$7-30. Snacks AR$10-18. Pizzas AR$15. Happy hour daily 6-10pm, 2-for-1 on certain drinks. Open M-Th and Su 6pm-6am, F-Sa 6pm-7am. Kitchen open daily 6pm-2am. Cash only.

**Granados Bar,** Chile 378 (☎4300 0999). [S] Independencia. This small bar, with its nifty all-white decor and neon lights, is the first of a two-block long line of bars, all of which are exceptionally popular on weekends. On summer nights, Granados and all its neighbors set up tables outside on the sidewalk along this section of Chile—you'll probably have to walk around a bit to find an open table. Open M-Sa until late. Cash only.

**Bar Británico,** Brasil 399 (☎4361 2107). [S] San Juan. Though this long-running bar, just across from Parque Lezama, was once condemned to become an Internet cafe, it was so popular that locals rallied to save it. Even after renovation, it retains a bohemian quality that prevailed when Ernesto Sábato penned *On Heroes and Tombs* here. Food AR$7-19. Beer AR$6.50-11. Mixed drinks AR$12-18. Open 24hr. Cash only.

**Gibraltar,** Perú 895 (☎4362 5310). [S] Independencia. A small, intimate pub that draws a mixed crowd with a good selection of beer and traditional, tasty pub grub. There's a pool table in the back. A run of the mill joint, but it gets the job done. Food AR$10-28. Drinks AR$7-20. Open daily 6pm-4am. Cash only.



### CLUBS

**Moliere,** Chile 299 (☎4343 2623; www.moliere-cafe.com). [S] Independencia. Relatively little distinguishes this club other than the fact that it's one of the only places to get your groove on in San Telmo. DJs mix a variety of Latin, electronica, and pop on the dance floor, which can be packed to capacity on weekends to the point where it restricts actual dancing; there's also a Latin dance, with salsa, samba, and *merengue,* on a smaller floor off to the side. Cover women AR$15, men AR$30. Open Th-Sa midnight-7am.

## RETIRO

Being a ritzy neighborhood, Retiro doesn't have the most varied or exciting nightlife scene—there are no clubs and the bars are often frequented by a businessy crowd unwinding post-work. There are still some excellent intimate options though for a relatively quiet night out.

### BARS

★ **Dadá,** San Martín 941 (☎4314 4787). [S] San Martín. This small, intimate bar has an alternative flair, a rarity in upscale, corporate Retiro. By day, businesspeople convene here for the highly regarded food, but at night, a crowd of tourists and *porteños* moves in for drinks and cool jazz. Entrees AR$19-37. Open M-Sa noon-late.

**Gran Bar Danzón,** Libertad 1161, 2nd fl. (☎4811 1108). [S] San Martín. This ultra-trendy bar draws hordes of businesspeople, as well as the fashionable and well dressed—most people are in suits or dresses, or at least mile-high heels. The menu includes pastas, seafood, sushi, and a huge selection of wine. There's usually a DJ at 11pm. Entrees AR$28-50. Open M-F 7pm-late, Sa 8:30pm-late, Su 8pm-late. AmEx/MC/V.

# Puerto Limón
## H O S T E L

*San Telmo neighborhood of Tango*

- 10 min. by foot to the principal turistic attractions: Plaza de Mayo, Casa Rosada, Obelisco, La Boca, Caminito & Puerto Madero

- 2 blocks from Plaza Dorrego

- 3 blocks from subway

**Services**
- ✓ Breakfast
- ✓ Hot showers 24 hs.
- ✓ Towels
- ✓ Daily room cleaning
- ✓ Internet free
- ✓ Bar
- ✓ Fully equipped kitchen
- ✓ BBQ

puertolimonhostel.com     WiFi™

msn  reservas@puertolimonhostel.com - info@puertolimonhostel.com
phone (+5411) **4361 9649** - **chacabuco st. 1080** - Buenos Aires, Argentina

**Kilkenny,** M.T. de Alvear 399 (☎4312 9179). Ⓢ San Martín. Kilkenny, a massive two-floor Irish pub, is a local institution with all the trappings of a traditional pub. On week-nights, the party gets started early on, and on weekends, those seeking a quiet drink will likely want to head elsewhere. Come early, or for lunch, if you want a seat. The second floor has a smoking section. Open daily 11am-2am. Cash only.

**Druid Inn,** Reconquista 1040 (☎4312 3688). Ⓢ San Martín. Smaller and quieter than other San Telmo offerings, this intimate Irish pub boasts an incredible selection of alcohol, including over twenty kinds of beer and one hundred types of whiskey. Try them all. There's also the usual roster of pub grub. Live music, including jazz, rock, and Celtic, Th-Sa. Open M-F noon-late, Sa 8pm-late. Cash only.

**Bárbaro,** Tres Sargentos 415 (☎4311 6856). Ⓢ San Martín. On a quiet, cobblestone pedestrian street, this bar draws a varied, somewhat older crowd for relaxation, conversation, and a few drinks. With its non-stodgy carved wood interior, painted columns, and modern art, it feels a bit like a funky, well-worn pub. Open daily noon-late. Cash only.

**Deep Blue,** Reconquista 920 (☎0800 444 2582; www.deepblue.com.ar). Ⓢ San Martín. A mixed crowd of tourists, young locals, and businesspeople frequent this strangely decorated bar. The drinks range in price from the affordable AR$11 to the insane AR$1000, though most mixed drinks are AR$19-25. There are a few pool tables in the center. Beer AR$11-15. Open M-Sa noon-2 or 3am. AmEx/MC/V.

**Zanzibar,** San Martín 986 (☎4312 9636). Ⓢ San Martín. Between Marcelo T. de Alvear and Paraguay. A description of the plush red stools and the shiny metal bar would fail to capture Zanzibar's laid-back attitude. It's far better to focus on the faded map of Africa and its menu, a tribute to rum "from all over the world" (it's actually

NIGHTLIFE

just Caribbean, but hey—we're not complaining). Beer AR$6-12. Mixed drinks $12-20. Open Tu-Th 6pm-3:30am, F-Sa 6pm-5am. Cash only.

# RECOLETA

A very upscale, wealthy neighborhood, Recoleta isn't known for partying until dawn. There are, of course, a number of bars, though they are spread out throughout the *barrio* and don't compose any real nightlife district. It is worth noting, however, that Recoleta's southern regions host a number of **GLBT bars and clubs** (p. 214), the beginning of a long district that continues through the northern regions of Balvanera and Almagro and southeastern Palermo.

## BARS

**Buller,** Presidente RM Ortiz 1827 (☎4808 9061). [S] Callao. It's slightly overpriced and crowded with tourists, but this small pub is worth a visit–it's one of the city's only microbreweries, churning out six varieties, from a basic lager and Oktoberfest to an IPA and stout. Pints AR$14-18. Pitchers AR$34-42. Entrees AR$19-38. Happy hour 7-9pm. Magic show Tu and Th 9:30pm and midnight. Open daily noon-late. AmEx/MC/V.

**Milión,** Paraná 1048 (☎4815 9925; www.milionargentina.com.ar). [S] Callao or Tribunales. If you're looking for a swanky night out on the town, head to this classy, sleek former mansion-turned bar and restaurant. The entrees (AR$31-80) can be a bit steep, but you can always indulge in the cheaper appetizer trios (AR$18) or tapas (AR$25-28). Beer AR$7-10. Wine by the bottle AR$32-196. Mixed drinks AR$15-28. Open M-F 11:30am-3:30am, Sa 8pm-4am, Su 8pm-2am. AmEx/MC/V.

**Shamrock,** Rodríguez Peña 1220 (☎4812 3584), between Juncal and Arenales. More chic bar than Irish pub, Shamrock's sea of tables seat BA's younger crowd, as well as a fair number of foreigners. Mixed drinks AR$9-18. Beer AR$7-26. Guinness AR$24. Happy hour until midnight with AR$6 shots and 2-for-1 beer. Open M-W and Su 6pm-4am, Th 6pm-5:30am, F-Sa 6pm-6:30am. Downstairs, the small, sweaty **Basement Club** spins electronica. Open Th 11pm-close, F-Sa 1am-6am. AmEx/MC/V: AR$20 minimum.

NIGHTLIFE

> **IT'S A DRINK, NOT A DRUG.** "Speed" means energy drink in Argentina, so if you see it on a menu in BA, it means vodka and Red Bull, not the illegal drug. The word for "speed" the drug is *amphetiminas.*

**Sitges,** Av. Córdoba 4119 (☎4861 3763; www.sitgesonline.com.ar). From cabaret to karaoke, this lively pre-club bar always has something going on. Well-dressed gay men sit at the tables, each equipped with occasionally working phones for drunk dialing the stranger across the room. The specialty drink, "Love" (vodka, strawberry, Sprite, and cream) is (deliberately?) just a bit too sweet. Mixed drinks AR$14-18. Beer AR$10-12. Fast food AR$5-35. AR$12 min. F all-you-can-drink AR$25. Sa drag night. Su karaoke. Open W-Th and Su 10:30pm-2:30am, F-Sa 10:30pm-5:30am. Cash only.

**Contramano,** Rodríguez Peña 1082 (☎4811 0494; www.contramano.com). This all-male nightclub caters to a laid-back, slightly older clientele. The mirror on the dance floor, which beats with house, pop, and techno, is perfect for subtly scoping out the man-candy behind you. Smoking lounge upstairs. Beer AR$5. Mixed drinks AR$10-30. Cover Th AR$10, F and Su AR$20, Sa AR$25. Open Th midnight-5am (only in summer), F-Sa midnight-6am, Su 10pm-5am. AmEx/MC/V.

**El Living,** M.T. de Alvear 1540 (☎4815 6574; www.living.com.ar). [S] Callao. Between Montevideo and Paraná. Outfitted to look like a living room (assuming that the standard living room includes 8 TVs and a huge projector screen), El Living starts off with comfort food for dinner, followed by well-priced drinks. Recent rock and pop favorites blast over the speakers, while the disco ball makes the back room more club-ish. *Menú* AR$37. Mixed drinks AR$8-16. Wine by the glass AR$5, by the bottle AR$11-38. Open Th 7pm for drinks, F-Sa 10pm-1:30am for dinner; continues as a bar late.

# PALERMO

Though other *barrios* have excellent bars and clubs, Palermo has the majority of the city's most popular nightlife establishments. **Palermo Soho** and **Palermo Hollywood** are packed with new bars and clubs, while **Las Cañitas** to the north has an additional concentration of bars. Nightlife here, however, shuts down relatively early for Palermo—usually around 3 or 4am. The opposite is true of **Costanera Norte** along the river, where the flashy clubs stay open until well after sunrise. Many of Palermo's bars and clubs are the domain of the city's wealthier 20-somethings and tourists, but there are a number of alternative, more relaxed establishments, particularly in Palermo Soho and in the southeastern corner, where there are several excellent **GLBT bars and clubs** (p. 214).

## PALERMO SOHO

### BARS

- **Antares,** Armenia 1447 (☎4833 9611; www.cervezaantares.com), between Cabrera and Gorriti. Noisy, full, kind of dark, but never smoky, Antares is the place to be for those interested in chilling over a pint of something other than Quilmes—they brew their own beer here. Occasionally hosts live music. Tapas, like *tortilla española*, AR$10 for one, AR$35 for the table. Salads AR$21-24. Entrees AR$24-36. Specialty pints AR$11-13. Mixed drinks AR$19-24. Open daily 7:30pm-4am. AmEx/MC/V.

  **CRÓNICO,** Jorge Luis Borges 1646 (☎4833 0708). Ⓢ Plaza Italia. It's right on Plaza Serrano, but this bar is about as anti-Palermo (a.k.a. not chic) as you can get. A young, sometimes rough-around-the-edges crowd cracks peanuts at a sea of tables in the dimly lit interior, while the rock and reggaeton blasting in the background enliven the atmosphere. A great place to wind down after a long night of clubbing—it's open well into the wee hours of the morning on weekends. Beer AR$7-9. Shots AR$7-15. Mixed drinks AR$14. Food AR$9-27. Open M-Th and Su 10am-6am, F-Sa 10am-8:30am. AmEx/MC/V.

  **Malasartes,** Honduras 4999 (☎4831 0743; www.malasartes.com.ar), on Plaza Serrano. This bar for "bad types" makes a seamless transition from day to night; they never close, and locals nosh on *mani* (peanuts)

## ON THE MENU

### BEER IN BAR-GENTINA

At first, Argentina seems like hell for beer-lovers. Good wine is everywhere, but in most bars, the only options are Quilmes, Quilmes, Schneider, and Quilmes, all of which only become drinkable after you're thoroughly sloshed.

But the future is bright. **Microbreweries** are popping up throughout the city and churning out their own delicious brews, and, surprisingly, Argentines are actually drinking them. A number of the city's microbreweries have their own popular bars and pubs, so if you're looking to revel in hops and malts instead of tannins and acids, you might want to try some of the following joints, which are among our favorites.

**1.** **Antares** (p. 209), in Palermo, serves up seven house brews, including an amazing Imperial Stout, in a massive, hopping bar.

**2.** Though a bit over-touristed and over-priced, **Buller** (p. 208), in Recoleta, brews six very good varieties; we'd go for the IPA.

**3.** If you're willing to wander far afield for some suds, head to **Cossab** (p. 214), in Boedo, where you can not only sample their excellent six brews—try the Honey—but also almost 100 beers from around the world.

**4.** Though slightly overdone, Dutch pub **Van Koning** (p. 212), in Las Cañitas, has an extensive menu, including top notch Otro Mundo and Europe's most popular exports. Compare the two, and we think you'll come away pleasantly surprised. And it's about time.

and nurse beers until the early morning. Sandwiches AR$12-26. Salads AR$15. Entrees AR$35. Chopp lager AR$9. Wines by the bottle AR$15-60. Open M-F 8am-2am, Sa 8am-5:30am, Su 9am-5:30am. Cash only.

**Congo,** Honduras 5329 (☎4833 5857). [S] Palermo. This medium-sized bar is one of Palermo's most popular and lasting nightlife spots. The atmosphere inside can either be chic and relaxed or packed and lively, depending on the night, but undoubtedly the best thing about the bar is its sprawling garden out back. Come early if you want one of the booths among the greenery. Open Tu-Sa 8pm-4am.

**Kim y Novak Bar!,** Güemes 4900 (☎4773 7521), at the intersection with Godoy Cruz. House music plays loudly in the basement of this gay-friendly bar/club named for a 1950s pin-up girl, so stay upstairs for conversation or to watch leopard-legging-clad pole dancers. Sometimes quiet on weekday nights, such as W, but chill enough not to be awkward. Heineken AR$7. Open W-Sa 11pm-5am. Cash only.

**Mundo Bizarro,** Serrano 1222 (☎4773 1967; www.mundobizarrobar.com). Everything seems off-kilter at this cocktail lounge, and we're sure it's not just the drinks talking—it's probably the cartoon pop art on the walls that would make even Wonder Woman feel welcome. The drinks are pricey, but they mix a mean martini. Mixed drinks AR$18-25. Open M-W and Su 8pm-2:30am, Th-Sa 8pm-5:50am. Cash only.

**Bar Taller,** Serrano 1595 (☎4831 5501). [S] Plaza Italia. This Plaza Serrano bar is a great place to hang out over a beer (AR$7-16) or a shockingly large shot (AR$7-18) amidst random machine parts (*taller* is Spanish for workshop). Sandwiches AR$4-18. Salads AR$9-18. Entrees AR$12.50-29. Mixed drinks AR$14-22. Open M-Th and Su 9am-2am, F-Sa 9am-5am. Cash only.

**Post,** Thames 1885 (☎15 5830 6465; www.poststreetbar.com.ar). [S] Plaza Italia. Another anti-Palermo establishment, this dim, grungy bar attracts a younger, relaxed crowd with rock and alternative music and drinks named after famous stars and songs; try the Eric Clapton (gin, grenadine, vodka, curaçao; AR$15). Art gallery on the second floor. Beer AR$5-12. Wine AR$10. Mixed drinks AR$12-15. *Pizzetas* AR$6-9. Sandwiches AR$8-14. Other snacks AR$7-35. Open daily 9am-3 or 4am. Cash only.

**Sugar,** Costa Rica 4619. [S] Scalabrini Ortiz. Hordes of hostel-based tourists and some locals pack this small bar pretty much every night. There's almost no chance of grabbing a table, so be prepared to fight for your own space in the crowd and rock out to American favorites. Happy hour 9pm-midnight: Quilmes AR$5. Beer AR$10. Mixed drinks AR$5. Cocktails AR$12-28. Wine by the bottle AR$15. Open Tu-Sa 9pm-late.

**Bulnes Class,** Bulnes 1250 (☎4861 7492; www.bulnesclass.com.ar). [S] Medrano. With its white leather couches, neon lighting, and photography adorning the walls, Bulnes Class is as sophisticated and cosmopolitan as the name implies. The place is large enough to meet people, but still intimate enough for conversation. Beer AR$10-12. Mixed drinks AR$15-25. Open F and Sa 11pm-late. Cash only.

## CLUBS

**Podestá Súper Club,** Armenia 1740 (☎4832 2776; www.elpodesta.com.ar). [S] Plaza Italia. This eclectic club can get packed to a breaking point on weekends with tourist and local 20-somethings. Downstairs, the crowd dances to 80s, 90s, and modern hits, while upstairs, a more sedate group relaxes on couches to electronica or grabs a seat at the bar. Beer AR$9. Mixed drinks AR$15-25. Happy hour 11pm-1am: 2-for-1 on certain cocktails. Cover women AR$20, men AR$30. Open F-Sa 11pm-late. Cash only.

**El Especial,** Av. Córdoba 4391 (www.fotolog.com/especialvideobar), at the intersection with Julián Álvarez. [S] Medrano. *Animal House,* meet Argentina. This BA underground scene in an unmarked apartment house is crowded with friendly partygoers with Monty Python on in the background. Think exotic frat party. Electronica plays in the first room, while rock and pop liven up the VIP lounge. Given its recent opening, don't be surprised if things change. Beer AR$8-12. Mixed drinks AR$13-20. Cover women AR$10, men AR$15; includes ■ **1L of beer.** Open F 10:30pm-late, Sa 11pm-late. Cash only.

**Kika,** Honduras 5339 (☎4137 5311; www.kikaclub.com.ar), at the intersection with Godoy Cruz. S Palermo or Plaza Italia. This huge club is especially popular on Sa, when well-groomed Argentines file in to groove to pop hits that range from Backstreet Boys to Billy Idol. In the back room, the music moves into more indie and eclectic genres. 21+. Cover Th AR$20, F-Sa women AR$30, AR$50 for men. Open Th-Sa 11pm-7am.

**Club Araóz,** Araóz 2424 (☎4832 9751; www.clubaraoz.com.ar), at the intersection with Santa Fe. S Scalabrini Ortiz. This smallish club runs a popular Th night hip-hop spot, officially called "Lost," which begins with a performance by break dancers at midnight. Big-name DJs take over other nights. Th hip-hop. F-Sa rock/pop. Su 80s. Cover AR$20-50, includes a Bud. Open Th and Su midnight-5am, F-Sa 1-7am. Cash only.

# PALERMO HOLLYWOOD

## BARS

■ **AcaBar,** Honduras 5733 (☎4772 0845 and 4776 3634). One part diner, one part bar, with plenty of flapper lampshades in between. AcaBar's funky decor and free board games have made it a neighborhood staple among 20-somethings looking to relax and have some good clean fun for the evening over a game of Monopoly and quiet music. Take the giant Jenga block challenge and try to build a tower with more than 20 rows. Entrees AR$11-30. Beer AR$6-14. Mixed drinks AR$14-17. Open M-Th noon-3pm and 8pm-2am, F noon-3pm and 8pm-5am, Sa 8pm-5am, Su 8pm-2am. AmEx/MC/V.

■ **Bangalore Pub & Curry House,** Humboldt 1416 (☎4779 2621). S Palermo. See p. 118 for food listing. This restaurant is also the ideal nightlife destination. The basement has an intimate atmosphere that actually feels like a pub—a rarity in BA. Beer AR$8-15. Mixed drinks AR$22-48. Open M-Th and Su 6pm-3am, F-Sa 6pm-6am. Cash only.

**Carnal,** Niceto Vega 5511 (☎4772 7582). S Palermo. This is one of BA's hippest night-time spots, so show up early or be prepared to wait. The downstairs bar, playing reggae in the background, is popular, but the prime real estate is upstairs on the garden veranda, where you can enjoy pricey, but excellent mixed drinks (AR$16-25) on a warm summer night. What's really impressive is the variety of brands of hard liquor; if you're looking for a particular whiskey or vodka, you'll hit the jackpot. Beer AR$7-14. Tapas AR$15-25. Entrees and snacks AR$25-40. Open Tu-W 8pm-3am, Th-Sa 8pm-6am. MC/V.

**Unico,** Honduras 5604 (☎4775 6693), at the intersection with Fitzroy. Unico's shining, colored Christmas lights make it a beacon for bargoers from blocks around. Buenos Aires' bright young things come here to sip expensive cocktails and make fractured conversation over the loud house music. The place is always busy—expect to wait if you want a table. Mixed drinks AR$15-30. Beer AR$9-15. Wine by the glass AR$8. Happy hour daily 6-9pm. Open M-F 8am-6am, Sa-Su 8:30am-6am. AmEx/MC/V.

**The Roxy Resto Bar,** Gorriti 5568 (☎4777 1230; www.theroxybar.com.ar), between Humboldt and Fitzroy. Another branch in Roxy's BA empire (p. 213), this nightlife spot starts the evening as a restaurant, and then spins pop as a bouncy dance club at night. Happy hour Tu-Th 8pm-midnight. Open Tu-Th 8pm-2am, F-Sa 8pm-6am. Cash only.

## CLUBS

**Niceto,** Niceto Vega 5510 (☎4779 9396; www.nicetoclub.com). DJs combine techno and strobe lights to make the hoodied masses move in a euphoric trance at this trendy nightspot. The club, which consists of a stage, dance floor, and upstairs "VIP" balcony, frequently plays host to popular music acts. Beer AR$5. Mixed drinks AR$18. On Th nights, Club 69, a dance troupe in drag, takes over. Cover AR$30. Open W-Su midnight-7am. Ticket counter open M-F noon-6pm.

NIGHTLIFE

## TOP TEN WAYS TO EXCESSIVELY BLEND IN

Looking to blend in with the locals? Sometimes, you can go too far. Stave off embarrassment and avoid these *faux pas:*

**1. Tangoing everywhere instead of walking.** When a casual walk will do, this is just excessive.
**2. Eating beef all the time.** No one actually does this. Save a cow, and save your heart.
**3. Swearing off all non-wine beverages.** Enticing, but please— spare your liver.
**4. Making frequent allusions to how BA is "soooo much like Paris!!!"** Lame travel guides invented this. *Porteños* won't appreciate the effort.
**5. Wearing a white uniform.** If you haven't noticed yet, only schoolchildren do this. So, basically, you'd look like an idiot.
**6. Painting your hostel dorm bright colors.** Leave it to El Caminito, where it's a schtick. You'd have a high damages bill, too.
**7. Riding a gaucho horse everywhere.** Can you imagine a horse on Buenos Aires' streets? We can, and it ain't pretty.
**8. Putting mayonnaise on everything.** It's true, they do like it as a condiment, but not *that* much. Again, save your heart.
**9. Suggesting Messi is the new Maradona.** We're sure this conversation has been had about... 1 billion times or so.
**10. Intravenous hook up to mate.** You would never sleep again.

# LAS CAÑITAS

## BARS

**Van Koning,** Báez 325 (☎4772 9909). Ⓢ Ministro Carranza. A haven for those missing decent, imported beer, Van Koning offers 75 international and national favorites, including Franziskaner, Tuborg, Karlsberg, and Staropramen (a favorite of *Let's Go: New York* editor Frank DeSimone), as well as a huge list of beer cocktails, like the Irish Car Bomb (AR$30). The Dutch-style interior is a bit overdone, but the atmosphere is still intimate and relaxed. Don't miss the terrace upstairs, or the collection of photos of the Dutch Princess Máxima, who happens to be Argentine. Beer AR$10-30. Mixed drinks AR$18-30. Snacks AR$7-20. Sandwiches AR$10-20. Pizzas AR$22-28. Open M-W and Su 7pm-3 or 4am, Th-Sa 7pm-5 or 6am. AmEx/MC/V.

**Drink Gallery,** Av. Chenaut 1794 (☎4775 3604; www.drink-gallery.com), at the intersection with Arce. Ⓢ Ministro Carranza. Beer pong tournaments every Tuesday? Flip cup on Wednesday? What *is* this place? Only the best place to watch football (American, of course) in BA, and perhaps a reincarnation of your college dorm. With a thoroughly American menu (anyone up for buffalo wings, chicken fingers, and hamburgers?) and beefy expats glued to the TV, only the zebra-striped couches strike an inauthentic note. Pitcher for beer pong AR$20. Wi-Fi access. Open daily 5pm-late. AmEx/MC/V.

**Jackie O.,** Báez 334 (☎4774 4844). Ⓢ Carranza. Between Arévalo and Chenault. One of many popular spots along the Báez strip, Jackie O., named for America's beloved former first lady, is a sleek, modern restaurant in the evenings, serving up American and Argentine favorites, but as the clock approaches midnight, the Las Cañitas pregaming crowd moves in to the bar and rooftop patio. Drinks AR$14-26. Open daily until late.

# COSTANERA NORTE

## CLUBS

**Caix,** at Av. Costanera Obligado and Av. Salguero (☎4805 6069; www.caix-ba.com.ar). For those who aren't ready to go home 7am Su morning, there's always the hugely popular Caix. The doors are open until well into the afternoon on Su, when the huge dance floor, outdoor riverside patio, and innumerable bars are still humming with people. Caix is very much the territory of locals; though many people here belong to the slick clubbing crowd, a rougher set is also represented, so it's wise to be careful. Open W and F 12:30-6am, Sa 12:30am to Su 2 or 3pm. 21+. Cover AR$25-40. Cash only.

**Crobar,** Paseo de la Infanta s/n (☎4778 1500; www.crobar.com.ar). Local prepsters party with their foreign tourist counterparts at this mammoth 2300-person capacity club. The speakers blast techno remixes of American pop favorites that will leave your ears ringing the next day. Beer AR$10. 21+. Cover AR$25. Open F-Sa 10:30pm-late.

**Rumi,** Av. Figueroa Alcorta 6442 (☎4782 1307; www.rumiba.com.ar), at La Pampa. Popular every night, the small dance floor at this club is dominated by the young and beautiful. It might not be worth the price, but you're bound to have a good time dancing to the techno. Cover AR$30-60, includes a Bud. Open Tu-Sa 1:30am-late.

**Pachá,** Av. Costanera Norte and Pampa (☎4788 4280; www.pachabuenosaires.com). Pick your way through the Porsche-packed parking lot to wait in line with the best (and no doubt brightest) of BA. Pachá makes its money by appealing to the jet set. Inside, you'll find a large dance floor, several bars, plenty of flashing lights, and blasting electronica and house. Regularly hosts big name DJs. 21+. Cover AR$60. Open Sa 1-8am.

**The Roxy Disco** (www.theroxybsas.com.ar), at the intersection of Casares and Sarmiento, in the Arcos del Sol, across from the Planetarium (p. 157). [S] Plaza Italia. Part of the Roxy franchise. Plays Latin rock and pop to a younger crowd. Beer AR$10-12. *Tragos* AR$12-20. Cover women AR$15, men AR$25. Open F-Sa 1:30am-7am. Cash only.



## VILLA CRESPO

### BARS

**878,** Thames 878 (☎4773 1098), between Loyola and Aguirre. [S] Plaza Italia. The big door guarding the entrance is the last reminder that 878 was once in the underground party scene. Since going legit, this bar has lost very little of its caché. The industrial chic-decor, lounge, and quiet music attracts good-looking 20-somethings. Drinks AR$25-30. Happy hour 8-10pm. Open daily 8pm-late. AmEx/MC/V: AR$20 minimum.

# BELGRANO

### BARS

👍 **Puerta Uno,** Juramento 1667 (☎4706 1522; www.puertauno.com). [S] Juramento. A relaxed, low-lit series of rooms decked out in palm fronds and flowers, Puerta Uno channels Southeast Asia without being self-conscious about it. Even more impressive than the decor are the drinks, which are pricey but high-quality and interesting. The Gancia Pear (AR$17), which combines pear juice and Sapphire, or the Pepete (AR$17), a mojito pepped up with honey, grapefruit, and ginger, are worth the trek to Belgrano. Tapas AR$15-30. Beer AR$10-18. Mixed drinks AR$15-30. Wine by the bottle AR$25-80, by the glass AR$12-30. Open Tu-Su 9pm-late. AmEx/MC/V: AR$50 minimum.

# BALVANERA

### CLUBS

**Azúcar,** Corrientes 3330 (☎4865 2102 or 4866 4439; www.azucarsalsa.com), between Agüero and Gallo. [S] Carlos Gardel. Near Abasto Shopping, green neon lighting and the blaring sound of the trumpet provide instant transport to the Caribbean. The club's weekend salsa attracts a mix of ages for hours of twirling. For the dance-shy out there, don't worry—the crowds are very friendly and supportive, and there's ample seating as a fallback. Beer AR$5. *Tragos* AR$10-15. Cover AR$15. Open F-Sa midnight-7am; classes offered during the week. Check website for details. Cash only.

# BOEDO

## BARS

**Cossab,** Carlos Calvo 4199 (☎4925 2505; www.pubcossab.com.ar). [S] La Plata. Looking for excellent beer? This relaxed pub is worth the trip from the center. The menu offers dozens of brands and varieties, from a slew of imported beers like Staropramen and Hoegaarden, to the local brews, including Cossab's own weizen and brown ale. Beer AR$8-27. Salads and sandwiches AR$10-27. Pizzas AR$17-32. W-Th all-you-can-eat pizza AR$14. Open W-Th 7pm-1:30am, F 7pm-4:30am, Sa 9pm-4:30am. Cash only.

## CLUBS

**Klub Killer,** Castro Barros 809 (☎4932 9261; www.klubkiller.com.ar). [S] Boedo. This place definitely has edge—though not quite as much as the name suggests. The local, alternative crowd that packs this small apartment-turned-bar is more relaxed than murderous—and mainly interested in conversation or in listening to the American and European rock and alternative playing in the background. Beer AR$8-15. Mixed drinks AR$15-20. Open F-Sa midnight-late. Cash only.



# GAY NIGHTLIFE

BA sports an active **GLBT** nightlife that rivals that of the top nightlife cities around the globe. The options are friendly and open and are scattered throughout capital federal, from the center to the outer *barrios*.

## BARS

**Flux,** M.T. de Alvear 980, Retiro (☎5252 0258; www.fluxbar.com.ar). [S] San Martín. New to the scene, this friendly, intimate bar draws small groups of 20- and 30-something gay men. The small tables and colorful, comfy couches are arranged to facilitate relaxed conversation. The extensive menu includes a huge variety of delicious mixed drinks (AR$12-22), though it has a limited beer selection. Happy hour 7-10pm, 2-for-1 mixed drinks. Open M-Sa 7pm-late. Cash only.

## CLUBS

**Bach Bar,** José Cabrera 4390, Palermo (☎5877 0919; www.bach-bar.com.ar), at the intersection with Julián Álvarez. [S] Scalabrini Ortiz. Get here too late on a weekend and be prepared to wait in line; this small bar and club is deservedly one of the most popular lesbian establishments in the city. Though some older women (and a few men) are regulars here, the crowd is mostly composed of hip 20-somethings pounding back drinks or dancing wherever they can find space to DJ-spun house and techno. Though entry is free, the way out is a little more interesting. Upon entry, you receive a chip, which you exchange, along with cash, for a drink and a ticket marked *"salida."* The ticket is the only way out, so you can't leave without spending at least AR$12 on drinks. This, of course, shouldn't be a problem. Drinks AR$12-25. Su karaoke. Open W-Su 11am-7am.

**Glam,** José Cabrera 3046, Recoleta (☎4963 2521; www.glambsas.com.ar). [S] Agüero. For one of BA's most popular gay clubs, Glam is surprisingly friendly and intimate. The dance floor draws a mixed crowd, but the majority of people are hip, young gay men (especially on Th and Sa) dancing to electronica. For those who need time away from the crowds, there is, of course, a semi-private room upstairs. Beer AR$10-12. Mixed drinks AR$10-25. Open Th-Sa 1-7am. Cover Th AR$25, F AR$15, Sa AR$30. Cash only.

**Angels,** Viamonte 2168, Balvanera (www.discoangels.com.ar). [S] Callao. Though this popular, two-story club includes a relaxed bar area, we don't think anyone bothers to stay there. Instead, it seems that everyone heads straight for one of the two dance floors, where DJs spin house, techno, pop, and rap. Join the crowd of fashionable, mostly gay 20- to 30-something men (plus a few women and transsexuals) and dance the night away. Whether you head into the small, semi-private room just behind the bar is up to you. Drinks AR$10-20. Cover F AR$15, Sa AR$25. Sa includes one drink. Open Th 12:30am-5am, F 12:30am-6am, Sa 12:30am-7am. Cash only.

**Amerika,** Gascón 1040, Almagro (☎4865 4416; www.ameri-k.com.ar). ⓢ Medrano. One of the city's most popular gay establishments, this massive club can get a bit crazy on weekends. Packed to the brim with a crowd of mostly young, gay men—though certainly welcoming of all others—the huge dance floor and numerous bars look both vaguely industrial and like a futuristic stage set. The music is mostly electronica, though the popular DJs do mix in some Latin pop and 80s music to shake things up. Mixed drinks AR$9-26. Open Th-Su midnight-7am. Cover Th and Su AR$25, F-Sa AR$40. Cash only.

**Alsina,** Adolfa Alsina 940, Monserrat (☎4331 3421; www.alsinabuenosaires.com.ar). ⓢ Piedras. This is one of the city's most beautiful clubs. It used to be known as Palacio Alsina, and with reason. Look up from the large dance floor at story after story of balconies drawn with red velvet curtains and you just might be distracted from the bodybuilders in briefs dancing on raised platforms around the floor. This is, after all, one of the city's hottest gay clubs, drawing a mixed, energetic, sometimes shirtless crowd with excellent electronica. If this is your scene, come on F or Su; Sa night, it hosts **Big One** (p. 204), BA's biggest electronica night, and the crowd is a bit different. Beer AR$12-14. Mixed drinks AR$15-25. Cover AR$30. Open F and Su 1am-late. AmEx/MC/V.

NIGHTLIFE

# DAYTRIPS

With all there is to see and do in Buenos Aires, the idea of leaving the city for something else may seem mind-boggling. There is a chance, though, after a week of noisy city life and staying up all night clubbing, that you'll want to get away from it all for a day. Fortunately, there's plenty to see afield from the borders of the metropolis, from the leafy riverside suburbs of San Isidro and Tigre to the traditional *gaucho* town of San Antonio de Areco. There's a reason we call these daytrips—plan to spend no more than one day each at these destinations. As such, we don't list any accommodations. We're sure you'll find Buenos Aires beckoning at the end of the day, anyway.

## SAN ISIDRO

For those weary of big city life, San Isidro, just forty minutes by train from the center of BA, offers the perfect escape. With winding cobblestone streets, beautiful old mansions, numerous green spaces, and a riverside location, this seriously wealthy northern *barrio* is a great place to relax on a sunny afternoon. For many years a popular summer retreat for the city's rich and well-connected, many *porteños* still come to the neighborhood on weekends for its *ferias* and museums. San Isidro may be wonderfully quiet during the week, but many of its attractions are also closed at that time.

### ⌂ TRANSPORTATION

**Buses:** Routes #60 and 168 travel from Constitución and La Boca, respectively, through the center and will drop you off near **Plaza Mitre,** San Isidro's central plaza; the trip, however, takes anywhere from an hour to an hour and a half depending on traffic.

**Trains:** Except for those staying in Palermo, train is the fastest option. From the station in Retiro, trains on the **Mitre line** (40min., every 10-30min. 6am-12:30am, AR$0.85) run to Estación San Isidro. To get to Plaza Mitre from the station, exit the station and turn in the direction the train was running; turn right on Belgrano, then veer left on 9 de Julio, which runs right into the Plaza. Alternatively, you can transfer at Olivos' Estación Mitre to the tourist **Tren de la Costa** (☎4002 6000), which runs along the coast and has its own Estación San Isidro right on Plaza Mitre (every 30min. 7am-11pm; AR$10, residents AR$6). Though more complicated and expensive than the local train, passengers can get off and on as often as they like, making it worthwhile for those planning to make several stops along the coast—and it does provide lovely views of the river.

### ✦🛈 ORIENTATION AND PRACTICAL INFORMATION

Most of San Isidro's sights cluster around the **Casco Histórico,** or "historic district," which stretches from the coast to **Avenida Libertador** and centers on **Plaza Bartolomé Mitre.** With its cobblestone streets and historic villas, this is also the best place to wander in the *barrio*. Southwest of here are the town's commercial streets, including the main street, **Belgrano.** Elsewhere along the coast, the streets are lined by the villas and mansions of San Isidro's wealthy denizens.

San Isidro's **tourist office,** Av. Libertador 16362, located on the southern end of Plaza Mitre, has information on restaurants and accommodations and hands out excellent maps that include detailed walking tours of the neighborhood. (☎4512 3209; www.sanisidroturismo.gov.ar. Open daily 9am-5pm.)

## 🍴 FOOD

It isn't difficult to find a place to eat in San Isidro. There are several well-touristed restaurants just north of **Plaza Mitre,** and a slew of local establishments along **Belgrano,** San Isidro's main commercial street, between Av. Libertador and the train station. More upscale options line **Boulevard Rocha,** which runs along the southeastern side of the **Hipodromo de San Isidro,** though many of these are only open late in the evening.

**Placeras Patagónicas,** J.B. La Salle 653 (☎4002 6068). If you don't want to wander too far afield, this restaurant, downstairs in the Tren de la Costa complex immediately north of the Plaza, serves up delicious Patagonian *tablas* (AR$40-100; serves 3-5 people), which include a selection of cheeses, smoked meats, and fish. There are also more traditional Argentine entrees and an inexpensive lunch *menú* (AR$23; M-F noon-4pm). Salads AR$17-23. Entrees AR$18-35. Open daily 9am-midnight. AmEx/MC/V. ❸

**La Cartuja,** Av. Libertador 16246, 2nd fl. (☎4747 4602). Also near the town center, and set across from the cathedral, this restaurant boasts a beautiful, quiet terrace perfect on any sunny day, along with an airy, rustic interior. The menu of Mediterranean cuisine, including a wide selection of seafood and pastas, is also supplemented by well-loved *parrilla* fare. Entrees AR$25-42. Open daily for lunch and dinner. AmEx/MC/V. ❸

**La Vaca,** Roque Sáenz Peña 1017 (☎4742 3715). For those heading in the direction of the coast, La Vaca is packed with locals at lunchtime scrambling for its *parrilla* fare. If you can, make sure to grab a table outside on the relaxed, expansive terrace under the leafy arbor. Entrees AR$20-36. Open daily for lunch and dinner. AmEx/MC/V. ❸

## 👁 SIGHTS

### CASCO HISTÓRICO AND AROUND

**PLAZA BARTOLOMÉ MITRE.** The center of the historic district, the beautifully terraced Plaza Mitre slopes down from Av. Libertador toward the river. Dotted with trees and small, manicured gardens, the Plaza is a fitting starting point for a tour of the neighborhood, though its only point of (vague) interest is the requisite statue of the Plaza's namesake, the president of Argentina from 1862 to 1868, at its southern edge. Each Saturday and Sunday from 10am to 6pm, the Plaza hosts the **Fería de Artesanos,** a crafts and souvenirs fair that runs year-round but has the most selection during the summer.

**CATEDRAL DE SAN ISIDRO.** Even from afar, it's hard to miss the tall spire of San Isidro's small neo-Gothic cathedral. Finished in 1898 and recently renovated, the pristinely beautiful white-and-gold interior is sparsely decorated but worth a visit for its beautiful stained glass windows and soaring ceiling. *(Av. Libertador 16200. On Plaza Mitre. ☎4743 0291. Open daily 8am-8pm. Free.)*

**ADRIÁN BECCAR VARELA AND SURROUNDINGS.** Beginning just behind the cathedral, winding **Calle Beccar Varela** is lined by lovely historic villas. Opposite the cathedral is the ornate stone **Casa de los Anchorena,** built in 1840 and once the home of the wealthy *porteño* **Anchorena** family (p. 152)—you can't really escape them, even when you leave BA. It now houses the **Colegio San Juan el Precursor.** Farther along the street, on the left at number 774, the plain colonial facade of the **Quinta Los Ombúes** once housed the street's namesake but is now the city's history **museum** (p. 220). The street ends at the **Mirador de los 3 Ombúes,** a lookout with views over the neighborhood and the Río de la Plata, which is as brown as ever. Immediately behind you is another villa, the very crumbling, very orange, and very sensibly named **Quinta Los Naranjos.**

DAYTRIPS

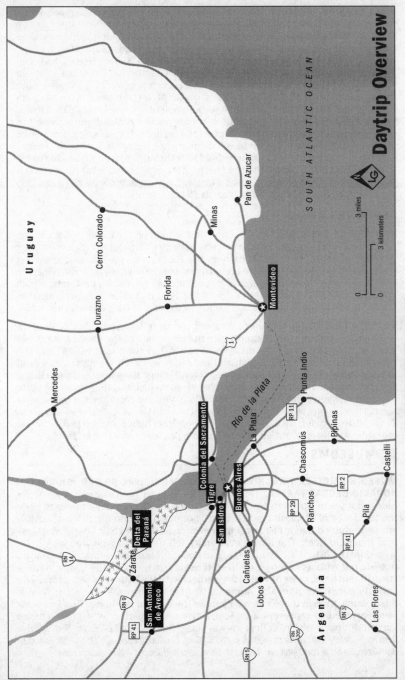

Daytrip Overview

SOUTH ATLANTIC OCEAN

Uruguay

Cerro Colorado

Durazno

Mercedes

Florida

Minas

Pan de Azucar

Montevideo

1

Río de la Plata

La Plata

Punta Indio

Colonia del Sacramento

Tigre

Buenos Aires

San Isidro

Delta del Paraná

Zárate

San Antonio de Areco

RN 14

RN 9

RP 41

RN 5

RN 205

Cañuelas

Lobos

Las Flores

RN 3

Pila

RP 41

Ranchos

RP 29

Chascomús

RP 2

Castelli

Pipinas

RP 11

Argentina

0 —— 3 miles

0 —— 3 kilometers

N

LG

**VILLA OCAMPO.** Built in 1890 by her father Manuel, this stunning French-Victorian mansion was the long-time residence of famous Argentine writer and millionaire **Victoria Ocampo.** The founder of the major literary publication *Sur*, Ocampo surrounded herself with some of the greatest minds of the 20th century, and major literary figures from Graham Greene and Aldous Huxley to Pablo Neruda and Jorge Luis Borges congregated at her home. Upon her death in 1979, she left the home to UNESCO, which is currently working to restore the building and turn it into a major cultural center of the type Ocampo envisioned. The only way to see the mansion is to take one of the weekend guided tours, which visit a number of the enormous rooms packed with art and antique furniture, as well as the beautifully landscaped gardens. If you can't make it here on the weekend and still want to see the mansion, it's worth having the tourist office call to see if there's a group guided tour that day; you might be able to tag along. *(Elortando 1837. From Plaza Mitre, head northeast on Av. Libertador, turn right on Uriburu, and right again on Elortando. ☎4732 4988; www.villaocampo.org. Guided Spanish-language tours every 30min. Sa-Su 12:30-6pm. AR$12, students $6.)*

### ALONG THE COAST

**PARQUES DE LAS RIBERAS.** Though San Isidro is on the **Río de la Plata,** much of the land bordering the river is private, making it difficult to reach the water. A series of **parks,** however, known as the Parques de las Riberas, allow for intermittent access to the shore and provide beautiful views over the river; the one nearest the *Casco Histórico* is located at the end of **Calle Centenera,** which winds around from the eastern edge of the Tren de la Costa station. Alternatively, there's another park farther south, at the end of **Calle General Pueyrredón.**

**RESERVA ECOLÓGICA.** Farther east along the river, the relatively tiny Reserva Ecológica is a great way to experience the landscape of the **Paraná Delta** if you can't actually make it to the delta itself (p. 223). A short trail winds from the reserve's entrance through marshland and out to an exceptionally tranquil (and exceptionally muddy) spot right on the river. Though the amount of trash lining the trail in places certainly doesn't improve on its beauty, other spots are quite lovely, and if you come here at the right time, you just might be the only one in the reserve. To get to the entrance, follow the Tren de la Costa tracks east from Plaza Mitre, turn left on Calle Lopez y Planes, then right on Av. de la Ribera; the entrance will be on your left after a half-block. *(Open daily 9am-6pm. Free.)*

### 🏛 MUSEUMS

**MUSEO BIBLIOTECA Y ARCHIVO HISTÓRICO MUNICIPAL DE SAN ISIDRO: DR. HORACIO BECCAR VARELA.** Built in the 18th century (and therefore one of the oldest houses in northern Buenos Aires), this lovely colonial home was once the residence of Mariquita Sánchez de Thompson, a famous patrician woman who entertained major historical figures such as General San Martín and General Belgrano here. The house eventually fell to Dr. Horacio Beccar Verela, who donated it to the city in 2005. The beautiful building, stark white on the outside but with a gorgeous, tiled, Mediterranean motif on the inside, houses six different halls, most of which are dedicated to the history of San Isidro. The collection includes portraits, documents, flags, uniforms, and other pieces of miscellania, though there's also a room in the back of the house that has been reconstructed to represent a typical 19th-century parlor, as well as a small garden out back with excellent views. *(Adrián Beccar Varela 774. Follow Beccar Varela from immediately behind the cathedral. ☎4575 4038. Captions in Spanish. Open Feb. Tu and Th 8am-3pm, Sa-Su 3-7pm; Mar.-Jan. Tu and Th 8am-noon and 2-6pm, F-Sa 2-6pm. Free.)*

**MUSEO HISTÓRICO MUNICIPAL BRIGADIER GENERAL J.M. DE PUEYRREDÓN.** Built in 1790 and first owned by **General Pueyrredón,** a major figure in the Argentine wars of independence (p. 55), this beautiful colonial home is worth visiting for the building alone, which is set among gorgeous gardens with views over the river. A number of rooms are devoted to a small collection of historical documents relating to Pueyrredón, though others have been furnished in the style of the time period. At the time of publication, the house was closed indefinitely for restoration. *(River Indarte 48. From Plaza Mitre, head five blocks down Av. Libertador and turn left on Roque Sáenz Peña; the museum is two blocks down on the right.* ☎*4512 3131. Open Mar.-Oct. Tu and Th 8am-6pm, Sa-Su 2-6pm; Nov.-Feb. Sa-Su 3-7pm. Guided tours Sa-Su Mar.-Oct. 4-6pm; Nov.-Feb. 5-7pm. Free.)*

# TIGRE

Settled as early as 1580, Tigre was a small port city until the beginning of the 20th century, when it became the preferred city escape for *porteños*, first for the elite and, nowadays, for everyone else. Named after the *tigres* (jaguars) that inhabited the delta until they were hunted to extinction, the small city is quite commercial and can get crowded on summer weekends. Still, it can be a great place to wander and relax on a sunny day, shopping at the market, visiting the stunning art museum, and eating and drinking along the river.

## TRANSPORTATION

**Trains:** Trains on the **Mitre line** depart for Tigre (1hr., every 10-30min. 6am-12:30am, AR$1.10) from Buenos Aires' Retiro station and terminate at Estación Tigre, located on Av. Ricardo Ubieto near the bridge over the Río Tigre, and return to Buenos Aires until 11:30pm. Alternatively, it is possible to transfer at Estación Mitre to the tourist **Tren de la Costa** (☎4002 6000; every 30min. 7am-11pm; AR$10, residents AR$6), which runs along the coast and terminates at the Estación Delta, opposite the amusement park and just blocks from Tigre's popular market, **Puerto de Frutos.** Though more complicated and expensive than the local train, passengers can get on and off as often as they like, making it worthwhile for those planning to make several stops along the coast.

## ORIENTATION

Located on a small island south of the **Río Lujan,** Tigre is divided into two halves by the smaller **Río Tigre.** On the coast east of the river, **Avenida Mitre** connects the passenger train station with the tourist office and leads to **Calle Vivanco,** where the Tren de la Costa station is located and which ends at the theme park and the **Puerto de Frutos** market. The eastern half is connected with the western half by a bridge near the train station. Following the river around the coast from the bridge in the western half, **Lavalle** leads to **Paseo Victorica,** the best place to walk along the river, and where most of the best restaurants and two major museums are located. The area inland from Paseo Victorica is also a great place for a quiet stroll among the crumbling older and newer villas of Tigre's inhabitants.

## PRACTICAL INFORMATION

**Tourist Office:** Av. Mitre 305 (☎4512 4497; www.tigre.gov.ar). In the Estación Fluvial (Boat Terminal), Tigre's helpful tourist office hands out maps and boat schedules and can suggest accommodations, boat trips on the river, and watersports operators. To get to the Boat Terminal from the passenger train station, head right across the roundabout and one block down Av. Mitre; it's just beyond the McDonald's. Open daily 8am-6pm.

**Banks:** Tigre's banks are located along Av. Cazón, which runs southeast from the bridge between the train station and boat terminal. Most have 24hr. ATMs, including **Banco de la Nación,** at the intersection of Av. Cazón and Emilio Mitre. Open M-F 10am-3pm.

**Pharmacy:** Farmácia del Pueblo, Av. Cazón 1550 (☎4749 0092). Open 24hr.

**Internet:** Indistinguishable *locutorios* along Av. Cazón offer Internet access for AR$2-3 per hr—one is at Cazón 1483 (☎4731 1559). Open daily 10am-8pm. AR$3 per hr.

**Post office:** Av. Cazón 1140. Open M-F 10am-6pm, though they sometimes close randomly around lunch.

## ▶ FOOD

It isn't difficult to find a place to eat in Tigre. Restaurants cluster around the major sights and more upscale establishments line **Paseo Victorica.** For cheaper eats, try the **Puerto de Frutos** or any of the number of **supermarkets** along **Avenida Cazón;** try **Ekí,** Av. Cazón 1340. (Open daily 8am-8pm. AmEx/MC/V.)

**Il Novo María Luján del Tigre,** Paseo Victorica 611 (☎4731 9613). One of Tigre's only restaurants with a patio on the river, Il Novo María is also one of the town's most popular—and with good reason. In addition to the Argentine staples of pasta and beef, the restaurant serves a variety of excellent seafood and more creative dishes; try the Singapore (chicken with pumpkin and fruits; AR$35). Table service AR$6. Appetizers AR$7-36. Salads AR$14-65. Seafood AR$26-78. *Parrilla* AR$19-39. Other entrees AR$32-44. Open daily 8am-midnight. AmEx/MC/V. ❹

**Literatos,** Av. del Libertador San Martín 440 (☎4749 8127). From the boat terminal, cross the bridge and continue straight for two blocks. If this small restaurant were on the riverbank, it would likely be packed. Luckily, it's not, and the rustic yellow dining room lined with modern art attracts a small in-the-know crowd with a delicious, inexpensive menu of seafood, interesting *milanesas,* and vegetable dishes. Entrees AR$21-35. Open M-F 9am-11pm, Sa 10am-4pm and 7:30-11pm, Su noon-3:30pm. MC/V. ❸

**Via Toscana,** Paseo Victorica 470 (☎4749 2972). This *heladería,* a local favorite, takes its ice cream seriously; just look for the charts on the counter expounding on the inferiority of other lowly shops. Flavors include a delicious *limón* and *dulce de leche.* Carry your sweets outside to enjoy on the leafy, shaded patio. Ice cream AR$7-12. Sundaes AR$16. Open W-Su noon-10pm. Cash only. ❶

## ◉ SIGHTS

**PUERTO DE FRUTOS.** Though for much of the 19th century, Tigre's harbor was a major fruit port, it's much better known nowadays for its crafts market. Set up along three different docks, the first two host lines of shops and stands selling leather, ceramics, and cheap clothing, though the focus is definitely on wicker products. The third, however, is open to ships, and you still can see the boats being unloaded. The market is open every day, but it's best to go on weekends, when the crowds are bigger and more shops are open. To get to the market, head down Av. Mitre from the station, veer right on Vivanco, and walk along the Tren de la Costa tracks to Sarmiento. *(Open daily 10am-7pm. Free.)*

**PARQUE DE LA COSTA.** Some might think it's a bit of an eyesore, but Tigre's large theme park is nonetheless very popular among *porteño* children for its rides, ferris wheels, playgrounds, and games. There are many rides intended for an older crowd, including several roller coasters. Many of the larger rides cost AR$5-10 extra, in addition to the price of admission. *(Bartolomé Mitre 2. ☎4002 6000. Open F-Su and holidays 11am-8pm. General admission AR$30; pasaporte, which includes unlimited access to several of the large rides as well, AR$40.)*

# 🏛 MUSEUMS

**🖼MUSEO DE ARTE TIGRE (MAT).** Even for those not particularly interested in art, Tigre's museum is worth visiting for the building alone. Built in 1909, the palatial, French-inspired edifice housed the Tigre Club, a major society casino, until gambling was outlawed in the 1930s. Purchased by the city in 1978 and recently refurbished, the interior is almost as ornate as the exterior, with beautiful stained glass, mirrors, chandeliers, and ceiling frescoes; don't miss the former ballroom, featuring a soaring painted ceiling, or the chance to stroll along the ornate terrace, which has stunning river views. The museum's actual collection rivals the best in Buenos Aires and is composed of mainly Argentine artists, including Antonio Berni, Eduardo Sívori, and Benito Quinquela Martín, and is arranged by theme as opposed to time period. The museum also hosts excellent temporary Latin American art exhibits. *(Paseo Victorica 972. ☎4512 4528; www.mat.gov.ar. Captions in Spanish. Open W-F 9am-7pm, Sa-Su and holidays noon-7pm. AR$5. Guided Spanish-language tours W-F 11am and 4pm, Sa-Su 1, 3, and 5pm. Free.)*

**MUSEO NAVAL DE LA NACIÓN.** Set in a soaring wooden hall, Tigre's naval museum is packed with a bewildering number of displays on the history of the Argentine naval force, as well as navigational history in general. Exhibits range from not-so-miniature reproductions of historic ships, to statues and portraits of famous personalities, to uniforms and dishes used on famous voyages. There's also a room of naval weapons you can mess with in back and an outdoor display of planes and parts of ships; keep an eye out for the twisted metal cabin of a ship bombed during the Falklands War. *(Paseo Victorica 602. ☎4749 0608. Captions in Spanish. Open M-F 8:30am-5:30pm, Sa-Su and holidays 10am-6:30pm. AR$2.)*

**MUSEO DE LA RECONQUISTA.** Housed in a lovely reconstructed colonial building, this museum was founded on the spot where **General Liniers** landed and began his march to retake Buenos Aires from the British in 1806. The collection, which includes rooms on the reconquest, the history of Tigre, the Tigre Club and Hotel, and a hall of uniforms, is a bit staid, but the pieces are definitely of high-quality and would be worth a visit for those interested in Argentine history. *(Liniers 818. ☎4512 4496. Some English captions. Open W-Su 10am-6pm. Free.)*

# 🏕 OUTDOOR ACTIVITIES

**BOAT TRIPS.** There are numerous ways to see the **Paraná Delta** from Tigre, and the town's excellent **tourist office** (p. 221) is very helpful in navigating the tour options. A slew of relatively indistinguishable companies offer quick, round-trip tours through a small part of the Delta near Tigre; though they don't go too far, they do offer a quick glimpse of the Delta and the river lifestyle. Most trips (AR$10-20) last one hour and are on either a larger catamaran or smaller launch, the latter of which are usually open and have fewer people and better views. The companies' small ticket kiosks are along the river banks, Bartolomé Mitre, at the Boat Terminal, and at the beginning of Paseo Victoria.

**FERRIES.** Longer cruises tend to be expensive. A great way to see more for less is to catch a ride on one of the regular ferries that service the smaller communities farther out on the Delta. Be sure to ask which round-trips are available, as many of the services are one-way. Trips last upwards from an hour and usually run AR$8-20. Three companies operate passenger services.

   **Intersleña,** at the Boat Terminal, ticket offices #3-4 (☎4749 0900).
   **Jilgüero,** at the Boat Terminal, ticket office #2 (☎4749 0900).

**Lineas Delta,** in front of the Boat Terminal at kiosk #6 (☎4731 1236).

**SPORTS.** Popular outdoor activities on the Delta include kayaking, rowing, and wakeboarding, and numerous operators offer lessons as well as guided trips of the Delta lasting anywhere from a few hours to a week. Most require prior reservation, so it's a good idea to call or email in advance.

**Puro Remo,** Lavalle 235, Tigre (☎15 5808 2237; www.puroremo.com.ar). One of the most conveniently located companies. Offers a variety of individual rowing classes, as well as half- and full-day kayaking trips through the Delta. Contact Tu-Su 7am-7pm.

**Rowing Trips** (☎15 5707 6957; www.rowingtrips.com.ar). Offers lessons as well as one- and two-day rowing trips in spring and summer W-Su at 9am to the Delta islands. Tours depart from the Regatas La Marina Club, located across the river from Paseo Victorica. English-speaking guides available. Reservations required.

**Kayak Tours** (☎4728 2865; www.nauticalescapes.com). Runs a huge variety of kayak tours, from two hours (AR$91) to a week (AR$3036), and rents kayaks (single half-day AR$61, full-day AR$91; double AR$106/152). Prices include transport from the train station to the company's base on the Río San Antonio. Reservations required.

**Wake School Gabriela Díaz** (☎4728 0031; www.wakeschool.com.ar). One of the world's top wakeboarders runs this school teaching wakesurfing, wakeboarding, and waterski- ing. Classes year-round. Equipment provided. The school is located on the Río San Antonio; to reach it, catch the Intersleña ferry to Gustanto. Contact daily 9am-7pm.

# SAN ANTONIO DE ARECO ☎02326

After staying in Buenos Aires, visiting San Antonio de Areco can be a definite culture shock. Located on the *pampas* just 113km away from the city, this tiny town, with its low colonial buildings, narrow cobblestone streets, and quiet parks, moves at a very different pace and is virtually silent on a weekday afternoon—if not on summer weekends, when there's an influx of tourism from the city. The long-time host of the beloved **Fiesta de la Tradición** (p. 226), San Antonio de Areco is considered the center of *gaucho* traditions, and most of the town's sights, including an excellent museum, a slew of talented artisans, and several famous *estancias*, focus on this theme. That said, you'll likely see more bicycles and mopeds circling town than *gauchos* on horseback (though there are a few of these, too), but even without them, the narrow cobblestone streets, lined with beautiful colonial buildings, are well worth a visit.

## TRANSPORTATION

**Buses:** Unless you're driving yourself, bus is the only way to get to San Antonio de Areco. **Chevallier,** kiosk #67 in Buenos Aires' Retiro station (☎4000 5255), runs buses (1hr. 45min.; 15 daily 6am-midnight; AR$20-25) to San Antonio de Areco's **Chevallier Station,** located at the corner of Avenida Smith and General Paz (☎453904); 15 daily buses return to Buenos Aires 4:45am-9:30pm. To get to the center from here, face the station and head straight down the street to its left, which is General Paz. After five blocks, turn right on Arellano, which runs right into the main square. To get to the tourist office, simply continue three more blocks down Arellano from the square; it's across the street at the corner with Av. Zerboni.

## ORIENTATION

The lack of signs away from the center can be a bit annoying, but San Anto- nio's strictly grid-pattern streets are still very easy to navigate. The small

DAYTRIPS

**Casco Histórico,** or old town, where most of San Antonio's sights are located, centers on **Plaza Arellano. Alsina** and **Arellano,** which border the Plaza to the east and west, are the city's main commercial streets and host most of the artisans. A few blocks from the Plaza, the **Río Areco** runs along the north side of town and is surrounded by a system of parks.

**WE DON'T NEED NO STINKIN' ADDRESSES.** You'll notice that for many of our listings, we only provide street intersections for the location rather than addresses. This is not an attempt to make things harder for you— we're not that cruel. Many places in San Antonio de Areco actually list their addresses this way. Thanks to the city's easily navigable grid, you shouldn't have any trouble. Addresses are overrated, anyway.

## 🖪 PRACTICAL INFORMATION

**Tourist Office:** Zerboni and Arellano (☎453165; www.sanantoniodeareco.com). In a small white building in Parque San Martín, the tourist office hands out maps as well as detailed lists of local services, accommodations, and artisans. Open daily 8am-8pm.

**Banks:** The town banks cluster near Plaza Arellano and along Alsina. **Banco Provincia,** at the intersection of Alsina and Bartolomé Mitre, has a 24hr. ATM. Open M-F 10am-6pm.

**Pharmacy:** Farmácia del Pueblo, at the intersection of Alsina and Bartolomé Mitre (☎452140).

**Internet: Planeta Virtual,** Alsina 158 (☎455555). Internet AR$2.50 per hr. Free Wi-Fi. Open daily 8am-2am.

**Post office: Correo Argentino,** at the intersection of Del Valle and Alvear (☎455609). Open M-F 10am-5pm.

## 🖪 FOOD

San Antonio de Areco has a reputation as a quiet, traditional *Pampas* town, and its many restaurants fit the bill with quiet, rustic flair. Establishments are scattered throughout the center, and **Zerboni,** which runs along the edge of the park, has the town's most popular *parrillas.* For cheaper eats, there's also a **supermarket** on the main square at the intersection of Arellano and Segunda Sombra. (Open M-Sa 8am-12:30pm and 4-8:30pm, Su 9am-12:30pm. AmEx/MC/V.)

**La Esquina de Merti,** on Plaza Arellano at the intersection of Arellano and Segunda Sombra (☎456705). Covered in old tin advertisements and signs, this brick-and-wood restaurant is a recreation of a *pulpería,* a type of old school general-provisions store that also serves as a bar and rural meeting point. You'll see locals lounging at the tables even outside of mealtimes, when it's a popular meeting spot for a drink. Serves all the Argentine standards; the tasty lunch-time *asado* (AR$23) is a great deal. Tortes AR$8. Sandwiches AR$3-13. *Parrilla* AR$10-28. Other entrees AR$13-30. Open daily noon-midnight. Lunch served noon-4pm. Dinner 8pm-midnight. Cash only. ❷

**La Vieja Sodería,** at the intersection of General Paz and Bolívar (☎456376). Tucked along a quiet sidestreet, this comfortable and relaxing cafe, covered with old advertisements and soda bottles, is an excellent place for breakfast, or for a mid-day drink or snack. Grab a seat inside or on the patio for coffee and delicious *picadas* (a type of stuffed tortilla; AR$8-28), or start the night early by selecting one of the many whiskey options, which take up nearly half of the menu (AR$6-45). Here's to whiskey in the middle of the day. Sandwiches AR$4-13. Breakfast AR$8-14. Beer AR$7-10. Mixed drinks AR$9-14. Open M-Sa 8am-10pm, Su 9am-10pm. Cash only. ❷

DAYTRIPS

## COWBOYS OF THE SOUTH

Every **November 10th** since 1939, people all over Argentina—no matter how *cheto* (snobbish) they may be—return to their roots and celebrate the **Día de la Tradición,** a festival dedicated to all things *criollo*—that is, all things to do with Argentine country culture. This, of course, involves consuming unholy amounts of beef at an *asado,* perhaps while washing it all down with a *mate* (p. 68) and grooving to folk tunes during the subsequent caffeine rush. This is all fine and well. But the center of it all is the *gaucho*—the wrangling Argentine cowboy of the *Pampas.* The date of the festival, after all, was chosen to coincide with the birthday of **José Hernández** (p. 76), author of the beloved *gaucho* epic **Martín Fierro.**

The place to be for the festival is **San Antonio de Areco,** Argentina's center of *gaucho* culture. Here, the festivities aren't limited to a single day—it's more like an entire week, usually the first or second week of November. The highlight, however, is the last Sunday, when *gauchos* parade through the town to the **Parque Criollo** (p. 226), where there's a public *asado* followed by displays of *gaucho* horseback skills. After experiencing it all, you might just never go back to the çity. Considering the massive popularity of the festival and the relatively small size of the town, it's a good idea to book bus tickets, as well as accommodations, well in advance.

**La Costa,** at the intersection of Zerboni and Belgrano (☎452481). Of the *parrillas* lining the park, La Costa is without a doubt the local favorite. The white adobe building stands out among the more traditional structures that surround it and has a patio overlooking the park. The menu includes homemade pasta, tortillas, and omelettes, as well as *bife* and *milanesas.* Sandwiches and salads AR$6-16. Pasta AR$15-22. *Parrilla* AR$8-21. Other entrees AR$13-29. Open Tu-Su noon-3:30pm and 8-11pm. MC/V. ❷

# ◉ SIGHTS

**PLAZA RUIZ DE ARELLANO.** Though it isn't particularly interesting in and of itself, the **Casco Histórico's** main plaza is nonetheless a lovely and relaxing green space. At its center stands a statue of **Juan Hipólito Vieytes,** an Argentine military officer, born in San Antonio de Areco, who participated in the reconquest of the city from the British in the early 19th century. The Plaza (and, in fact, most of the town) occupies land that once belonged to **José Ruiz de Arellano,** who sponsored the building of the town's first chapel in 1730.

**IGLESIA PARROQUIAL SAN ANTONIO DE PADUA.** The first version of this simple but impressive church, a basic adobe chapel built in 1730 under the auspices of José Ruiz de Arellano, was rebuilt twice to create a grander edifice. The plain colonial exterior of the current church, finished in 1870, gives way to a lovely and eerily quiet rectangular interior, worth stepping into for a look at the massive carved altarpiece crammed into one end. It looks like it could use a bit more space. *(On the south side of the Plaza Ruiz de Arellano.)*

**PARQUE SAN MARTÍN.** To get a feeling for the wide open expanse of the plains surrounding this tiny town, head to its northern edge, where the Río Areco winds through a system of rather barren, if expansive, tree shaded parks. North of here, paved streets give way to dirt roads where you might actually see *gauchos* trotting on horseback, as well as some excellent views across the *Pampas.*

# 🏛 MUSEUMS

**PARQUE CRIOLLO AND MUSEO GAUCHESCO "RICARDO GÜIRALDES".** North of town along a picturesque dirt road, this museum is more of a complex than a single building. It's set in the **Parque Criollo,** a rambling, grassy field that is the main setting for the *gaucho* games of the town's popular **fes-**

**tival** (p. 226). Visitors enter the complex through the 150-year-old **La Blanqueada**, a *pulpería* (general store) located on the **Camino Royale**. The *pulpería* makes a famous appearance in Argentine author Ricardo Güiraldes' renowned 1926 novel *Don Segundo Sombra*, which is still well-loved for its positive depiction of the *gaucho* culture and which, of course, gives its name to the museum. Beyond the general store, a path winds by a small chapel and some farm equipment to the museum building, a 1930s reproduction of an 18th-century *estancia* (farm). Its collection, with *gaucho* costumes and gear, clearly focuses on rural culture, but also includes portraits of famous Argentine writers and General Rosas' (p. 56) bed. There's also a collection of *gaucho* artwork. *(Camino Ricardo Güiraldes. To get to the museum, head through the parks north of town, cross the brick Puente Viejo (old bridge) and head down the dirt road in front of you; the museum will be on your left. ☎455839. Some English captions. English pamphlets available. Open M and W-Su 11am-5pm. AR$4.)*

**CENTRO CULTURAL Y TALLER DRAGHI.** This excellent museum and workshop, run for over forty years by the town's most famous silversmith, who passed away in 2008, has sent its hand-made pieces to the rich and aristocratic all over the world. Upon arrival, visitors are given a short tour of the workshop explaining the process by which each piece is painstakingly made and are then left to marvel at the museum's impressive collection, which mixes silver pieces from the 19th and 20th century with some of the workshop's own products. Wonderfully intricate saddles, spurs, whips, stirrups, knives, and *mates* line the walls; don't miss the bridles that took three years to make. *(Lavalle 387. On the north side of the Plaza Ruiz de Arellano. ☎454219. Captions in English and Spanish. Open M-Sa 9am-1pm and 3:30-8pm, Su 10am-1pm. AR$5. Guided tours available.)*

**MUSEO ATELLIER DEL PINTOR LUIS GASPARINI.** This small museum, which is actually the artist's house, displays the works of local painter and drawer Luis Gasparini. Though the collection is limited, the charismatic and enthusiastic artist shows and explains his paintings and drawings, which focus mainly on *gaucho* themes and Argentine symbols. If you're lucky, he may also give you a live demonstration. *(Alvear 545. ☎02325 1540 1330. Open daily 8am-8pm. Free.)*

## ◤ RANCHES (ESTANCIAS)

Some of the country's most famous *estancias*, or ranches, surround San Antonio de Areco; staying in them, however, can be a very, very expensive proposition. It is possible—and much cheaper—to spend the day at **Cinacina**, located just outside of San Antonio de Areco's **Casco Histórico**. This beautiful, rambling *estancia* offers day packages that start at 11am and include several meals, a horseback or carriage ride over their lands, dance shows, and *gaucho* demonstrations. To get to the *estancia*, head west on Lavalle from the main plaza— you'll end up at the gates 10 minutes later. *(Lavalle 9. ☎452045; www.lacinacina.com. ar. Day-package AR$95. Cash only. Advance reservations recommended.)*

DAYTRIPS

# EXCURSIONS

Even farther beyond BA's traditional daytrips are longer excursions that will completely remove the traveler from the city world. Treks out to Argentina's western plains and mountains lead to vineyards and adventure activities, while the jungles of the north hold some of the world's most spectacular natural wonders. Closer to Buenos Aires' own neighborhood are the sands and sleepy old towns of Uruguay, the oft-forgotten country across the Río de la Plata.

## WESTERN ARGENTINA

### MENDOZA                                                                ☎0261

Located over 1000km west of Buenos Aires, Mendoza, the capital of the eponymous province, has become a massively popular excursion for travelers visiting Buenos Aires. Founded in 1561 and completely leveled by an earthquake exactly 300 years later, this rambling, relaxing city, featuring wide streets and numerous plazas, has few sights to speak of—save for several decent museums and an excellent, enormous park—but most travelers come to Mendoza for what lies around the city, not for what's in it. Mendoza is known as the country's premier 🗹**wine-producing region,** and some of Argentina's main vineyards are within easy reach of the city center. Additionally, the city lies only 100km from the Andes Mountains, making it a hot spot for adventure.

### ▣ INTERCITY TRANSPORTATION

**Buses: Andesmar,** kiosk #27 (☎4313 4242); **Central Argentino,** kiosk #47 (☎4315 1868); **Chevallier,** kiosk #67 (☎4000 5255); **El Rápido Internacional,** kiosk #33 (☎4313 3757); **Flecha Bus,** kiosks #56 and 145 (☎4000 5200); and **Tramat,** kiosk #45 (☎4314 1258), run buses (12-18hr.; AR$120-235) from the Retiro station in Buenos Aires to Mendoza and back. Buses usually depart early evening and arrive early to late morning at Mendoza's station, **Terminal del Sol,** Av. de Acceso and Costanera (☎431 3001), located just across the city's eastern border in the suburb of Guaymallén. The station has a small bank with **ATM, tourist office** (open 7am-10pm), and a number of shops. To get to the center, about a 15min. walk away, head to the very end of the ticket hall and exit the station; you'll see an underpass lined with kiosks in front of you. Walk through this underpass and the next and continue west along the street that lies at the end; this is Av. Alem, which becomes Montevideo and runs right into the center. **Taxis** and **remises** are also at the station; the 5min. drive should cost around AR$5-8.

> ⚠ **TERMINAL DEL SOL SAFETY.** Many thefts have been reported recently at the bus station. Watch your baggage and valuables.

### ▣ LOCAL TRANSPORTATION

**Buses:** Local buses are identified by two numbers: a single-digit number that indicates direction and a secondary multi-digit number. Make sure you have both numbers right or you'll end up going in the wrong direction. They run 6am-2pm and cost AR$1.10 for shorter journeys and AR$1.40 for longer trips. Tickets are bought on board at automatic machines, which only accept change. Mendoza proper is compact enough that taking buses is rarely necessary within the center; travelers will have to take buses, however, to reach the wineries or airport.

**Taxis:** Though taxis ply the center, they can sometimes be hard to find; call or be prepared to wait. Base fare AR$2.50. **Radio Móvil** (☎445 5855). **Radio Taxi** (☎430 3300).

**Bike rental: Bikes and Wines,** 25 de Mayo 981 (☎410 6686). Also with locations in Maipú (p. 235). Naturally, the logo for this company features a biker riding while drinking wine. Price includes a free drink and map with self-guided city tour. Half-day (4hr.) AR$20; full-day AR$34. Open 10am-6pm. Cash only.

## ✴ ORIENTATION

After the earthquake, Mendoza's streets were rebuilt in a regular grid pattern centering on the four-block-square **Plaza Independencia.** Four satellite squares lie at the corners; the area surrounding these plazas is known as the **Microcentro** (hey, that sounds familiar) and is bordered by the city's main commercial streets: **Avenida Colón** to the south, **Avenida Las Heras** to the north, **Avenida San Martín** to the east, and **Belgrano** to the west.

**TAKING POTHOLES TO THE NEXT LEVEL.** The occasional, very deep ditch between the sidewalk and the street in Mendoza can be quite horrifying. Take care, especially when drunk—they can appear out of nowhere.

## ⚐ PRACTICAL INFORMATION

**Tourist Offices:** Av. San Martín 1143 (☎420 2800). Offers maps and can help book excursions. Also deals with permits to climb nearby Aconcagua, South America's highest mountain. Open daily 8am-9pm. Additional branches at Av. San Martín and Garibaldi (☎420 1333) and Av. Las Heras 341 (☎429 6298). Open 9am-9pm.

**Banks:** The city's main banks and exchange offices line Av. San Martín between Av. Las Heras and Av. Colón; virtually all have **24hr. ATMs.** Try **Banco de la Nación,** Av. San Martín and Gutierrez (☎425 9482). Open M-F 10am-5pm.

**Laundromat: Laveráp,** Av. Colón 502 (☎435 2035). Same-day wash and dry AR$12. Open M-Sa 8:30am-9pm. Cash only.

**Emergency:** Police ☎101, Fire ☎100, Ambulance ☎107.

**Police: Policía Federal,** Perú 1049 (☎423 8710). Also houses the tourist police.

**Pharmacy: Farmacia del Puente,** Av. Las Heras 201 (☎425 9209). Open 24hr.

**Hospital: Hospital Central,** Salta and L.N. Alem (☎429 7100).

**Internet Access: WH Internet and Games,** Peatonal Sarmiento 219 (☎423 3398). Wi-Fi AR$2 per hr. Internet AR$4 per hr. Offers copy, fax, and CD-burning services. Open daily 7:30am-1am. Additional locations at Av. San Martín 1178 and Av. Las Heras 61.

**Post Office:** Av. Colón and Av. San Martín (☎429 1190). Open M-F 8am-8pm, Sa 10am-1pm. **Postal Code:** 5500.

## ⌂ ACCOMMODATIONS

As tourism in Mendoza has increased, so has the number of accommodation options. Hostels in Mendoza are particularly excellent, and virtually all will help travelers book tours and excursions and arrange for transportation.

EXCURSIONS

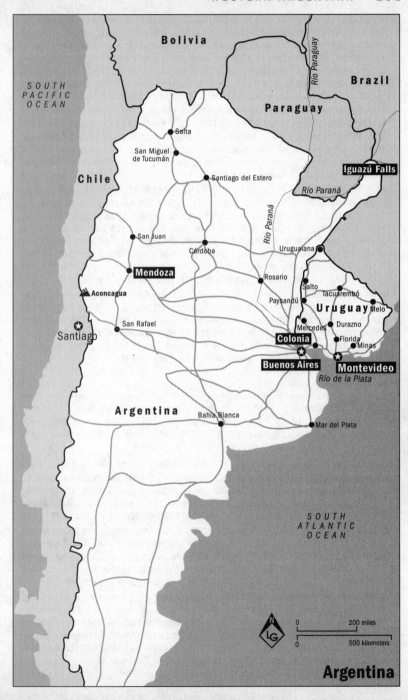

**Hostel Lao,** La Rioja 771 (☎438 0454; www.laohostel.com). Heading up Alem from the bus station, turn left on La Rioja. This hostel, one of the most popular in South America, sports clean, top-notch dorms and a relaxed and sociable atmosphere. Facilities include a common room with TV, a kitchen, and a large garden with hammocks and a pool. Arranges tours. Breakfast included. Free wine Tu-Su nights. F night *asado* AR$45. Laundry service AR$12. Free Internet and Wi-Fi. Reception 24hr. Check-out 10:30am. 4-bed dorm with A/C and private bath AR$42; 6-bed dorms with A/C AR$40; doubles with shared bath AR$120, with private bath, TV, and A/C AR$160. Cash only. ❷

**Hostel Independencia,** Mitre 1257 (☎423 1806; www.hostelindependencia.com.ar). Located in the block north of Mendoza's main plaza, this large, sociable hostel is set inside a gorgeous yellow townhouse with a bar, dining room, common room with TV, patio, and kitchen. Arranges tours, including Aconcagua trips. Bike rental available. Breakfast included. Free Internet and Wi-Fi. Reception 24hr. Check-out 10am. 6-bed dorms AR$34; doubles with private bath AR$75; triples AR$108. Cash only. ❷

**Break Point,** Arístides Villanueva 241 (☎423 9514; www.breakpointhostel.com.ar). From the center, follow Av. Colón, which becomes Arístides Villanueva. On the street with most of the city's bars, this hostel also has its own patio bar out front and a backyard pool and barbecue pit. Arranges tours. Breakfast included. Free Internet and Wi-Fi. Reception 24hr. Check-out 11am. 5- to 6-bed dorms with shared bath AR$40; 6- to 10-bed dorms with private bath AR$45; doubles with private bath and bunk bed AR$110, with full bed AR$140; quads with private bath AR$240. Cash only. ❷

**Hotel Zamora,** Perú 1156 (☎425 7537 or 423 3614; www.hotelzamora.netfirms.com). Walk west on Sarmiento from Plaza Independencia and turn right on Perú; the hotel will be on the left after a half-block. Set in an old neocolonial townhouse, this small hotel offers basic, clean rooms with simple wooden furniture, private baths, telephones, A/C, and TVs, all around a green patio. Breakfast included. Reception 24hr. Check-out 10am. Singles AR$75; doubles AR$110; triples AR$140. Cash only. ❷

# FOOD

Mendoza's city center is covered with restaurants, so you'll likely run into something tasty within minutes of setting out. Many of these are relatively run-of-the-mill establishments serving the Argentine basics, though some have unique flair, such as pleasant seating out on the sidewalk.

**La Tasca de la Plaza,** Montevideo 117 (☎420 0603). Across the street from Plaza España, one of the city's most beautiful squares, this tiny restaurant serves excellent, inexpensive Spanish cuisine. The seafood *tapas*, including snails, clams, and mussels, are the stars of the menu; be sure to give the spiced calamari (AR$9) a try. Tapas AR$4-9. Entrees AR$11-36. Desserts AR$4-7. Open daily 8pm-midnight. Cash only. ❷

**Arrope,** Primitivo de la Reta 927 (☎420 3090). Just a block from Plaza Pellegrini, this tiny vegetarian restaurant has great-value salad and hot entree buffets. Eat all you want for AR$22, or purchase food by the kg. (AR$25); a stacked plate should only run around AR$16. Though it's possible to stay and eat in the bright, simple dining room, most locals come for the cheap take-out. Open M-Sa 8am-midnight. Cash only. ❷

**La Carmela,** Av. Arístides Villanueva 298. Though along the city's main street for nightlife, this large restaurant with a distinct, arched-brick facade is packed even during the day. The expansive menu has standard but excellent Argentine fare. The daily rotating *menú* often features seafood. Be warned, however: as the menu advises, nothing here is done in a hurry. Sandwiches AR$8-25. Pizza AR$12-45. Calzones AR$32-98. Other entrees AR$15-45. Open M-Sa 8am-3:30pm and 8:30pm-late. Cash only. ❸

EXCURSIONS

## Mendoza

**ACCOMMODATIONS**
Break Point, **3**
Hostel Independencia, **2**
Hostel Lao, **1**
Hotel Zamora, **4**

**FOOD**
Arrope, **5**
La Carmela, **6**
La Tasca de la Plaza, **7**

**MUSEUMS**
Museo del Área Fundacional, **8**

**NIGHTLIFE**
Believe, **9**
El Palenque, **10**
Por Acá, **11**

GUAYMALLEN

Jesuit Church Ruins

Parque O'Higgins

Montecasero

Terminal de Omnibus

Basilica de San Francisco

Pza. Pedro de Castillo

Hospital Central

Salta

Roma

San Juan

Garibaldi

L.N. Alem

Av. José Vicente Zapata

9 de Julio

España

Patricias Mendocinas

Av. Mitre

Chile

25 de Mayo

Coronel Plaza

J.A. Maza

Perú

Av. Las Heras

Pza. Chile

Recochea

Espejo

Av. Sarmiento

Gutiérrez

San Martín

Pza.

Pza. Independencia

Pza. Montevideo

Pza. Italia

Av. Colón

Pza. España

Av. San Martín

Hipolito Trigoyen

Belgrano

Parque Cívico

Laverap

Bikes and Wines

Av. Emilio Civic

N. Avillaneda

I.L. Aguirre

Av. Juan B. Justo

Arístides Villanueva

Ciascoaga

Marínaz de

Gran De

Ciudad Universitaria
Universidad Naciónal de Cuyo

Caballitos de Marly

Park Entrance

Fuente de los Continentes

Rosedal

El Lago

200 meters
200 yards

EXCURSIONS

## 👁 🏛 SIGHTS AND MUSEUMS

**PLAZA INDEPENDENCIA.** After the 1861 earthquake leveled all of Mendoza, the center of the new city was moved to this massive, four-block-square plaza, which was designed to be quake-proof (i.e., so big that if you stood at the center, you wouldn't be crushed by falling buildings). Shaded by beautiful trees and always buzzing with energy, the Plaza draws crowds of the city's residents, who come here to relax, stroll, eat lunch, make out, etc.—the usual. On the side of the square along Mendocinas, there's a popular **crafts fair**, which is definitely at its best on weekends, though a few stalls are open virtually all the time.

**PARQUE SAN MARTÍN.** On Mendoza's western edge—and seemingly bigger than the town itself—lies the city's best and most popular sight, Parque San Martín. This massive piece of greenery was designed in 1897 by **Carlos Thays** (p. 157) and now contains a small lake, a zoo, the city's natural sciences museums, Mendoza's university, and a sprawling sports complex. Covering the whole park on foot would be a seriously non-relaxing activity, but luckily, the best areas for wandering lie at the park's eastern edge (near the city) and public transport carries visitors to the complexes out west. Near the park's entrance, hundreds of trees shade countless green open spaces where locals come to picnic and play soccer. If you're short on time (or energy), a short walk around the **lake** in this area is probably your best option.

**MUSEO DEL ÁREA FUNDACIONAL.** At the eastern edge of Plaza Pedro de Castillo, this museum was built right over the ruins of a series of pre-earthquake buildings and occupies a spot once held by the town hall, a public market, and a slaughterhouse. At the front of the museum, it's possible to peer through the glass floor at the various foundations, including the pits where cows were slaughtered—don't miss the old blood channel on the floor. Yeah, we know—morbid, but it's history. To the left of the foundations, a series of exhibits explains Mendoza's history. (*At the intersection of Betran and Videla Castillo, in Plaza Pedro de Castillo.* ☎ 425 6927. *Open Tu-Sa 8:30am-8pm, Su 3-8pm. Captions in Spanish, but the price of admission includes a short English- or Spanish-language guided tour. AR$4, students AR$3.*)

## 🍸 NIGHTLIFE

Though Mendoza doesn't stay up as late or party as hard as Buenos Aires, the city still has some excellent bars and clubs. Most of the hip establishments cluster along Arístides Villanueva, west of Mendoza's Microcentro toward Parque San Martín. Mendoza's **clubs** are a bit harder to reach; virtually all are located 15km out of town along the **Ruta Panamericana** near the tiny town of **Chacras de Coria.** Local favorites include **Alquimia,** Ruta Panamericana and Cerro Aconcagua (☎ 15 659 8080), which has two packed dance floors, and **Apeteco,** Barraquero and San Juan (☎ 15 454 4870).

**Believe,** Colón 241 (☎ 429 5567). It's hard to call this Irish pub an Irish pub. Sure, it has the necessary trappings—beer ads on the walls, Irish flag on the ceiling, random motorcycle on the wall, etc.—but, packed as it is with young locals, it feels more like your basic raucous bar on weekend nights. The atmosphere, however, is excellent and very friendly; English and American favorites play in the background, and there's a great selection of international beers, including Asahi, Bass, and Franziskaner. Tapas AR$7-9. Pizza AR$9-29. Sandwiches and salads AR$11-29. Other entrees AR$18-29. Beer AR$5-33. Shots and mixed drinks AR$7-90. Open M-F 11am-4am, Sa-Su 8pm-4am. Cash only.

**El Palenque,** Arístides Villanueva 287. Located right in the heart of Mendoza's nightlife district, this tiny, rustic bar, covered with various *Pampas* memorabilia, is popular among a young crowd of Mendocinos for its Argentine snacks and relaxed atmosphere. Food AR$4-32. Beer AR$6-14. Wine AR$12-56. Open Tu-Sa 8pm-late. Cash only.

**Por Acá,** Arístides Villanueva 557 (☎420 0364). Dive bar meets mod decor: this two-story bar, set in an old townhouse, is stylishly grungy. On weekends, downstairs on the tiny dance floor, a young, local crowd dances to American tunes, mostly rock, while others sprawl out in the tiny side rooms or upstairs at a row of quieter tables, where there's a second bar. If you'd like a tamer experience, come earlier in the evening or on a weeknight for some excellent pizza and a beer. Sandwiches AR$13-20. Pizzas AR$9-29. Beer AR$8-16. Mixed drinks AR$9-25. Open daily 8pm-4:30am. Cash only.

## 🏂 ADVENTURE ACTIVITIES

With highlands and the Andes Mountains beyond nearby, Mendoza offers a number of adventure tours for visitors that will surely elicit that "you're crazy" response you're looking for once you get home. Though many tour operators are based out of town, the numerous companies that offer excursions to the mountains congregate along Mendoza's main commercial streets and along Av. Sarmiento. Recommended operators include:

**Colangüil Aventura** (☎15 657 1328; www.colanguiladventure.com.ar). Runs full-day ice climbing (AR$140 plus equipment), rock climbing (AR$105), and trekking expeditions (AR$125), as well as several multi-day treks in the mountains.

**Mendoza Parapente** (☎426 8424; www.mendozaparapente.com.ar). Leads very popular paragliding trips in the Andes for AR$200 per person.

**Campo Base Adventures,** Av. Mitre 946 (☎429 0775; www.campo-base.com.ar). Offers a huge variety of tours, from more low-key excursions, like winery tours, city tours, and drives through the Andes, to more involved options, such as rappelling, mountain biking, rafting, and horseback riding trips.

**Aymara,** 9 de Julio 1023 (☎420 2064; www.aymara.com.ar). This long-running, trusted company runs trips to Aconcagua, ranging from three-day excursions around the base to the traditional full ascent, as well as more unique routes to the peak.

## 🏂 DAYTRIPS FROM MENDOZA

Most travelers to Mendoza only spend evenings in the city itself; the rest of the day, everyone seems to be out on daytrips, whether to the vineyards around the tiny town of **Maipú,** to the budget ski resort **Los Penitentes,** or to the mountains for a huge variety of **adventure activities,** including rafting, trekking, climbing, rappelling, horseback riding, mountain biking, or paragliding.

🏂**MAIPÚ.** Just 15km from Mendoza along Route 7, the tiny town of Maipú is one of the main centers of **wine** production in Mendoza and is a great daytrip for those wanting to visit the vineyards independently. The most accessible vineyards line the area around **Calle Urquiza,** a road that winds south of town through a region known as **Coquimbito.** Over the course of 12km, roads branch off Urquiza and lead to ten different vineyards, where tours give guests an overview of the facilities and several wines to taste (AR$10-15). Most are open year-round and daily from 10am-6pm, but some close during winter and/or on Sundays, so it's best to check Maipú's **tourist office** (p. 236) in advance.

The most popular and pleasant way to visit the vineyards is to rent a bike from one of the numerous shops near **Plaza Rutini,** located along Urquiza; most shops will give you a complete map of the vineyards. Walking is, of course, possible, but considering the distances between the vineyards, you'll only be able to see the one or two closest in this fashion. If you do decide to rent a bike, be aware that for much of the route, Urquiza is more of a busy street than a country road, and cars will be zipping around you constantly, making the ride a bit less relaxing than it could be. At other points, the roads become more picturesque, and through the breaks in the trees, it's possible to catch glimpses of the mountains. The best rental company is **Bikes and Wines,** at Urquiza 1606, just across from the plaza. (☎410 6686; www.bikesandwines. com. Full-day rental AR$34, half-day AR$20. Open 10am-6pm).

Before setting out along Urquiza, a popular first stop is **Bodega la Rural,** Montecaseros 2625, along the road that branches off east from the plaza. In this massive, old vineyard, there's also a museum containing over 5000 wine artifacts, including old tools and machines. The free tour also includes a sub-par glass of wine. (☎497 2013; www.bodegalarural.com.ar/ingles. Guided visits M-Sa every 30min. 9am-1pm and 2-5pm, Su every hr. 10am-1pm.) Of the other vineyards along the route, recommended options include: **Carinae,** Videla Aranda 2899, a small boutique winery owned by an expat French couple; **Club Tapiz,** along Route 60, Familia de Tommaso, an old, rustic winery along Urquiza where you can also pick up an excellent meal (entrees AR$29-58); **Trapiche,** along Mitre (closed during winter); and **Historias and Sabores,** along Gómez, where you can take a break from wine and enjoy a variety of liqueurs instead (closed Su).

To get to Maipú, take **bus** #10/171, 172, or 173 (daily 6am-2am, AR$1.40) from the Mendoza city center and ask the bus driver to let you off on Plaza Rutini, which lies along Urquiza and where you can rent bikes. There's also a **tourist kiosk** on the Plaza. (Open M-F 9am-6pm, Sa 9am-5pm.)

◪**LOS PENITENTES.** The ski resort of choice for most budget travelers, tiny Los Penitentes lies along the **Alta Montaña Route,** otherwise known as RN 7, a mountain highway eventually leading into Chile. The resort itself is a small conglomeration of bright houses at the base of the decent-sized mountain (4300m). Skiing and snowboarding here get mixed reviews (ranging from decent to excellent), and be warned that some of the trails aren't in the best condition and can be quite icy—or not even maintained in any noticeable manner. Still, the resort provides a very inexpensive day of good skiing and boarding.

**WHY SOUTH AMERICAN SKIING?** Well, save for the expensive airfare it takes to get down there, why the hell not? It's one of the few places in the world where you can get excellent skiing conditions during the Northern Hemisphere summer. Many resorts also allow off-piste (a.k.a. backcountry skiing) trails, which are illegal in many parts of the United States. Let's Go does not recommend skiing out of bounds.

Upon entering the village, purchase a lift ticket at the kiosk in front of you; you can choose between three tickets (AR$70-140) allowing access to three different parts of the mountain: just the lower regions, up through the mid-level, or all the way to the top. It's possible to rent ski and snowboard gear right next to the entrance, though if you're picky, you can always get gear in advance in Mendoza, where ski and snowboard shops line Peatonal Sarmiento.

Expreso Uspallata runs **buses** (3hr.; AR$15) from the terminal in Mendoza to the resort, usually departing the city at 6am and 10am and returning at 2pm and 5pm, though it's a good idea to drop by the station to check out the most recent schedule before showing up in the wee hours and still being too late.

# IGUAZÚ FALLS

Iguazú's *cataratas,* or waterfalls, exhaust most superlatives; they are simply one of the most stunning, beautiful, dramatic, and powerful natural sights in the world. Straddling the Argentine-Brazilian-Paraguayan border, a system of over 200 separate falls plummets over the sharp cliffs of the Río Iguazú Superior and plunges into the mist-shrouded Río Iguazú Inferior below—all amid a dense, intensely green jungle setting. The falls certainly aren't undiscovered, but the drama of the sight—as well as the steam-engine sound effects produced by the falls themselves—somehow manages to overpower the groups of camera-toting tourists also partaking in the experience. Luckily for those coming from Buenos Aires, the best views, as well as most of the falls themselves, lie within Argentina, just 18km from the surprisingly pleasant town of **Puerto Iguazú,** where there are plenty of accommodation and food options. Many travelers, however, do take a quick, two- or three-hour trip over to the **Brazilian side,** which provides a better overall panorama of the falls, though American tourists will have to pay US$100 in visa fees.

 **MEDICAL PREPARATION.** Since Iguazú is in a tropical climate, some medical preparation may be required, including, but not limited to, a yellow fever vaccination and malaria pills. See p. 30 for more information.

## WHEN TO GO

The falls are stunning at any time of year and in any weather, and though heavier rainfall will indeed produce more thunderous cascades, you're bound to get a good show regardless. It's usually best to visit during the **Argentine winter,** when the sweltering heat fades into a pleasant, sunny warmth. However, this rule does not apply during July, when the falls are swarmed with South American tourists, but the crowds aren't so bad as to destroy the experience. The falls are pretty big and rivaled only by Africa's Victoria Falls in scope.

# PUERTO IGUAZÚ                          ☎03757

Despite the fact that it's the closest town to one of Argentina's most popular attractions, Puerto Iguazú retains an authentic, untouristed feel. With most visitors at the falls during the day and clustered in the restaurants at night, locals actually seem to outnumber tourists on the street, making the small, rambling town a relaxing place to pass a few days.

### ✈ INTERCITY TRANSPORTATION

**Flights:** Iguazú's small **airport** (☎420595) is located close to the entrance to the falls, almost 20km from the town itself. Though there's no real tourist office here, the **tour company kiosks** in the arrivals terminal can provide information on the park and the town. A **taxi** to Puerto Iguazú runs AR$60-70, though a much cheaper option is to hitch a ride on the shared mini-bus (25min., every 30min. as long as flights are arriving, AR$15) run by **Four Tourist Travel** (☎422962, 420681), which will drop you at any hotel in Puerto Iguazú or along the highway between the park and the town. The company's desk is located just to the left as you exit the baggage claim; call in advance to reserve a return trip to the airport at the end of your stay.

**Buses:** Numerous companies, including **El Rápido Argentino,** kiosk #193 (☎0800 333 1970); **Crucero del Norte,** kiosk #125 (☎4315 1652); **Empresa Rio Uruguay,** kiosk #120 (☎4312 1828); **Expreso Singer,** kiosk 117 (☎4313 3927); and **Via Bariloche,** kiosk #121 (☎4315 7700), run buses (17-19hr.; 20 per day; *semi-cama* AR$150-175, *cama* AR$180-195, first-class AR$200-220) to and from Puerto Iguazú. Most depart late afternoon and early evening. Buses arrive at Iguazú's **Terminal de Omnibus**

(☎423006), located at the intersection of Av. Córdoba and Misiones in the town center. Though there's no official tourist office here, **tour and bus company kiosks** throughout the terminal offer information on the falls and the national park. Follow the signs at the terminal's entrance for luggage storage (open 7am-9pm; AR$4).

## ⊟ LOCAL TRANSPORTATION

**Taxis:** Many taxi companies cluster around the bus station. Try **Agencia de Remises,** Córdoba 44 (☎423500). Set fares to the airport and the falls run around AR$60-70.

**Bike Rental:** Av. Victoria Aguirre 552. AR$10 per hr. AR$40 per day. Open 9am-midnight.

## ✈🛈 ORIENTATION AND PRACTICAL INFORMATION

Despite the fact that Puerto Iguazú's street plan isn't exactly the most regular, the town center is small enough that it's quite difficult to get lost here. Most establishments, including virtually all the town's accommodations and restaurants, are along **Avenida Victoria Aguirre,** the town's main street, and **Avenida Misiones,** which run roughly parallel to each other and are connected by **Avenida Córdoba,** where the bus station is located.

**Tourist Office:** Av. Victoria Aguirre (☎422938). Open daily 9am-8pm.

**Consulate: Brazil,** Córdoba 264 (☎421348). Open M-F 9am-1pm.

**Banks:** Puerto Iguazú's few banks are located along Av. Victoria Aguirre. **Banco de la Nación,** Av. Victoria Aguirre 179, has a **24hr. ATM.** Open M-F 9am-1pm.

**Laundromat:** Av. Misiones 42. Same-day wash and dry AR$15. Open daily 8am-noon and 3-8pm.

**Emergency:** Police ☎102, Ambulance ☎107, Fire ☎100.

**Police:** Av. Victoria Aguirre and San Martín (☎420016).

**Pharmacy: Macrofarma,** located directly in front of the bus station at the intersection of Av. Misiones and Córdoba (☎423790), has a rotating list of pharmacies currently on night duty in its front window. Open M-Sa 7am-midnight, Su 8-10am.

**Hospital:** Av. Victoria Aguirre and Ushuaia (☎420288).

**Internet Access: La Web,** Av. Misiones 117. AR$3 per hr. Open M-Sa 9am-midnight, Su 5pm-midnight. **Internet,** Av. Victoria Aguirre 294. AR$4 per hr. Also serves as a *locutorio.* Open M-W and Su 7am-midnight, Th-Sa 7am-1am.

**Post Office:** Av. San Martín 780, with a more accessible branch in the Internet cafe/*locutorio* at Av. Victoria Aguirre 294 (see above).

## ⌂ ACCOMMODATIONS

▩ **Hostel Inn (HI),** Kilometer 5, Ruta 12 (☎421823; www.hostel-inn.com). Along the highway between Puerto Iguazú and the national park/airport, this enormously popular hostel is the place to do anything except sleep. Young, party-hungry travelers converge at its huge pool out front, restaurant and bar inside, TV room, and shared kitchen. There are even sporadic tango and Brazilian dance shows and lessons. The hostel is far from town, but it's closer to the falls, and you can grab the bus to the park right out front. Jungle excursions available. Breakfast included. Free Internet and Wi-Fi. Reception 24hr. Check-out 11am. 6-bed dorms HI-members AR$34, non-HI-members AR$36; doubles $140/150; triples $165/175; quads $180/200. Cash only. ❷

**Timbó Posada,** Av. Misiones 147 (☎422698; www.timboiguazu.com.ar). Turn left out of the bus station and make an immediate left on Av. Misiones; the hostel is 2 blocks

EXCURSIONS

down on the left. Travelers at this small, friendly hostel are all about the falls and don't really come here to party; the vibe is definitely early-to-bed, early-to-rise, which makes it a perfect alternative to Hostel Inn. The hostel itself, with its basic, brightly painted rooms, is a great place to relax, and there's a small shared kitchen and common room with TV in a wooden building in the leafy garden out back, where there's also a small pool. Breakfast included. Free Internet. Laundry service AR$18. Reception 24hr. Check-out 10am. Dorms AR$36; singles with shared bath AR$70; doubles with shared bath AR$80, with private bath and A/C AR$165; triples with private bath and A/C AR$195; quads with private bath and A/C AR$220. Cash only. ❷

**Hosteria Los Helechos,** Paulino Amarante 76 (☎420338; www.hosterialoshelechos. com.ar). Exiting the bus station, head straight onto Paulino Amarante 76; the hotel will be on your right. Though not unique, this 3-star hotel is a great value. The simple, bright rooms—all with private bath—include TVs and telephones, and there's a garden with pool out back as well as a rambling sitting room, breakfast room, and bar. Buffet breakfast included. Reception 24hr. Check-out 11am. Singles AR$108, with A/C AR$130; doubles AR$130/166; triples AR$166/216. 10% discount for students. AmEx/MC/V. ❷

## 🍴 FOOD

**Tierra,** Av. Misiones 125. 2 blocks down Misiones from the bus station. This small cafe and restaurant has a relaxed, intimate atmosphere and unique decor—enjoy it, because both are rare qualities in Puerto Iguazú. Grab a seat outside or indoors for delicious Argentine basics and imaginative international fare, including a great vegetable and pasta stir-fry (AR$20). Also popular among backpackers for drinks or coffee, but, then again, what place in town isn't? Salads and sandwiches AR$9-18. Stir-frys AR$18-30. Pasta AR$20-28. *Parrilla* AR$35-42. Open M-Sa 2pm-midnight. Cash only. ❷

**El Quincho del Tío Querido,** Bompland 110 (☎420151 or 422223). Head down Misiones from the bus station and turn left on Bompland; it will be on your immediate left. Get here early, or forfeit your chance at a table on the beautiful patio right next to this massive establishment's *asado;* the only other option is to venture into the cavernous dining room blasting easy-listening music. It specializes in *bife,* but try the *lomo* marinated with baked apples (AR$36). The local grilled fish, *surubí,* is also top-notch. Salads AR$8-30. Pasta AR$19-25. 3-course set *menús* AR$30-34. *Parrilla* AR$22-68. Other entrees AR$36-80. Open daily 8pm-late. AmEx/MC/V. ❺

**Pizza Colór,** Córdoba 135 (☎420206). Just to the right exiting the bus station. A great place for a relaxed, inexpensive, and convenient meal of Argentine favorites, including delicious, stone-baked pizza, this cavernous restaurant, with its unoriginal tiled floor and colorful tablecloths, definitely benefits from its single strange feature: a tree growing in the middle of the dining hall. Salads AR$9-13. Pizzas AR$12-32. Pasta AR$19-35. *Parrilla* AR$14-43. Open daily noon-midnight. Cash only. ❷

# PARQUE NACIONAL IGUAZÚ

On the Argentine side, the falls are enveloped by the small Parque Nacional Iguazú, which also includes pieces of the surrounding sub-tropical forest. Be aware that creativity is not encouraged here; camping and striking out on your own are not allowed, and you'll have to follow the beaten path to see both the falls themselves and the surrounding forest. Though you should only need a single day for all the park's activities, it's doubtful that you'll feel you've wasted any extra time you do decide to spend here—it's *that* breathtaking.

## LOCAL LEGEND

### LEGEND OF THE GURANÍ

Waterfall formation seems simple enough. You have your flowing stream of water, an erosion-resistant cliff, and boom—cascades ensue. Right? Not so fast. The process wasn't simple for Iguazú Falls, at least according to legend.

Long before European explorers and camera-toting tourists were stomping around the jungles, the **Guraní** Indians lived in the region surrounding the present-day falls. In fact, they were around back when the falls didn't even exist, when it was just the **Iguazú River.** Things were peaceful, except for one problem—the river was the lair of **M'Boi,** the **Serpent God,** who demanded a sacrifice of virgin Guraní girls. Further complicating matters was the fact that M'Boi's father, as you will remember, was **Tupa,** the **Supreme God of All.** So if the Guraní failed to offer sacrifices, they would anger M'Boi, which would enrage the Supreme God of All. Needless to say, you didn't want to piss off dad.

Things came to a head one day when M'Boi spotted the reflection of **Naipi,** a beautiful Guraní girl. M'Boi immediately demanded that the villagers give up the girl as a sacrifice. They were reluctant at first, since Naipi was to be wed to the great warrior **Taruba,** but, not wishing to anger the Supreme God of All, they ultimately caved in.

Taruba and Naipi, understandably, were more than a little upset. Rather than lose his future wife to the river, Taruba decided to challenge M'Boi and orches-

**YOU WILL GET WET.** It goes without saying, since you are at one of the largest waterfalls in the world, but just a reminder—bring an extra set of dry clothes with you or you might be an unhappy camper.

## TRANSPORTATION

Argentine company **El Practico** runs daily buses (30min., at least every 30min. 7:10am-7:10pm, AR$5) from the bus station in Puerto Iguazú to the park's entrance. Buy tickets at kiosk #19, from where the buses also depart. To get to the kiosk, enter the bus station and veer right and up the stairs until you see a metal causeway in front of you; cross the causeway and descend on the other side of the station's parking lot; the kiosk will be immediately on your right.

## PRACTICAL INFORMATION

A variety of **tour operators,** usually based both within Puerto Iguazú and the park itself, run guided tours of the falls and surrounding jungle. If you don't want to spend a huge amount of on tours, most travelers recommend choosing the boat trip under the falls over the jungle safaris, as you won't see many animals on the safari trips. Recommended operators include:

**Iguazú Jungle Explorer,** based within the park (☎421696; www.iguazujunglexplorer.com/ingles_home.htm). Runs jungle safaris in a 4X4, short rafting trips down the Río Iguazú, and a popular boat ride under the falls (AR$75).

**Explorador Expediciones,** based within the park (☎491800; www.rainforestevt.com.ar) and at Petito Moreno 217, in Puerto Iguazú (☎421632). Runs two daily safaris departing at 10:30am and 4:30pm.

**Yguazú Extreme,** based within the park (☎423660 or 15 441864), offers rafting trips within the park as well as rappelling and climbing trips, and has a zipline (a suspended, inclined cable that you ride down via pulley). Open daily 8am-3pm.

## SIGHTS

**THE PARK ENTRANCE.** After getting off the bus, head immediately to the **Visitor's Center,** where you'll pay the AR$40 entrance fee and where you can pick up very helpful **maps** of the park. If you're planning on visiting the park again, be sure to hang onto your ticket and get it stamped as you exit, as it entitles you to a 50% discount the second day. (Open daily Oct.-Feb. 8am-7pm; Mar.-Sept.

8am-6pm.) Leaving the visitor's center, to your right there's a tiny, but worthwhile **museum**, which has displays on the flora, fauna, and history of the park. As soon as you pass the museum, you'll be surrounded by tour operators offering various guided visits to the park, including **jungle safaris**, brief **speedboat trips** below the falls, and **rafting trips** on the river (see **Other Activities**, p. 242).

To get to the falls themselves from this entrance, you can either wait in line to hop on the park train at the **Estación Central**, or simply take the **Sendero Verde**, a beautiful, 15min. pathway that winds its way through the jungle—and one of the few places you're likely to see too many tourists—both of which end at the **Estación Cataratas.**

## THE FALLS

From Estación Cataratas, two well-marked paths, the **Paseo Inferior**, or "Lower Circuit," and **Paseo Superior**, or "Upper Trail," wind through the jungle around, below, and above a number of the falls and to **Isla San Martín**, located in the middle of the Río Iguazú. A train also leaves from here for the **Estación Garganta**, from where a series of causeways leads to the mammoth ▓ **Garganta del Diablo**, or "Devil's Throat," by far the park's biggest and most impressive waterfall.

**PASEO SUPERIOR.** The shorter of the two *paseos*, the Paseo Superior is a great place to start your visit. Winding along the edge of the cliffs, it provides excellent views of the falls and river from above, as well as some of the best panoramas of the falls taken all together.

**PASEO INFERIOR.** As its name implies, the Paseo Inferior lies below the cliff-edge and gets up-close-and-personal with a number of the waterfalls—so close, in fact, that you can choose to let some of the larger falls soak you to the skin, if that's your thing. About half-way along the *paseo*, signs point the way down a separate path to a small dock, from where a free **ferry** (last boat 3:45pm) departs for **Isla San Martín**, a stunning, rocky island in the middle of the river. Paths criss-cross the islet, leading through dense vegetation and providing excellent views of a number of the falls. In summer, the island's small **beach** is open to swimmers. This dock is also the departure point for the exciting, soaking **motorboat trips** that pass right under the falls.

**GARGANTA DEL DIABLO.** To get to Iguazú's single biggest waterfall, catch the train from the Estación Cataratas to the Estación Garganta. From here, a series of metal causeways crosses the river—all the time providing beautiful vistas through the jungle—

trate a daring escape with Naipi by canoe on the river. Yes, that's right—in a slight lapse of judgment, to escape from the Serpent God, Taruba decided it would be a good idea to head right into the Serpent God's lair.

Unsurprisingly, M'Boi quickly spotted the fleeing lovers and worked himself up into a furious rage. Growing to massive size, he slithered and squirmed violently, creating new curves and bends in the river and forming an enormous crack in the earth—**the waterfalls.** The canoe spiraled downward into the water, separating Taruba and Naipi on opposite sides of the cascades. So that they could never be together again, M'Boi turned Taruba into a **tree** and Naipi into a **rock.** The Serpent God stayed in between to monitor things, living in what is today the most spectacular section of the falls, the **Garganta del Diablo** (Devil's Throat). Some would call it overkill. For the Serpent God, it was just another day at the office.

So, gentle reader, there's a chance you have M'Boi to thank for the magnificent cascades you see before you. Today, whenever a rainbow forms between the two falls, stretching from a palm tree in Brazil to a rock in Argentina, it's no leprechaun and his pot of gold—people say it's Naipi and Taruba showing their love for each other, in defiance of M'Boi. It makes a great Kodak moment, by the way.

and leads to a lookout point over the "Devil's Throat," which actually does look, strangely enough, like a massive throat. Here, the river is funneled into an almost circular set of cliffs, and the sheer volume of water thundering across the edge and into the misty void below will likely stagger even the most jaded traveler.

 **BUG OFF.** In doing battle with the fearsome creatures of the jungle, bug spray is an essential ally. Come prepared with DEET.

## OTHER ACTIVITIES

**SENDERO MACUCO.** It's easy to forget that Iguazú also happens to contain lush jungle—except, of course, as a background to the falls. Still, there's only one official **trail** providing access to the forest itself, called the Sendero Macuco. Follow the signs from the visitor's center to reach the trail's entrance, from which it's a 3.2km hike to the trail's end at a lookout point over the jungle and a small, secluded pool and waterfall. Along the trail, it's possible that you'll see wildlife, including monkeys, though it's likely that you'll only see birds, including toucans, considering the number of people on the trail.

## THE BRAZILIAN SIDE

Although the Argentine side provides the best up-close views of the falls, many travelers take a few-hour side-trip to the Brazilian side to catch the **overall panorama** from above, an undeniably stunning sight. For people of most nationalities, this is a rather uncomplicated proposition involving only brief border formalities; citizens of the United States, however, will have to pick up a visa at the Brazilian consulate (US$100; see p. 238) in Puerto Iguazú beforehand. Some travelers say it's possible to briefly enter Brazil without getting this visa by simply not getting off the bus and reporting yourself at the border, but it's officially necessary to obtain one, and if you choose not to, you'll be potentially setting yourself up for major problems upon returning to Argentina.

From the bus station in Puerto Iguazú (p. 237), El Prático runs a **bus** (at least every hour 7am-6pm) to **Foz do Iguaçu,** the Brazilian access point for the falls and where buses to the Brazilian side depart. Upon entering Brazil, people of all nationalities—except Brazilians, Paraguayans, and Argentines—should ask to get off the bus to go through the necessary border formalities and get exit and entrance stamps. Though the bus may not always wait around for such passengers, it's an easy enough proposition to catch the next bus coming across the border. Alternatively, you can simply exit immigration and wait for the next bus coming from Foz do Iguaçu and heading to the Brazilian national park, which will save you time overall. To do this, however, you'll need to have exchanged a small amount of currency in Puerto Iguazú before departure.

In the national park on the Brazilian side, a short walkway winds above most of the falls on the Argentine and Brazilian sides, providing a stunning overview of the sight—especially of the Gargantua del Diablo.

# URUGUAY

Squished between Argentina and Brazil, Uruguay sometimes seems like the dowdy second cousin who received the pity-invite for Thanksgiving. It's, well, just kind of there, forever condemned to "Switzerland of South America" sta-

EXCURSIONS

tus by many travel guides. On the contrary, for the traveler, Uruguay is no neglected cousin at the Thanksgiving dinner table, but rather the perfect place to be if you've got the big-city blues in BA. Life here is just more laid back than in Argentina—and that is by no means synonymous with boring. It's simply a world apart, a destination that will provide some thrilling contrasts, and some similarities (they like soccer and beef here, too), with Argentina.

**ENTRANCE REQUIREMENTS.** Getting into Uruguay should be a piece of cake, as long as you have a valid passport. Citizens of Australia, Canada, Ireland, New Zealand, the United Kingdom, and the United States will receive a tourist card upon entry—the card allows you to stay in Uruguay as a visitor for up to 90 days. Nationals of other countries require visas. It's critical that you **hold on to your tourist card throughout your journey.** If you return to Argentina, or your other point of origin, without it, you may be fined.

# GETTING TO URUGUAY

## BY FERRY AND BUS

Ah, the open sea—or river, we should say. It may feel like an ocean, but taking a boat between Argentina and Uruguay amounts to nothing more than the longest river crossing—ever. Ferries traverse the Río de la Plata on a daily basis, whizzing (or slowly lumbering along, if it's an old vessel) passengers between Buenos Aires, Colonia, and Montevideo. It is by far the cheapest and most practical way to travel between Argentina and Uruguay. Book far in advance, especially if it's summer (Dec.-Mar.) or a weekend—or, for the double whammy, a summer weekend. Expect fares to be higher during the summer and even more expensive on weekends. Some companies recommend arriving 90 minutes before your departure time. While this may be unnecessarily lengthy, allow for at least 45 minutes to check luggage and go through customs, and to accommodate traffic or any other hurdles. Keep your passport handy throughout ticket purchasing and customs. If you're afraid of ◤sea monsters, we're pretty sure there's no cause for concern. The brown waters of the Río de la Plata probably wouldn't be very fun to live in, even for a monster.

The main company providing ferry service to Uruguay is Buquebus (www. buquebus.com). Their **offices** in Colonia (open daily 8am-8pm) are at the bus terminal at Av. Roosevelt and Manuel Lobo, and at the **dock,** just south of the bus station on Florida. The Montevideo office is at the **Terminal de Buquebus** in the **Ciudad Vieja,** at the intersection of Rambla 25 de Agosto de 1825 and Colon (☎+598 2 916 0910). Offices in Buenos Aires are at:

**Puerto Madero,** Av. Antártida Argentina 821 (☎+54 11 4316 6500). Open M-F 7am-7pm, Sa-Su 7am-2pm.

**Microcentro,** Av. Córdoba 879. Open M-F 9am-7pm, Sa 9am-2pm.

**Recoleta,** Posadas 1452. Open M-F 9am-7pm, Sa 9am-2pm.

**Retiro,** Av. Antártida Argentina y Calle Diez, at the bus station. Open M-F 9am-7pm, Sa 9am-2pm.

Boats sailing from BA to Colonia and Montevideo depart from the **Terminal Buquebus,** north of *Dique 4* in Puerto Madero. **Catamarans** run to **Colonia** (1hr.; 1-7 per day; one-way AR$124, UR$848), and **Montevideo** (3hr.; 1-2 per day; AR$236, UR$1,493). Slower **ferries** only run to Colonia (3hr.; AR$89, UR$555). Bus con-

nections from Colonia to Montevideo and Punta del Este are available for catamarans and ferries. Buses connecting from Colonia arrive in Montevideo at **Tres
Cruces,** at the intersection of Artigas and Dr. Ferrer Serra (☎+598 2 408 8601;
www.trescruces.com.uy; open 24hr.), just due west of Parque Batlle. From the
station, **buses** #21, 64, 180, 187, 188, and 330 run to the center of the city. From
there, buses #14, 64, 104, and 121 run to Punta Carretas and Pocitos.

---

**THINGS YOU SHOULD KNOW:**

**Currency:** Uruguay uses the **Uruguayan peso.** Prices on the ground will be
denoted using the $ symbol, but to avoid confusion with AR$ and US$, in
this guide we will use UR$. At the time of publication, the **exchange rate**
was roughly US$1 to UR$19 and AR$1 to UR$6.

**Yerba mate:** Argentina's favorite drink is even more popular in Uruguay. We
know, it's hard to believe, but it's true. You'll see, and taste, for yourself.

**Sports:** As in Argentina, soccer is a way of life in Uruguay. The national team
is only of only 5 squads in history to win the FIFA World Cup at least twice
(1930 and 1950). The other teams to accomplish this feat—Argentina (2),
Germany (3), Italy (4), and Brazil (5).

**Economy:** The Uruguayan economy is mostly based in agriculture (a.k.a. beef
and wine), which accounts for roughly 10% of the GDP.

---

# COLONIA DEL SACRAMENTO ☎052

Grit under your fingernails got you down? Just one hour from BA by catama-
ran, Colonia's tree-lined avenues and uneven colonial streets provide a breath
of fresh air after the big city, and, if the well-preserved *Barrio Histórico* is any
indication, time here really does move in a different dimension. Since its declaration as an UNESCO World Heritage site in 1995, Colonia has developed into
a tourist mecca, included in most itineraries from Buenos Aires as a daytrip, or
even a longer excursion. Of course, a journey to Colonia is particularly important for travelers looking for more impressive-looking passport stamps.

**COLONIA MANIA.** Things are quiet in Colonia during the low season,
but in summer, expect more buzz and prices 10-30% higher than normal.

## ✈ INTERCITY TRANSPORTATION

**Buses:** Colonia's bus **terminal,** at Manuel Lobo and Av. Roosevelt, is just north of the
ferry dock. If you're coming from the port, it'll be on your right. Lockers are available for
luggage storage (ask a guard or at the Berruti y Cia desk). There are other services available as well, including an **ATM, exchange bureau,** and **Internet** kiosks. Two companies,
Turil and COT, offer frequent, direct bus service to Montevideo (2½hr., UR$167). Quality
and frequency of service is about the same. Note that some companies require payment in UR$. Turil (☎1990 25246 25247; www.turil.com.uy) runs buses from Colonia
to **Montevideo** (M-F 5, 6, 8:30, 10:30am, 2, 4:30, 6, 8pm; Sa-Su 6, 8:30, 10:30am,
2, 4:30, 6, 8, 9:15pm). COT (☎3121; www.cot.com.uy) has service from Colonia to
**Montevideo** (M-F 6:45, 9:15, 11am, 1, 4, 5:30, 7, 8:30, 10pm).

**Ferries:** For ferry transportation between Buenos Aires and Colonia, see p. 243.

Rio de la Plata

TO BODEGA BERNARDI

Av Artigas

AV ROOSEVELT

Terminal de Omnibus

TO (50m)

Rivera

Rivadavia

Av. General Flores

18 de Julio

Manoel Lobo

Méndez

Fosalba

Lavalleja

Plaza 25 de Agosto

Intendente Suárez

Florida

Washington Barbot

Av General Flores

18 de Julio

Manoel Lobo

Ituzaingó

Florida

Portón de Campo

San Antonio

BARRIO HISTÓRICO

Iglesia Matriz

Vasconcellos

Plaza de Armas
Manoel Lobo

Virrey Cevallos

España

Portugal

De La Playa

San José

San Rita

8 De Octubre

Del Colegio

Comercio

Misiones De Los Tapes

De Las Flores

San Gabriel

Plaza Mayor
25 de Mayo

Suspiros

San Pedro

Solis

Los

El Faro and
Convento de
San Francisco

100 meters

100 yards

**Colonia del Sacramento**

ACCOMMODATIONS
Hostel Colonial, 1
El Viajero Hostel, 5

FOOD
La Bodeguita, 2
Meson de la Plaza, 3
Parrilla El Portón, 4

EXCURSIONS

## ⌐ LOCAL TRANSPORTATION

**Buses:** Within the city, COTUC and ABC Cooperativa run buses between the *centro* and Real San Carlos (30min.; 2 per hr. M-F 6am-2pm, 1 per hr. 3pm-1am; 1 per hr. Sa-Su 5am-1am; UR$13). Stops line Av. General Flores. The route to Real San Carlos takes D. Baque, while the return trip follows Av. Artigas. Buses from Real San Carlos to the *centro* (30min.; 2 per hr. M-F 5:30am-1:30pm, 1 per hr. 2:30pm-12:30am; UR$13).

 **"UR PESOS, PLEASE."** Once on the ground, you'll find that many accommodations and restaurants take UR$, AR$, and US$. However, for public transportation, many buses only take UR$. Have some pesos handy.

**Taxis:** Taxi stands line the corners of Av. General Flores. For service at General Flores and Lavaleja (☎22858); at Intendente Suarez and General Flores (☎22556). A taxi to Real San Carlos runs about UR$100, to the Bodega Bernardi UR$300.

## ▰ ▰ ORIENTATION AND PRACTICAL INFORMATION

Colonia is situated on a small peninsula directly across the Río de la Plata from Buenos Aires. At roughly ten blocks long and four blocks wide, the city is easy to navigate. Most services, including **ATMs, taxis,** and local **buses,** can be found on the town's main street, **Avenida General Flores,** which runs east-west from the **Centro** to the **Barrio Histórico** right on the shore, where most of the major sights are. The **ferry dock** and **bus terminal** are on the southeastern shore of the peninsula, about a 10-minute walk from the center. Stretching up the coast to **Real San Carlos,** Colonia is mostly residential, except for the now defunct **Plaza de Torros,** a 45 minute ramble away.

**Tourist Offices:** Main tourist office in the *Barrio Histórico,* 224 Manuel Lobo (☎28506). Open daily 9am-6pm. For details on restaurants and clubs, pick up a **Güear** guide.

**Bike, Moped, Go-Kart, and Golf Cart Rental:** Yes, this sounds like a listing for a family fun center or a country club, but that's the way things go in Colonia's narrow streets.

**Thrifty,** Av. General Flores 172 (☎22939; www.thrifty.com.uy), with an additional location at the port, rents bikes (US$1.50-3 per hr., US$9-15 per day), mopeds (US$7 per hr., US$30 per day), go-karts (US$10 per hr., US$50 per day), and golf carts (US$12-15 per hr., US$50-60 per day). Open M-Th 9:30am-7pm, F-Su 9am-8pm.

**MotoRent,** Virrey Cevallos 223 (☎29665; www.motorent.com.uy), across from Thrifty. Rents golf carts (UR$270 per hr., UR$1100 per day), buggies (UR$330/hr., $UR 1100/day), and mopeds (UR$130/hr., $UR440/day). Additional location at the port. Open daily 10am-8pm. Cash only.

**Banks, ATMs, and Currency Exchange:** It's best to exchange some money before you leave Argentina, but if you still need to withdraw money upon arrival, the **Banco Comercial,** Av. General Flores 356 (☎23220) has **ATMs.** Open daily 1-6pm.

**Emergency:** Police ☎911, Ambulance ☎24300 or 26170.

**Police:** Av. General Flores 364, facing Plazza 25 de Agosto (☎23348). The tourist police, also at this location, distribute the ▨ **best map of Colonia.**

**Pharmacy: Farmácia del Sacramento,** Manuel Lobo 454 (☎20413), at the intersection with Alberti Mendez. Open daily 8am-8pm and 10pm-8am. MC/V.

**Hospital:** The pink headquarters of Colonia's local hospital is at the intersection of Av. 18 de Julio and Av. Mendez (☎22994 or 26161). Cash only.

**Internet:** *Locutorio* inside Galería Peñarol, Av. General Flores 285 (☎29046) has Internet (UR$25 per hr.) and phones (UR$10 per min. to the US). Open daily 10am-10pm.

EXCURSIONS

**Post Office:** Lavallejos 226 (☎22116; www.correo.com.uy). Postcards UR$17. Letters UR$37. Accepts only UR$. Open M-F 9am-5pm. **Postal Code:** 70000.

# ACCOMMODATIONS

Colonia's budget accommodations lie outside the historic center, and there isn't much of a transportation problem, given the minuscule size of the town—all are within a short five-minute walk of the ferry dock and the bus terminal.

**Hostel Colonial,** Av. Grl. Flores 440 (☎30347; hostelling_colonial@hotmail.com). Hostel Colonial is without question the best joint in town. The spacious, well-lit rooms are set around a series of interior patios and are a steal for the price. Though most beds in the dorms are bunked, it's sometimes possible to snag an unbunked bed. The excellent bathrooms have plenty of privacy and room for changing. Inquire at the front desk about their 3hr. horseback riding excursions. Minimum 2 people UR$450. Breakfast UR$70-170. Linens included. Free Internet and Wi-Fi. Free bikes available. Check-out 10:30am. 6-bed dorms UR$190; singles UR$460; doubles UR$230. ❷

**El Viajero Hostel,** Washington Barbot 164 (☎22683; www.elviajerohostel.com). Out of all the accommodations in town, El Viajero is the closest to the *Barrio Histórico*. It's also more social than its rivals, featuring a barbecue, bar, and common room with TV. Though the rooms are, overall, decent (the dorms have ensuite bathrooms, which is always a plus), the doubles can be a bit cramped. Tours of the region available. Breakfast included. Linens included. Free Internet and Wi-Fi. Dorms UR$300; doubles with twin beds UR$950; M-Th and Su doubles with matrimonial UR$950, F-Sa UR$1050. ❷

# FOOD

The *Barrio Histórico* has many restaurants that cater to Colonia's daytripping crowd. Though the eats are affordable, especially compared to Montevideo, the closer you are to a colonial building, the more expensive it will be. Most locals eat at spots along the main street, **Avenida General Flores.**

**A TIP ON TIPS.** Taxi drivers often expect a 10% tip. Servers at restaurants should also receive the same amount.

**La Bodeguita,** Calle del Comercio 167 (☎25329; www.labodeguita.net). La Bodeguita's prime location in the *Barrio Histórico*, complete with an outdoor deck overlooking the river, could have made it a tourist trap. Thankfully, it isn't—it remains packed to the brim with local families and young people because of its delicious, crazy cheap thin-crust pizza. Individual pizzas UR$45-60. Pastas UR$165. *Parrilla* UR$260-285. Open Tu-F 7:30pm-midnight, Sa-Su noon-3pm and 7:30pm-midnight. Cash only. ❷

**Mesón de la Plaza,** Vasconcellos 153 (☎24807; www.mesondelaplaza.com). This eatery, right in the *Barrio Histórico*, has a reputation as the best restaurant in town. A patio in the back and frequent live music class up the experience, but it's still refreshingly affordable. The menu has Uruguayan classics but also, thankfully, includes some other options for variety, including dishes like salmon with arugula (UR$275). Open M 8-11:30pm, Tu-F noon-3pm and 8-11:30pm, Sa-Su noon-3pm and 8pm-1am. ❹

**Parrilla el Portón,** Av. Grl. Flores 333 (☎25318; www.elporton-colonia.com). A cheerful *parrilla* renowned for its plentiful, affordable food and wine. Salads UR$65-165. Pastas UR$70-95. Fish UR$120-290. *Parrilla* for two UR$300. ½L of house wine UR$40. Open daily noon-4pm and 8pm-midnight. AmEx/MC/V: UR$250 min. ❸

## ◉ 🏛 SIGHTS AND MUSEUMS

**▨BARRIO HISTÓRICO.** Thanks to its varied Spanish and Portuguese past, Colonia has parts with a distinctive Spanish colonial flair (i.e., a grid pattern of streets), while the older part of town, the *Barrio Histórico*, has a more Portuguese style, with a rebellious, distinctly non-Spanish mess of terrain conforming alleys. Situated at the tip of Colonia's promontory, the main entrance to the old city is along **Manoel Lobo,** over a drawbridge, and through the **Portón del Campo,** a glitzy remnant of the old city wall. After passing through the gates, you'll find yourself in the **Plaza Mayor,** the heart of the *Barrio Histórico*.

Just north of Plaza Mayor on San Antonio is another public square, **Plaza de Armas Manoel Lobo,** where the walkways outline the ruins of the old governor's house. The Plaza is also home to one of the most prominent buildings in Colonia: the **Iglesia Matriz.** The church was built in the late 1600s, making it the oldest place of worship in the country. Back in Plaza Mayor, in the southeastern corner, is the cobblestone alley **Calle de los Suspiros,** lined with some of the city's most distinctive buildings, some of which are over 250 years old. A notable pink stucco private residence, at the intersection with San Pedro, perhaps best captures the city's old school colonial feel.

**▨MUSEO NAUFRAGIOS Y TESOROS.** This newest contributor to Colonia's tourist economy, a warehouse devoted entirely to ☑pirates and buried treasures found in the Río de la Plata, ranks as the most high-tech and hokey of them all. It's also, astonishingly, the best. The museum answers seafaring questions you never thought to ask, including how many rats stowed away on a standard 18th-century ship, through exhibits assembled with enthusiasm and humor (plastic models of the aforementioned rats make a strong showing). The star of the show is the guided tour of the *Bruja del Mar* (Witch of the Sea), a life-size reproduction of one of the ships that used to sail around the river. Located near the Plaza de Toros in Real San Carlos, the museum is a 45min. walk north along the coast from the center—it's an ideal bike ride destination. Buses ABC and COTUC (p. 246) also drop you off at the corner and run about every half hour. *(At the intersection of Roger Balet and Calle de los Argentinos. Open daily 10:30am-5:30pm; closed summer Tu, except in July. UR$100, children 6-12 UR$40.)*

**IMPRESS YOUR FRIENDS WITH THIS FUN FACT.** The frequent fights between the Spanish and the Portuguese didn't only affect the town's unique street patterns—it also left its mark on the town's architecture. The easiest way to tell which house belonged to which nationality is to look at the roofs. In general, if it's **flat,** it was **Spanish,** and if it's **slanted,** it was probably **Portuguese.** Many buildings feature both styles. Crazy.

**ELSEWHERE IN COLONIA.** There are 118 steps to the top of the town's distinctive 19th-century lighthouse, **El Faro.** A visit affords a phenomenal workout and a view of the muddy Río de la Plata below, laundry hung out to dry in neighbors' backyards, and the two spires of the town church. On clear days, you might be able to see BA on the horizon. Perhaps more interesting than the lighthouse are the ruins near its base, the origins of much of the stone used in El Faro's construction. They're the remains of the oldest convent in the country, the **Convento de San Francisco,** founded in 1685 but summarily destroyed during one of the region's many colonial wars. *(Near the intersection of Comercio and San Pedro. Open winter M-F 2-5:30pm, Sa-Su 11am-5:30pm; summer M-F 11am-8:30pm.)* Just 5km outside the center down Luis Casanello is the **Playa Farrando,** the best beach in town.

EXCURSIONS

Toward the end of the route, the path widens into an avenue, with trees down the middle. At the end of the road, veer right. Walking is a bad idea given the sketchy sectors of town in between, so it's better to rent a bike or a moped.

>  **PLAYA FARRANDO SAFETY.** Since the route to Playa Farrando runs through Colonia's poor neighborhoods, Let's Go does not recommend bringing any valuables to the beach. Not that you'd really need them, anyway.

For ⚡wine aficionados, the 19th-century **Bodega Bernardi,** just 7km up Route 1 at kilometer 171.5, provides the opportunity to test your palate. The vineyard specializes in red wines, complete with accompanying cheeses and *empanadas*, but also makes some white wines. Guided tours of the winery are free and are offered in English, Italian, and Spanish, but call ahead and give advance notice to ensure a tour in your language. Though buses run to the *bodega*, the distance is short enough for a bike ride. (*Ruta 1, km. 171.5, Laguna de los Patos.* ☎24752; www.bodegabernardi.com. Open summer M-Sa 9am-noon and 3-7pm; winter M-Sa 9am-noon and 2-5:30pm; Su 10am-2pm. Last entrance 30min. before close. Free. To get there by bus, take any of the several local buses that leave via Ruta 1. Compania Colonia offers buses M-F 6:45, 10:20, 10:30am, 12:15, 1:30, 3:30, 4, 6, 7, 8:10pm; Sa 6:45, 10:20, 10:30am, 3:30, 4, 6, 7, 8:10pm; Su 8, 10:20, 10:30am, 6, 8, 8:20pm. UR$25.)

# MONTEVIDEO ☎02

Many travelers dismiss Uruguay's capital as a smaller, less flashy, and more expensive version of Buenos Aires. While it's true that Montevideo is less populous than BA, with 1.4 million inhabitants to Buenos Aires' 13 million, the other comparisons couldn't be farther from the truth. From the classic old town, *Ciudad Vieja*, dotted with plazas and markets grilling unholy amounts of *bife*, to the beautiful string of sandy beaches and trails lining the coast, Montevideo still has something to offer for the intrepid traveler—a tranquility and sense of ease unrivaled by the Argentine capital.

>  **WHAT'S IN A NAME?** The origin of the Montevideo's name remains a mystery. Some theories attribute it to mis-transcription by cartographers of Magellan's notoriously bad handwriting. Others didn't even know Magellan had bad writing. Still others say it actually comes from the Portuguese phrase *"Monte vide eu,"* which means "I see a hill"—though not the most original of names, you have to think that early explorers, after sailing across an entire ocean, might have had a sort of "screw this" mentality about city naming.

## ✈ INTERCITY TRANSPORTATION

**Buses:** Montevideo's main bus terminal, **Tres Cruces,** at the intersection of Artigas and Dr. Ferrer Serra (☎+598 2 408 8601; www.trescruces.com.uy; open 24hr.), is just due west of Parque Batlle. Buses #21, 64, 180, 187, 188, and 330 run to the center of the city. From there, take bus #14, 64, 104, or 121 to get to Punta Carretas or Pocitos. Turil (☎1990; www.turil.com.uy) runs buses from Montevideo to **Colonia** (UR$167; daily 5:30, 6:50, 10am, 12:30, 2:30, 4:30, 6:30, 10:30pm). COT (☎409 4949; www.cot.com.uy) also offers routes from Montevideo to **Colonia** (UR$167; daily 5, 7:45, 9:30, 11:30am, 1:30, 3:30, 5, 7:15, 9, 10pm). COPSA, with offices in Tres Cruces (☎902 1818; www.copsa.com.uy; open 24hr.), runs buses about every hour to the beaches of **Punta del Este** (2hr., UR$138).

**Ferries:** For ferry transportation between Buenos Aires and Montevideo, see p. 243.

EXC

## ⌐ LOCAL TRANSPORTATION

**Buses:** Local buses run out of the Terminal Omnibus Río Branco, Rio Branco 1409. At 11pm, buses run only hourly. Regular service starts up again at 7am. UR$13.50, paid to the man sitting opposite the driver after boarding.

**Taxis:** You can pick them up anywhere on the street. For immediate service, try any of the number of Radio taxi services, including **Fono-Taxi** (☎203 7000), **Radio Taxi Cooperativo** (☎311 1030), and **Radio Taxi Scot** (☎208 0810). At night, taxis charge an additional initial fee of UR$20-30.

## ✴ ORIENTATION

Most tourists are based in the **Ciudad Vieja,** the historic center. Though the area was seen as a rough neighborhood for many years, recent revitalization campaigns have proved successful, resulting in some new pedestrian streets and a series of bars and clubs. The old town is set on a peninsula jutting out into the city harbor. The city's main square is the **Plaza Independencia** (p. 253), based roughly on the border between the *Ciudad Vieja* and the city's downtown, **Centro.** The bustling **Avenida 18 de Julio** runs east from the Plaza Independencia through Centro. North of Centro is the port and **Aguada,** which tourists visit for the **Palacio Legislativo** (p. 253), the base of the country's parliament. From the *Ciudad Vieja*, the coastal **Rambla** runs east to **Pocitos** and **Punta Carretas.**

## ✴ PRACTICAL INFORMATION

**Tourist Offices: Ministerio de Turismo** (☎188 5111), at the intersection of Rambla 25 de Agosto and Yacaré, right next to the ferry terminal.

**Bike Rental: Bicicletería Sur,** 1100 Durazno (☎901 0792), rents bikes for UR$20 per hr. or UR$80 per 6hr. Must be 18+ with telephone number and ID. Open M-F 9am-1pm, 3-7pm; Sa 9am-1pm, 3-5pm.

**Embassies:**

**Argentina,** Cuareim 1470 (☎902 8166; emb-uruguay.mrecic.gov.ar). Open M-F 10am-1pm, 3-6pm.

**Canada,** Plaza Independencia 749, office 102 (☎902 2030; http://geo.international.gc.ca/latin-america/uruguay), above the Aerolineas Argentinas office. Open M-F 9-11am; extra hours for Canadians M-Th 2-4:30pm.

**United Kingdom,** Marco Bruto 1073 (☎622 3630), just west of Pocitos. Open M-F Mar.-Dec. 9am-1pm, 2-5:30pm; Jan.-Feb. 8:30am-2:30pm.

**United States,** Lauro Muller 1776 (☎418 7777; http://montevideo.usembassy.gov). Open M-F 8:30am-5:30pm.

**Banks, ATMs, and Currency Exchange:** Banks and currency exchange services can be found throughout the city offering similar rates. Though some have longer hours, others are only open 1-5pm. Most ATM cards will work with BANRED, the Uruguayan ATM network, which accesses Banelco and Visa and Mastercard networks.

**Emergency:** For all emergencies, dial ☎911.

**Police:** Carlos Quijano 1310 (☎1909). The tourist police are based at Colonia 1021 (☎0800 8226/908 3303/909102).

**Pharmacy:** There are many 24hr. pharmacies—your hostel should be able to direct you to the closest one. One central location is **Farmacia San Antonio,** Av. 18 de Julio 841 (☎900 0368). Open 24hr.

**Hospital: Hospital de Clínicas,** Av. Italia (☎480 1222; www.hc.edu.uy), just after A. A Navarro, is the public hospital.

EXCURSIONS

## Montevideo

▲ **ACCOMMODATIONS**
Che Lagarto Hostel, **1**
El Viajero, **2**
Hotel Palacio, **3**

● **FOOD**
El Fogón, **4**
La Posada Don Tiburón, **5**
San Rafael, **6**
El Tigre, **7**

🏛 **MUSEUMS**
Museo Torres García, **8**

♦ **NIGHTLIFE**
Bar Fun Fun, **9**
Pony Pisador, **10**
W. Lounge, **11**

Puerto de Montevideo

Río de la Plata

TO PLAYA POCITOS (2km)

TO PALACIO LEGISLATIVO (500m)

Mercado del Puerto

Rbla. República de Argentina

**Internet:** *Locutorios,* with telephones and Internet, are plentiful in the center near Av. 18 de Julio. Just around the corner from the Plaza Independencia, **Centro,** Andes 1363 (☎902 4522), has computers with microphones and Skype. Internet UR$16-50 per hr. Calls to the US UR$7 per min. Open 24hr.

**Post Office: Correo Central** (☎916 0200) takes up an entire block between Sarandí and Buenos Aires. Open M-F 9am-5pm. Postcards UR$17. Letters UR$55. There's also a **FedEx,** Juncal 1321 (☎628 0100), on the Plaza Independencia. Open M-F 10am-1pm, 2-7pm. **Postal Code:** 10000-20000.

## ACCOMMODATIONS

Montevideo's budget accommodations are clustered in the center and the **Ciudad Vieja,** convenient to many sights and nightlife spots. If you're looking for a single, it's often surprisingly cheaper to go to a hotel than a hostel. Expect to pay in cash, either with Uruguayan pesos or American dollars.

**El Viajero,** Ituzaingó 1436 (☎915 6192; www.elviajerohostels.com). This tidy, mid-sized hostel in the heart of the *Ciudad Vieja* manages the rare combination of sociability and cleanliness and features two kitchens, a terrace for outdoor barbecues, and a common room with piano. The dorms are standard fare, but the twin doubles sport some classier furnishings, such as bookshelves. If you care about solitude, ask for a room set away from the common room, which can get noisy from time to time. 6- to 8-bed dorms UR$300; singles UR$724. Accepts both UR$ and US$. ❷

**Che Lagarto Hostel (HI),** Plaza de la Independencia 713 (☎903 0175; www.chelagarto.com/montevideo-hostels.php). This big, sociable HI-affiliate, part of a chain of hostels around South America, has balconies that overlook the Plaza de la Independencia, giving it the best location hands-down (albeit the noisiest) in the city. Music pulses regularly from the common room with TV and pool table, and the bar does brisk business in 1L beers. The hostel also occasionally organizes barbecues. Breakfast included. Free Internet and Wi-Fi. 4-bed dorms UR$305; 6-bed dorms with ensuite bath UR$324; 8-bed dorms UR$267; doubles UR$667-762. Accepts both UR$ and US$. ❷

**Hotel Palacio,** Bartolomé Mitre 1364 (☎916 3612; www.hotelpalacio.com.uy). For a private room, Hotel Palacio is a steal. The antique elevator is perhaps more charming than the antique feel of some of the mattresses, but the location in the *Ciudad Vieja* and helpful staff compensate. The slightly more expensive top rooms get more light and boast private balconies with harbor views. Singles US$22-25; doubles US$23-26, with additional bed US$27-30; balcony rooms US$28-30. MC/V. ❸

## FOOD

Pizza and *parrilla* reign supreme in Montevideo's dining scene, which is more expensive (though still very affordable) and less varied than in Argentina. Proximity to the Río de la Plata may explain the appearance of more fish on the menu, but can't account for the presence of more salads. Despite this extra greenery, vegetarians will find it as difficult as ever to satisfy their hunger.

**San Rafael,** Zelmar Michelini 1301 (☎900 5214), at the intersection with San José. San Rafael doesn't look like much from the outside, but focus too much on the paper placemats and *telenovelas* and you'll miss some of the best bang-for-your-buck eats in the city. Locals come here when they don't feel like cooking—there's nary a tourist in sight. The portions of well-flavored Uruguayan basics are plentiful, and there are also some more inventive options, such as the *arroz a la cubana* (UR$96). Entrees UR$55-255. Open daily 7am-2am. AmEx/MC/V: UR$250 min. ❸

**El Fogón,** San José 1080 (☎900 0900; www.elfogon.com.uy). Past the Art Nouveau lamp at the entrance is the old-fashioned interior of this restaurant and grill, complete with penguined waiters. The selection is huge, the desserts are even bigger, and the tourist crowds are epic. Appetizers UR$73-380. *Parrilla* UR$160-450. Pastas UR$169-215. Fish UR$170-380. Open daily noon-4pm and 7pm-1am. AmEx/MC/V. ❹

**La Posada Don Tiburón,** Pérez Castellano 1569 (☎915 4278). A meal of grilled meat and vegetables at the Mercado del Puerto (p. 254) is practically a requirement for visitors to Montevideo. There are many options, and this is merely one of them. Serves up one of the cheaper *entrecotes* (steaks) around at UR$220. Salads UR$90-195. *Parrilla* UR$140-320. Fish UR$290-320. Desserts UR$85-150. Beer UR$70. Open daily 9am-midnight; closes 5pm in July. 5pm. MC/V. ❸

**El Tigre,** Scocería 2501 (☎710 7081). On an innocuous corner in Pocitos, this noisy steakhouse showcases some tasty dishes at excellent prices. At night, the increasingly lively restaurant attracts a younger crowd looking for drinks, a good time, and a look at the tiger tucked discreetly over the television. When you're done, hit the road and pick from one of the many other bars nearby. Entrees UR$65-320. Wine by the carafe UR$75. Open daily noon-3:30pm and 6pm-4am. MC/V. ❸

---

**URU FOOD IS GUAY DELICIOUS!** Argentina is by no means the only place in the Río de la Plata neighborhood with some distinctive eats. Uruguay gets the job done with some tasty treats of their own.

**Chivito:** This signature Uruguayan sandwich stars a thin piece of meat completely overwhelmed by its toppings, which include fried egg, cheese, grilled peppers, lettuce, tomato, and mayonnaise.

**Almíbar:** An orange-colored syrup similar to Jell-o in taste, but sweeter and often made out of pumpkin.

**Chajá:** White cake topped with cream and meringue.

**Fainá:** A sort of pizza crust made out of cornmeal.

**Pamplona:** Meat stuffed with ham, red peppers, and cheese.

---

## ◎ 🏛 SIGHTS AND MUSEUMS

◪**PLAZA INDEPENDENCIA AND SURROUNDINGS.** The heart of the *Ciudad Vieja*, palm-studded, 19th-century Plaza Independencia is Montevideo's largest square and the site of political protests and impromptu *tambor* (drum) sessions. You may recognize the prominent, early 20th-century tower at Artigas' one o'clock, on the southeastern corner of the square. That's because the building, the **Palacio Salvo**, was designed by the same architect who planned Palacio Barolo (p. 144) in Buenos Aires. When completed in 1928, the structure ranked as the tallest building in Latin America, and continues to hold its place as the most photographed building in the city, despite the ugly antenna at the top. *(At the intersection of Av. 18 de Julio and Plaza Independencia.)* From the western end of the Plaza, **Sarandí,** a pedestrian street, leads through **market** stalls and the smaller, 18th-century **Plaza Constitución,** home to two of the oldest buildings in the city, the 1790 **Catedral Metropolitana** and the 1804 **Cabildo,** the government headquarters during the Viceroyalty of the River Plate.

◪**PALACIO LEGISLATIVO.** Uruguay's magnificent parliament building, designed by **Vittorio Meano,** the mastermind behind BA's Congreso (p. 144), was completed in 1925, just in time for the 100th anniversary of the country's declaration of independence from Brazil. The **General Assembly of Uruguay** has 30 senators and 99 *diputados*, some of whom you can glimpse roaming the corridors. Try and snag the autograph of your favorite Uruguayan representative. Excellent Spanish-language **guided visits** give an account of the building's history, as well as explanations of how the government operates. *(From Plaza Fabini, head north along Av. del Libertador—the walk takes 30min. Alternatively, take bus #141 or 142 from the stop on Calle Buenos Aires, one block from Teatro Solís. You can't miss the building itself, which is on Av. de las Leyes. The entrance is on Av. General Flores. ☎142 2528; www.parlamento.gub.uy. Guided 45min. visits M-F 9, 10, 11am, noon, 2:30, 3:30, 4pm. Free.)*

**BLAST FROM THE PAST.** In 2004, Parliament designated August 24th the *Noche de la Nostalgia*, a night when everyone wears out of fashion clothes and all discos go retro. Informally, the custom has been in practice since 1978. If you happen to be in town then, get down and get funky.

**◼THE RAMBLA, PLAYA POCITOS, AND SURROUNDINGS.** Montevideo's seaside **Rambla** runs along nearly 14 miles of uninterrupted Río de la Plata coast, from the *Ciudad Vieja* to Pocitos. On weekends, the **bike paths** transform into a chaotic riot of dogs, soccer balls, and running suits, with the inevitable *mate* drinker thrown into the mix. At the far eastern end of the path in Pocitos is the city's most centrally located beach, the beautiful **Playa Pocitos.** *(To go straight to Playa Pocitos, take bus #121, get off at Av. Brasil, and walk towards the shoreline. Bus #104 starts on Av. 18 de Julio and runs along the entire coast to Carrasco.)*

**MUSEO TORRES GARCÍA.** Joaquín Torres García, painter, theorist, and (for a curveball here) toy manufacturer, ranks as Uruguay's most influential artist of the 20th century. The museum displays pieces from the start to the finish of his career, and includes watercolors, some of the toys he produced to support himself financially, and the work for which he is perhaps most famous—a **sketch** of the world with the ◼**south on top.** *(Sarandí 683. Just off Plaza Independencia and behind the Puerta de la Ciudadela on the right. ☎916 2663 or 915 6544; www.torresgarcia.org.uy. Captions in English. Open M-F 9:30am-7:30pm, Sa 10am-6pm. Suggested contribution UR$20-50.)*

**TEATRO SOLÍS.** The imposing Neoclassical Teatro Solís, Montevideo's main cultural space since the 19th century, was daring enough and had enough doubters upon completion that engineers marched the army through the edifice to prove it wouldn't collapse. Obviously, it was still standing afterwards, though perhaps dirtied by stamping military boots. The sun on the front pediment was not the origin of the building's name—that honor goes to 16th-century Spanish explorer **Juan Díaz de Solís** (p. 53), who named the Río de la Plata. **Guided tours** walk visitors through the building's history, take you into the sumptuous main theater, and may include impromptu performances. *(At the intersection of Buenos Aires and Ciudadela, just southwest of Plaza Independencia. ☎1950 3323 or 1950 3325; www. teatrosolis.org.uy. Guided tours Tu, Th 4pm; W, F-Su 11am, noon, 4pm. Spanish-language UR$20, other language UR$40. W Spanish-language tours. Performance tickets UR$200-2000.)*

**MERCADO DEL PUERTO.** Designed in 1868 as the largest market in Latin America, the Mercado now operates as a mecca for tourists and locals looking for a bite to eat, but don't expect anything more than meat and seafood. The wrought-iron structure that houses the market was built in England, and at least one apocryphal story claims that the structure was, in fact, originally destined for Chile, before a storm sunk the ship and carried it conveniently close to the Montevideo harbor. Next door, the **Museo del Carnaval** displays instruments and costumes from **Carnaval,** the country's hugely popular 40-day celebration that starts in February. *(Rambla 25 de Agosto 218, at the intersection with Maciel. ☎916 5493; www.mercadodelpuerto.com.uy. Open Tu-Su 11am-5pm. Free.)*

## ■ NIGHTLIFE

Nightlife clusters in the *Ciudad Vieja* along a series of streets that spoke off from **Bartolomé Mitre,** making it easy for tourists to barhop from place to place. The city's clubs, which are usually open only for Friday and Saturday nights, are virtually indistinguishable—dancers can expect to encounter *cumbia* and pop more than anything else pretty much everywhere they go. There are also bars and clubs scattered in **Pocitos** and **Punta Carretas,** especially along **Avenida España,** but these are more difficult to get to without a car. Things get going slightly earlier than in Buenos Aires; though the streets teem with people at all hours, the lines snaking around the corners are longest at around 2am.

> **CIUDAD VIEJA SAFETY.** Montevideo is a safe town for nightlife on the whole, but *Ciudad Vieja*, which used to be a poor neighborhood during the 1973-1985 dictatorship, still retains some of its past grittiness and can be dangerous at night. Exercise caution.

■ **Bar Fun Fun,** Ciudadela 1229 (☎915 8005; www.barfunfun.com), at the Mercado Central just of Plaza Independencia. Bar Fun Fun, in operation since 1895, actually manages to meet the expectations generated by its name with chill live music acts. Photographs on the wall document the bar's storied past, which most famously includes a 1933 visit by tango great Carlos Gardel (p. 79). Legend has it that one sip of the Uvita, the bar's secret recipe drink, prompted him to dedicate a song to the mysterious beverage. Uvita UR$36. W rock. Th tango and rock. F and Sa tango and *candome.* Cover UR$50-100. Open Tu-Sa 8pm-4am. Cash only.

■ **W. Lounge,** Rambla Wilson and Requena Garcia (☎712 1177), in the Parque Rodo. Renowned as Montevideo's most popular dance spot, W. Lounge has adapted the one-size-fits-all mentality to club form, with different dance floors spinning music as varied as salsa and electronica. F nights attract the city's sleek 20-somethings, while on Saturdays the teen set tries to scam its way inside. Occasional visiting DJs. Mixed drinks UR$80. Cover F UR$160, Sa UR$150. Open F midnight-10am, Sa midnight-7am.

**Pony Pisador,** Bartolomé Mitre 326 (☎957470; www.elponypisador.com.uy). The Pony Pisador is the Ciudad Vieja's most popular watering hole, a noisy bar with live music and tables spilling out into the street. Inside, 20-somethings crowd around bar stools or head upstairs for table seating. Across the street, the Pony Pisador **disco** spins mostly Latin pop, with electronica, *cumbia,* and hip-hop mixed in. Beer UR$60-85. *Tragos* UR$85-115. Open M-Th 5pm-close, F-Su 8pm-close. AmEx/MC/V: UR$200 minimum.

EXCURSIONS

# APPENDIX

## CLIMATE

You could consider this excessive mothering, but it's essential to mention it somewhere, so bear with us—in the **Southern Hemisphere,** June-September is winter and December-March is summer. We know, it's crazy. Almost as crazy as the toilets flushing the opposite direction in the Southern Hemisphere (this is actually false; see p. 33). Buenos Aires itself, in "sciencey," technical terms, has what's called a **humid subtropical climate.** This means that it's very hot during the summer and mild in winter. Here's another way to think of it: by latitude, Buenos Aires is as far south of the equator as Florida is north, so the climate is, not surprisingly, remarkably similar to Florida's.

| MONTH | AVG. HIGH TEMP. | | AVG. LOW TEMP. | | AVG. RAINFALL | | AVG. NUMBER OF WET DAYS |
|-------|------|------|------|------|--------|---------|----|
| January | 28°C | 83°F | 20°C | 68°F | 99mm | 3.9 in. | 9 |
| February | 27°C | 81°F | 19°C | 67°F | 107mm | 4.2 in. | 9 |
| March | 25°C | 77°F | 18°C | 64°F | 124mm | 4.9 in. | 9 |
| April | 22°C | 71°F | 14°C | 58°F | 89mm | 3.5 in. | 9 |
| May | 18°C | 64°F | 11°C | 52°F | 71mm | 2.8 in. | 8 |
| June | 15°C | 59°F | 8°C | 47°F | 56mm | 2.2 in. | 6 |
| July | 14°C | 58°F | 8°C | 46°F | 61mm | 2.4 in. | 7 |
| August | 16°C | 60°F | 9°C | 48°F | 66mm | 2.6 in. | 8 |
| September | 18°C | 64°F | 11°C | 51°F | 66mm | 2.6 in. | 7 |
| October | 21°C | 69°F | 13°C | 56°F | 112mm | 4.4 in. | 10 |
| November | 24°C | 75°F | 16°C | 61°F | 104mm | 4.1 in. | 10 |
| December | 27°C | 80°F | 18°C | 65°F | 97mm | 3.8 in. | 9 |

To convert from degrees Fahrenheit to degrees Celsius, subtract 32 and multiply by 5/9. To convert from Celsius to Fahrenheit, multiply by 9/5 and add 32.

| °CELSIUS | -5 | 0 | 5 | 10 | 15 | 20 | 25 | 30 | 35 | 40 |
|----------|----|----|----|----|----|----|----|----|----|-----|
| °FAHRENHEIT | 23 | 32 | 41 | 50 | 59 | 68 | 77 | 86 | 95 | 104 |

## MEASUREMENTS

Like the rest of the rational world, Argentina uses the metric system. The basic unit of length is the meter (m), which is divided into 100 centimeters (cm) or 1000 millimeters (mm). One thousand meters make up one kilometer (km). Fluids are measured in liters (L), each divided into 1000 milliliters (mL). A liter of pure water weighs one kilogram (kg), the unit of mass that is divided into 1000 grams (g). One metric ton is 1000kg.

| MEASUREMENT CONVERSIONS | |
|---|---|
| 1 inch (in.) = 25.4mm | 1 millimeter (mm) = 0.039 in. |
| 1 foot (ft.) = 0.305m | 1 meter (m) = 3.28 ft. |
| 1 yard (yd.) = 0.914m | 1 meter (m) = 1.094 yd. |

| MEASUREMENT CONVERSIONS | |
|---|---|
| 1 mile (mi.) = 1.609km | 1 kilometer (km) = 0.621 mi. |
| 1 ounce (oz.) = 28.35g | 1 gram (g) = 0.035 oz. |
| 1 pound (lb.) = 0.454kg | 1 kilogram (kg) = 2.205 lb. |
| 1 fluid ounce (fl. oz.) = 29.57mL | 1 milliliter (mL) = 0.034 fl. oz. |
| 1 gallon (gal.) = 3.785L | 1 liter (L) = 0.264 gal. |

# LANGUAGE

Spanish is the official language of Argentina, where it is known more commonly as *castellano* (from the Castile region of Spain, where modern-day Spanish originated). Argentine *castellano* is very similar in pronunciation to traditional Spanish, but there are several notable differences. Thanks to Argentina's rich history of immigration, the *castellano* accent has a strong connection to Italian. Furthermore, Argentina is one of the few large Spanish-speaking countries that utilizes *voseo*—the use of the pronoun *vos* instead of *tú* for English "you." Although many *porteños* speak English, especially in the tourist-mobbed central *barrios*, knowing at least some basic Spanish will go a long way. *Porteños* will appreciate the effort, and it will prove useful when you encounter a region where there are few English speakers. It will happen. Trust us.

## PRONUNCIATION

Each vowel has only one pronunciation: *a* ("ah" in "father"); *e* ("eh" in "pet"); *i* ("ee" in "eat"); *o* ("oh" in "oat"); *u* ("oo" in "boot"); *y*, by itself, is pronounced the same as the Spanish i ("ee"). Most consonants are the same as in English. Important exceptions are: *j* ("h" in "hello"); *ll* ("y" in "yes"); *ñ* ("ny" in "canyon"); and *r* at the beginning of a word or *rr* anywhere in a word (trilled). *H* is always silent. *G* before *e* or *i* is pronounced like the "h" in "hen"; elsewhere it is pronounced like the "g" in "gate." *X* has a bewildering variety of pronunciations; depending on dialect and word position, it can sound like the English "h," "s," "sh," or "x." *B* and *v* have similar pronunciations. Spanish words receive stress on the syllable marked with an accent. In the absence of an accent mark, words that end in vowels, *n*, or *s* receive stress on the second to last syllable. For words ending in all other consonants, stress falls on the last syllable. The Spanish language has masculine and feminine nouns, and gives a gender to all adjectives. Masculine words generally end with an *o*, feminine words generally end with an *a*. Pay close attention—slight changes in word ending can have drastic changes in meaning. For instance, when receiving directions, mind the distinction between *derecho* (straight; more commonly *recto*) and *derecha* (right). Sentences that end in ? or ! are also preceded by the same punctuation upside-down: *¿Cómo estás? ¡Muy bien, gracias!*

## PHRASEBOOK

### ESSENTIAL PHRASES

| ENGLISH | SPANISH | PRONUNCIATION |
|---|---|---|
| Hello. | Hola. | OH-la |
| How are you? | ¿Cómo está? | KOH-mo es-TA |

APPENDIX

| | | |
|---|---|---|
| Good, thanks | Muy bien, gracias | MWEE bee-en, GRA-see-ahs |
| Goodbye. | Adiós. | ah-dee-OHS |
| Yes/No | Sí/No | SEE/NO |
| Please. | Por favor. | POHR fa-VOHR |
| Thank you. | Gracias. | GRA-see-ahs |
| You're welcome. | De nada. | DAY NAH-dah |
| Do you speak English? | ¿Habla inglés? | AH-blah en-GLACE |
| I don't speak Spanish. | No hablo español. | NO AH-bloh ehs-pahn-YOHL |
| Excuse me. | Perdón. | pehr-DOHN |
| I don't know. | No sé. | NO SAY |
| Can you repeat that? | ¿Puede repetirlo? | PWEH-day reh-peh-TEER-lo |

## INTERPERSONAL INTERACTIONS

| ENGLISH | SPANISH | ENGLISH | SPANISH |
|---|---|---|---|
| What is your name? | ¿Cómo se llama? | Do you come here often? | ¿Viene aquí a menudo? |
| Pleased to meet you. | Encantado(a)/Mucho gusto. | How do you say...in Spanish/English? | ¿Comó se dice...en español/inglés? |
| Where are you from? | ¿De dónde es? | I'm (twenty) years old. | Tengo (veinte) años. |
| This is my first time in Buenos Aires. | Esta es mi primera vez en Buenos Aires. | I have a boyfriend/girlfriend/spouse. | Tengo novio/novia/esposo(a). |
| What a shame: you bought *Lonely Planet*! | ¡Qué lástima: compraste *Lonely Planet*! | What does...mean? | ¿Qué significa...? |

## YOUR ARRIVAL

| ENGLISH | SPANISH | ENGLISH | SPANISH |
|---|---|---|---|
| I am from (the US/Europe). | Soy de (los Estados Unidos/Europa). | What's the problem, sir/madam? | ¿Cuál es el problema, señor/señora? |
| Here is my passport. | Aquí está mi pasaporte. | I lost my passport. | Perdí mi pasaporte. |
| I will be here for less than six months. | Estaré aquí por menos de seis meses. | I have nothing to declare. | No tengo nada para declarar. |
| I don't know where that came from. | No sé de donde vino eso. | Please do not detain me. | Por favor no me detenga. |
| Where is customs? | ¿Dónde está la aduana? | Where do I claim my luggage? | ¿Dónde puedo reclamar mi equipaje? |

## DIRECTIONS

| ENGLISH | SPANISH | ENGLISH | SPANISH |
|---|---|---|---|
| (to the) right | (a la) derecha | (to the) left | (a la) izquierda |
| next to | al lado de/junto a | across from | en frente de/frente a |
| straight ahead | derecho | turn (command) | doble |
| near (to) | cerca (de) | far (from) | lejos (de) |
| on top of/above | encima de/arriba | beneath/below | bajo de/abajo |
| traffic light | semáforo | corner | esquina |
| street | calle/avenida | block | cuadra |

## GETTING AROUND

| ENGLISH | SPANISH | ENGLISH | SPANISH |
|---|---|---|---|
| How can you get to...? | ¿Cómo se puede llegar a...? | Is there anything cheaper? | ¿Hay algo más barato/económico? |
| Does this bus go to (Retiro)? | ¿Va este autobús a (Retiro)? | On foot. | A pie. |

| ENGLISH | SPANISH | ENGLISH | SPANISH |
|---|---|---|---|
| Where is (Florida) street? | ¿Dónde está la calle (Florida)? | What bus line goes to..? | ¿Qué línea de buses tiene servicio a...? |
| When does the bus leave? | ¿Cuándo sale el bús? | Where does the bus leave from? | ¿De dónde sale el bús? |
| I'm getting off at... | Bajo en... | I have to go now. | Tengo que ir ahora. |
| Can I buy a ticket? | ¿Podría comprar un boleto? | How far is...? | ¿Qué tan lejos está...? |
| How long does the trip take? | ¿Cuántas horas dura el viaje? | Continue forward. | Siga derecho. |
| I am going to the airport. | Voy al aeropuerto. | The flight is delayed/canceled. | El vuelo está atrasado/cancelado. |
| Where is the bathroom? | ¿Dónde está el baño? | Is it safe to hitchhike? | ¿Es seguro pedir aventón? |
| I lost my baggage. | Perdí mi equipaje. | I'm lost. | Estoy perdido(a). |
| I would like to rent (a car). | Quisiera alquilar (un coche). | Please let me off at the zoo. | Por favor, déjeme en el zoológico. |
| How much does it cost per day/week? | ¿Cuánto cuesta por día/semana? | Does it have (heating/air-conditioning)? | ¿Tiene (calefacción/aire acondicionado)? |
| Where can I buy a cell-phone? | ¿Dónde puedo comprar un teléfono celular? | Where can I check email? | ¿Dónde se puede chequear el email? |
| Could you tell me what time it is? | ¿Podría decirme qué hora es? | Are there student discounts available? | ¿Hay descuentos para estudiantes? |

## SURVIVAL SPANISH

| ENGLISH | SPANISH | ENGLISH | SPANISH |
|---|---|---|---|
| Again, please | Otra vez, por favor | Could you speak more slowly? | ¿Podría hablar más despacio? |
| Does this bus go to...? | ¿Este autobús va a...? | What bus line goes to...? | ¿Cuál línea de buses tiene servicio a...? |
| Where is (Lavalle) street? | ¿Dónde está la calle (Lavalle)? | From where/when does the bus leave? | ¿De dónde/cuándo sale el autobús? |
| Can you let me know when we get to...? | ¿Me podría avisar cuando lleguemos a...? | Could you tell me what time it is? | ¿Podría decirme que hora es? |
| I'm getting off at... | Me bajo en... | How far/near is... | ¿Qué tan lejos/cerca está...? |
| Can I buy a ticket? | ¿Podría comprar un boleto? | Can you take me to (the train station)? | ¿Podría llevarme a (la estación de tren)? |
| How long does the trip take? | ¿Cuánto tiempo dura el viaje? | The flight is delayed/cancelled. | El vuelo está atrasado/cancelado. |
| Round-trip/one-way | Ida y vuelta/ida | Is it safe to hitchhike? | ¿Es seguro hacer autostop? |
| I am going to the airport. | Voy al aeropuerto. | I'm lost. | Estoy perdido(a). |
| I'm in a hurry! | ¡Tengo prisa! | Please let me off at (the zoo). | Por favor, déjeme en (el zoológico). |
| I would like to rent (a car). | Quisiera alquilar (un coche). | Where can I check email? | ¿Dónde se puede chequear el correo electrónico? |
| How much does it cost per day/week? | ¿Cuanto cuesta por día/semana? | Are there student discounts available? | ¿Hay descuentos para estudiantes? |

## ACCOMMODATIONS

| ENGLISH | SPANISH | ENGLISH | SPANISH |
|---|---|---|---|
| Is there a cheap hotel around here? | ¿Hay un hotel económico por aquí? | Are there rooms with windows? | ¿Hay habitaciones con ventanas? |
| Do you have rooms available? | ¿Tiene habitaciones libres? | I am going to stay for (four) days. | Me voy a quedar (cuatro) días. |
| I would like to reserve a room. | Quisiera reservar una habitación. | Are there cheaper rooms? | ¿Hay habitaciones más baratas? |

| English | Spanish | English | Spanish |
|---|---|---|---|
| Can I see a room? | ¿Podría ver una habitación? | Do they come with private baths? | ¿Vienen con baño privado? |
| Do you have any singles/doubles? | ¿Tiene habitaciones sencillas/dobles? | Is there hot water? | ¿Hay agua caliente? |
| Does it have (heating/A/C)? | ¿Tiene (calefacción/aire acondicionado)? | Who's there? | ¿Quién es? |
| I need another key/towel/pillow. | Necesito otra llave/toalla/almohada. | My bedsheets are dirty. | Mis sábanas están sucias. |
| The shower/sink/toilet is broken. | La ducha/pila/el servicio no funciona. | I'll take it. | Lo tomo. |
| There are cockroaches in my room. | Hay cucarachas en mi habitación. | Dance, cockroaches, dance! | ¡Bailen, cucarachas, bailen! |

## EMERGENCY

| ENGLISH | SPANISH | ENGLISH | SPANISH |
|---|---|---|---|
| Help! | ¡Socorro!/¡Ayúdeme! | Call the police! | ¡Llame a la policía! |
| I am hurt. | Estoy herido(a). | Leave me alone! | ¡Déjame en paz! |
| It's an emergency! | ¡Es una emergencia! | They robbed me! | ¡Me han robado! |
| Fire! | ¡Fuego!/¡Incendio! | They went that way! | ¡Fueron en esa dirección! |
| Call a clinic/ambulance/doctor/priest! | ¡Llame a una clínica/una ambulancia/un médico/un padre! | I will only speak in the presence of a lawyer. | Sólo hablaré en presencia de un abogado(a). |
| I need to contact my embassy. | Necesito contactar mi embajada. | Don't touch me! | ¡No me toque! |

## MEDICAL

| ENGLISH | SPANISH | ENGLISH | SPANISH |
|---|---|---|---|
| I feel bad/better/fine/worse. | Me siento mal/mejor/bien/peor. | What is this medicine for? | ¿Para qué es esta medicina? |
| I have a headache. | Tengo un dolor de cabeza. | Where is the nearest hospital/doctor? | ¿Dónde está el hospital/doctor más cercano? |
| I'm sick/ill. | Estoy enfermo(a). | I have a stomachache. | Me duele el estómago. |
| I'm allergic to... | Soy alérgico(a) a... | Here is my prescription. | Aquí está la receta médica. |
| I think I'm going to vomit. | Pienso que voy a vomitar. | I haven't been able to go to the bathroom in (four) days. | No he podido ir al baño en (cuatro) días. |
| I have a cold/a fever/diarrhea/nausea | Tengo gripe/una calentura/diarrea/náusea. | Call a doctor, please. | Llame a un médico, por favor. |

## NUMBERS, DAYS, AND MONTHS

| ENGLISH | SPANISH | ENGLISH | SPANISH | ENGLISH | SPANISH |
|---|---|---|---|---|---|
| 0 | cero | 12 | doce | 40 | cuarenta |
| 1 | uno | 13 | trece | 50 | cincuenta |
| 2 | dos | 14 | catorce | 100 | cien |
| 3 | tres | 15 | quince | 1000 | un mil |
| 4 | cuatro | 16 | dieciseis | 1 million | un millón |
| 5 | cinco | 17 | diecisiete | Sunday | domingo |
| 6 | seis | 18 | dieciocho | Monday | lunes |
| 7 | siete | 19 | diecinueve | Tuesday | martes |
| 8 | ocho | 20 | veinte | Wednesday | miércoles |
| 9 | nueve | 21 | veintiuno | Thursday | jueves |
| 10 | diez | 22 | veintidos | Friday | viernes |
| 11 | once | 30 | treinta | Saturday | sábado |

| ENGLISH | SPANISH | ENGLISH | SPANISH | ENGLISH | SPANISH |
|---|---|---|---|---|---|
| today | hoy | night | noche | May | mayo |
| tomorrow | mañana | month | mes | June | junio |
| day after tomorrow | pasado mañana | year | año | July | julio |
| yesterday | ayer | early/late | temprano/tarde | August | agosto |
| day before | anteayer | January | enero | September | septiembre |
| weekend | fin de semana | February | febrero | October | octubre |
| morning | mañana | March | marzo | November | noviembre |
| afternoon | tarde | April | abril | December | diciembre |

## EATING OUT

| ENGLISH | SPANISH | ENGLISH | SPANISH |
|---|---|---|---|
| breakfast | desayuno | Do you have anything vegetarian/without meat? | ¿Hay algún plato vegetariano/sin carne? |
| lunch | almuerzo | I would like to order (dulce de leche). | Quisiera (dulce de leche). |
| dinner | comida/cena | This is too spicy. | Es demasiado pica. |
| dessert | postre | Can I see the menu? | ¿Podría ver la carta/el menú? |
| drink (alcoholic) | bebida (trago) | Where is a good restaurant? | ¿Dónde está un restaurante bueno? |
| spoon | cuchara | Do you have hot sauce? | ¿Tiene salsa picante? |
| cup | copa/taza | Table for (one), please. | Mesa para (uno), por favor. |
| knife | cuchillo | Do you take credit cards? | ¿Aceptan tarjetas de crédito? |
| fork | tenedor | Disgusting! | ¡Guácala!/¡Que asco! |
| napkin | servilleta | Delicious! | ¡Qué rico! |
| bon appétit | buen provecho | Check, please. | ¡La cuenta, por favor! |

## MENU READER

| SPANISH | ENGLISH | SPANISH | ENGLISH |
|---|---|---|---|
| a la plancha | grilled | legumbres | vegetables/legumes |
| al vapor | steamed | lima | lime |
| aceite | oil | limón | lemon |
| aceituna | olive | limonada | lemonade |
| agua (purificada) | water (purified) | locos | abalone (white fish) |
| ajo | garlic | lomo | steak or chop |
| almeja | clam | macedonia | syrupy dessert |
| arroz | rice | maíz | corn |
| bistec | beefsteak | mariscos | seafood |
| café | coffee | miel | honey |
| caliente | hot | naranja | orange |
| camarones | shrimp | nata | cream |
| carne | meat | pan | bread |
| cebolla | onion | paps | potatoes |
| cerveza | beer | papas fritas | french fries |
| chorizo | spicy sausage | parrillas | various grilled meats |
| coco | coconut | pasteles | desserts/pies |
| congrio | eel | pescado | fish |
| cordero | lamb | pimienta | pepper |

APPENDIX

| dulces | sweets | plato | plate |
|--------|--------|-------|-------|
| dulce de leche | caramelized milk | pollo | chicken |
| gallo pinto | fried rice and beans cooked with spices | puerco | pork |
| ensalada | salad | queso | cheese |
| entrada | appetizer | sal | salt |
| gaseosa | soda | sopa | soup |
| kuchen | pastry with fruit | tragos | mixed drinks/liquor |
| leche | milk | vino tinto/blanco | red wine/white |

# GLOSSARY

**aduana:** customs
**agencia de viaje:** travel agency
**aguardiente:** strong liquor
**aguas termales:** hot springs
**ahora:** now
**ahorita:** "now in just a little bit," which can mean anything from 5min. to 5hr.
**aire acondicionado:** air-conditioned (A/C)
**a la plancha:** grilled
**al gusto:** as you wish
**alemán:** German
**almacén:** (grocery) store
**almuerzo:** lunch, midday meal
**alpaca:** shaggy-haired, long-necked animal in the cameloid family
**altiplano:** highland
**amigo/a:** friend
**andén:** platform
**arroz:** rice
**arroz chaufa:** Chinese-style fried rice
**artesanía:** arts and crafts
**avenida:** avenue
**bahía:** bay
**bandido:** bandit
**baño:** bathroom or natural spa
**barato/a:** cheap
**barranca:** canyon
**barro:** mud
**barrio:** neighborhood
**biblioteca:** library
**bistec/bistek:** beefsteak
**bocaditos:** bar appetizers
**bodega:** convenience store or winery
**boletería:** ticket counter
**bonito/a:** pretty/beautiful
**borracho/a:** drunk
**bosque:** forest
**botica:** drugstore
**bueno/a:** good
**buena suerte:** good luck

**buen provecho:** bon appétit
**burro:** donkey
**caballero:** gentleman
**caballo:** horse
**cabiñas:** cabins
**cajeros:** cashiers
**cajeros automáticos:** ATMs
**caldera:** coffee or tea pot
**caldo:** soup, broth, or stew
**calle:** street
**cama:** bed
**camarones:** shrimp
**cambio:** change
**caminata:** hike
**camino:** path, track, road
**camión:** truck
**camioneta:** small, pickup-sized truck
**campamento:** campground
**campesino/a:** person from a rural area, peasant
**campo:** countryside
**canotaje:** rafting
**cantina:** drinking establishment, usually male-dominated
**carne asada:** roast meat
**capilla:** chapel
**caro/a:** expensive
**carretera:** highway
**carro:** car, or sometimes a train car
**casa:** house
**casa de cambio:** currency exchange establishment
**casado/a:** married
**cataratas:** waterfalls
**casona:** mansion
**catedral:** cathedral
**centro:** city center
**cerca:** near/nearby
**cerro:** hill
**cerveza:** beer

APPENDIX

APPENDIX

**ceviche:** raw fish marinated in lemon juice, herbs, and veggies
**cevichería:** ceviche restaurant
**chico/a:** boy/girl, little
**chicharrón:** bite-sized pieces of fried meat, usually pork
**chuleta de chancho:** pork chop
**churrasco:** steak
**cigarillo:** cigarette
**cine:** cinema
**ciudad:** city
**ciudadela:** large city neighborhood
**coche:** car
**colectivo:** shared taxi
**coliseo:** coliseum/stadium
**comedor:** dining room
**comida típica:** typical/traditional dishes
**con:** with
**consulado:** consulate
**correo:** post office
**cordillera:** mountain range
**crucero:** crossroads
**Cruz Roja:** Red Cross
**cuadra:** street block
**cuarto:** room
**cuenta:** bill/check
**cuento:** story/account
**cueva:** cave
**curandero:** healer
**damas:** ladies
**desayuno:** breakfast
**descompuesto:** broken, out of order; spoiled/rotten food
**desierto:** desert
**despacio:** slow
**de turno:** 24hr. rotating schedule for pharmacies
**dinero:** money
**discoteca:** dance club
**dueño/a:** owner
**dulces:** sweets
**edificio:** building
**email:** email
**embajada:** embassy
**embarcadero:** dock
**emergencia:** emergency
**encomiendas:** estates granted to Spanish settlers in Latin America
**entrada:** entrance
**estadio:** stadium
**este:** east
**estrella:** star
**extranjero:** foreign/foreigner
**farmacia:** pharmacy

**farmacia en turno:** 24hr. pharmacy
**feliz:** happy
**ferrocarril:** railroad
**fiesta:** party, holiday
**finca:** plantation-like agricultural enterprise or a ranch
**friajes:** sudden cold winds
**frijoles:** beans
**frontera:** border
**fumar:** to smoke
**fundo:** large estate or tract of land
**fútbol:** soccer
**ganga:** bargain
**gobierno:** government
**gordo/a:** fat
**gorra:** cap
**gratis:** free
**gringo/a:** North American
**guanaco:** cameloid animal
**habitación:** a room
**hacer una caminata:** take a hike
**hacienda:** ranch
**helado:** ice cream
**hermano/a:** brother/sister
**hervido/a:** boiled
**hielo:** ice
**hijo/a:** son/daughter
**hombre:** man
**iglesia:** church
**impuestos:** taxes
**impuesto valor añadido (IVA):** value added tax (VAT)
**indígena:** indigenous, refers to the native population
**isla:** island
**jarra:** 1L pitcher of beer
**jirón:** street
**jugo:** juice
**ladrón:** thief
**lago/laguna:** lake
**lancha:** launch, small boat
**langosta:** lobster
**langostino:** jumbo shrimp
**larga distancia:** long distance
**lavandería:** laundromat
**lejos:** far
**lente:** slow
**librería:** bookstore
**lista de correos:** mail-holding system in Latin America
**loma:** hill
**lomo:** chop (such as pork)
**madre:** mother
**malo/a:** bad

**malecón:** pier or seaside thoroughfare
**maletas:** luggage, suitcases
**maneje despacio:** drive slowly
**manjar blanco:** a whole-milk caramel spread
**mar:** sea
**mariscos:** seafood
**matas:** shrubs, jungle brush
**matrimonial:** double bed
**menestras:** lentils/beans, or bean stew
**menú del día/menú:** fixed daily meal often offered for a bargain price
**mercado:** market
**merienda:** snack
**mestizaje:** crossing of races
**mestizo/a:** person of mixed European and indigenous descent
**microbus:** small, local bus
**mirador:** observatory or lookout point
**muelle:** wharf
**muerte:** death
**museo:** museum
**música folklórica:** folk music
**nada:** nothing
**niño/a:** child
**norte:** north
**obra:** work of art/play
**obraje:** primitive textile workshop
**oeste:** west
**oficina de turismo:** tourist office
**padre:** father
**pampa:** a plain (geographical)
**pan:** bread
**panadería:** bakery
**panga:** motorboat
**parada:** stop (on a bus or train)
**parilla:** various cuts of meat, grilled
**paro:** labor strike
**parque:** park
**parroquia:** parish
**paseo turístico:** tour covering a series of sites
**payaso:** clown
**pelea de gallos:** cockfighting
**peligroso/a:** dangerous
**peninsulares:** Spanish-born colonists
**peña:** folkloric music club
**pescado:** fish
**picante:** spicy
**pisa de uvas:** grape-stomping
**pisco sour:** drink made from pisco, lemon juice, sugarcane syrup, and egg white
**plátano:** plantain
**playa:** beach

**población:** population, settlement
**policía:** police
**pollo a la brasa:** roasted chicken
**pueblito:** small town
**pueblo:** town
**puente:** bridge
**puerta:** door
**puerto:** port
**queso:** cheese
**rana:** frog
**recreo:** place of amusement, restaurant/bar on the outskirts of a city
**refrescos:** refreshments, soft drinks
**reloj:** watch, clock
**río:** river
**ropa:** clothes
**sábanas:** bedsheets
**sabor:** flavor
**sala:** living room
**salida:** exit
**salto:** waterfall
**salsa:** sauce (can be of many varieties)
**seguro/a:** lock, insurance; adj.: safe
**semáforo:** traffic light
**semana:** week
**Semana Santa:** Holy Week
**sexo:** sex
**shaman/chaman:** spiritual healer
**SIDA:** Spanish acronym for AIDS
**siesta:** mid-afternoon nap; businesses often close at this time
**sillar:** flexible, white, volcanic rock used in construction
**sol:** sun
**solito/a:** alone
**solo/a:** alone
**solo carril:** one-lane road or bridge
**soltero/a:** single (unmarried)
**supermercado:** supermarket
**sur:** south
**tarifa:** fee
**tapas:** small appetizers served in bars
**telenovela:** soap opera
**terminal terrestre:** bus station
**tienda:** store
**tipo de cambio:** exchange rate
**trago:** mixed drink/shot of alcohol
**triste:** sad
**trucha:** trout
**turismo:** tourism
**turista:** tourist
**valle:** valley
**zona:** zone

# PORTEÑO GLOSSARY

**alfajores:** shortbread cookies sandwiched together with *dulce de leche* or jam

**asado:** grilling/barbecue

**barbaro:** awesome

**barrabrava:** hooligan

**barullo:** noise

**bife:** beef

**bomba:** another word for the *mate* gourd

**bombilla:** the metal straw used to drink *mate*

**borracho/choborra/escavio:** drunk

**carasucias:** buns topped with brown sugar

**caudillo:** a military dictator

**ceviches:** raw seafood salad

**cheto:** snob, or dude

**churro:** pot

**cumbia:** a Colombian folk dance and dance music

**dulce de leche:** a condensed milk-based syrup similar in taste to caramel

**empanada:** a stuffed pastry

**estancia:** a large farm

**estoy jodiendo:** I'm hanging out and bullshitting/pulling one over on you

**estoy roto:** I'm exhausted

**facturas:** pastries

**falopeado:** high (drug induced)

**fideos:** noodles

**forro:** condom

**fuegos artificiales:** fireworks

**garchar:** fuck

**gitanos:** gypsies

**guardapolvo:** the white smocks that are part of the Argentine public school uniform

**heladería:** ice cream parlor

**licuado:** smoothie

**locro:** a thick, heavy stew

**macana:** make a mistake/put your foot in your mouth

**Martín Fierro:** the Argentine national epic, the encapsulation of the *gaucho* experience

**mate:** the infused drink made from *yerba mate;* also the name of the gourd from which mate is drunk

**me cagó:** he/she cheated me

**menu del dia:** daily specials

**milanesas:** seasoned, breaded, and fried meat

**milonga:** a place where tango is performed

**mina:** chick/girl

**ñoquis:** a small dish of pasta, made from potatoes (gnocchi)

**pachanguear:** dance (in a party-like way)

**palmeritas:** flaky, sweet concoctions

**patear:** give the brush off

**pegar:** to buy drugs (Let's Go does not endorse illegal narcotics)

**perros:** dogs

**picada:** a type of stuffed tortilla

**playa:** beach

**porro pot:** a joint

**porteño:** people of the port (a resident of Buenos Aires)

**pulpería:** a general store

**purée:** mashed potatoes

**putear:** talk shit

**quinta:** a little plot of farmland and prairie, sometimes with a few horses and cattle, kept by some town-dwelling Argentines

**sandwiches de miga:** small, tea-time sandwiches made with crustless bread

**soda:** carbonated water

**tenedor libres:** all-you-can-eat buffets

**tipo:** guy

**vuelve usted mañana:** come back tomorrow

**yerba mate:** the species of holly used to make *mate*

# MAP APPENDIX

## SUGGESTED ITINERARIES:

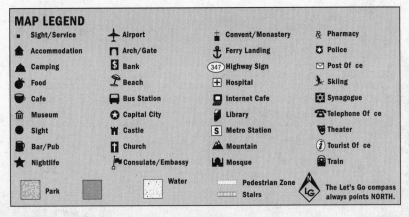

**MAP LEGEND**

| | | |
|---|---|---|
| ▪ Sight/Service | ✈ Airport | ‡ Convent/Monastery | ℞ Pharmacy |
| 🏠 Accommodation | ⌂ Arch/Gate | ⚓ Ferry Landing | ✪ Police |
| ▲ Camping | $ Bank | (347) Highway Sign | ✉ Post Of ce |
| 🍖 Food | 🏖 Beach | ✚ Hospital | ⛷ Skiing |
| ☕ Cafe | 🚌 Bus Station | 💻 Internet Cafe | ✡ Synagogue |
| 🏛 Museum | ✪ Capital City | Library | ☎ Telephone Of ce |
| ● Sight | 🏰 Castle | S Metro Station | Theater |
| ☕ Bar/Pub | ✝ Church | ⛰ Mountain | (i) Tourist Of ce |
| ★ Nightlife | Consulate/Embassy | Mosque | 🚂 Train |

| | | | |
|---|---|---|---|
| Park | | Water | Pedestrian Zone |
| | | | Stairs |

The Let's Go compass
always points NORTH.

MAP APPENDIX

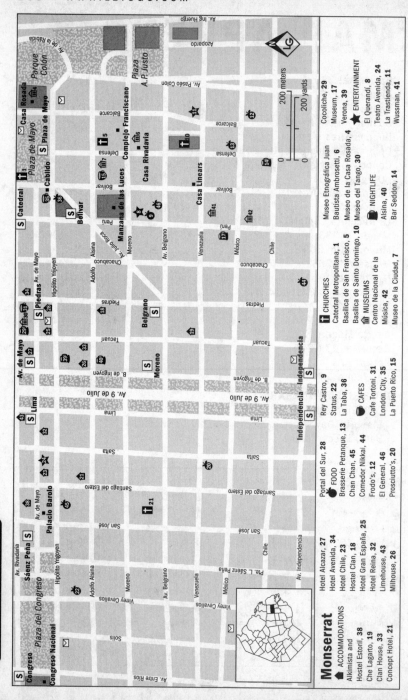

MAP APPENDIX

# Monserrat

## ▲ ACCOMMODATIONS
Alkimista and
Hostel Estoril, **38**
Che Lagarto, **19**
Clan House, **33**
Concept Hotel, **21**
Hotel Alcazar, **27**
Hotel Avenida, **34**
Hotel Chile, **23**
Hostel Clan, **18**
Hostel Gran España, **25**
Hotel Reina, **32**
Limehouse, **43**
Milhouse, **26**
Portal del Sur, **28**
Rey Castro, **9**
Status, **22**
La Taba, **36**

## ● FOOD
Brasserie Petanque, **13**
Chan Chan, **45**
Comedor Nikkai, **44**
Frodo's, **12**
El General, **46**
Prosciutto's, **20**

## ☕ CAFES
Cafe Tortoni, **31**
London City, **35**
La Puerta Rico, **15**

## 🏛 MUSEUMS
Centro Nacional de la
Música, **42**
Museo de la Ciudad, **7**
Museo Etnográfica Juan
Bautista Ambrosetti, **6**
Museo de la Casa Rosada, **4**
Museo del Tango, **30**

## ✝ CHURCHES
Catedral Metropolitana, **1**
Basílica de San Francisco, **3**
Basílica de Santo Domingo, **10**

## 🎵 NIGHTLIFE
Alsina, **40**
Bar Seddon, **14**
Cocoliche, **29**
Museum, **17**
Verona, **39**

## ★ ENTERTAINMENT
El Querandí, **8**
Teatro Avenida, **24**
La Trastienda, **11**
Wussman, **41**

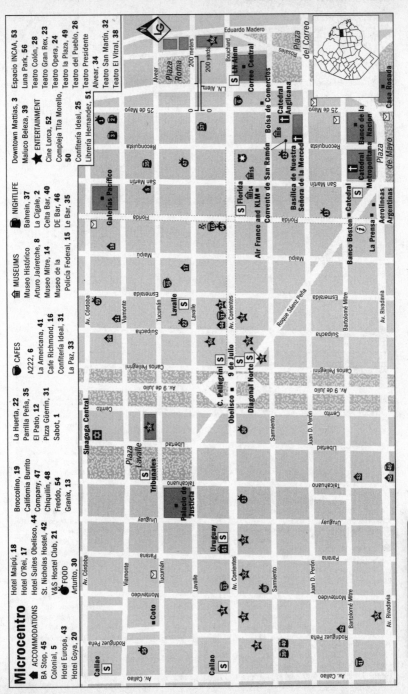

# Microcentro

| | | | |
|---|---|---|---|
| **ACCOMMODATIONS** | Broccolino, 19 | La Huerta, 22 | Espacio INCAA, 53 |
| BA Stop, 45 | California Burrito | Parrilla Peña, 35 | Luna Park, 56 |
| Colonial, 5 | Company, 47 | El Patio, 12 | Teatro Colón, 28 |
| Hotel Europa, 43 | Chiquilín, 48 | Pizza Güerrin, 31 | Teatro Gran Rex, 23 |
| Hotel Goya, 20 | V&S Hostel Club, 21 | Sabot, 1 | Teatro Opera, 24 |
| Hotel Maipú, 18 | 🍴 **FOOD** | | Teatro la Plaza, 49 |
| Hotel O'Rei, 17 | Arturto, 30 | 🟧 **CAFES** | Teatro del Pueblo, 26 |
| Hotel Suites Obelisco, 44 | | A222, 6 | Teatro Presidente |
| St. Nicholas Hostel, 42 | | La Americana, 41 | Alvear, 34 |
| | | Cafe Richmond, 16 | Teatro San Martín, 32 |
| | | Confitería Ideal, 31 | Teatro El Vitral, 38 |
| | | La Paz, 33 | |

| | | |
|---|---|---|
| 🏛 **MUSEUMS** | ⭐ **ENTERTAINMENT** | Downtown Mattias, 3 |
| Museo Histórico | Cine Lorca, 52 | Maluco Beleza, 39 |
| Arturo Jaúretche, 8 | Compleja Tita Morello, | |
| Museo Mitre, 14 | 50 | 🍸 **NIGHTLIFE** |
| Museo de la | Confitería Ideal, 25 | Bahrein, 37 |
| Policia Federal, 15 | Librería Hernandez, 51 | La Cigale, 2 |
| | | Celta Bar, 40 |
| | | DE Bar, 46 |
| | | Le Bar, 35 |

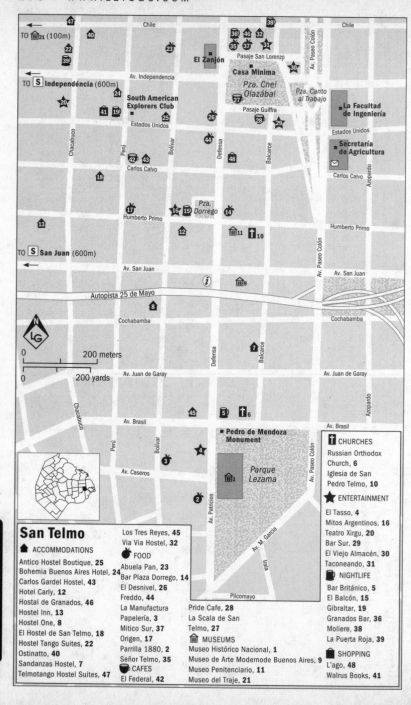

TO 21 (100m)

Chile

El Zanjón

Pasaje San Lorenzo

Casa Minima

TO [S] Independéncia (600m)

Av. Independencia

Pza. Cnel Olazábal

Pza. Canto al Trabajo

South American Explorers Club

Estados Unidos

Pasaje Guiffra

La Facultad de Ingeniería

Estados Unidos

Secretaría de Agricultura

Carlos Calvo

Carlos Calvo

Pza. Dorrego

Humberto Primo

Humberto Primo

TO [S] San Juan (600m)

Av. San Juan

Av. San Juan

Autopista 25 de Mayo

Cochabamba

Cochabamba

0        200 meters

0        200 yards

Av. Juan de Garay

Av. Juan de Garay

Av. Brasil

Av. Brasil

Av. Caseros

Pedro de Mendoza Monument

Parque Lezama

Pilcomayo

**CHURCHES**
Russian Orthodox Church, 6
Iglesia de San Pedro Telmo, 10

★ **ENTERTAINMENT**
El Tasso, 4
Mitos Argentinos, 16
Teatro Xirgu, 20
Bar Sur, 29
El Viejo Almacén, 30
Taconeando, 31

**NIGHTLIFE**
Bar Británico, 5
El Balcón, 15
Gibraltar, 19
Granados Bar, 36
Moliere, 38
La Puerta Roja, 39

**SHOPPING**
L'ago, 48
Walrus Books, 41

## San Telmo

**ACCOMMODATIONS**
Antico Hostel Boutique, 25
Bohemia Buenos Aires Hotel, 24
Carlos Gardel Hostel, 43
Hotel Carly, 12
Hostal de Granados, 46
Hostel Inn, 13
Hostel One, 8
El Hostel de San Telmo, 18
Hostel Tango Suites, 22
Ostinatto, 40
Sandanzas Hostel, 7
Telmotango Hostel Suites, 47

Los Tres Reyes, 45
Via Via Hostel, 32

**FOOD**
Abuela Pan, 23
Bar Plaza Dorrego, 14
El Desnivel, 26
Freddo, 44
La Manufactura
Papelería, 3
Mitico Sur, 37
Origen, 17
Parrilla 1880, 2
Señor Telmo, 35

**CAFES**
El Federal, 42

Pride Cafe, 28
La Scala de San Telmo, 27

**MUSEUMS**
Museo Histórico Nacional, 1
Museo de Arte Modernode Buenos Aires, 9
Museo Penitenciario, 11
Museo del Traje, 21

**MAP APPENDIX**

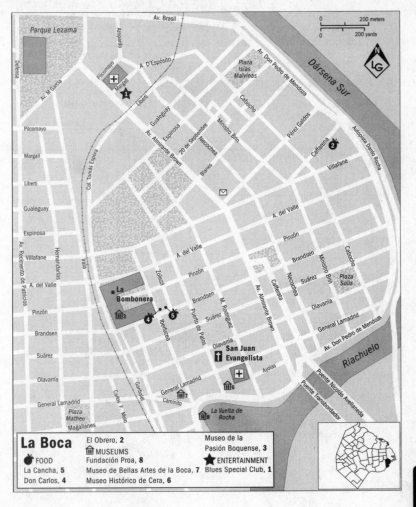

Parque Lezama

Av. Brasil

Av. Don Pedro de Mendoza

Dársena Sur

Plaza Islas Malvinas

0    200 meters
0    200 yards

**La Boca**

El Obrero, **2**

🏛 MUSEUMS

Museo de la Pasión Boquense, **3**

🍴 FOOD

La Cancha, **5**

Don Carlos, **4**

Fundación Proa, **8**

Museo de Bellas Artes de la Boca, **7**

Museo Histórico de Cera, **6**

★ ENTERTAINMENT

Blues Special Club, **1**

Av. Cordóba

⚓ **Terminal Busquebus**
**(Ferries to Uruguay)**

C. Grierson

Viamonte

Alvear

**10**

V. Campo

T. Guevara

Bou-chard

Rosales

Sarmiento

**1**

ⓘ

*Dique 4*

O. Cossentini

J. Manso

*Parque Forner*

T. Guevara

Juan Perón

M. Güemes

🏛 **3**

Av. Carlos M. Noel

Reserve Entrance

**Reserva Ecológica Costanera Sur**

*Laguna de las Gaviotas*

🏛 **5**

M. Saénz

Av. de los Italianos

*Dique 3*

*Parque Mujeres Argentinas*

J. Manso

O. Cossentini

Av. Eduardo Madero

Libertador

Moreno

**Aduana**

**4**

M. Lynch

Av. Belgrano

**9**

A. Villaflor

0    200 meters
0    200 yards

N LG

Venezuela

Mexico

Chile

Av. Ing. Huergo

A. Moreau de Justo

*Dique 2*

M. Salotti

Aimé Painé

Eyle

**6**

O. Cossentini

Ezcurra

*Parque Bastidas*

J. Lanten

Av. T. Achával Rodríguez

Calabria

*Laguna de los Coipos*

*Laguna de los Patos*

Av. Independencia

**8**

Azopardo

Estados Unidos

**7**

R. Vera Peñaloza

Carlos Calvo

Humberto Primo

San Juan

Pierina Dealessi

*Dique 1*

Elvira R. de Dellapiane

J. Balbin

Alf. F. Pareja

Reserve Entrance

Av. España

Cochabamba

Av. Juan de Garay

Av. Brasil

Benjamin Lavaisse

**MAP APPENDIX**

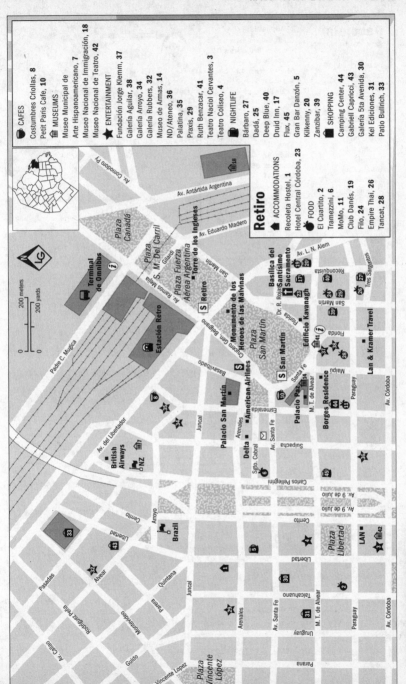

**CAFES**
Costumbres Criollas, **8**
Petit París Cafe, **10**

**MUSEUMS**
Museo Municipal de
Arte Hispanoamericano, **7**
Museo Nacional de Immigración, **18**
Museo Nacional de Teatro, **42**

★ **ENTERTAINMENT**
Fundación Jorge Klemm, **37**
Galería Aguilar, **38**
Galería Arroyo, **34**
Galería Rubbers, **32**
Museo de Armas, **14**
ND/Ateneo, **36**
Palatina, **35**
Praxis, **29**
Ruth Benzacar, **41**
Teatro Naciol Cervantes, **3**
Teatro Coliseo, **4**

**NIGHTLIFE**
Bárbaro, **27**
Dadá, **25**
Deep Blue, **40**
Druid Inn, **17**
Flux, **45**
Gran Bar Danzón, **5**
Kilkenny, **20**
Zanzíbar, **39**

**SHOPPING**
Camping Center, **44**
Gabrieli Capricci, **43**
Galería 5ta Avenida, **30**
Kel Ediciones, **31**
Patio Bullrich, **33**

## Retiro

▲ **ACCOMMODATIONS**
Recoleta Hostel, **1**
Hotel Central Córdoba, **23**

**FOOD**
El Cuartito, **2**
Tramezzini, **6**
MoMo, **11**
Club Danés, **19**
Filo, **24**
Empire Thai, **26**
Tancat, **28**

## Recoleta

**ACCOMMODATIONS**
Hotel Castillo, 9
Hotel Lion d'Or, 15
Juncal Palace Hotel, 6

**FOOD**
Amaranta, 14
Artesano, 3
La Bourgogne, 43
Club Sirio, 13
Cuatro Hojas, 8
Un Altra Volta, 31
Lotos, 12
Los Maestros, 7
Maria de Bambi, 28
Mirta Rovagna, 35
Sake, 5
El Sanjuanino, 23

**CAFES**
La Biela, 26
Clásica y Moderna, 29
Confitería La Rambla, 22

**MUSEUMS**
Centro Cultura Recoleta, 41
Museo de Bellas Artes, 19
Museo de la
Deuda Externa, 19
Museo Xul Solar, 2
Palais Glace, 20

**NIGHTLIFE**
Buller, 27
Contramano, 45
El Living, 36
Glam, 40
Milión, 37
Shamrock, 39
Sitges, 44

**SHOPPING**
Ateneo Grand Splendid, 32
Bond Street Galeria, 46
Buenos Aires Design, 38

**ENTERTAINMENT**
Notorious, 30

Pza. Rep. de Chile

Chile

Pza. Rep. del Uruguay

Pza. Naciones Unidas

Lucena

Jose Leon Pagano

Peru

Austria

Tagle

Av. Pte. Figueroa Alcorta

Floralis Genérica

Pza. Cap. Grl. J. J. de Urquiza

Facultad de Derecho

E. J. Couture

Brig. Grl. J. F. Quiroga

Pza. R. Darío

Biblioteca Nacional

Pza. Mitre

Av. del Libertador

🏛19

Parq. C. Thays

J. M. Gutiérrez

Grl. Gelly Y Obes

Dr. Lagleyze

UK

Av. Pueyrredón

Pza. Francia

Pza. Int. Alvear

🏛20

Ed. Schiaffino

Pza. San Martín de Tours

22

Ireland

23

Posadas

38

🏛41

Basílica Nuestra Señora de Pilar

Haedo

Av. Alvear

43

Av. Callao

Pza. Tte. Grl. E. Mitre

La Recoleta Cemetary

Av. Las Heras

Pza. Recoleta ℹ

27

26

34

28

Palacio Hume

Quintana

33

31

Palacio Duhan

Rodríguez Peña

14

Uruguay

Guido

35

Montevideo

Acuénaga

Uriburu

Junín

Ayacucho

15

V. López

13

31

Juncal

Larrea

6

7

Pza. V. López

Juncal

39

Juncal

Arenales

8

Riobamba

Av. Callao

Arenales

Av. Santa Fe

46

32

31

Pte. J. E. Uriburu

Junín

Ayacucho

45

Rodríguez Peña

37

9

Universidad de Buenos Aires

M. T. de Alvear

Montevideo

Paraná

Uruguay

Talcahuano

30

Pza. Rodríguez Peña

36

Pza. B. Houssay

Paraguay

29

Facultad de Medicina S

Callao S

12

Av. Córdoba

🏛42

# Palermo

**♦ ACCOMMODATIONS**
Alma Petit Hostel, **2**
Casa Esmeralda, **13**
La Otra Orilla, **24**
Te Adoro Garcia, **1**

**🍴 FOOD**
Anden Restaurant, **8**
Artemisia, **42**
Bangalore Pub
& Curry House, **18**
Bella Italia, **34**
Las Cholas, **6**
Novecento, **43**

Oui Oui, **11**
Tonno, **3**

**☕ CAFES**
Santos Sabores, **9**
Patricia Villobos
Delicatessen, **31**

**🏛 MUSEUMS**
Casa Museo Ricardo Rojas, **4**
MALBA, **30**
Museo de Arte Popular
José Hernández, **32**
Museo de Artes Plásticas
Eduardo Sívori, **44**

Museo Evita, **40**
Museo del Hombre, **10**
Museo Metropolitano, **36**
Museo Nacional de
Arto Decorativo, **29**
Planetario Galileo Galilei, **37**

**🌙 NIGHTLIFE**
878, **47**
AcaBar, **14**
Bach Bar, **21**
Bulnes Class, **23**
Caix, **39**
Carnal, **17**

Club Aráoz, **25**
Jackie O., **7**
Crobar, **38**
Drink Gallery, **33**
El Especial, **20**
Niceto, **19**
Pácha, **46**
The Roxy Disco, **48**
The Roxy Resto Bar, **16**
Rumi, **45**
Sitges, **22**
Unico, **15**
Van Koning, **5**

**🛍 SHOPPING**
Alto Palermo, **27**
Paseo Alcorta, **35**
Las Pulgas

Antiguedades, **12**

**★ ENTERTAINMENT**
Cinemark Palermo, **28**
La Peña del Colorado, **26**
Thelonious, **25**
Virasoro, **41**

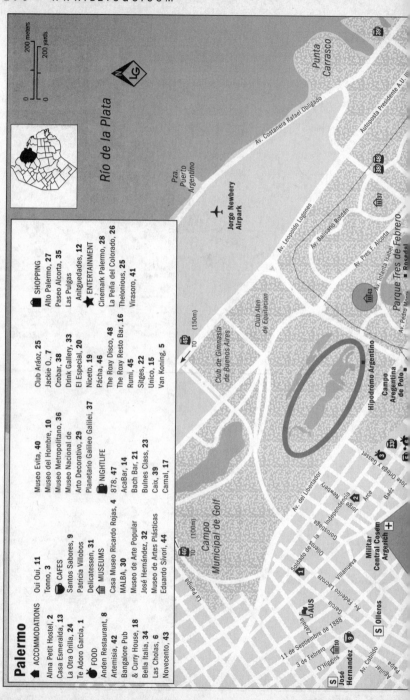

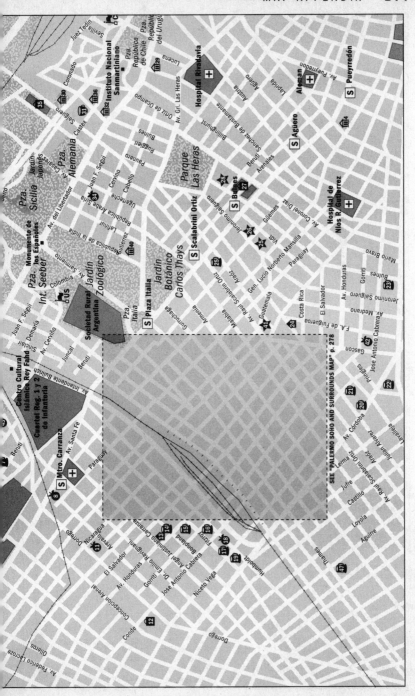

MAP APPENDIX

SEE "PALERMO SOHO AND SURROUNDS MAP" p. 278

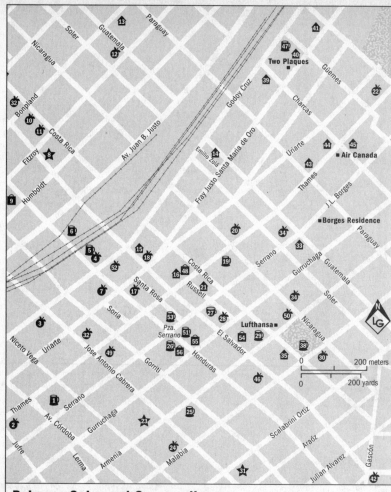

# Palermo Soho and Surroundings

## ACCOMMODATIONS

Casa Babylon Art Hostel, **33**
Casa Jardín, **44**
Che Lulu Trendy Hotel, **14**
Cypress Inn, **21**
Gecko Hostel, **13**
Hostel-Bar Giramondo, **40**
Giramondo Suites, **41**
Back in Town—
Buenos Aires, **15**
Hostel Suites Palermo, **39**
Palermo House, **16**
So Hostel, **45**
Tango Backpackers, **43**
Zentrum Hostel, **35**

## FOOD

Al Andalus, **52**
Bar Uriarte, **7**
Bereber, **50**
Boutique del Libro, **48**
La Cabrera, **49**
La Casa Polaca, **34**
Ceviche, **10**
El Chef Iuseff, **24**
Club Eros, **17**
Cluny, **46**
La Cupertina, **3**
Freud y Fahler, **28**
Gardelito, **20**
Green Bamboo, **32**
Krishna, **30**

Miranda, **11**
Parrilla, **22**
La Peca, **42**
Pekin, **4**
Prâna, **18**
Sarkis, **2**
Sudestada, **12**

## CAFES

Meridiano 58, **27**

## SHOPPING

Calma Chica, **55**
Eterna Cadencia, **9**
Rapsodía, **54**
Salsipuedes, **56**

## NIGHTLIFE

Antares, **25**
Bar Taller, **26**
Congo, **6**
CRÓNICO, **53**
Kim y Novak Bar!, **47**
Kika, **5**
Malasartes, **51**
Mundo Bizarro, **1**
Podestá Súper Club, **29**
Post, **19**
Sugar, **38**

## ENTERTAINMENT

Tiempo de Gitanos, **8**
Salón Canning, **31**
La Virutá, **23**

**MAP APPENDIX**

Conde

Conde 15 Superí

Freiere

Zapiola Freiere

Zapiola 16

La Pampa

Sucre

Av. Crámer Echeverría Juramento Mendoza Olazábal Blanco Encalada Av. Monroe

Vidal

Moldes

Moldes Amenabar

Amenabar **Mercado Modelo de Belgrano** Roosevelt Pedro Rivera M. Ugarte Av. Crámer

Ciudad de la Paz **J. Hernández** Ciudad de la Paz Vidal

**S** Moldes

Av. Cabildo **S Juramento** Amenabar

Vuelta de Obligado **Iglesia de la Inmaculada** Av. Cabildo **14** **S** Ciudad de la Paz

Cuba **Concepción** **Congreso de Tucuman**

Arcos **Plaza** 12 Vuelta de Obligado

O'Higgins **Belgrano** 11 Cuba 10 Iberá

3 de Febrero Arcos

11 de Septiembre 13 1 O'Higgins

8 Arribeños 3 de Febrero Quesada

Av. Virrey Vértiz 5 11 de Septiembre

7 6 Arribeños

Montañeses 4 2

Av. del Libertador 3

Migueletes Av. del Libertador

Miñones Av. Congreso

Campo **Municipal de Golf** Artilleros

Av. Valentín Alsina Cazadores

Hernández Echeverría Juramento Mendoza Olazábal Blanco Encalada Av. Monroe Sáenz Valiente V. de la Plaza Almte. García Almte. Gral Brown Dr. R. Hernández P. Agote

Húsares

Dragones 0 200 meters

Ramsay 0 200 yards **Estadio Monumental Núñez**

Av. Figueroa Alcorta

# Belgrano

**ACCOMMODATIONS**
Pampa Hostel, **9**
La Rosada de Belgrano, **10**

**FOOD**
Asia Oriental, **4**
Los Chinos, **8**
Lai Lai, **5**
La Más Querida, **7**
El Pobre Luis, **2**

**MUSEUMS**
Casa de Yrurtia, **1**
Museo Histórico
Sarmiento, **11**

Museo Larreta, **12**
Museo Libero Badii, **13**
**SHOPPING**
Kel Ediciones, **15**

Palacio de las Artes, **16**
**NIGHTLIFE**
Puerta Uno, **6**

**ENTERTAINMENT**
Gen. Paz, **14**
Showcase Cinemas, **3**

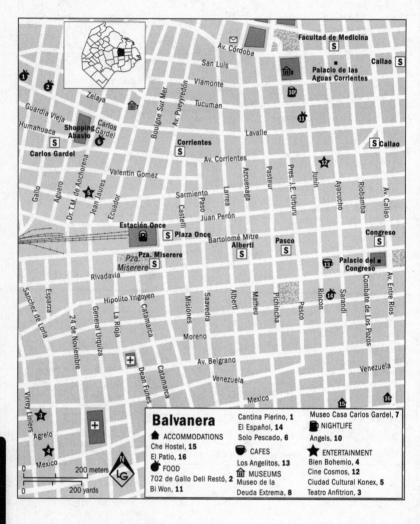

Av. Córdoba
San Luis
Viamonte
Tucuman
**Facultad de Medicina** S
**Palacio de las Aguas Corrientes**
Callao S
Lavalle
Zelaya
Guardia Vieja
Humahuaca
Boulogne Sur Mer
Av. Pueyrredón
**Shopping Abasto**
Carlos Gardel
Corrientes S
Av. Corrientes
**Carlos Gardel** S
Valentin Gomez
Arcuenaga
Pasteur
Pres. J.E. Urburu
Junín
Ayacucho
Riobamba
Av. Callao
S Callao
Gallo
Aguero
Dr. T.M. de Anchorena
Jean Jaures
Ecuador
Sarmiento
Paso
Larrea
Juan Perón
Castelli
**Estación Once** S **Plaza Once**
Bartolomé Mitre
**Alberti**
**Pasco** S
**Congreso** S
**Pza. Miserere** S
Rivadavia
Hipolito Yrigoyen
Catamarca
Saavedra
Alberti
Matheu
Pichincha
Pasco
Rincon
Sarandi
**Palacio del Congreso**
Combate de Los Pozos
Av. Entre Rios
Esparza
Sanchez de Loria
24 de Noviembre
General Urquiza
La Rioja
Misiones
Moreno
Av. Belgrano
Venezuela
Venezuela
Mexico
Virrey Liniers
Agrelo
Mexico
Dean Funes
Catamarca
Combate de Los Pozos

0  200 meters
0  200 yards

**Balvanera**

🏠 ACCOMMODATIONS
Che Hostel, **15**
El Patio, **16**
🍴 FOOD
702 de Gallo Deli Restó, **2**
Bi Won, **11**

Cantina Pierino, **1**
El Español, **14**
Solo Pescado, **6**
☕ CAFES
Los Angelitos, **13**
🏛 MUSEUMS
Museo de la
Deuda Extrema, **8**

Museo Casa Carlos Gardel, **7**
🍺 NIGHTLIFE
Angels, **10**
★ ENTERTAINMENT
Bien Bohemio, **4**
Cine Cosmos, **12**
Ciudad Cultural Konex, **5**
Teatro Anfitrion, **3**

MAP APPENDIX

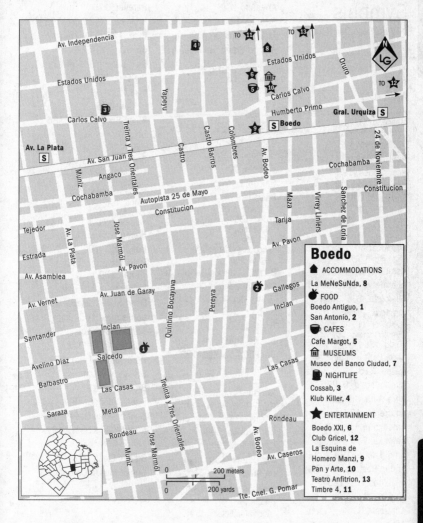

**Boedo**

🔺 ACCOMMODATIONS
La MeNeSuNda, **8**

🍗 FOOD
Boedo Antiguo, **1**
San Antonio, **2**

☕ CAFES
Cafe Margot, **5**

🏛 MUSEUMS
Museo del Banco Ciudad, **7**

📓 NIGHTLIFE
Cossab, **3**
Klub Killer, **4**

⭐ ENTERTAINMENT
Boedo XXI, **6**
Club Gricel, **12**
La Esquina de
Homero Manzi, **9**
Pan y Arte, **10**
Teatro Anfitrion, **13**
Timbre 4, **11**

# INDEX

INDEX

RICE PUBLIC LIBRARY
8 WENTWORTH ST.
KITTERY, MAINE  03904
207-439-1553

# SMART TRAVELERS KNOW:
## GET YOUR CARD BEFORE YOU GO

An HI USA membership card gives you access to friendly and affordable accommodations at over 4,000 hostels in more than 85 countries around the world.

HI USA Members receive complementary travel insurance, airline discounts, free stay vouchers, long distance calling card bonus, so its a good idea to get your membership while you're still planning your trip.

Hostelling International USA

JENNIFER BURKE
8401 COLESVILLE ROAD
SILVER SPRING, MD 20910

060-0010001                    **ADULT**
02/01/10                       10/18/84
Expires                        Date of Birth
Signature  *Jennifer Burke*

**Get your card online today:**

# hiusa.org

# We'd rather be traveling.

# LET'S GO
# BUDGET TRAVEL GUIDES
## www.letsgo.com